PROCEEDINGS OF THE SECOND INTERNATIONAL CONGRESS FOR THE STUDY OF CHILD LANGUAGE

Volume II

Edited by

Carol Larson Thew
Carolyn Echols Johnson

KLINCK MEMORIAL LIBRARY
Concordia College
River Forest, IL 60305

UNIVERSITY
PRESS OF
AMERICA

LANHAM • NEW YORK • LONDON

Copyright © 1984 by

The International Association for the Study of Child Language

University Press of America,™ Inc.

4720 Boston Way
Lanham, MD 20706

3 Henrietta Street
London WC2E 8LU England

All rights reserved

Printed in the United States of America

Co-Published by arrangement with
The International Association for the Study
of Child Language.

Library of Congress Cataloging in Publication Data
(Revised for volume 2)

International Congress for the Study of Child Language
    (2nd : 1981 : Vancouver, B.C.)
    Proceedings of the Second International Congress for
the Study of Child Language.

    Includes bibliographies.
    1. Language acquisition–Congresses. I. Johnson,
Carolyn Echols. II. Thew, Carol Larson. III. Title.
P118.I57   1981   401'.9   82–16145
ISBN 0–8191–2738–8 (v. 1)
ISBN 0–8191–2739–6 (pbk. : v. 1)
ISBN 0–8191–3694–8 (v. 2 : alk. paper)
ISBN 0-8191 -3695-6 (pbk.)

PREFACE

This book is the second of two volumes containing papers prepared for the Second International Congress for the Study of Child Language, held August 9-14, 1981 in Vancouver, British Columbia, Canada. The Congress was sponsored by the International Association for the Study of Child Language and the University of British Columbia.

We judge the Congress to have been a particularly successful one. Scholars from eighteen countries presented more than one hundred papers on a wide range of language acquisition topics. The Proceedings contain seventy-eight papers in two volumes. Volume I was published by University Press of America in September, 1982, and contains forty-five articles. For the reader's convenience, the Table of Contents for Volume I is reprinted in this volume beginning on page 516. This second volume contains thirty-three articles. It completes the sections Prespeech, Phonology, Morphology and Syntax, Semantics, and Language Development in Exceptional Children. It includes new sections on Language and Cognition, and Bilingualism, and a section retitled Pragmatics, Discourse, and the Interaction Context.

The publication of the Proceedings marks the end of five years of work--from the initial planning of the Congress by international and local committees to the editing of the camera-ready manuscripts. Thanks are due to Natalie Waterson, Terry Myers, and Els Oksaar for their communication and policy decisions, and to the local committee members Deborah Gibson, John Gilbert, David Ingram, Carolyn Johnson, Ken Reeder, Carol Thew, Darcy Dybhavn, and Maura O'Melinn. We especially thank David Ingram, now President of the Association, for his help in selecting the publisher and in sending out the call for completed papers. We are also grateful to the School of Audiology and Speech Sciences at the University of British Columbia for the use of its facilities and for providing an environment supportive of both planning the Congress and making its papers available to an international readership.

                Carol Larson Thew
                Department of Language Education
                University of British Columbia

                Carolyn Echols Johnson
                School of Audiology and Speech Sciences
                University of British Columbia

TABLE OF CONTENTS

VOLUME II

PRESPEECH

Kristine S. MacKain, Michael Studdert-Kennedy, Susan Spieker & Daniel Stern
INFANTS' LATERALIZED PERCEPTION OF AUDITORY-VISUAL RELATIONS FOR SPEECH ... 1

PHONOLOGY

Jean Aitchison & Shulamuth Chiat
RECALL ERRORS AND NATURAL PHONOLOGY ... 17

Mary Schramm Coberly
PHONOLOGICAL PROCESSES AFFECTING CONSONANTS IN THE ACQUISITION OF AMERICAN ENGLISH: THE OLMSTED DATA ... 27

Michael A. Crary, Terrel Welmers & Stephen E. Blache
A PRELIMINARY LOOK AT PHONOLOGICAL PROCESS SUPPRESSION ... 42

Natalie Waterson
EVIDENCE FOR NON-SEGMENTAL, WHOLE-PATTERN SPEECH PERCEPTION AND PRODUCTION FROM A CHILD'S FIRST RECITATIONS OF NURSERY RHYMES ... 57

MORPHOLOGY AND SYNTAX

George Branigan & William Stokes
AN INTEGRATED ACCOUNT OF UTTERANCE VARIABILITY IN EARLY LANGUAGE DEVELOPMENT ... 73

Paul Fletcher
LEXIS AND GRAMMAR IN THE DEVELOPMENT OF VERB-FORMS ... 89

Lise Menn & Brian MacWhinney
AVOIDING REPETITIONS: ENOUGH IS ENOUGH ... 100

SEMANTICS

Nancy Budwig, Michael Bamberg, & Amy Strage — 112
A CASE FOR LITERAL METAPHOR IN CHILD LANGUAGE

Esther Dromi — 127
THE WORD-CONTEXT PRODUCTION STRATEGY IN THE EARLY ACQUISITION OF MEANING

Michael J. Evans — 142
COMPLEMENTARITY, ANTONYMY, AND SEMANTIC DEVELOPMENT: A METHOD AND SOME DATA

Alison Gopnik — 163
"GONE" AND THE CONCEPT OF THE OBJECT

Hannelore Grimm & Werner Kany — 179
MEANING AND FUNCTION OF COMMON, PROPER AND NICK NAMES: HOW SCHOOLCHILDREN VIEW THE RELATION BETWEEN WORDS AND THEIR REFERENTS

Stan A. Kuczaj II — 194
DEVELOPMENT OF THE KINSHIP TERM SEMANTIC SYSTEM IN ENGLISH SPEAKING CHILDREN

Roy D. Pea & Ronald Mawby — 204
SEMANTICS OF MODAL AUXILIARY VERB USES BY PRESCHOOL CHILDREN

H. Stephen Straight — 220
LANGUAGE AND THE COGNITIVE BREAKTHROUGH AT AGE SIX

LANGUAGE AND COGNITION

Shizuko Amaiwa — 232
THE RELATION OF REASONING, MEMORY AND VERBAL ABILITY OF CHILDREN

Nelson Cowan & Lewis A. Leavitt — 243
TALKING BACKWARD: SPEECH PLAY IN LATE CHILDHOOD

Kim Plunkett & Anna Trosborg — 251
SOME PROBLEMS FOR THE COGNITIVIST APPROACH TO LANGUAGE

Adriana L. Schuler & Christiane Bormann 269
THE INTERRELATIONS BETWEEN COGNITIVE AND
COMMUNICATIVE DEVELOPMENT: SOME IMPLICATIONS
FROM THE STUDY OF A MUTE AUTISTIC ADOLESCENT

Gisela E. Speidel 283
THE ACQUISITION OF LINGUISTIC STRUCTURES
AND COGNITIVE DEVELOPMENT

Jeni E. Yamada 297
ON THE RELATIONSHIP BETWEEN LANGUAGE
AND COGNITION: EVIDENCE FROM A
HYPERLINGUISTIC RETARDED ADOLESCENT

PRAGMATICS, DISCOURSE, AND THE INTERACTION CONTEXT

Barbara Bokus & Grace Wales Shugar 322
WHAT DO YOUNG CHILDREN SAY TO START PEER
INTERACTION? SOME DISCOURSE PROCESSES AT PRESCHOOL
AGE IN THE CHILD-CHILD DYADIC RELATION

Toni Cross, Gillian Parmenter, Maryla Juchnowski, 337
& Gillian Johnson
EFFECTS OF DAY-CARE EXPERIENCE ON THE
FORMAL AND PRAGMATIC DEVELOPMENT OF YOUNG
CHILDREN

Maggie Kirkman & Toni Cross 360
FUNCTIONAL DIVERSITY AS A DEVELOPMENTAL
PHENOMENON IN CHILD AND PARENT CONVERSATION

Maureen Shields 379
DISCOURSE UNIVERSALS AND THE DEVELOPMENT
OF LINGUISTIC STRUCTURES FROM THE FIRST
TO THE FIFTH YEAR. PART 1. FIRST
WORDS.

Anne Van Kleeck & Richard Street 401
TALKATIVENESS AS A SOURCE OF INDIVIDUAL
VARIATION IN CHILDREN'S LANGUAGE USE

BILINGUALISM

Marlene Dolitsky 423
A MODEL OF BILINGUAL SEMANTICS:
INTERSECTING AND NON-INTERSECTING MORPHEMES
AND THEIR ACQUISITION

Mel Greenlee 438
LANGUAGE ELICITATION TECHNIQUES IN BILINGUAL
DISCOURSE: A COMPARISON

Els Oksaar 462
THE ACQUISITION OF INTERACTIONAL COMPETENCE
IN BI- AND TRILINGUAL ENVIRONMENTS

Robert R. Roy 475
A COMPARISON OF ORDER OF GRAMMAR ACQUISITION
BETWEEN FRENCH IMMERSION STUDENTS AND
FRANCOPHONES

LANGUAGE DEVELOPMENT IN EXCEPTIONAL CHILDREN

Eila Alahuhta 487
ON THE PREDICTIVE VALUE OF THE LINGUISTIC
LEVEL AND PRIMARY SYMPTOMS CONFIRMED IN PRE-
SCHOOL AS REGARDS SUBSEQUENT SCHOOL AND
LINGUISTIC PERFORMANCES

Jillian Ball, Toni Cross, & Kim Horsborough 502
A COMPARATIVE STUDY OF THE LINGUISTIC
ABILITIES OF AUTISTIC, DYSPHASIC AND NORMAL
CHILDREN

TABLE OF CONTENTS REPRINTED FROM VOLUME I   516

Infants' Lateralized Perception of Auditory-Visual Relations for Speech

Kristine S. MacKain (Cornell University Medical College), Michael Studdert-Kennedy (Haskins Laboratories), Susan Spieker (Cornell University), and Daniel Stern (Cornell University Medical College)

Background

We perceive speech more easily if we can see the speaker's face when he or she is talking. When the speaker's face is in view, speech perception is a bimodal (auditory-visual) process whereby information obtained via the visual modality is used to either supplement or disambiguate information obtained via the auditory modality.

For example, under conditions of no auditory input Dodd (1977) found that her subjects could identify 24% of consonant-vowel-consonant syllables correctly. When the facial display was combined with masked auditory input, her subjects reported 58% of the CVC's correctly, an increase of 34% over the condition in which only visual information was available.

A dramatic effect occurs when, through experimental manipulation, auditory and visual information are placed in conflict (e.g., a voice is heard saying "ba" while the face you are seeing is silently articulating "ga"). In this situation, the information transmitted via each modality is not veridically perceived; instead, a blending or integration occurs, resulting in the percept "da" (Summerfield, 1979). Under similar circumstances of auditory-visual conflict, McGurk & MacDonald (1976) have shown similar effects with children as young as three years.

Two recent published studies of infants'

1

bimodal perception have investigated infants' sensitivity to auditory-visual correspondences in speech. Spelke and Cortelyou (1981) presented four-month-old infants with moving pictures of two women projected side by side. The women spoke spontaneously, while the speech of one woman was played through a central loudspeaker. Infants preferred to look at the face that matched the voice. Similarly, in an earlier study, Dodd (1979) found that 10- to 16-week-old infants looked at the mirrored reflection of a woman's face repeating nursery rhymes significantly <u>less</u> when the woman's speech and articulation were out of synchrony by 400 msec, than when they were in their natural temporal relation.

There are two possible interpretations of this finding. Both require that infants be sensitive to correspondences and discrepancies between auditory and visual dimensions of continuous speech. The first interpretation supposes that infants prefer points of change in auditory and visual structure to be synchronized, very much as they apparently prefer auditory-visual synchrony in non-speech events (Spelke, 1979).

However, if it is mere synchrony that infants prefer, we would expect them to be satisfied with any pattern of auditory-visual correspondence whatever. A second interpretation of these two studies is that infants prefer not mere synchrony, but a natural pattern of qualitative correspondence between the auditory and visual dimensions of an event; for example, a rapid rise in the amplitude and upward shift in overall spectral structure being the correlate of an opening rather than a closing mouth.

A test of this second interpretation was the goal of the present study. We investigated whether infants would apprehend auditory-visual correspondences in speech structure when the synchrony between competing displays was maintained.

Our pilot work suggested that intermodal recognition of speech was enhanced when infants were attending to the right rather than the left video display. Kinsbourne (1970, 1974) and others (Lempert & Kinsbourne, 1982) have shown, with a diversity of stimulus materials, that when adults look to the right (or left) as they complete a task, their performance is facilitated if the task demands are best subserved by the hemisphere contralateral to gaze direction. We expected that only rightward attending would significantly enhance recognition of auditory-visual correspondences in speech structure.

Method

Subjects. Eighteen infants, 8 males and 10 females, (with a mean age of 5 months, 25 days), participated. Infants were healthy and full-term with no familial history of congenital hearing or vision defects and no reported postnatal defects.

Stimulus materials. (see DESIGN handout). The displays were drawn from three pairs of consonant-vowel-consonant-vowel (CVCV) disyllables, spoken with a terminal pitch contour and equal stress on both syllables:

/mama/ /lulu/
/bebi/ /zuzi/
/vava/ /zuzu/

We attempted to optimize the conditions for detecting these correspondences by making the articulatory dynamics of the contrasting video displays maximally discriminable. To this end we paired disyllabic spondees that differed as much as possible in both consonant and vowel.

We chose consonants with forward, but different places of articulation (labial versus alveolar) and vowels that differed in lip-rounding (with the exception of the final vowel in /bebi/ and /zuzi/). To facilitate the maintenance of synchrony during the sequence of repetitions, all disyllables were of about equal duration.

Each CVCV was spoken in a General American dialect by an adult female (S) in synchrony with the corresponding or contrasting articulations of another adult female (A). Thus, to the beat of a metronome, (S) spoke one CVCV (e.g., mama) while (A) silently articulated the other CVCV member of the pair (e.g., lulu). The voice of (S) and the face of (A) were simultaneously recorded to appear on one vertical half of a 13 inch video monitor screen. At the end of the second syllable of each CVCV, (A) held her mouth open until she began the next CVCV disyllable. This procedure eliminated possible discrepances, across video displays of different disyllables, between vowel sound offset and mouth closure onset at the termination of each CVCV.

After the first recording, the video recording procedure was repeated: this time A was videotaped to appear on the other half of the screen while silently repeating the second CVCV in the pair (e.g., mama) in synchrony with the audio playback of the original /mama/. The entire procedure was repeated until each member of each pair had occurred as an audio recording and the articulatory pattern corresponding to each recorded disyllable had been recorded to appear on both left and right sides of the video monitor screen.

Each recording lasted 20 seconds and comprised 11 repetitions of the CVCV pairs, spoken approximately one every 1900 msec. Each CVCV was about 1100 msec. long with interstimulus intervals of 800 msec.

It was possible that auditory-visual asynchronies could have resulted which might be detected by infants. In order to determine the extent of auditory-visual asynchronies, we had the two video displays measured at a film production studio in Manhattan. For each audio presentation, asynchronies were tracked in 16 msec units along visible points of articulation between the two different video displays for each contrasting consonant and vowel in the CVCV pair (e.g., $C_1V_1C_1V_1$ versus $C_2V_2C_2V_2$). Timing differences were measured for each pair between 1) the onset of lip opening or protrusion for both V_1-V_2 pairs, 2) the point of maximum mouth opening or lip protrusion for both V_1-V_2 pairs, 3) the onset of change in mouth position from the maximum point of excursion towards the next articulatory target, and 4) the onset of articulatory closure for both C_1-C_2 pairs. In no case did asynchronies exceed 1 1/2 video frames or about 48 msec. On the assumption that one of the video displays was in synchrony with the audio display, 48 msec is the maximum auditory-visual asynchrony on any trial. This value is well below the auditory-visual asynchrony detection threshold found for adults listening to speech as they watch a video display of someone talking. Dixon & Spitz (1980) found mean thresholds in detecting asynchronies of 258 msec. when the video display preceded the audio display and 131 msec. when the audio display preceded the video one.

Despite the close alignment of the two video displays, we needed to test our assumption that one of the video displays was in synchrony with the auditory CVCV. To do this, we had seven adults naive to the purposes of the experiment make perceptual judgments of synchrony and asynchrony for all the experimental CVCV (auditory-visual matching and mismatching) presentations.

Subjects were shown examples of the audio-video CVCV matches and mismatches. They were reminded of movies where the dubbing was poor and the voice and articulation seemed to be out of synchrony. Subjects were asked to try to ignore any auditory-visual mismatches in the particular consonants and vowels, while attending closely to the timing relation between auditory and visual events. For each auditory-visual CVCV occurrence, subjects were asked to judge whether the events they saw and heard seemed in- or out-of-synchrony.

T-tests revealed no significant differences in judgments of temporal discrepancy for auditory-visual CVCV matches versus mismatches on any of the six disyllables.

Apparatus. An "infant theater" was constructed so that one split screen on each of the two of TV video monitors could be viewed by the infant (see APPARATUS handout). The box-like theater rested on a table which was open at the front where the infant sat. The inside of the theater was painted white, making the TV screens contrastive objects in the infant's visual field. The TV's were placed in two rear wall windows, separated by 10 inches. Centrally placed between the windows was a camera for filming the infant's visual responses. On the floor of the theater, at the open, front end of the box, was a shallow round cut-out for the infant's abdomen to assure a proper viewing position for the infant when held on the mother's lap. The ceiling of the theater extended above the infant's head, but below the mother's so the mother could not see the video displays.

The speech corresponding to one of the two video displays was played from the speaker of both monitors. Before each session, the loudness levels were balanced between the two speakers of each video monitor so that the perceived location of the sound source was between the video monitor at the center of the theater's back wall. The infant's looking patterns were recorded with the camera and a Sony TV recording deck.

Procedure

Each session began with a warm-up exercise designed to draw the infant's gaze toward both right and left video monitors: a talking puppet alternated between the monitors, attracting the infant's attention to each in turn.

Infants were presented with each of the three

stimulus pairs on four trials, making a total of twelve trials presented to each infant. (see DESIGN handout). Each member of a stimulus pair (e.g., mama, lulu) occurred twice as an audio signal, with its matching video display occurring once on the left video monitor and once on the right. The 12 trials were randomized across conditions under the constraint that no two trials which contained the same video output (e.g., audio "mama", video "mama, lulu" and audio "lulu", video "mama, lulu") immediately followed one another. This constraint was imposed to discourage habituation to the video and/or audio displays and to distribute order effects over the three disyllabic pairs. We used nine different randomizations and assigned two infants to each randomization. The length of the experimental session was approximately four minutes.

Results

From video recordings, independent observers recorded direction of gaze and first fixation times to each video display. The observers could not see the video displays.

Observer reliability, based on 19% of the trials, was r = .96 for left looking time and r = .98 for right looking time (Pearson Product Moment Correlation).

The data were categorized according to auditory-visual matches and mismatches. For each trial, we measured the duration of each infant's first fixation to the left video display and the duration of first fixation to the right video display rather than the fixation durations to each side for the entire trial period. We preferred first fixation time as a response measure because it was not as vulnerable to contamination by extraneous factors such as attentional lapses.

For each infant and for each disyllable, we transformed fixation times into proportions since total first fixation time durations for a given disyllable varied across infants. In addition, the conversion to proportions took into account the potential infuence of a right-turning tendency.

We obtained proportions of first fixation time spent looking at auditory-visual matches from each infant for each disyllable. Proportions were computed by dividing the time spent looking at a match (right, left, or combined sides) by the total first fixation time for that comparison. For each comparison, total first fixation times were summed across two trials. Table 1 summarizes the comparisons we made and the means of these computations.

The overall proportion of total, right and left, first fixation time spent looking at matches was significantly greater than for mismatches ($z < -2.64$, $p = .004$; Wilcoxon Matched Pairs Signed Ranks Test, one-tailed).

On the right side, the proportion of total first fixation time spent looking at matches was significantly greater than for mismatches overall ($z \leq 2.66$, $p = .004$, one-tailed) and for three of the six disyllables: mama, bebi, and zuzu (with respective values of $z < -2.46$, $p = .007$, $n = 17$, one-tie; $z < -1.94$, $p = .03$, $n = 17$, one-tie; $z < -2.27$, $p = .01$). All tests were one-tailed. Proportions were in the correct direction (>.50) for all six disyllables (Table 1). On the left side, the proportion of total first fixation time spent looking at matches was not significantly greater than for mismatches overall nor on any of the six disyllables. Proportions were greater than .50 for only three of the disyllables.

On the right side, the number of infants who spent more than half of their first fixation time looking at matches versus mismatches was significant, on a binomial test, for two disyllables (mama, 13/18, $p = .05$; zuzu, 14/18, $p = .02$), but corresponding tests for left-side looking were not significant.

In a right-left comparison, the proportion of total first fixation time spent looking at auditory-visual matches was significantly greater on the right side than on the left side overall ($z \leq -2.02$, $p=.02$) and for three out of the six disyllables: (mama, bebi, and zuzu (respectively, $z<-1.87$, $p=.03$; $z\leq-1.68$, $p=.05$; $z\leq-1.96$, $p=.03$). All tests were one-tailed. Right side proportions were greater than left for all six disyllables (Table 1).

The direction of infants' first look following trial onset was to the right side on 58% of the total trials ($N=215$).

One potential source of response bias, a preference for a visual articulatory pattern irrespective of the auditory pattern that accompanied it, might have influenced these results. To check this, Spearman Rank Order Correlation coefficients were computed for preferences to a video display when the auditory signal matched the video display and when it did not match the video display. We computed correlations for right and left sides combined as well as for each side separately. A strong positive correlation would indicate infants preferred to look at a particular articulatory pattern irrespective of the CVCV to which they were listening. None of the correlations was significant.

In summary, infants looked significantly longer at synchronized video displays of a woman articulating a disyllable that matched what they were hearing, than at an alternative display that did not match what they were hearing. Moreover, the preference for auditory-visual matches occurred exclusively when infants were attending to the right side: we found significant preferences only for right matches over right mismatches, and for right matches over left matches.

Discussion

These findings indicate mutual facilitation of two left-hemisphere functions: rightward orientation of attention and intermodal speech perception. The relation between prelinguistic infants' recognition of intermodal speech properties and their remarkable capacity to reproduce speech seen and heard (de Boysson-Bardies, this Conference; de Boysson-Bardies, Sagart, and Bacri, 1981) may rest in a predisposition of the left hemisphere to discover sensorimotor links between perceived speech structure and its articulatory source.

Two opposing accounts have been offered for the convergence of visual and auditory information in intermodal speech perception. One proposes a combination of modality-specific information, represented by discrete, phonetic features (MacDonald & McGurk, 1978). The other proposes that an abstract, modality-free prelinguistic pattern emerges from the active integration of two continuous sources of information, acoustic and optic, about the dynamics of articulation (Summerfield, 1979).

These findings are consistent with the view proposed by Summerfield (1979) in that his explanation makes unnecessary the attribution of a priori phonetic knowledge to prelinguistic infants in recovering speech structure during perception in order that it may be reproduced during the prelinguistic, babbling period.

We are parsimoniously assuming that infants' sensitivity to auditory-visual correlates of articulation are made on the basis of prelinguistic, intermodal properties which provide equivalent information about articulation. Of these three possible auditory dimensions for speech - fundamental frequency, amplitude, and the distribution of spectral energy -- only the last two seem to have natural correlates in the visual domain. Distribution of spectral energy and amplitude vary directly with mouth opening. Infants may be sensitive to some pattern of change shared by, for example, degree of mouth opening or of lip rounding and either (or both) of the two auditory dimensions. Whatever the structure of the auditory-visual correlates, we know that the language learner eventually comes to perceive auditory-visual relations for speech according to phonological correspondences. The infant's acquisition of these relations might be facilitated if the information linking auditory and visual speech events were first apprehended according to prelinguistic properties which subsequently give rise to linguistic parameters as the child acquires a phonology.

References

de Boysson-Bardies, B., Sagart L. & Bacri, N. Phonetic analysis of late babbling: a case study of a French child. Journal of Child Language, 1981, 8, 511-524.

Dixon, N.F. & Spitz, L. The detection of auditory visual desynchrony. Perception, 1980, 9, 719-721.

Dodd, B. The role of vision in the perception of speech. Perception, 1977, 6, 31-40.

Dodd, B. Lip-reading in infants: attention to speech presented in- and out-of-synchrony. Cognitive Psychology, 1979, 11, 478-484.

Kinsbourne, M. Cerebral basis of lateral asymmetrics in attention. Acta Psychologica, 1970, 33, 193-201.

Kinsbourne, M. The control of attention by interaction between the cerebral hemispheres. M.S. Kornblum (Ed), Attention and Performance IV. New York: Academic Press; 1973.

Lempert, H. & Kinsbourne, M. Effect of laterality of orientation of verbal memory. Neuropsychologia, 1982, 20, 211-214.

MacDonald, J. & McGurk, H. Visual influences on speech perception processes. Perception and Psychophysics, 1978, 24, 253-257.

McGurk, H. & MacDonald, J. Hearing lips and seeing voices: A new illusion. Nature, 1976, 264, 746-748.

Spelke, E.S. Infants' intermodal perception of events. Cognitive Psychology, 1976, 8, 5530560.

Spelke, E.S. Perceiving bimodally specified events in infancy. Developmental Psychology, 1979, 15, 626-636.

Spelke, E.S. & Cortelyou, A. Looking and listening in infancy. In M.E. Lamb and L.R. Sherrod (Eds), Infant Social Cognition: Empirical and Theoretical Considerations, Hillsdale: Earlbaum, 1981, 61-84.

Summerfield, Q. Use of visual information for phonetic perception. Phonetica, 1979, 36, 314-331.

DESIGN

Conditions	Audio	Video
		Left	Right
	mama	mama	lulu
1		lulu	mama
	lulu	lulu	mama
		mama	lulu
	bebi	bebi	zuzi
		zuzi	bebi
2			
	zuzi	zuzi	bebi
		bebi	zuzi
	vava	vava	zuzu
3		zuzu	vava
	zuzu	zuzu	vava
		vava	zuzu

APPARATUS

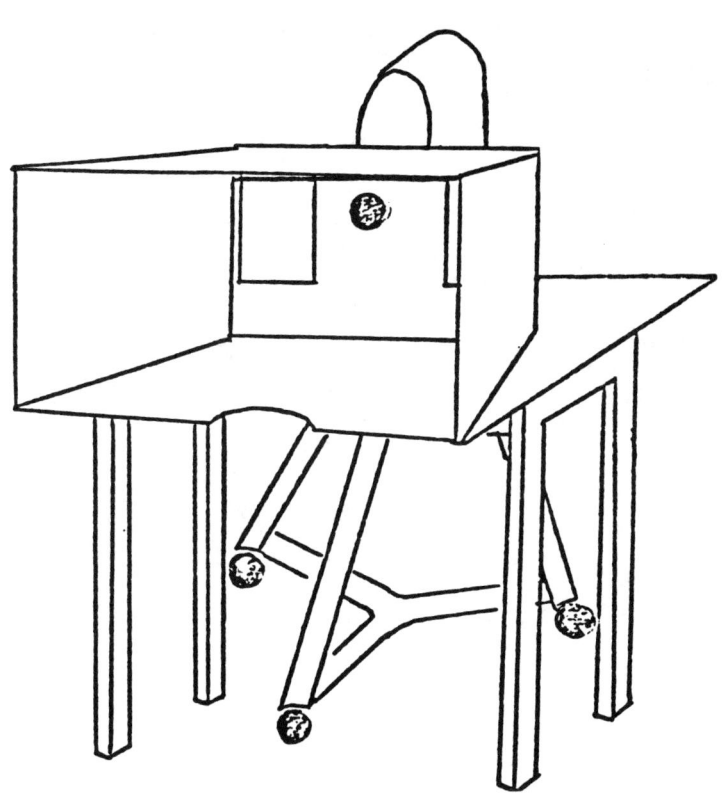

15

Table I

Proportion of first fixation time, averaged over 18 infants, spent looking at matches vs. mismatches, right vs. left matches, right matches vs. right mismatches, and left matches vs. left mismatches.

Proportion of time of time spent looking at	bebi	zuzi	Disyllable mama	lulu	vava	zuzu	Overall
Right Matches vs. Right Mismatches	.59	.52	.62	.53	.52	.61	.57
Left Matches vs. Left Mismatches	.54	.50	.54	.49	.49	.52	.51
Right vs. Left Matches	.57	.57	.61	.52	.58	.59	.57

RECALL ERRORS AND NATURAL PHONOLOGY

Jean Aitchison
(London School of Economics and Political Science)

and

Shulamuth Chiat
(School for the Study of Disorders of Human Communication)

Linguists have now identified a number of so-called natural processes in the speech of young children (Chiat, 1979; Ingram, 1979). To give a few well-known examples, we find extensive consonant harmony, as [kɔ:k] for 'talk', or [gʌk] for 'duck'. We find a tendency to omit final consonants, as in [du:] for 'juice', which is in turn part of a tendency to reduce syllables to a simple consonant-vowel structure, as in [di:] for 'eat'. And there are several others.

Why exactly these processes exist remains a puzzle. A few of them may be attributed to perception and production problems. But these explanations are only partial, and a number of processes remain a mystery.

This paper[1] is an attempt to shed light on the problem. We would like to argue that a number of these natural processes may be memory filters -- that is, processes applied when there is too much pressure on the memory to recall lexical items accurately. The processes reveal themselves in situations where perception and production problems can be shown to be absent, but where memory overload is guaranteed. These 'natural memory' processes, as we may call them, became apparent when we presented a number of new words to children aged between four and nine. The children in our study could correctly imitate these new words. Yet after a short delay, their attempts to recall the words showed deformations which included a number of the natural processes noted in younger children.

Our subjects were 90 children between the ages of four and nine drawn from two schools in a predominantly middle class area on the outskirts of London (Harrow). We interviewed each child separately, and the session was recorded. In the interview, the child was shown picturebooks containing animals, and was asked to talk about the pictures. The children could name most of the animals without difficulty, since they were common ones such as pig, rabbit, elephant. Scattered among the common animals were a number of uncommon ones: armadillo [ɑːməˈdɪləʊ], bandicoot [ˈbændɪkuːt], cuscus [ˈkʊskʊs], kudu [ˈkvduː], lemming [ˈlemɪŋ], mongoose [ˈmɒŋguːs], raccoon [rəˈkuːn], tapir [ˈteɪpɪə], and yak [jæk].

When a strange animal appeared, the child was either baffled, "I've never seen one like that before', or made a wrong guess, "Is it a kind of buffalo?". At this point, we introduced the animal's name, and explained a little about it. The strange animals recurred at intervals throughout the books, much to the frustration of some children, "Oh no, not that one again!" We aimed to show each new animal at least four times, and we also checked that each child could perceive and produce the word concerned.[2]

In this task, we tried to provide the kind of situation which children of this age often meet. Four to nine year olds are bombarded with sets of new words, and find it quite normal to be told the names of new things. Most of them joined in willingly.

Our experiment was designed to discover which phonological aspects of a word were consistently maintained by children, and which tended to be unstable. In order to do this, we examined the erroneous attempts at the strange animals in respect of the following seven phonological variables: (1) initial consonant; (2) final consonant; (3) stressed vowel; (4) number of syllables; (5) stress placement; (6) consonant preceding vowel with primary stress; (7) consonant(s) preceding vowel with primary stress. Owing to lack of time, we will (in this paper) concentrate on the first four.

We discovered that there was wide variation in the recall of each variable, depending on the word involved. We therefore attempted to identify some of the factors which affected the variables. We found certain recurring phonological processes which were not necessarily linked to any one variable.

We will now outline the processes which affected the phonological variables, and then give our general conclusions.

As we can see, recall of initial consonants showed wide variation (see Table 1). The need to consider a word as a whole is shown by the fact that [k] was better recalled at the beginning of kudu than at the beginning of cuscus, in spite of the fact that both are two-syllable words with initial stress, beginning with [kʊ].

An initial consonant was remembered best when it directly preceded the stressed vowel, and agreed in voicing with the following consonant, as in bandicoot, lemming, and tapir. In raccoon these conditions did not hold, and the initial consonant was disrupted both by consonant harmony, and the loss of the initial syllable. Of the 19 errors on this word, seven were due to consonant harmony, as in [gəku:n], and six to loss of the first syllable, as in [ku:n]. (British children are not familiar with raccoons, so this was a totally new word to them.)

Kudu was another word in which consonant harmony disrupted the initial consonant (see Figure 1). Those who failed to preserve the initial [k] mostly made it agree in voicing with the following [d], producing attempts such as ['gʊdu:], though agreement in place of articulation was also found as in [tu:du:]. Meanwhile, those who preserved the initial [k] tended to harmonize the following consonant, as in [kə'gu:].

In armadillo, which began with a vowel, we found five examples of an inserted initial consonant, as in ['mɑ:mədɪ-ləʊ]. This error suggests a preference for a consonant-vowel syllable structure, especially since the reverse error, deletion of an initial consonant, was rare, occurring on average once per animal.

In a number of errors, children substituted a sound from the same natural class, usually differing in one feature from the target, as in goose-goose for cuscus.

To summarize our findings on initial consonants, we noted four major phonological processes which caused errors: consonant harmony, loss of an unstressed initial syllable, a tendency towards consonant-vowel syllable structure, and confusion with another phoneme from the same natural class as the target. Together, these tendencies accounted for 72% of the errors on initial consonants.

Table 1.

Percentage of children whose erroneous attempts were identical to the target in respect of 4 variables

	INITIAL CONSONANT	FINAL CONSONANT	STRESSED VOWEL	NUMBER OF SYLLABLES
ARMADILLO N=23	70	91	61	61
BANDICOOT N=21	81	24	86	86
CUSCUS N=54	41	61	9	93
KUDU N=52	69	85	4	83
LEMMING N=36	86	22	75	81
MONGOOSE N=16	50	62	62	69
RACCOON N=17	18	88	100	65
TAPIR N=29	90	72	55	45
YAK N=17	35	65	55	76

FIG. 1

KUDU CONSONANT HARMONY

(The figures in round brackets indicate the number of children who produced each error).

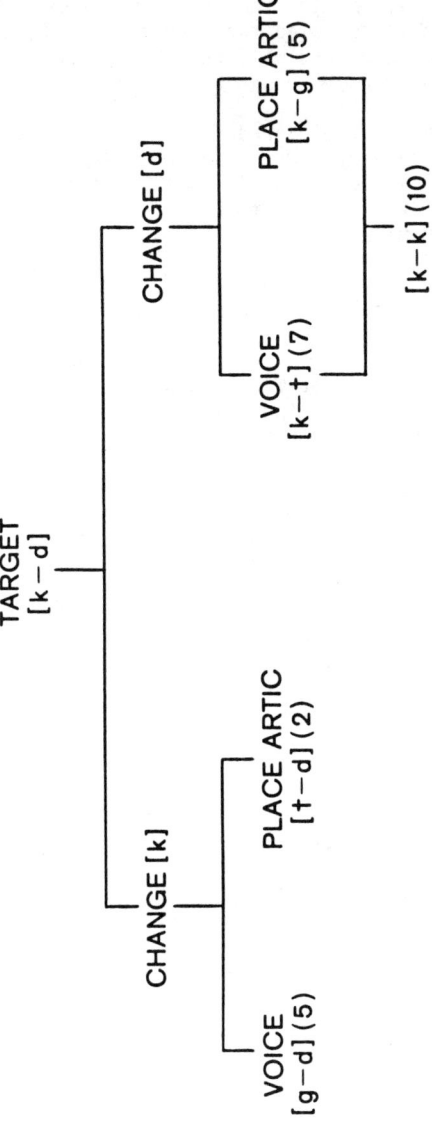

Let us now look at the treatment of final consonants (see Table 1). A final consonant was reasonably well recalled when it followed the stressed vowel, as in raccoon and yak, but not very well remembered when the final syllable was unstressed as in bandicoot.

The most notable error was simple omission. This supports the tendency towards consonant-vowel syllable structure noted earlier. In line with this tendency, the children had little difficulty in remembering that armadillo, kudu, and tapir had no final consonant.

Once again, children tended to replace a final consonant with one from the same natural class, as in ['bændɪku:p] for bandicoot.

Overall, loss of final consonant, and confusion with another phoneme from the same natural class accounted for 66% of the final consonant errors.

Now for the stressed vowel. Errors on this variable tended to be vowels adjacent to the target typically preserving the frontness or backness of the target better than its height, as in ['ku:sku:s] for cuscus.

On a number of occasions, the original stressed vowel was reduced or omitted due to shifting of stress. In kudu, for example, [ʊ] was realized as [ə] in 33 attempts, as in [kə'du:], an error apparently due to the shifting of stress to the following tense vowel.

Overall, 76% of the errors on the stressed vowel were accounted for by the substitution of an immediately higher or lower vowel, or by the reduction of the stressed vowel due to stress shift.

Finally, number of syllables (see Table 1). This variable was preserved best in the word cuscus, where the reduplication presumably helped, since children sometimes remembered this and little else, with attempts such as choo-choo, moose-moose. Elsewhere, the number of syllables tended to be well recalled when the word had initial stress, as in bandicoot, lemming.

The most prominent error was the omission of an unstressed syllable. This tendency was particularly strong initially, as in [kuːn] for raccoon, though examples occurred in other parts of the word also, as in ['dændiː], ['bæŋkuːt] for bandicoot.

The word tapir, which we treated as bisyllabic, presented an interesting problem for the children. They clearly had difficulty in deciding whether the final diphthong [ɪə] contained one or two syllables. There were 10 attempts with triphthongs at the end, as in ['teɪpɪəʊ], and 6 with three syllables, as in ['tæridə].

Overall, 65% of the errors in number of syllables were accounted for by unstressed syllable omission, and the problem over the final diphthong in tapir.

Let us now conclude. The erroneous attempts at the target words revealed a number of tendencies:

(i)   Consonant-vowel syllable structure.
(ii) Omission of unstressed syllables.
(iii) Consonant harmony.
(iv) Substitution of a consonant from the same natural class as the target.
(v)   Substitution of a vowel adjacent to the target.
(vi) Placement of stress on a tense vowel.
(vii) Confusion over the number of syllables in a falling diphthong.

These seven tendencies accounted for 71% of errors on the four variables discussed: initial consonant, final consonant, stressed vowel, number of syllables (see Table 2). Considering the number of random errors which could have been made, this figure is striking.

Our list of faulty recall characteristics looks remarkably like a summary of the phonological processes typically found in the speech of very young children. It seems unlikely that the resemblance is accidental. We suggest that our results reflect a relationship between the two. We tentatively propose two explanations, which possibly interact with one another:

1. A number of the processes found in the speech of very

Table 2.

Percentage of errors accounted for by seven phonological tendencies

	INITIAL CONSONANT	FINAL CONSONANT	STRESSED VOWEL	NUMBER SYLLABLES	TOTAL
	N=116	N=112	N=210	N=95	N=533
(i)	4	35	0	0	8
(ii)	10	0	0	48	11
(iii)	19	0	0	0	4
(iv)	39	31	0	0	15
(v)	0	0	57	0	22
(vi)	0	0	19	0	8
(vii)	0	0	0	17	3
TOTAL	72	66	76	65	71

young children may be due to faulty recall. That is, in learning new words, a child's memory is overloaded, so that not all features of new words are stored.

2. Faulty recall may reflect the ordering of perceptual features in memory. That is, those phonetic features which are most perceptually salient may also be those that are most salient in auditory memory.

These tentative explanations need to be explored in greater depth, along with alternative possibilities. For example, some of these tendencies may reflect an inability to organize the stored form into the required phonetic shape.

These observations raise a number of further questions:

(1) Are the tendencies we have noted a subset of the natural phonological processes found in the speech of very young children, or are the two sets co-extensive?

(2) Are the tendencies we have observed universal, or are they due to the phonological structure of English?

(3) Are the same tendencies found in the faulty recall of words by adults? These are some of the questions which we are currently investigating.

To summarise, we have demonstrated that patterns of recall errors made by four to nine year olds in a word-learning task closely resemble certain phonological processes found in the speech of very young children. We suggest that the role of memory, which has hitherto been virtually ignored by linguists, needs to be taken into consideration.

NOTES

[1].This paper is the actual text of the paper given at Vancouver. A fuller account can be found in Aitchison and Chiat (1981). The research is part of a project entitled 'The Dissimilarity Hypothesis: Differences between Child and Adult Lexical Storage and Retrieval' supported by the Social Science Research Council and carried out by the authors at the London School of Economics.

[2.] For a more detailed account of the methodology see Aitchison and Chiat (1981).

REFERENCES

AITCHISON, J. and CHIAT, S. (1981), 'Natural phonology or natural memory? The interaction between phonological processes and recall mechanisms.' Language and Speech 24, 311-326.

CHIAT, S. (1979), 'The role of the word in phonological development.' Linguistics 17, 591-610.

INGRAM, D. (1979), 'Phonological patterns in the speech of young children.' In P. Fletcher and M. Garman (eds.), Language Acquisition (Cambridge University Press), 133-148.

Phonological Processes Affecting Consonants in the
Acquisition of American English: the Olmsted Data

Mary Schramm Coberly
University of Colorado

It is of interest to identify the more widespread strategies in children's phonological acquisition because they may point to the phonetic constraints that most or all children are faced with in learning to speak. The data collected by David Olmsted for the research reported in Out of the Mouths of Babes (1971) is of special value for this purpose. It is based on a sample of 100 children, and thus is one of the few large-sample studies, like Wellman et al. (1931), Templin (1957), Snow (1963), and Ingram's study of initial fricatives (1980). The Olmsted sample contains very young children; as Table 1 shows, 43 of the sample analyzed in this paper were under 30 months, considerably more than in the other studies. It is also the only study based entirely on spontaneous conversation, with suspected imitations thrown out, in contrast to the other studies which have used picture identification and description, or direct imitation.

Age	Girls	Boys
16-23 mos	9	5
24-29 mos	14	15
30-35 mos	7	8
36-41 mos	6	4
42-47 mos	3	2
48-53 mos	3	2
TOTALS	42	36

Table 1. Distribution of age and sex in the sample analyzed in this paper.

Because of the way they are grouped, the data presented in Olmsted's book are not fully usable for comparing frequencies of pronunciation errors. The number of children not attempting a sound is lumped with the number consistently mispronouncing it, and thus one cannot tell whether sounds that are rare in certain environments are seldom pronounced correctly in those environments, or simply seldom attempted.

For this study of error patterns in consonants, therefore, I have reanalyzed the original interview data for 78 children, kindly supplied by David Olmsted. Data on the 22 others were in use for other research at the time of this study, but had been selected randomly rather than for their linguistic content, according to Olmsted.

Data Analysis

The data on each interview consists of transcriptions of recordings and notes of the utterances of (usually) a single child during one interview, elicited by conversation with the transcriber. Transcription is broad, capturing allophone-sized deviations. Each child's utterance is paired with a transcription of its presumed target utterance in the mother's pronunciation, according to the combined judgments of transcriber and mother. Discrepancies between child's utterances and their targets provide the basic data on errors, listed in Table 2.

Correct interpretation of target utterances is one of the main difficulties in this study. Reinterpretations were made during my analysis, and further reinterpretations are suggested by the results. I have consulted with David Olmsted and he concurs with the following comments on Table 2. (1) Most [h] substitutions for [w] which are listed in the table are probably really [h] substitutions for [hw]. Some [w] substitutions for [hw] probably occurred, which are not listed in the table. (2) The number of voicing errors with intervocalic [t] is probably too high in the table, due to underestimation of tapping in target utterances. But since strong intervocalic voicing also occurs with [p] and [k], which are not tapped in adult speech, voicing is apparently a real error pattern. Thus the proportion of children making voicing errors out of total number attempting [t] intervocalically in Figure 1 is probably not greatly inflated. (Instead, the number attempting is inflated.) (3) The number of substitutions of [n] for [ŋ] in the table is too high due to underestimation of fronting in the target utterances. While .57 of the children attempting target [ŋ]'s fronted them, only .08 children fronted [ŋ] in words like "ring" and "thing", which are not fronted in informal adult usage. This latter must be closer to the real rate of phonological error.

The following method of analysis was used. Data were

Targets ↓	Substitutions Initial	Substitutions Intervocalic	Substitutions Final
p	b 9	b 8	∅ 5, k
t	d 7, k 5, ∅,p,č	∅ 17, d 14, ʔ,khly	∅ 42, d, ʔ
k	g 8, h,d,b	g 7, p	∅ 11, ʔ,t
b	w 7, m 4, p,∅,v,h	∅,w,β,d	∅
d	g 10, b	∅ 18, g 4, l,y,tʔ	∅ 22, t 10
g	k,∅	k 8, d 4, ∅	k 9, ∅
f	v,ps,z,čy,tw	∅	d,v,∅
θ	s	t	∅ 8, f
s	θ 7, š 7, t 5, h, d,č	θ	∅ 15, θ 7, t 5, š
š	s 15, ž,∅,č,h,y, θ,sy	∅	θ 7, ∅ 6, s 4
c	t 8, š 6, d,ts	t 4, ty	t
v	b	b,d	b
ð	d 55, ∅ 15, y 8, z,t,g,ǰ,w	d 5, ∅	not attempted
z	∅,dy	s	s 19, ∅ 10, š,θ,ð
ǰ	d 5, ž 4	∅	∅,z,d,ž
m	∅ 6, b 5, w	∅ 4, n	∅ 11, n
n	d,m,∅	∅ 13, d 4	∅ 35, m,ʔ,ŋ,t
ŋ		no errors	n 20, ∅ 6
r	w 16, ∅	∅ 8, w 6	∅ 34, vowel 20
l	w 12, ∅ 7, y 4, d	∅ 20, w 5, d,n,r,vowel	∅ 34, w
w	∅ 11, h 5, f	∅,t,l,r	
y	∅ 4, w	not attempted	
h	∅ 22, ʔ,b,t	not attempted	

Table 2. Major substitution errors and numbers of children making them in three environments.

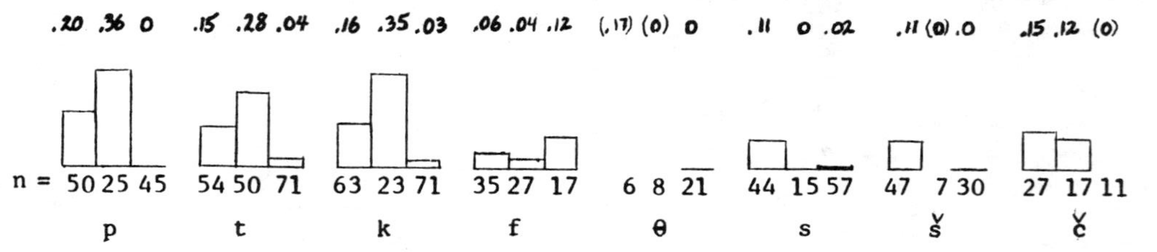

Figure 1. Proportions of children substituting voiced segments for voiceless obstruents. Each set of bars represents (left to right) initial, medial, and final positions. n = number attempting.

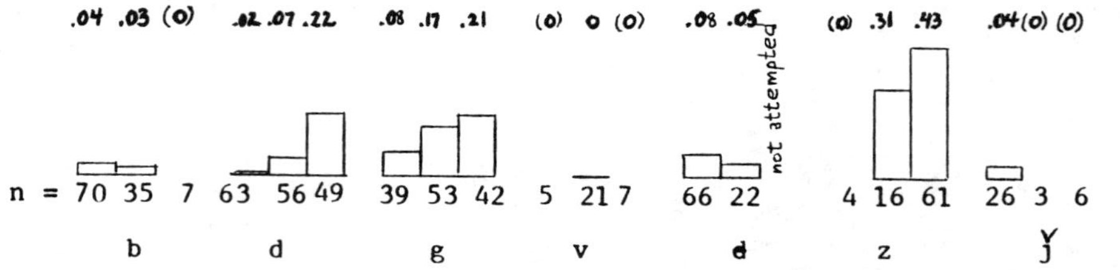

Figure 2. Proportions of children substituting voiceless segments for voiced obstruents. Each set of bars represents (left to right) initial, medial, and final positions. n = number attempting.

punched on cards by the investigator and computer-sorted into lists of utterances for each correct and incorrect consonant in each environment. Errors and correct tokens were then hand-counted from each list. Errors that seemed likely to be morphological or even stylistic rather than phonological ("baby go" for "baby goes"; "gonna" for "going to") were thrown out. In the end, all single-consonant suffixes were thrown out because it was impossible to distinguish morphological from phonological final dropping. Three environments were then isolated for study that seemed to produce the most clearcut error patterns: utterance-initial, utterance-final, and medial within morphemes. (Thus [t] in "bottle" was counted, but [t] in "bought a pig" was not, being on a morpheme boundary.) Because of limits on presentation time and publication space, only singlet consonants, not clusters, were studied for the final analysis. Syllabic consonants and syllable-final glides were considered vowels, but syllable-final liquids were counted as consonants. Numbers of children producing errors or correct tokens were counted, rather than total numbers of tokens, since the question of most interest was the proportion of children following various strategies, which might have been distorted by large differences between the numbers of times consonants were attempted by different children.

Results

In the graphs in Figures 1 - 6, error (or correct) patterns are presented as proportions of children attempting each consonant who produced at least one incorrect (or correct) token. The number attempting each consonant in each position is listed under that bar. It was necessary to count numbers attempting because not all children attempted each consonant in each environment. Thus, in Figure 1, for example, 50 children attempted initial [p], and .20 of those produced voiced substitutions. Measures of statistical significance were not applied because the separate observations were not independent, owing to the large overlap in children attempting different consonants. It is not certain how large a sample would be needed, to be representative of the population of middle-class American English-learning children. Subsamples under about 15 children seemed particularly erratic, and hence bars were not drawn for them in the figures; the proportions for such subsamples are parenthesized.

1. Major voicing substitution patterns

Final, and occasionally intervocalic devoicing of obstruents is shown in Figure 2. All voiced obstruents attempted by large enough subsamples to be representative show greater substitution of voiceless consonants in final position than elsewhere. The dramatic absence of voicing errors in final position, shown in Figure 1, provides further evidence that voicing is disfavored finally.

There are two possible cues which transcribers could hear as final devoicing: failure to lengthen the preceding vowel, and early cessation of vocal fold vibration, probably owing to the difficulty of maintaining the air pressure gradient for voicing against increasing impedance at the end of a breath group. Both types of error have been reported in children (Naeser 1970, Raphael et al. 1974, Smith 1977, Greenlee 1977). As Figure 3 shows, final devoicing does not decrease with age, in contrast to the other major patterns. Possibly therefore the transcribers focussed on the vocal fold vibration cue, which adults often do not produce for final voicing, and which children might not develop with increasing age. Of course the absence of a decline in errors might be an artifact of the small subsamples.

Substantial devoicing also occurs intervocalically with [g] and [z], but not [d], [b], or [ɖ]. The tendency for devoicing to happen with back obstruents but not front again suggests that the vocal fold vibration cue is not being produced owing to difficulty in maintaining air pressure, especially with a small supraglottal cavity.

Intervocalic and initial voicing of stops, affricates, and fricatives is shown in Figure 1. Initial voicing of stops is usually thought to be a response to the difficulty of coordinating precise timing of the tongue and vocal folds. A similar constraint should affect initial affricates: it should be easier to set the vocal folds in position for voicing at any time before the release of the stop portion of the affricate (as with [ǰ]) than to begin voicing and release of fricative occlusion at approximately the same time, as required to produce [ɣ]. The same difficulty should affect voiceless initial fricatives, since voicing must be timed to start as fricative occlusion is released.

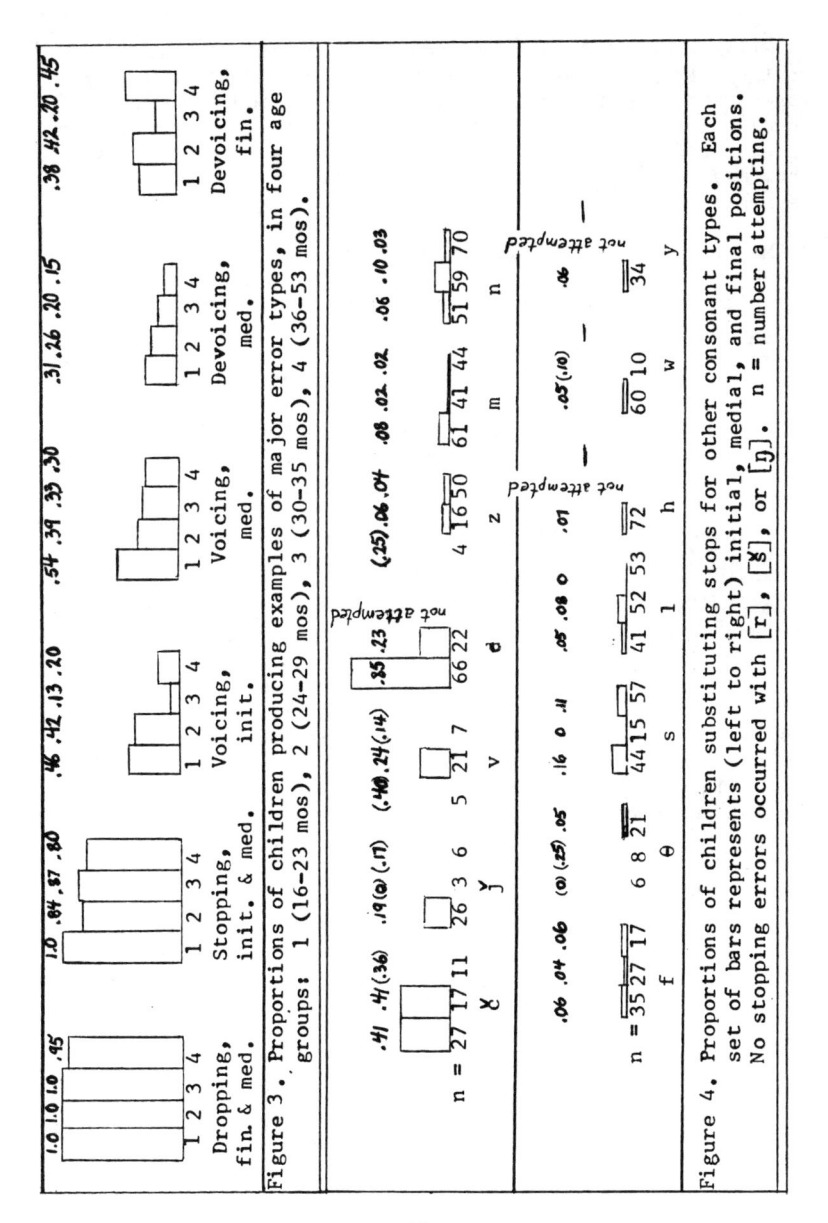

Figure 3. Proportions of children producing examples of major error types, in four age groups: 1 (16-23 mos), 2 (24-29 mos), 3 (30-35 mos), 4 (36-53 mos).

Figure 4. Proportions of children substituting stops for other consonant types. Each set of bars represents (left to right) initial, medial, and final positions. No stopping errors occurred with [r], [š], or [tʃ]. n = number attempting.

Intervocalic voicing strategy is probably a response both to the difficulty of coordinating vocal fold with tongue gestures, and also to the rapidity of release and resumption of vocal fold vibration. Perhaps the second difficulty is lessened for fricatives because of their longer durations, and that may be why intervocalic voicing of fricatives appears to be negligible.

2. Major manner substitution patterns

Stopping of affricates and voiced front fricatives [v] and [ð] is shown in Figure 4. Because of the small subsamples, one cannot tell from this data whether stopping is more frequent initially than elsewhere, as suggested by Ferguson (1973), Ingram (1978, 1980), and Edwards (1979). The extremely frequent stopping of initial [ð] probably represents alveolar substitution rather than actual stopping, since interdental stops would be transcribed as [d̪].

Interestingly, the stopping of the voiced labial fricative [v] is matched by a similar tendency toward manner substitution (spirantizing and gliding) in the voiced labial stop [b](Table 2). This may reflect auditory perceptual confusions. Wang & Bilger (1973, Tables II-IX) show that [f] and [v] are misheard as stops more often than other fricatives, and [b] is misheard as a fricative more often than other stops, in initial position. (In final position, all obstruents are misheard as other manners fairly often.)

Gliding and vocalizing of liquids can be seen in Table 2. The gliding consists mainly of [w] substitutions, chiefly in initial position where adults are more likely to round the lips in pronouncing liquids. Vowel substitution occurs mainly for final [r].

3. Major place substitution pattern

Initial velar substitutions for alveolar stops, shown in Table 2, occurred frequently in apparent consonant harmony forms, such as "goggy" for "doggy" and "guck" for "duck". All 10 children substituting [g] for initial [d], in fact, did so in consonant harmony forms. A preference for velar harmony has been noted by Ferguson, Peizer & Weeks (1973), and reported for several children (Smith 1973, Menn 1975), but was not prominent in Vihman's 1978 cross-language sample

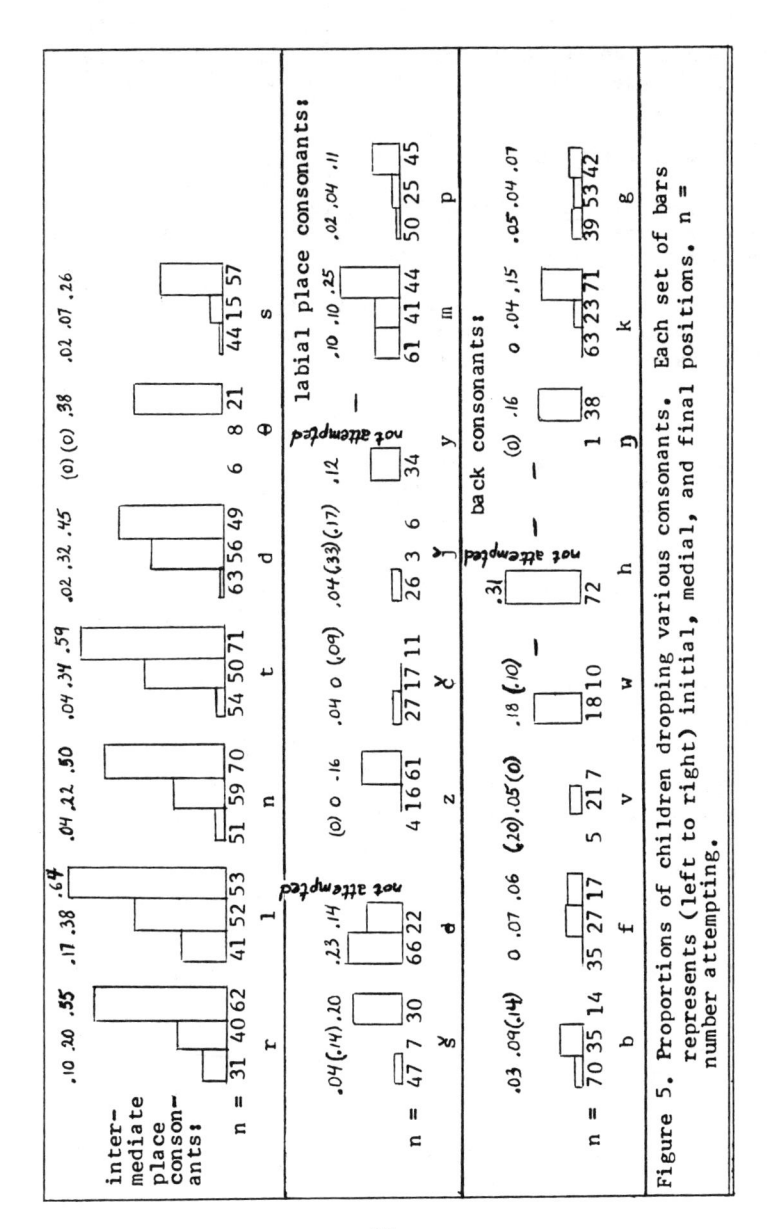

Figure 5. Proportions of children dropping various consonants. Each set of bars represents (left to right) initial, medial, and final positions. n = number attempting.

of 13 children producing consonant harmony. Perhaps it is more characteristic of English than of certain other languages.

4. Major dropping patterns

Final, and to a lesser extent intervocalic dropping of consonants can be seen in Figure 5, and as ∅ substitutions in Table 2. This pattern would be the expected outcome of a syllable-final dropping strategy, with intervocalic consonants interpreted by children as sometimes syllable-initial and sometimes syllable-final. It undoubtedly represents the often noted tendency in early speech (as well as world languages, Bell 1971) to prefer CV syllable form.

An exception, [d], is dropped more often initially than intervocalically, mainly in the words "that", "this", "the", and "there". This may be direct imitation of adult informal norms as in "atta boy".

Dropping of intermediate place consonants to a greater extent than extreme front or back consonants is evident in Figure 5. Alveolar, interdental, and palatal consonants are dropped by larger proportions of children than labial or velar consonants, a pattern that has not been noticed previously, to my knowledge.

Dropping of liquids, nasals, stops, and [h] to a greater extent than fricatives, affricates, or semivowels is also apparent in Figure 5. Intermediate place fricatives and [y] tend to be dropped by fewer children than intermediate place liquids, nasals, and stops. Labial fricatives and [w] are also dropped by fewer children than labial nasals or stops. This tendency not to drop fricatives, affricates, and semivowels has also not been noticed before, to my knowledge.

5. Relative rates of acquisition of various consonant classes

Figure 6 shows the proportions of children producing correct tokens of various consonants out of numbers of children attempting them. While these are not measures of order of acquisition, they tend to parallel claims that have been made about order of acquisition. The relationship between these success rates and similar statistics on error rates is a direct one: consonants that show high success rates show low error rates, and vice versa.

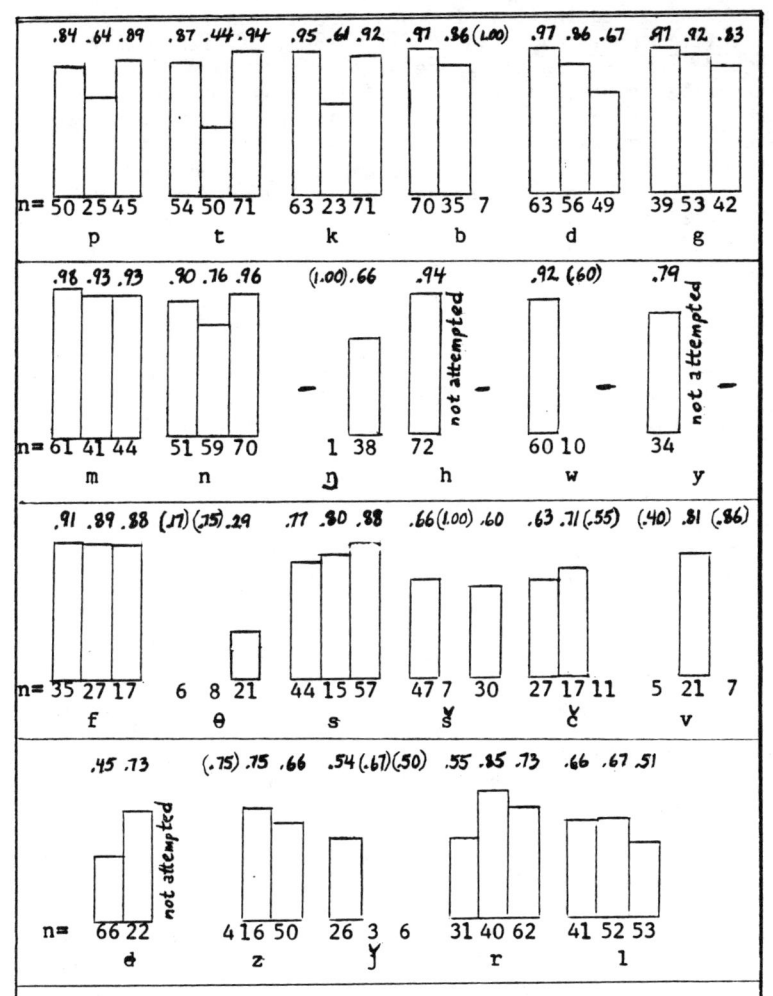

Figure 6. Proportions of children producing correct tokens of various consonants. Each set of bars represents (left to right) initial, medial, and final positions. n = number attempting.

Faster acquisition of stops, nasals, and glides (mainly in initial position) than of fricatives, affricates, or liquids can be seen in Figure 6. The advantage is not as strong intervocalically and finally, mainly because of errors other than manner substitutions: voicing and devoicing of stops, intervocalic dropping of [n], and absence of data on glides in those positions. The greater frequency of stopping and gliding errors than of spirant or liquid substitutions (Table 2) also indicates greater ease of acquisition of stops and glides; it is not clear whether stopping and gliding are more likely to occur initially than in other positions. It is striking that nasals, although acquired correctly quite rapidly, very rarely substitute for other manners.

Faster acquisition of labial than other places, except for [p] can be seen in Figure 6. [b] does not appear to have an advantage over other voiced stops in Figure 6, but it is in fact acquired faster in the youngest two age groups. (The data are not illustrated for lack of space.) [p] is not ahead of other voiceless stops even in the younger age groups. This may correspond to the weakness of [p] and [g] to which Ferguson (1975) has called attention. [g] is also acquired more slowly than [k] in the youngest two age groups.

Slower acquisition of interdental than other places is apparent in Figure 6 in spite of the small subsamples. The weakness of interdentals in child speech and their scarcity in world languages (Hockett 1955) may be due in part to perceptual constraints. Wang & Bilger (1973, Tables II-IX) show lower rates of correct identification of interdental fricatives than of any other consonants utterance-initially, and almost any other utterance-finally.

Faster acquisition of voiceless than voiced fricatives can be seen in Figure 6, although based only on comparisons of intervocalic [f] and [v], intervocalic and final [s] and [z], and initial [č] and [ǰ]. The errors that contributed most strongly to the disadvantage of voiced fricatives were not devoicing, however, except in the case of [z], but were mainly stopping errors.

Faster acquisition of some fricatives than some stops intervocalically and finally can be seen in Figure 6. Ferguson (1973) has observed that fricatives are frequently acquired first intervocalically or finally, where they often precede stops. In the Olmsted data, some voiceless fricatives are acquired faster than the voiced stops finally, and all fricatives are acquired faster than voiceless stops intervocalically, due to the strong voicing and devoicing errors among stops.

Conclusions

The main surprises in the Olmsted data are children's preferences for dropping intermediate place rather than front or back place consonants, and for dropping liquids, nasals, stops, and [h] rather than fricatives, affricates, or semivowels. The strategy of initial fronting and final backing, noticed by Ingram (1974) and Bleile (at this conference) is not a significant pattern in this data; possibly it is characteristic of only a small minority of children. The more rapid acquisition of some fricatives than some stops intervocalically and finally, and the more rapid acquisition of voiceless than of voiced fricatives, seem to be artifacts of other, phonetically diverse strategies, rather than directly reflecting phonetic constraints. Aside from these points, the Olmsted data confirms previous widely held generalizations about English-learning children's error tendencies.

References

Bell, A. 1971. 'Some patterns of occurrence and formation of syllable structures.' Working Papers Linguistic Universals 6. Stanford.

Edwards, M.L. 1979. 'Phonological processes in fricative acquisition.' PRCLD 17.98-105.

Ferguson, C.A. 1973. 'The acquisition of fricatives.' PRCLD 6.61-86.

_____ 1975. 'Sound patterns in language acquisition.' 26th Annual Georgetown Round Table, March 13.

_____, Peizer, D.B. & Weeks, T.E. 1973. 'Model and replica grammar of a child's first words.' Lingua 31. 35-65.

Greenlee, M. 1977. 'Learning the phonetic cues to the voiced-voiceless distinction: preliminary study of four American English speaking children.' Seventh Annual Meeting California Linguistics Association, Fresno, Cal. April 30-May 1.

Hockett, C.F. 1955. A manual of phonology. (Pt. I, IJAL 21, No. 4).

Ingram, D. 1974. 'Fronting in child phonology.' JCL 1. 233-41.

_____ 1978. 'The role of the syllable in phonological development.' in Bell, A. & Hooper, J.B. eds., Syllables and segments, North Holland, 143-55.

_____, Christensen, L., Veach, S. & Webster, B. 1980. 'The acquisition of word-initial fricatives and affricates in English by children between two and six years.' in Yeni-Komshian, G., Kavanagh, J.F., & Ferguson, C.A. eds., Child phonology volume I; production. Academic Press. 169-92.

Menn, L. 1975. 'Counterexample to 'fronting' as a universal of child language.' JCL 2.293-96.

Naeser, M.A. 1970. 'The American child's acquisition of differential vowel duration.' Univ. Wisconsin Research and Development Center for Cognitive Learning, Technical Report No. 144.

Olmsted, D.L. 1971. Out of the mouths of babes. Mouton.

Raphael, L.J., Dorman, M. & Geffner, D. 1977. 'Voicing-conditioned durational differences in vowels and consonants in English.' Journal Phonetics 3.25-33.

Smith, B. 1977. 'Phonetic aspects of 'devoiced' stop consonants in children's speech.' Ninth Meeting ASA, Miami Beach, Fla., December.

Smith, N. 1973. The acquisition of phonology: a case study. Cambridge UP.

Snow, K. 1963. 'A detailed analysis of articulatory responses of 'normal' first grade children.' JSHR 6.277-90.

Templin, M.C. 1957. Certain language skills in children. Minnesota UP.

Vihman, M.M. 1976. 'Consonant harmony: its scope and function in child language.' in Greenberg, J.H., ed. Universals of human language, volume 2: phonology. Stanford UP. 281-334.

Wang, D.M. & Bilger, R.C. 1973. 'Consonant confusions in noise: a study of perceptual features.' JASA 54.1248-66.

Wellman, B.L., Case, I.M., Mengert, E.G. & Bradbury, D.E. 1931. Speech sounds of young children. Univ. Iowa Studies in Child Welfare 5 (2). Iowa UP.

A PRELIMINARY LOOK AT PHONOLOGICAL PROCESS SUPPRESSION

Michael A. Crary, Ph.D.

Terrel Welmers, M.A.

Stephen E. Blache, Ph.D.

Department of Communication Disorders and Sciences
Southern Illinois University - Carbondale
Carbondale, IL   USA

Recently, much attention has been given to the study of phonological development and disorders via phonological process analyses. One aspect of this area which has received limited research is the suppression of simplifying phonological processes by normal children and the relation of these processes to grammatical development in general. The purpose of the present study was to describe patterns of phonological process suppression by language-normal children and to investigate relations between these processes and chronological age and mean length of utterance.

METHOD

Subjects:

Twenty preschool children participated in this investigation. All children were Caucasian from monolingual (American-English) families. Physical examination records were checked to determine that each child had normal hearing, normal intellect, and no structural or functional motor problems. Ages ranged from 2.0 to 4.0 years. Each child demonstrated age appropriate speech and language development as determined by the Preschool Language Scale (Zimmerman, Steiner, and Pond, 1979).

Speech Samples:

Each child was seen individually for two sessions. The first session was used to complete the normative speech and language battery. During the second session each child was engaged in conversation using pictures and toys to elicit verbal productions. From these conversations a sample of 100 words was selected for analysis based on the following criteria: 1) only one production of a given word unless subsequent productions were phonologically different, 2) no words were included that were subject to phonological reduction resulting from normal stress variations (e.g. a̠, a̠n, t̠he, etc.), 3) no automatic or rote sequences such as counting were included, and 4) no word was selected unless the transcriber was certain of the adult form of the intended target. Using broad phonetic notation the 100 words were transcribed from sequential utterances near the middle of the conversations. It is important to note that not all of the productions demonstrated phonological errors. Correct productions were also included in the samples in an attempt to represent more completely each child's phonological system.

In addition to the selection of words for phonological analysis, each conversational sample was analyzed for mean length of utterance (MLU) according to procedures outlined by Brown (1973).

Phonological Process Analysis:

Each of the twenty samples was subject to a phonological process analysis following procedures suggested by Crary (1980). Once the data base has been organized onto transcription analysis sheets, productions are compared to intended targets (adult forms) in reference to general phonological process patterns described by Ingram (1976). Next, a frequency of occurrence is calculated for each identified process. This frequency of occurrence value is termed the Relative Strength (RS) of the process and is obtained by dividing the total number of actual occurrences by the number of potential occurrences of each identified process. A potential occurrence is defined as the normal phonological pattern subject to alteration by a particular process. Hence, all final consonants form potential occurrences for final consonant deletion and all clusters form potential occurrences for cluster reduction. Utilization of this simple procedure permits numerical representation of phonological patterns and facilitates statistical comparisons.

Data Comparisons:

Following the phonological process analysis and calculation of the RS values, two types of data comparisons were completed. The first comparison was an attempt to identify descriptive developmental trends in phonological process suppression. Toward this goal, the subject group was subdivided by chronological age into four equal groups. Group 1 consisted of children between the ages of 2.0 and 2.5, Group 2 between 2.5 and 3.0, Group 3 between 3.0 and 3.5, and Group 4 between 3.5 and 4.0. Within each group the number of subjects demonstrating each process was tallied along with the mean and maximum RS values. The second comparison reflects an attempt to identify significant relationships among the identified processes and between these phonological error patterns, chronological age, and MLU. These comparisons were completed through three statistical procedures: zero-order correlation, stepwise regression, and multiple regression.

As seen in Table 1, only six phonological processes were identified in the obtained speech samples. These include: final consonant deletion (DFC), cluster reduction (CR), stopping (ST), gliding (GL), weak syllable deletion (WSD), and fronting (FR). This list reflects those processes that were consistently verified in the spontaneous samples.

The most prevalent process observed was cluster reduction; occurring in 15 out of 20 samples. As shown in Table 2, cluster reduction was followed by gliding, stopping, final consonant deletion, fronting and weak syllable deletion in descending order.[1] The data presented in this table provide a descriptive analysis of phonological process suppression in normal children. The most general statement about these data is that the children involved in this study did not produce a great amount of phonological errors. By looking at the N' and MAX RS values for each process in the respective subgroups, several descriptive points may be extracted. First, only cluster reduction and gliding appear in samples from all age groups. The strength of cluster reduction appears to inversely correlate with chronological age as indicated by a decrease in

---

[1] Weak syllable deletion was observed in only one subject (in the youngest group) and therefore not included in the table.

RESULTS AND DISCUSSION

TABLE 1: PROMINENT PHONOLOGICAL PROCESSES IDENTIFIED IN SPONTANEOUS SPEECH SAMPLES OF TWENTY PRESCHOOL CHILDREN (2.0 - 4.0)

PROCESS	DESCRIPTION	EXAMPLE
Deletion Final Consonants (DFC)	Omission of final C	mus → mu
Cluster Reduction (CR)	Simplification of cluster by a) omission of one member b) replacement of one member c) omission of entire cluster	 frag → fag frag → fwag frag → ag
Stopping (ST)	Producing a stop for a) a fricative b) an affricate	 sut → tut tʃit → tit
Gliding (GL)	Replacing a liquid with a glide	rod → wod luz → juz
Weak Syllable Deletion (WSD)	Omission of an unstressed syllable in a polysyllabic word	artitʃok → artok
Fronting (FR)	Producing a palatal or velar sound as an alveolar sound	ku → tu ʃo → so

both the mean and maximum RS values as well as the number
of children demonstrating this process across age groups.
The gliding process also seemed to have an inverse correlation with chronological age; however, it is a "weaker"
process than cluster reduction. The increase in RS values
in the oldest group of children results from a very specific
difficulty with the /l/ phoneme in the two children demonstrating this process. Both children substituted /w/ for
the /l/ in the prevocalic position of words; however, both
of these subjects produced the /r/ phoneme correctly and
demonstrated no errors in stop-liquid clusters involving /r/.

TABLE 2: DESCRIPTIVE ANALYSIS OF PHONOLOGICAL PROCESS
SUPPRESSION ACROSS FOUR AGE LEVELS: MEAN RS VALUE,
MAXIMUM RS VALUE, NUMBER OF SS
DEMONSTRATING PROCESS

		AGE LEVELS				
		2.0-2.5	2.5-3.0	3.0-3.5	3.5-4.0	N
DFC	$\bar{x}$	.05	.01	.05	---	
	Max	.12	.01	.23	---	
	N'	2	1	1	---	4
CR	$\bar{x}$	.29	.09	.05	.03	
	Max	.40	.19	.12	.07	
	N'	5	4	3	3	15
ST	x	.05	.05	---	---	
	Max	.13	.11	---	---	
	N'	3	5	---	---	8
GL	$\bar{x}$	.13	.07	.03	.06	
	Max	.18	.14	.05	.16	
	N'	4	3	4	2	13
FR	$\bar{x}$	---	.05	.04	.02	
	Max	---	.25	.22	.12	
	N'	---	1	1	1	3

Weak syllable deletion was observed in only 1 sample from the youngest age group. Apparently, linguistically normal children in this age range have sufficient prosodic control to produce poly-syllabic words. Stopping was present in the two youngest groups but was not a strong process as evidenced by maximum RS values of .13 and .11 respectively. No examples of this process were observed in children beyond 3 years of age (oldest child in second group was 2;11 while the youngest child in third group was 3;3). Final consonant deletion was not a prominent process among these subjects. Only four of the twenty children made errors involving syllable closure. The frequency of occurrence of these errors was extremely low for children below 3 years of age (.12 and .01). The single child in subgroup three (age 3;3) who demonstrated this process at RS = .23 produced single words without errors and this was considered normal based on criterion testing. The final consonant deletions in conversational speech may result from producing longer strings of words and/or from producing more complex grammatical units. Too, the possibility that this child has a subclinical phonological delay should not be ruled out. The final identified process, fronting, was observed in only three samples. No examples of fronting were identified in the youngest group of children. One child in each of the remaining age groups demonstrated the fronting process. In each case RS values were high compared to other processes observed within the subgroups. From these data, it seems that fronting is not a frequent phonological error pattern in linguistically normal preschool children, but when it does appear in the phonological system it becomes a major error pattern for the individual child.

Once these descriptive developmental trends were identified, the next step was to look for significant relations among phonological error patterns and between these patterns and chronological age and MLU. The correlation matrix presented in Table 3 reveals only one significant ($p < .05$) correlation between the processes of cluster reduction and stopping. Though significant for this particular sample size, this positive correlation (.547) is viewed as marginal, accounting for less than 30% of the common variance between the two variables. The base of this relationship may be simply the ability of certain children in this group to produce fricatives. In isolation fricatives may be produced as stops and in blends they may be omitted. Though not specifically evaluated in the present study, this relationship does merit further investigation. The lack of significance among the remaining intra-process correlations suggest that these processes are independent phenomena, i.e., that they reflect different behaviors.

Multiple processes yielded significant negative correlations with both age and MLU. Too, age and MLU were highly related (+.859). However, with the exception of cluster reduction, different phonological processes were significantly correlated with age or MLU. Age significantly correlated with the processes of cluster reduction (-.814), stopping (-.595), and gliding (-.447). MLU was significantly related to final consonant deletion (-.458), and weak syllable deletion (-.466) in addition to cluster reduction (-.841). Again, with the exception of cluster reduction, the significant correlations to age or MLU are viewed as marginal, accounting for only a small percentage of common variance between variables.

TABLE 3: CORRELATION MATRIX FOR NORMAL SUBJECTS (N = 20)

	AGE	MLU	DFC	CR	ST	GL	WSD	FR
Age		+.859*	-.231	-.814*	-.595*	-.447*	-.310	-.109
MLU			-.458*	-.841*	-.434	-.226	-.466*	+.092
DFC				+.346	-.237	-.162	+.372	+.418
CR					+.547*	+.418	+.383	-.176
ST						+.378	-.143	-.167
GL							-.244	-.283
WSD								-.092
FR								

*p < .05

The fact that different phonological processes correlated significantly with age vs. MLU must be addressed. The significant correlations between age and cluster reduction, stopping, and gliding seem to reflect a paradigmatic view of phonological (speech sound) acquisition. Clusters, certain fricatives, and liquids represent sound classes mastered relatively late in phonological development. The negative correlations between each of these error patterns and age indicate that these errors decrease as age increases. This observation is substantiated by the descriptive data. The fact that other phonological processes have low, nonsignificant correlations with age may indicate that the normal phonological patterns altered by these processes are mastered by very young children - prior to age 2 years. Again, the descriptive data support this impression. The remaining processes occur less frequently than cluster reduction, stopping, or gliding, both in total occurrence and in the respective age subgroups.

The significant correlations between MLU and final consonant deletion, cluster reduction, and weak syllable deletion may reflect an organizational strategy in the developing language system. Both final consonant deletion and weak syllable deletion occur infrequently in the samples and predominantly in the youngest children. The single occurrence of weak syllable deletion was observed in the child with the lowest MLU value and co-existed with both final consonant deletion and cluster reduction. Also, as mentioned earlier, final consonant deletion was primarily confined to children under three years of age. MLU values for these children indicated primarily two word productions. These observations may indicate a sequential constraint stage or sequential reduction strategy employed in expressive grammar of young children. The essence of the evidence is that cluster reduction, final consonant deletion, and weak syllable deletion are phonological processes which involve some type of sequential simplification. These processes are most prominent in younger children with low MLU values. Obviously, low MLU values reflect limited linguistic sequences. The possibility should not be excluded that the co-existence of these phenomena is a result of some underlying linguistic programming strategy or limitation related to memory, performance constraints, or grammatical organizational abilities. Admittedly, the argument for a sequential limitation or constraint strategy is not strong based on these data. These observations should be viewed as hypotheses for future research rather than conclusions based on present data.

TABLE 4: STEPWISE REGRESSION ANALYSES:

NORMAL SUBJECTS (N = 20)

Dependent Variable = MLU

Variable	R	Prop. Var. Red.	F for Ent. Var.	P
CR	.84	.708	43.542	<.001
DFC	.86	.032	2.061	NS
WSD	.87	.012	0.795	NS
ST	.88	.017	1.080	NS
FR	.88	.002	0.137	NS
GL	.88	.000	0.018	NS

Dependent Variable = Age

Variable	R	Prop. Var. Red.	F for Ent. Var.	P
CR	.81	.662	35.268	<.001
ST	.83	.032	1.769	NS
WSD	.84	.008	0.435	NS
GL	.85	.020	1.050	NS
FR	.86	.010	0.532	NS
DFC	.86	.003	0.140	NS

Cluster reduction emerged as a dominant process in both the descriptive and correlation analyses. It was the most frequently occurring process, the strongest process, and had a high correlation to both age and MLU. A stepwise regression analysis was completed to identify which process best predicted MLU or age respectively. Given the dominance of cluster reduction in the preceding analyses, it was expected that this process would be the best phonological predictor of both developmental indices. As seen in Table 4, this expectation was realized. Cluster reduction was the only significant predictor of either age or MLU. In fact, the remaining processes had very little influence on the proportion of variance reduced in the respective analyses. In view of this significant relationship to age and MLU independently, and given the high correlation between these measures, a multiple regression analysis was completed using cluster reduction to predict a composite of age and MLU. Results produced a significant multiple correlation (R = .86) with 74% accountable variance. Collectively, these analyses suggest that cluster reduction shares much "common ground" with the developmental indices of age and MLU. From a phonological perspective, a child's ability to produce clusters may be a good index of that child's linguistic development. As such, more information needs to be gathered regarding the suppression of cluster reduction in normal and delayed children.

TABLE 5: FORECASTING MODEL OF AGE PREDICTING CLUSTER REDUCTION (RS)

Age	CR	+ .072	− .072
1.0	.42	.492	.348
1.5	.35	.422	.278
2.0	.27	.342	.198
2.5	.19	.262	.118
3.0	.12	.192	.048
3.5	.04	.112	----
4.0	---	----	----

Toward the goal of projecting a developmental model of the suppression of cluster reduction, simple regression analyses were completed using age or MLU to predict RS values for this phonological process. Table 5 presents the forecasted model for age and cluster reduction. According to the model, children should be producing clusters appropriately by four years of age. Even as young as three or three and a half years children should demonstrate limited errors in attempts to produce clusters.

TABLE 6: FORECASTING MODEL OF MLU
PREDICTING CLUSTER REDUCTION (RS)

MLU	CR	+ .067	− .067
1.0	.394	.461	.367
2.0	.315	.382	.248
3.0	.235	.302	.168
4.0	.156	.223	.089
5.0	.076	.143	.009
6.0	----	----	----

Table 6 presents the forecasted model for MLU and cluster reduction. Once MLU has reached a level of four, five, or six words few, if any, cluster errors would be expected.

These types of models are useful not only in generating hypotheses about normal developmental progression, but also, for making clinical decisions about the normalcy of a given child's phonological development. As a brief example of clinical utilization, cluster reduction RS values from ten (10) phonologically delayed subjects were plotted onto graphic representations of the forecasted models. The first comparison uses age as the developmental index (see Figure 1). Note the distance between the normal model and all delayed subjects. The MLU comparison (Figure 2) provides similar results except it appears as if one of the normal subjects fits more closely with the delayed subjects than with other linguistically normal children. A review of the raw data revealed this to be a two-year-old child with an MLU value of 3.6. This child also demonstrated relatively high values for stopping and gliding compared to other children of a similar age. Also, this child's

52

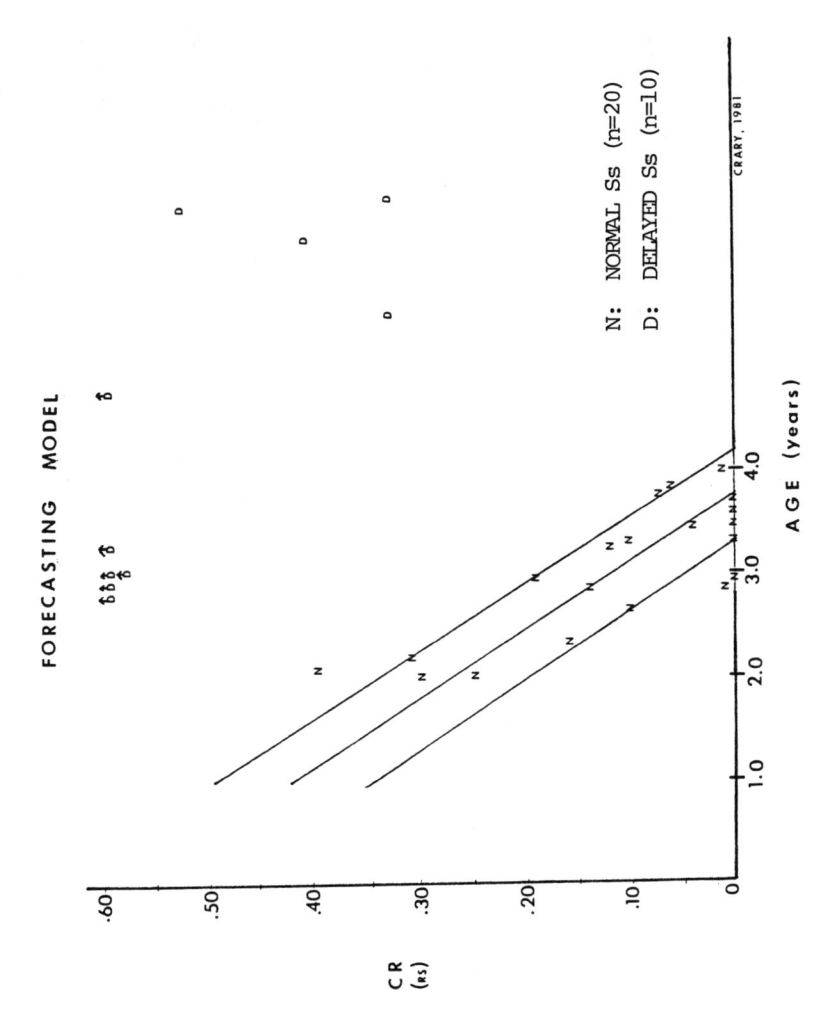

FIGURE 1: Comparison of normal vs. disordered subjects on regression model for age and cluster reduction.

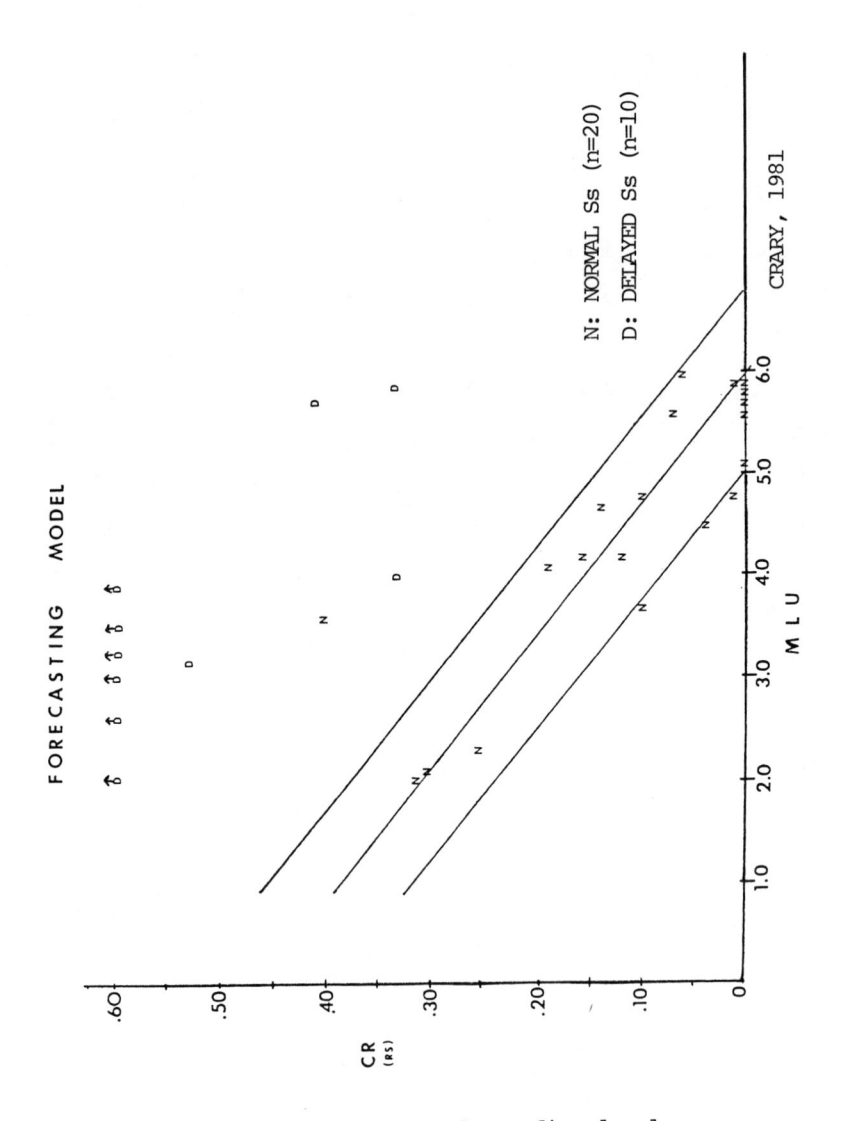

FIGURE 2: Comparison of normal vs. disordered subjects on regression model for MLU and cluster reduction.

MLU was nearly 2 morphemes longer than three other children of the same age. Perhaps the apparent phonological discrepancy reflects the influence of a more highly developed expressive grammar for this child. The regression model identified this child as being delayed in the ability to produce clusters given a specific MLU value. However, as presented, other factors must be considered when making judgments regarding the normalcy of an individual child's phonological system.

SUMMARY AND CONCLUSIONS

This descriptive investigation has generated many observations. The purpose of this study was to describe patterns of phonological process suppression in language-normal children and to investigate the relations between these error patterns and the developmental indices of age and MLU. The major findings of this investigation may be summarized as follows:

1 - Few phonological errors were produced by the children in the age range studied (2.0 to 4.0 years).

2 - Those errors that were produced could be categorized into six prominent phonological processes: cluster reduction, deletion of final consonants, stopping, gliding, weak syllable deletion, and fronting.

3 - Of the identified processes, cluster reduction and gliding were the most persistent, occurring in samples of more than half of the subjects across all age categories. Final consonant deletion, fronting, and weak syllable deletion were infrequently observed in the samples.

4 - A correlation analysis revealed only one significant correlation among all phonological processes: cluster reduction and stopping. Cluster reduction, stopping and gliding correlated significantly with age while final consonant deletion, weak syllable deletion, and cluster reduction correlated with MLU.

5 - Cluster reduction was the only process to significantly predict age or MLU. Too, this process had a high

correlation with age and MLU combined. It was suggested that a child's ability to produce clusters may be a good indication of linguistic development. A simple regression analysis was used to produce a forecast model of cluster reduction RS values from age and MLU.

Beyond the obvious description of phonological processes in the speech patterns of these normal children, all other findings should be viewed as hypotheses requiring additional investigation. Foremost among these is the relation of cluster reduction to other linguistic developmental indices. Follow-up work along this line of research with larger subject pools should prove useful to those who describe normal language development and to those who intervene in cases of abnormal language development.

REFERENCES

Brown, R., A First Language: The Early Stages. Cambridge: Harvard University Press (1973).

Crary, M., RX x RA = RIU: Quantifying speech sample analysis. Paper presented at American Speech-Language and Hearing Association Convention, Detroit (1980).

Ingram, D., Phonological Disability in Children. New York: Elsevier (1976).

Zimmerman, I., Steiner, V., Pond, R., Preschool Language Scale. Columbus: Charles E. Merrill Pub. Co. (1979).

Evidence for non-segmental, whole-pattern speech perception
and production from a child's first recitations of nursery
rhymes.
Natalie Waterson, Dept. of Phonetics & Linguistics, S.O.A.S.,
University of London.

The learning of nursery rhymes (N.R.s) by the writer's child
P was recorded as part of a diary study of his speech and
other development. The recitation of N.R.s is one of the
modes of social interaction that takes place between parents
and babies and as such has a useful function. In many ways
N.R.s are very suitable for young children. They have
strong rhythm, very clear and definite intonation patterns,
and they tend to be repetitive. Also the meaning is relatively unimportant. Parents do not usually try to explain
what N.R.s mean, and children do not seem to attach much
meaning to them but just enjoy the sound.

N.R.'s were recited frequently to P and were also read to
him from books. When he began to ask for them by name, and
was able to identify them in his books, the parents played
the game with him, as many do, of leaving off the last word
of each line for him to fill in, for instance:
>   Ride a cock-horse to Banbury...
>   To see a fair lady upon a white..
>   With rings on her fingers and
>   bells on her...
>   She shall have music wherever
>   she...

and P filled in [ḳɔs] 'cross', [hɔs] 'horse', [tɔs] 'toes'
and [gɔs] 'goes'. At this time he was using multiple-word
utterances such as [bʌbu: 'tɔ:kən 'babɪ, 'ʔʌlɪ 'ʔʌlɪ 'baɪ],
'P's talking to Bobby, lovely lovely boy' (said when patting
the dog and kissing his face), and ['ɪtɪ 'dɪŋk 'ʔɔ:tə] 'a
little drink of water', and then ['bɪt mɔ: 'dɪŋk 'ʔɔ:tə]
'another drink of water'.

The first N.R. recited was Ding dong bell, at 1;8.20. It
was not recorded but a note in the diary says that the
rhythm sounded familiar but some of the words were not
quite recognisable. The next day P recited another rhyme
which was not at first recognised. It may be noted that P's
efforts sounded like N.R.s although the content was not
recognisable. This is because they contained various

essential features of N.R.s: he was attempting wholes without too much effort being expended on getting the words right. That same day further attempts were made at Ding dong bell. The next day both rhymes were repeated several times and an attempt was made at Sing a song of sixpence. Again the whole was recited but in reduced form, as was the case with the other two. In the next eight weeks, between the ages of 1;8.20 and 1;9., various other N.R.s were recited: Little Bo Peep; Goosey, goosey, gander; Old mother Hubbard; Baa baa black sheep; One, two, buckle my shoe; Old King Cole; Little Boy Blue; Ride a cock-horse; Dickory, dickory, dock; Hey diddle diddle, the cat and the fiddle; Humpty Dumpty; Jack and Jill; Hush-a-bye baby; Little Miss Muffet, and Tom the piper's son. Of these, eight were recorded. Limitations of space preclude the discussion of more than one. Ding dong bell was selected for consideration as it is not too long; it was also the first, and several versions were recorded for it; also its acquisition was typical. The first recorded version is given on p 70 Ding dong bell II; the second, with variations, on p71 Ding dong bell III; and the last, which was recorded about 20 days after the first attempt, is given on p72 Ding dong bell IV.

Most of P's recitations took place at mealtimes in his high chair. There was no book present to provide visual cues so he had to rely entirely on his auditory memory. Recording was by pencil and paper using the I.P.A.. As P kept repeating his efforts, it was possible to check and re-check the transcriptions. A slightly broader transcription is used here than in the original because of the difficulty of reproducing a very narrow one but it is narrow enough for the purposes of this paper. From the start, each rhyme was attempted as a whole unit: there was no evidence that learning was additive, that is to say, no line by line or word by word addition. The N.R.s were first produced in very simple form and were gradually modified until they became a closer match to the parents' version (the model). Rhythm, intonation, and rhyme were quite a good match from the start, and it was the most salient words or parts of words that were acquired first, the less salient were filled in later. This is the same as was the case with the child's early words and sentences (Waterson, 1971, 1976, 1978). Thus the same non-segmental, whole-pattern production, and hence in all probability perception was involved in this child's

acquisition of N.R.s as in the acquisition of words and
sentences.

Since parents and others recite N.R.s as complete texts,
one would expect a child's perception of them to be as
whole units, and hence also his production. A N.R. is self-
contained, bounded by silence, and the whole is repeated
unchanged on separate occasions. Each N.R. can be viewed
as a text with its own internal cohesion which is accounted
for by features such as intonation, rhyme, repetition in
various guises, and semantic content, and even syntactic
structure. P produced his own texts in reduced form, which
were clearly his own constructions just as his early words
were (Waterson, 1971). A rough indication of the reduction
in overall length of the N.R.s can be given by comparing
the number of words and syllables in the child's version with
the model. Taking as a sample the last recorded version of
Ding dong bell (Ding dong bell IV), the model has 35 words:
41 syllables; 27 stressed and 14 unstressed, whereas P's
version has 24 words: 29 syllables; 23 stressed and 6 unstressed. A brief description of the N.R. as recited by
P's parents now follows to demonstrate the characteristics
which mark it as a single unit. It will then be possible to
show how these are produced by the child in his early efforts,
thus demonstrating his Gestalt treatment of the N.R. There
are, of course, many ways of reciting a N.R. but here the
form used by the family is given. There was a difference in
the father's and mother's usage in the sixth line of Ding
dong bell: the father used 'Johnny' and the mother 'Tommy'
and this may account for P's preference for [dʌnɪ] rather
than [tæmɪ] in this line. By this age, P's speech was
closer to his mother's type of Southern British English than
to his father's Dublin English so it is the mother's pronunciation that is given in the transcription of the adult
version in Ding dong bell I p 69. The orthographic form is
also given. The lines are marked (1) through (9) for easy
reference.

The unity of the N.R. is marked 1) semantically 2) syntactically and 3) phonologically. It is marked semantically by
the single topic of the cat in the well - the whole N.R.
centres round this. Syntactically it is marked by the
sequence of related sentence types: a calling for attention
in (1), followed by an announcement in (2), then two related

questions and answers (3) and (4), (5) and (6), which being structurally the same, echo each other, and final comment - (7) (8) (9) - which relates to one of the questions and answers, namely (3) and (4). As far as syntax and semantics go, there is nothing to prevent a further comment or question, etc., on the same topic being added, that is to say, there is no real marker of finality, and in fact, although some versions end on (9), 'poor pussy cat', two more lines are sometimes added: 'Who never did him any harm But caught rats and mice in his father's barn'. It seems it is the phonology that makes the greatest contribution to marking the N.R. as a complete text as will be shown in Fig.1. below. The intonation is represented graphically. The pitches of the first and last syllables of each line are marked variously as H (high), M (mid), L (low), Lev. (level), F (fall), R (rise), HF (high fall), LF (low fall), RF (rise-fall). Stressed syllables are marked ━, unstressed ─.

	Stress and intonation	Onset and Ending	
(1)		H ───── R	a
(2)		M ───── HF	a
(3)		H ───── R	b
(4)		M ───── HF	b
(5)		H ───── R	c
(6)		M ───── HF	c
(7)		H ───── RF	d
(8)		M ───── Lev.	
(9)		H ───── LF	d

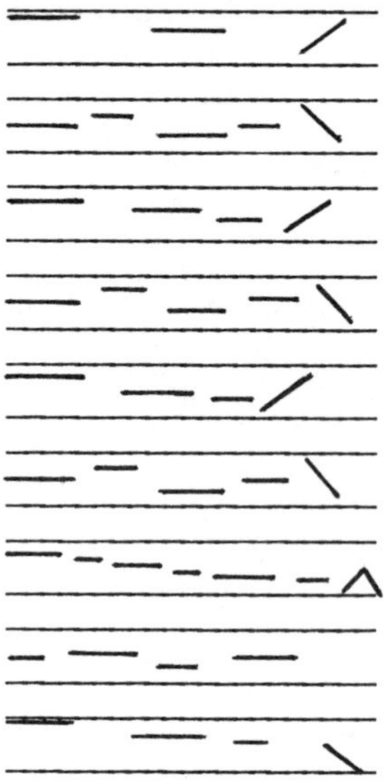

Fig. 1 Rhythm and intonation of parent's version.

What are written as lines are auditorily recognisable as such because of the rhythmic and intonation patterns and the rhyming. There is a strong rhythm marked by three stresses in (1) through (6), with a change in (7) and (8) where the number of stresses changes to four in (7) and two in (8), and then returns to three again in (9). The break in rhythm brings these lines into focus, as does the extra strong stress on 'naughty' in (7); this is required because (7) and (8) carry the moral of the N.R. The ends of the lines rhyme in pairs: aa, bb, cc, dd, (8) not rhyming with anything. The endings are also marked by terminal contours such as are found at the ends of clauses and sentences in discourse: alternate rises and falls from (1) through (6), a rise-fall in (7), level in (8), and a low fall in (9). The onsets are also marked by pitch: high pitch on the first stressed syllable of the first line of each related pair, namely (1), (3), (5), (7), and (9), and mid pitch at the onset of the even numbers, as shown in Fig. 1 above.

Any text that is going to be memorised has to be broken up into manageable 'chunks' (Miller, 1956): the N.R. is now examined to find possible candidates for such chunks.

The lines have been shown to have their own unity and may be looked upon as small chunks which make up the text of the N.R. However, there are also units intermediate between lines and whole text. These are units of more than one line which have their own internal cohesion. This is marked in several ways: by the rhyming, the rhythm, and intonation which link the lines into groups. The rhyming as aa, bb, cc, dd, links (1) and (2), (3) and (4), (5) and (6) into pairs, or two-line chunks, and (7) and (9), which include (8), into a three-line group or chunk. The rhythm of (1) and (2) is basically repeated in (3) and (4), and (5) and (6) (with the addition of a penultimate unstressed syllable in (3) and 5)), thus strengthening the links between the lines grouped by rhyming. These pairs of lines are also linked by the repetition of the intonation pattern in that the first of each pair starts on a high pitch and ends on a rise, and the second starts on a mid pitch and ends on a fall (See Fig.1). (1) and (2), (3) and (4), and (5) and (6) may thus be described as three chunks; (7), (8) and (9) as another chunk. The fact that (7) and (9) rhyme and (8) does not confirms this as a unit; the difference in rhythm from the other lines and pairs of lines, and the shorter pauses at the end of (7) and (8) accompanied by suspension type intonation: rise-fall and level, also mark these lines as part of a larger unit, a three-line chunk, the fall in (9) marking the end.

The N.R. has its own internal cohesion which marks it as a text or large chunk. This unity is marked phonologically by the use of intonation and variation of pitch levels, by the patterned rhyming mentioned earlier, and by the strong rhythm of three stresses per line, interrupted at (7) and (8) but returning again at (9). The step-down intonation of each line also marks the unity of the whole as does the alternation of high and mid onsets throughout (See Fig.1). The highest pitches are found at the onset of (1) and of (9). This extra high pitch on (1) marks the beginning of the whole text, and the low fall in (9) which falls to the bottom of the voice range marks the end of the whole text in the same way as described by Couper-Kuhlen for English discourse (Couper-Kuhlen, 1982). The extra high pitch in (9) is for emphasis. The high falls in (2), (4), and (6) which do not reach the bottom of the voice range, leave an expectation that something will follow, as do the rises at the ending of (1), (3), (5), the rise-fall on (7), and the mid level pitch in (8). There is thus a clear beginning, middle, and ending so that the N.R. can be analysed as a text or large chunk which is comprised of four chunks, each made up of two or three lines, the lines themselves being the smallest chunks. Consideration will now be given to whether these chunks, established for the parents' version of the N.R., have any validity for the child, that is, whether there is any evidence of him using these chunks in his own production of the N.R.

The first attempt at a N.R., Ding dong bell, was not recorded but it was an attempt at the whole. The next day several attempts were made. These are shown on p 70 Ding dong bell II. What is omitted in the child's versions is placed in brackets in the model. It will be seen that P's version has a beginning and an ending but much of the middle is missing. This suggests the recognition of the N.R. as a unit or chunk. There is rhythm, intonation, and rhyming, all of which have a regular correspondence to the model. (1) and (2) start with three stresses as in the model, but a fresh start is then made with three stresses in (1) and two in (2), and this is

the rhythmic pattern that was kept in versions in 2 and 3
(Ding dong bell III and IV) for lines (1) through (6). It
seems that a rhythm of three plus three stresses would have
made the N.R. too long for the child to manage at the current stage of development. The middle of the rhyme, (3)
through (5) was not attempted: this could have been due to
memory failure, or just too much information to process at
this point. In (6) there are two stresses corresponding to
'Tommy' and 'Stout'; these are the last two stressed words in
the model, the first, 'little', is not responded to. In (7)
in one variant, only one stress is produced, on 'naughty',
which has the extra prominence of emphasis; in the other 'boy
was that' which has two stresses in the model, is telescoped
into ['bat] with one stress, so that there are two stresses
instead of the four. (8) is not attempted and (9) has three
stresses as in the model. The resulting rhythm is strong
like the model though with fewer stresses. The intonation
is a close match, onsets and endings of the lines produced
are as shown for the model (Fig.1), except that (7) ends in
a fall. (1) and (2) rhyme as in the model but so do (6) and
(7), unlike the model. This is the result of the non-
production of the closing element of the diphthong [aʊ] in
'Stout', and P's use of the [a] vowel instead of [æ]. Much
of what is produced is what is auditorily salient and what is
omitted is non-salient. Beginnings and endings are generally
more salient as far as memory goes: beginnings usually have
the attention concentrated on them and can be coped with as
the memory does not yet have a heavy load; endings are more
recent, with no further load to follow, so are freshest in
the memory; the middle is a non-salient position and P omits
a large portion of it. Similarly, only stressed words were
responded to, none of the unstressed like 'the', 'her', 'a',
'to', and 'was' were attempted. Even though parts of the
N.R. are missing, P's use of high pitch at the start and low
fall at the end mark the beginning and end of the N.R. in the
same way as in the model, and he has the same step-down intonation with a rise at the end of (1) and a fall in (2).
The fall in (6) also matches the model but (7) ends on a fall
instead of a rise-fall. P thus made use of rhythm and intonation similar to but not identical with the model, which
shows his attempt to be his own construction.

What about the four chunks which comprise the large chunk or
text? P's treatment of (1) and (2) together in the two

attempts suggests that he is treating this pair as a unit.
(6) rhymes with (7) and has the same rhythm so seems to be
paired with it but both end on a fall, so are not a pair
like (1) and (2) in this respect. The production of (7) and
(9) without (8) may mean that (7), (8), (9) are being
treated as a chunk, particularly in view of version 2, where
(7) and (9) are taken together, and then (8) and (9) (Ding
dong bell III p 71). It is not clear whether P was processing
in terms of these chunks in version I, but version 2 which
was recited on the same day, provides evidence that he does;
he is, however, certainly treating lines as chunks. He
attempts the rhythm and intonation of each line he produces;
he uses matching onset pitch and ending pitch even though he
does not always produce the first word of the line of the
model, 'little' in (6) and 'what' in (7) for instance. His
onset pitch is on the second stressed words, 'Tommy' and
'naughty' but they have the pitches of the first stressed
words of the model. Thus not all the stressed words are
produced, and none of the unstressed. However the fact that
the child produces both stressed and unstressed syllables of
words, in 'pussy', 'Tommy' and 'naughty', show his recognition of the word as a unit.

Version 2 was produced on the same day and with the variants
given (Ding dong bell III p 71). It was repeated several
times and was in use in the three weeks that followed. The
features marking the cohesion of the whole text as used in
version 1 are maintained. Now P attempts all the lines. The
step-down intonation is used throughout; high and mid pitches
are used alternately at the onset of lines as in the model
(See Fig.1) even though he still does not produce the first
word of the line in each case. In (4) and (6) his onset
pitch is on the second words: 'Johnny' and 'Tommy' and in (7)
on 'naughty'. The endings alternate with rises and falls as
in the model, and (8) ends on a level pitch but (7) still
falls in place of the rise-fall. The lines rhyme in pairs
but (5) through (9), excluding (8) all have the same rhyme;
this does not necessarily mean that they are not rhyming in
pairs as the reason for it is that P is still not making a
distinction between [a], [æ], and [aʊ].

The rhythm, intonation and rhyming are now well established
although the rhythm differs from the model which has three
stresses in each of (1) through (6). P has a three-stress

line alternating with a two-stress line and this provides
additional evidence that he is chunking the lines into
pairs in his own construction; the repetition of this pattern of pairs is an extra marker of the linking of these
chunks into the larger chunk or text. The rhythm change
at (7) is maintained but P is apparently still having difficulty in coping with such a long line, and the non-salient combination of sounds [wəz ðə] may have been difficult
to identify, so he continues to use the telescoped form
[bat], and (7) is a two-stress line as in version 1. This
is followed by a three-stress line (9). He then attempts
(8) (which has one stress and the only unstressed word,
'to', in his text), and follows it with (9). It is interesting to see that (7) and (9) appear to be paired into a
chunk because they rhyme, but both end on a fall which
suggests that they may not constitute a chunk (cf. (6) and
(7) in version 1). (8) then follows with (9) and these
are paired by intonation, (8) ending on a level pitch,
marking non-finality, and (9) on a fall, marking finality.

The first stressed words of (4), (6), (7) and (8) of the
model are not produced. 'Little' in (4) and (6) is relatively non-salient. In (7) 'What' is relatively non-salient because of the following emphatic 'naughty', so it is
'naughty', 'boy' and 'that' which are responded to.
Support for the view that 'little' is not produced because
of its non-salience, is provided by the fact that the word
was familiar to P and he often used it in his speech as
['ItI]. (8) starts on an unstressed non-salient word 'to'
and this may have had something to do with the non-production of 'try'.

A point worthy of note is that in the second line of each
pair there is at least one stressed word less than in the
model, and this, added to the fact that no unstressed
words bar one are produced, shows that in his own construction of the N.R., P is producing much shorter chunks
than the adults. One could argue that as he is able to
produce three-stress lines, he could be expected to produce them wherever the model has them. That he does not
is an argument for his treating pairs of lines as chunks
because whereas three stresses for a chunk is not too
much, six stresses could be too much as his

hypothesized chunks at this point do not exceed five stressed
words:
```
    Child's (1) + (2) = 5    Adults' = 6
           (3) + (4) = 5            = 6
           (5) + (6) = 5            = 6
           (7) + (9) = 5
           (8) + (9) = 4
```
Child's (7) (8) (9) = 9 Adults' (7) (8) (9) = 9
(7) (8) (9) is plainly too big a chunk so the child splits
it into (7) + (9) with five stresses, and (8) and (9) with
four, which add up to a total of nine as in the model.

From the description given of P's production of the N.R., it
is clear that the main concentration is on the prosodic
features of the text. Rhythmic, intonation and rhyming
patterns appear to be recognised and are responded to;
pronunication of words, however, is less accurate than that
of everyday speech. For example, the velar nasal [ŋ] which
P used early in his speech, is not used in 'Ding dong';
[d] is used for [dʒ] of 'Johnny' and [dr] of 'drown' although
he used an affricate [dz] in 'John' and 'Geoffrey', and
'drive' and 'dry'; [g] is used for [gr] in 'Green' although
he used [gj] for [gr] in 'grass'; 'try' was not attempted
but [tr] was regularly produced as [tʃ] in 'train'. 'Boy'
was [baɪ] in speech but was not used in (7) although it was
a familiar word. All this again points to problems of
planning and producing articulatory contrasts in longer
stretches of utterance (cf. Waterson, 1978).

The last version of the N.R. to be recorded was at age 1;9
(Ding dong bell IV p72). This version 3 came into use three
weeks after version 2 was first recited. The biggest change
is in the chunk comprised of (7) (8) (9). (9) is no longer
repeated, and (7) now has four stresses, the child responding
to all four stresses of the model. (8) still has only one
stress, so (7) and (8) now add up to five stresses, and (9)
has three, making eight stresses where the model has nine.
Although the chunk now has fewer stresses than the model, it
is a closer match. There are some changes in the pronunciation of words, though not very many. The velar nasal is now
used in 'Ding dong'; 'naughty' is now [nɔ:tɪ], and [bat] 'boy
was that', is now unscrambled to [ˈbaɪ ˈdat] 'boy that';
[da:n] for 'drown' [draʊn] is an improvement on [dan] as
there is length though not yet diphthongisation.

Conclusions.

Just as intonation, stress, and rhythm appear to be very salient for young children and are learnt early, so they are also accorded high priority in the learning of N.R.s. The child P produced the non-segmental characteristics of the N.R. which mark it as a whole unit from the start, and appeared to respond to the chunks which comprise the model as recited by his parents. He was able to pick out patterns of rhythm, intonation, and rhyme, and constructed his own versions of the N.R. very much as he has been shown to construct his own words and sentences (Waterson, 1978). P must have been learning the N.R.s for some time before he started to produce them, judging by the short time within which he produced several once he got started. Hearing the N.R.s must have provided him with the opportunity to develop his speech processing capability to cope with longer texts than before and may also have helped to increase his memory span. If this is so, it seems that N.R.s have a useful function to play in language learning by providing self-training in the processing of longer utterances in advance of their use in speech, and may be a useful tool for speech therapy if used wisely. As mentioned earlier, a child is not particularly concerned with meaning in N.R.s nor is original syntactic construction required, because he is given a model. But he has the opportunity to plan and produce long utterances at the phonetic and phonological levels - to develop the physiological and neurological processes for this in a pleasurable way so that when he comes to use longer utterances in a text, as in discourse, he will be well-practised in producing a large number of articulatory contrasts within rhythmic utterances, with different intonation patterns in various sequences, and so will be free to concentrate on other aspects, such as the semantics and syntax. One may speculate that the so-called 'jargon' that children use has a similar function. Some children, either before they begin to use one-word utterances or at the same time, use long strings with the rhythm and intonation of the language they are learning which sound like the language and yet are incomprehensible (Peters, 1977). Some children indulge in verbal play, producing long strings of words, as Weir's child did in his pre-sleep monologues (Weir, 1962). Babbling too is coming to be recognised as an important phase in acquiring control of the vocal tract. All these may be means whereby children get practice which enables them to develop different aspects of speech processing.

References.

Couper-Kuhlen, E. (1982) Intonational macrostructures: Aspects of prosodic cohesion. Paper given at the BAAL Seminar on Intonation and Discourse, University of Aston, Birmingham.

Miller, G.A. (1956) The magical number seven, plus or minus two: Some limits on our capacity for processing information. Psychological Review, 63.

Peters, A.M. (1977) Language learning strategies: Does the whole equal the sum of the parts? Language, 53, 3.

Waterson, N. (1971) Child phonology: a prosodic view. Journal of Linguistics 7.
(1976) Perception and production in the acquisition of phonology. In W. von-R.-Engel and Y. Lebrun (eds.) Baby Talk and Infant Speech, Swets and Zeitlinger, Amsterdam.
(1978) Growth of complexity in phonological development. In N. Waterson and C.E. Snow (eds.) The Development of Communication. Wiley, Chichester.

Weir, R.H. (1962) Language in the Crib. Mouton, The Hague.

Ding dong bell: Adult version

(1) Ding dong bell, (1) ˈdɪŋ ˈdɒŋ ˈbel
(2) Pussy's in the well. (2) ˈpusiz ˈin ðə ˈwel
(3) Who put her in? (3) ˈhu: ˈpʊt ər ˈɪn
(4) Little Johnny Green. (4) ˈlɪtl ˈdʒɒnɪ ˈgri:n
(5) Who pulled her out? (5) ˈhu: ˈpʊld ər ˈaʊt
(6) Little Tommy Stout. (6) ˈlɪtl ˈtɒmɪ ˈstaʊt
(7) What a naughty boy was that (7) ˈwɒt e ˈnɔ:tɪ ˈbɔɪ wez ˈðæt
(8) To try to drown (8) tʊ ˈtraɪ tʊ ˈdraʊn
(9) Poor pussy cat. (9) ˈpɔə ˈpʊsi ˈkæt

Ding dong bell I

69

	Child (1;8.21) Version 1		Adult
(1)	ˈdɪŋ ˈdɒn ˈbeʊ	(1)	ˈdɪŋ ˈdɒŋ ˈbel
(2)	ˈpuːsɪ ˈɔː ˈeʊ	(2)	ˈpʊsi(z) ˈɪn (ðə) ˈ(w)el
(1)	ˈdɪŋ ˈdɒn ˈbeʊ	(1)	ˈdɪŋ ˈdɒŋ ˈbel
(2)	ˈpuːsɪ ˈweʊ	(2)	ˈpʊsi(z) ɪn ðə ˈwel
(3)	—	(3)	ˈhuː ˈpʊt ər ˈɪn
(4)	—	(4)	ˈlɪtl̩ ˈɪnʤn̩ ˈgriːn
(5)	—	(5)	ˈhuː ˈpʊld ər ˈaʊt
(6)	ˈtæmɪ ˈtʌt/ˈeːnɪ ˈdat	(6)	(ˈlɪtl̩) ˈtɒmɪ ˈ(s)ta(ʊ)t
(7)	ˈcnɪ/ˈeːnuːda ˈbat	(7)	ˈ(wɒt (ə ˈnɔːtɪ ˈbɔɪ) wəz ˈðæt
(8)	—	(8)	(tʊ ˈtraɪ tʊ ˈdraʊn)
(9)	ˈenɪ ˈpʊhʊ ˈkʌt	(9)	ˈenɪ ˈpʊsi ˈkæt

Ding dong bell II

	Child (1;8.21) Version 2		Adult
(1)	ˈdɪŋ ˈdɒn ˈbeʊ	(1)	ˈdɪŋ ˈdɒŋ ˈbel
(2)	ˈpuːsɪ ˈʔeʊ/ˈweʊ	(2)	ˈpʊsi(z ˈɪn ðə) ˈwel
(3)	ˈhuː/ˈuː ˈpʊʔ ˈɪn	(3)	ˈhuː ˈpʊt (ɚ) ˈɪn
(4)	ˈdʌnɪ ˈgiːn	(4)	(ˈlɪtl) ˈdʒɒnɪ ˈg(r)iːn
(5)	ˈuː ˈpʊʔ ˈat	(5)	ˈ(h)uː ˈpʊ(l)d (ɚ) ˈa(ʊ)t
(6)	ˈdʌnɪ ˈgat/tat	(6)	(ˈlɪtl) ˈtɒmɪ/ˈtɒn(ʒ)ɪ ˈ(s)ta(ʊ)t
(7)	ˈnɔːteʊ ˈbat	(7)	(ˈɒt ə ˈcʊːtɪː ˈbɔ)b, ˈzæt
(9)	ˈpɒd ˈpʊhʊ ˈkat	(9)	ˈənd ˈpʊsi ˈkæt
(8)	tə ˈdan	(8)	tʊ ˈtraɪ) tʊ ˈd(r)a(ʊ)n
(9)	ˈpɒd ˈpʊhʊ ˈkat	(9)	ˈənd ˈpʊsi ˈkæt

Ding dong bell III

	Child (1;9) Version 3		Adult
(1)	ˈdɪŋ ˈdɒŋ ˈbeʊ	(1)	ˈdɪŋ ˈdɒŋ ˈbel
(2)	ˈpuːsɪ ˈeʊ	(2)	ˈpusi(z ˈɪn ðə) ˈ(w)el
(3)	ˈuː ˈpʊʔ ˈɪn	(3)	ˈ(h)uː ˈpʊt (ər) ˈɪn
(4)	ˈdʌnɪ ˈgiːn	(4)	(ˈlɪtl) ˈd(ʒ)ɒnɪ ˈg(r)iːn
(5)	ˈuː ˈpʊʔ ˈat	(5)	ˈ(h)uː ˈpʊ(l)d (ər) ˈa(ʊ)t
(6)	ˈdʌnɪ ˈdat	(6)	(ˈlɪtl) ˈtɒmɪ/d(ʒ)ɒnɪ ˈ(s)ta(ʊ)t
(7)	ˈʌt ˈnɔːtɪ ˈbaɪ ˈdat	(7)	ˈ(w)ɒt (e) ˈnɔːtɪ ˈbɔɪ (wəz) ˈðæt
(8)	te ˈdaːn	(8)	(tʊ ˈtraɪ) tʊ ˈd(r)a(ʊ)n
(9)	ˈpʊə ˈpʊhʊ ˈkat	(9)	pʊə ˈpʊsi ˈkæt

Ding dong bell IV

An Integrated Account of Utterance Variability in
Early Language Development

George Branigan   William Stokes
Stonehill College   Lesley College

Individual differences in children's approaches to the discovery of syntax have received considerable attention during the last ten years. Nelson (1973) and Bloom (1970, 1973) established a mode of inquiry which continues to influence the intent and nature of recent investigations (Peters, 1977, 1978). What has typified their work has been the tendency toward dichotomous classifications of children's strategies for discovering syntax. Some children have been found to prefer the semantic certainty of single word expressions (referers, nominal expressions, use of substantives) while others have been found to prefer the exploitation of syntax and the flexibility of multi-word expressions (expressors, pronominal expressions, use of relational words). Peters has enriched and complicated this view by identifying analytic and gestalt approaches to the discovery of syntax. Each of these studies differs in significant detail from the others making summary treatment most difficult (Bowerman 1978; Nelson 1980). The matter is made yet more difficult, although at the same time more reasonable, when it is acknowledged that the dichotomous classifications represent the more or less arbitrary division of nondiscrete phenomena; "...it was not claimed nor was it intended that all children were exclusively one type or the other" (Nelson 1980, p.11). What is common to these views is the interest in characterizing and then explaining apparently diverse approaches to discovering the rules of the language.

Variation has also been reported in the acquisition of phonological segments, in the phonological structure of early words and in the strategies children use to solve the problem of learning to pronounce the language (Menyuk and Menn, 1979; Menn, 1981). Variability has been demonstrated in the word-form classes represented in children's early vocabularies and differences have been found in the types of utterances children produce during the one word period (Nelson, 1973; Bloom, 1973; Scollon, 1974; Branigan, 1979).

Our interest in these matters has been spurred by

three additional influences. In a series of papers,Branigan (1976,1977,1979 and in preparation) has explored the consequences of more precise techniques for analyzing the character of children's early utterances. By making use of spectographic analyses of utterances he has uncovered a wealth of form and variety in child language which, in some cases, is incapable of being described by the currently available vocabulary. Secondly, the explorations of variation in phonology have considered the role of production constraints in the account of that variability (Ferguson, 1978). McNeill (1974) has provided a conceptually similar account of aspects of syntax. Observed variation need not be accounted for exclusively by appeal to "input" factors such as perception, cognition or experience, but may also be accounted for by appealing to "output" factors of organization and production constraints. Finally, Stokes (1977) has explored aspects of within-child variation including variation in performance across turns in conversations and Stokes and Holden (1980) have documented unusual occurrences in the early stages of language development such as the very early but very infrequent use of original two word utterances by children who, near their first birthday, are otherwise clearly within the one word period.

In this paper, we will briefly describe the variety of utterance forms which children produce in the early periods of language development and provide an account of the within-child variation we have encountered. The evidence we offer will rely upon the occurrence of pauses (temporal fragmentation), the coexistence of different forms in children's output and the incidence of revisions during production.

Subjects-Methods

Thirteen children (0;9-5;0) were observed in home and laboratory settings at irregular intervals for periods from three to twenty-four months. The subjects and some of the observations made have appeared in previous published and unpublished works by the authors. Observations were recorded in three forms: audio, video and diary. Analyses that attend to segmental, prosodic, and temporal aspects of utterances are based principally upon spectographic tracings. On some occasions, analyses are based solely upon the author's perception of the children's productions (c f. Stokes and Branigan, 1978, where the unreliability of perceptual judgments is treated). We recognize that perceptual judgments and diary entries are generally unreliable, but we have found that they provide the only reasonable means for gathering rare events in the language of these children. We have collected over 30 hours of audio recordings and more than 3000 spectrograms have been prepared. We have thus combined formal and informal data collection procedures.

Definition of Utterance and Notational System

We are employing a neutral, operational definition of utterance (c f. Branigan, 1979): an utterance is any vocalization which is bounded by 1000 msec of silence (on either side). This definition avoids the inevitable difficulties associated with defining utterance in terms of intention, structure or function, and it permits an unprejudiced examination of the data in our effort to uncover the variety of utterance forms which may exist. Within the category of utterance, five types of utterance forms are identified.

These five forms are determined by two criteria:

1) Whether they contain sufficiently intelligible information to be given a meaningful interpretation.

2) The duration of silence which intervenes between lexical items.

This latter criterion, since it derives from spectrographic information, is capable of locating silent intervals which are below the threshold of perceptual detection. The five utterance forms we identify are:

1) A babbling form: the vocalization contains no recognizable lexical items.
2) A one word form: the vocalization is comprised of a single lexical item.
3) A successive form: the vocalization is separated from the next vocalization by 400-1000 msec of silence.

4) A multiple form: the vocalization is separated from the next vocalization by 100-400 msec of silence.
5) A compressed form: continuous vocalization with silent intervals of no more than 100 msec.

Two things are evident from these definitions. First, the burden of distinguishing a lexical (meaningful) from a non-lexical item still rests with the researcher. Second, the superordinate category "utterance" can be either a single sub-category or a combination of the subcategorical forms. Within this system, traditional descriptions of utterance forms are expanded. The system still permits us to identify babbles, single word utterances and multiple word utterances. But because it utilizes a temporal criterion to define both the superordinate and subordinate forms it allows for a richer description of children's productions.

For example this system expands our capacity to describe "successiveness". In earlier accounts, pauses between words were typically discussed with reference to separations between single words (e.g., wear/shoes). Our system allows us to treat two-word combinations separated from other two-word combinations by a pause (e.g.,I want/wear shoes) as a similar phenomenon. Furthermore it allows us to classify both "I want/wear shoes" and "I want wear shoes" as whole utterances on the superordinate condition (both bounded by 1000 msec of silence) but to distinguish between them according to their internal structure based on the subordinate conditions. This system increases our descriptive range and maximizes our ability to discover unique, distributional or developmental features of a wide variety of utterance forms.

A coding system is used to distinguish utterance forms in the following manner: 1) a natural typist's space indicates silence of less than 100 msec; 2) a raised period indicates a silence of between 100-400 msec; and 3) a slash indicates a silence of between 400-1000 msec.

The outline in Table 1 derives from our operational definition for utterance. First we distinguish between intelligible and unintelligible utterances, the common distinction between babbles and utterances with lexical content. Next we distinguish utterances by form or developmental history or both.

TABLE 1   Partial Variety of Utterance Forms

I. UNINTERPRETABLE
   A. VARIABLE (RANDOM): dawidado, dedrumtutut di
   B. STABLE
      1. DIFFERENTIATED SYLLABLES: wídə̀, gɔkIŋ, bᵁda
      2. REDUPLICATED SYLLABLES:
          bababab a, gᵛdʌgᵁdʌgᵁdʌ

II. LEXICAL CONTENT
   A. WORD
      1. VARIABLE (EVOLVING)
        a. PROGRESSIVE REORGANIZATION
          ki→kikæ →kikæk → kikæt → kIʔikæt → kIDikæt
        b. SUDDEN REORGANIZATION
          wawa→ O→wɔDæ
        c. REGRESSIVE REORGANIZATION
          dæ di → dæ dæ → dæ → dɔ → dɔdi → dædi
      2. STABLE: mama, no, etc.
   B. CONSTRUCTIONS
      1. TEMPORALLY FRAGMENTED

        a. SYLLABLES: pakI/bᵁk
        b. WORDS: dog/house
        c. PHRASES: I want/wear shoes

      2. PROSODICALLY INTEGRATED
        a. MULTIPLE WORD COMBINATIONS
          1) NOMINAL: baby cookie
          2) PRONOMINAL: see it
        b. COMPRESSED SENTENCES
          1) FROZEN IMITATIONS: I'll get it,
                Me carry you, etc.
          2) FLEXIBLE
            a) FORMULAS (FRAMES) wanna drink of ____
            b) UNIQUE: making the boot slide
                 juice in my sock
                 they don't sit up

Although the outline gives the impression that utterances can be easily classified under one of the headings, the fact is that an utterance, as defined here, can result from the combination of the types with each other. For example, one of our children produced "[detrumtututɔdi]/they don't sit up" combining a random babble and a unique compressed sentence within the 1000 msec boundaries used to identify an utterance. The two utterance types were separated by a 460 msec interval of silence giving the whole utterance the temporal pattern which is characteristic of successive forms. The data we will present below illustrates how within-child variability is typified by such combinations of forms across the separate categories.

We will discuss three features of our children's utterances, although other phenomena in the data bear on the issue of variation as well. First we find that the temporal organization of utterances varies, for all of our children, from one utterance occasion to the next. Second, we find that linguistic features (e.g., pronouns vs. nouns) that are intended to distinguish between children, in fact, coexist for our children. Third, we find that some utterances undergo reorganization as a child is speaking.

RESULTS
Temporal Organization

One feature which has been used to distinguish between children is the temporal unity of their utterances. Some children primarily produce single word utterances while others produce prosodically well-integrated phrases along with single words. The difference between the two types of multi-word structures is the presence or absence of pauses between lexical units. We have observed our children to use both fragmented and unified utterances at the same time.

TABLE 2 Co-occurrence of temporal forms

mama·David·touch/microphone	me/close it
mama·David/touch microphone	me·close it
mama·David·touch microphone	me close it
mama/more/glass/water	stick/here
mama·more·glass·milk	here·the ball
mama/more/glass/juice	here/car/bIba

```
is this ball        see a/more/is this some more/more
is·that ball        is that·more
is this/doggie      a more/is that more
```

All of the utterances in Table 2 exhibit an alternation between temporal forms, i.e., the utterances are either temporally fragmented or temporally unified (prosodically integrated). In each set, the semantic intentions appear to be the same. But the form varies from utterance to utterance and the distribution of pauses, that is where they occur, appears to be totally unpredictable. The clearest example is probably the first set of utterances from David who was telling his mother that he hit his head on the microphone. Here we find one totally integrated utterance, one with a pause between the verb and object and one with two pauses - one between the subject and verb and the other between the verb and object. Why is it, we ask, that a child who can produce a prosodically unified, multiple word utterance on one occasion will produce a similar (or identical) utterance with temporal fragmentation on another occasion just moments apart?

Coexistence of Linguistic Features

The previous examples illustrate the coexistence of forms with different degrees of temporal unity and demonstrate that our children alternated between temporal forms. Within a more specific category that has been discussed in the literature on variation, nominal vs. pronominal use, we have found these two categories to coexist not only within children but within a single utterance as well. For the examples in Table 3 the nominal referent for the pronominal form appears either before or after the pronoun. That is, the object of reference is either specified first and then referred to or referred to and later specified.

It is clear from these examples that the nouns to which the pronouns refer are available for use. The single most illuminating example, here, demonstrates the availability of the noun "window" from its use singly (window) and from its use in the phrases "in here window", "out the window". The contrast between the selection of the noun and the choice of a pronominal form is apparent from the frequent use of the expression "close it" which was used to talk about the activity of opening the window (on a toy house), putting a figure through and closing the window. The availability of both forms is more strikingly demonstrated by their mutual occurrence in "oh close it/window".

TABLE 3   Coexistence of Nouns and Pronouns

                    in here window
                    out the window
                    window
                    me close it (ref.=window)
                    oh close it/window

this isn't cookie	truck/what's that
where is it·truck	water/get it · water away
what's that/truck	ball/ball see it
what's that/oh vacuum	boat/see it
I'll get it·egg	
see it/that is/carrot	A: What are you doing Ben?
is it/kitty·cat	C: Is·this a·sponge?
is·this a·sponge	A: Yes, that's a sponge.
it here·boat	C: Oh, drop it.
	A: You dropped it.

The other examples demonstrate simultaneous use within or across utterances as well. What is intriguing, however, is that the pronominal forms virtually always occur in construction with other words while the nominals could occur either in construction or singly.

Reorganization

The third type of within-child variation in our data reveals that, from as early as the one word period, children alter the form of what they intend to say as they speak. They reorganize both the form and/or the composition of their utterances either spontaneously or as a consequence of being misunderstood. The data in Table 4 illustrate ongoing reorganization of utterance form.

TABLE 4 On line reorganization

bakibo ──────→ paki/bʊk   water/get it ə · water away
kiki ──────→ kʊ/ki   see a/more/is this same more/more
IzI·Izæ · Izæʌmʊn   bear/bear/bear here
dIsʌ /dIsʌ nɔgʌ   [he]   doll/more/more ə doll more
hwɛ /wɛ yugoIn   out/pull out
                              airplane/is a airplane

Segmental reorganization is evident in the reformulation of the less segmentally precise forms [bakibo] and [kiki] to their more precise representations [pakI/bʊk] and kʊ/ki . But notice in both cases how reorganization and greater segmental specification affected the produced form; each reorganized word appeared with a pause between syllables.

Reorganization of output is evident in the other examples as well. In

[IzI · Izæ · Izæʌmʊn]

the child initiates an utterance, reorganizes one part, and then integrates this new part in the longer phrase [Izæʌmʊn]. Similarly, in [dIsʌ /dIsʌ nɔgʌ] and [hwɛ /wɛ yugoIn] , the child begins to speak, pauses and resumes with the initial portion integrated into a longer phrase.

Furthermore, reorganization can occur across utterance turns,

George/mic
George · microphone

with the dual effect of more fully specifying the incomplete word and of prosodically integrating the original, temporally fragmented form.

These instances of reorganization do not always result in the subsequent integration of elements into a longer phrase. Occasionally, the reorganization simply focuses on an incomplete word

[oʌʔæiə mIfʌ · maikIfon]
oh what's that a mic·microphone
see a [bʊ] / ball

or it evidences the selection of a different lexical item

Apple
App-/another/apple

Here the child was naming objects in a picture book. He had just said "apple", noticed another one on the same page and began to name it, stopped in mid-word and reorganized his utterance to "another/apple". Notice that the output still contains pauses typical of temporally fragmented forms.

Our older children demonstrated reorganization during speaking or across utterance turns as well. Some reformulations also contained the pauses which frequently punctuated the younger subjects' reorganizational efforts.

TABLE 5   Older children's reformulations
C: I'm gonna let one dry out.
A: Huh?
C: I'm gonna let one/I'm gonna let one dries out.

C: Nobody cares do/does anyone.

C: Somebody else wants to be ates.
A: What?
C: Eaten.
A: Huh?
C: Somebody else wants to be eaten.

The utterances in Table 5 illustrate changes which are at a morphological or syntactic level rather than those which are at the lexical or segmental level. Nonetheless, the revisions in "Nobody cares do/does anyone" and "I'm gonna let one dries out" are quite similar to those reported above. In both of these examples, a pause occurs just at that point where a change is made in the organization of the utterance.

Comparisons to Previous Reports

Earlier reports of one word speech, although focusing on differences between children, never claimed that their data neatly divided types of children. Bloom (1973) never claimed that children who use substantive forms don't also use relational forms. Nor did she claim that successive single word utterances exist to the exclusion of multiple word combinations. Nelson (1973) never argued that expressors never used referential words; neither did she claim that referers never uttered whole phrases. Peters (1977) never reported that Minh exclusively used Gestalt phrases nor that all such phrases were pre-fabricated routines.

We have no intention of setting the analyses of these researchers up as straw-men and then arguing vacuously that they were wrong in their accounts. We will, however, compare our findings to those previously appearing in the literature and suggest how it is that everybody could be right.

If one examines Bloom's data carefully, there are examples in Allison's transcript which parallel the data we have reported. In sessions I and II, Allison always referred to her toy doll as "baby". When she began to use the compound "baby doll" at session III, the two words were occasionally separated by a pause.

>babydoll/diaper
>baby/doll/clean diaper

In other cases, we find the simultaneous occurrence of utterances with temporal fragmentation followed by temporally integrated utterances.

>baby eat/baby eat/cookie
>baby eat cookie

>baby doll ride/truck
>baby doll ride truck

Finally we find longer utterances with intervening pauses at the later sessions V and VI.

>I want/you want some·cocoa
>I want/I don't want to wear it
>no/that my/that not my cookie
>I guess it/I guess I broke it

Nelson (1973) and Peters (1977) have both reported the use of whole phrases by children in the one-word period. Although a limited number of examples are given, these utterance forms are generally described as unanalyzed wholes, prefabricated routines or formulaic utterances. Certainly our data contain examples of phrases which could fit these descriptions (e.g., what's that, I don't know where it is). But on the whole most of the longer phrasal forms, the prosodically integrated forms we are calling compressed sentences, were unique.

>making the boot slide
>I'm gonna read the book
>juice in my sock

Furthermore, compressed sentences combine in a variety of temporal forms with other vocalizations to form longer utterances.

>no/don't like my·book/here
>again/more out close it
>is a new hat·no a·Ben hat

Moreover, the fact that they are sometimes the final product of reorganizational efforts

$$[\text{IzI·Iz}æ \cdot \text{Iz}æ \wedge \text{m}\Lambda\text{n}]$$

and that the separate words are sometimes segmented out of the compressed sentence

>out/pull out
>up/pull up
>you slided/slide
>beddie-bye·him·up/it go beddie-bye

argue that these forms are constructed by the child rather than excised from adult speech as unanalyzed wholes.

Just as we have argued that temporally fragmented and temporally unified forms coexist, we are proposing that within the temporally unified forms, formulas and unique, constructed compressed sentences coexist.

Conclusions
As noted above, observed individual differences, or variability, in early child language development have most often been described by means of dichotomous categories. Some children were described as "referers" and were observed making proportionally greater use of one word utterances which tended to contain "nominals" or "substantives". Other children were described as "expressors" and were observed making proportionately greater use of multi-word utterances which contained "pronominals" and "functors". We have sought to enrich these characterizations in the following ways: (1) as our capacity for more precise description was increased through the use of spectrographic analyses, we have noted a far greater number of descriptive categories - simple bifurcation is no longer adequate; we have identified five categories of utterances and have suggested that these may "conjoin" into more complex utterances: (2) we have also found that all our subjects produced all forms of utterances. That is, not only are there more than two kinds of utterances (e.g., gestalt or analytic) but all children evidence all forms. The only individual differences are the frequency of occurrence of differ-

ent forms. We have found the simultaneous occurrence of different forms for all children more interesting than the statistical differences in proportion of use. We have therefore directed our efforts toward accounting for the within-child variety.

We believe that the observed variation is not the consequence of more or less pervasive differences in children, but rather is the consequence of the variable application of available production strategies. One further example from Kate, our youngest subject, may make the matter clear. In one word utterances the words bye-bye, Mommy, Daddy and Amy were each bisyllables. The last was produced as [memi] introducing an initial nasal through assimilation. Her output was constrained to producing monosyllabic or bisyllabic forms. When any of the proper names was combined with the salutation to form a two word utterance, Kate was faced with a dilemma, the organization of a 4 syllable utterance with a system which imposed a bisyllabic upper limit on utterance length. She evidenced an interesting simplification strategy, however, by always deleting the second syllables producing [baima] [baidæ] and most interestingly [baie]. She deleted second syllables evidently to maintain the bisyllabic nature of the output. She never produced meaningful four syllable utterances at that time - the production constraint operated on all available forms, even those which had two underlying words. The return to [e] as the first syllable of Amy in the two word expression [baie] suggests that although Amy always appeared as [memi] in isolation, the underlying form did not contain the initial nasal; it was introduced, instead, as the result of a phonological rule during production.

In this case as well as those above, we are suggesting that the variability in temporal forms, in the use of nominals and pronominals, and in the "on-line" reorganization of utterances can be accounted for by the influence of organizational principles and production constraints. The interaction between the number of elements (e.g., segments, syllables, words) and temporal form (e.g., fragmentation or unity) suggests that the type of utterance a child will produce varies according to the number of distinctions which are specified in an utterance plan. For example, as segmental distinctions become more precise, fragmentation and/or lengthening is the result (e.g., bakibo→paki/bʊk).Conversely as the number of distinct words (or syllables) increases in an utterance plan, with a unified intonational pattern, the result is compression and/or deletion of segmental or syllabic specifications (e.g., [baibai mama]→[baima] or [hwʌtzðæt → ʌzæ]). Organizational effects are further supported by the presence of reformulations, both spontaneous and elicited.

McNeill (1974) claimed that "normal speech seems to be uttered...as it is organized." Children, we assume, are often confronted with the dilemma that their intentions exceed their organizational and productive capacity, thus their performance is often hesitant and characterized by repetition, redundancy and revisions as they seek to both clearly and simply convey their intentions.

Under this account variability is an aspect of language which joins all children together in a common struggle to overcome or outgrow organizational and production limitations. Variability is a weaker basis for dividing children into dichotomous groupings (distinguished perhaps, as Peters (1977) speculated, by differences in cerebral hemispheric functioning) than is commonly suggested. Moreover, this account fits more comfortably with accounts of phenomena in phonology, (e.g., Ferguson & Macken, 1980) and in cognitive psychology (e.g., Miller, 1956). We have also reported that temporal fragmentation and reorganization during production are characteristic of children's performance at ages from one year to five years. No doubt, similar data could be obtained for adults as well when their organizational capacity and production constraints are tested against their underlying knowledge as in second language learning. Thus we have begun to explore a characteristic that is present in some form, perhaps in different contexts, across development.

Bibliography

Bloom, L. (1970). Language Development: form and function in emerging grammars. Cambridge, Mass: M.I.T. Press.

Bloom, L. (1973). One Word at a Time. The Hague: Mouton.

Bowerman, M. (1978) Words and sentences: uniformity, individual variation and shifts over time in patterns of acquisition. In F. Minifie and L. Lloyd (Eds.), Communicative and Cognitive Abilities - Early Behavioral Assessment. Baltimore: University Park Press, 349-396.

Branigan, G. (1976). Durational constraints during the one word period. Paper presented at The First Annual Boston University Conference on Language Development.

Branigan, G. (1977). If this kid is in the one word period... so how come he's saying whole sentences? Paper presented at The Second Annual Boston University Conference on Language Development.

Branigan, G. (1979). Some reasons why successive single word utterances are not. The Journal of Child Language, 6,3,411-421.

Branigan, G. (in preparation) Sentences children use - but shouldn't.

Ferguson, C. (1978). Learning to pronounce: the earliest stages of phonological development in the child. In F. Minifie and L. Lloyd (Eds.), Communication and Cognitive Abilities - Early Behavioral Assessment. Baltimore: University Park Press, 273-297.

Ferguson, C. and Macken, M. (1980). Phonological development in children: play and cognition. Papers and Reports on Child Language Development, 18, 138-177.

McNeill, D. (1974). Semiotic extension. Paper presented at the Loyola Symposium on Cognition, Chicago.

Menn, L. (1981). Theories of phonological development. Pre-publication draft. To appear in The Proceedings of the

New York Academy of Sciences.

Menyuk, P. and Menn, L. (1979). Early strategies for the perception and production of words and sounds. In P. Fletcher and M. Garman, (Eds.). Language Acquisition. Cambridge: Cambridge University Press, 49-70.

Miller, G. (1956). The magical number seven plus or minus two, or, some limits on our capacity for processing information. Psychological Review, 63, 81-96.

Nelson, K. (1973). Structure and strategy in learning to talk. Monograph of the Society for Research in Child Development, 38 (1-2), Serial no. 149.

Nelson, K. (1980). Individual differences in language development:implications for development and language. Address delivered at The Fifth Annual Boston University Conference on Language Development.

Peters, A. (1977). Language learning strategies: does the whole equal the sum of the parts? Language, 53, 560-573.

Peters, A. (1978). Units of acquisition. Ms. University of Hawaii.

Scollon, R. (1974). A real early stage: an unzippered condensation of a dissertation on child language. University of Hawaii Working Papers in Linguistics, 6,67-81.

Stokes, W. (1977). Motivation and language development. Paper presented at Society for Research in Child Development, New Orleans.

Stokes, W. and Branigan, G. (1978). On the definition of two-word utterances: or when does 1+1=2? Paper presented at The Third Annual Boston University Conference on Language Development.

Stokes, W. and Holden, S. (1980). Individual patterns in early language development: is there a one word period? Paper presented at The Fifth Annual Boston University Conference on Language Development.

LEXIS AND GRAMMAR IN THE DEVELOPMENT OF VERB-FORMS

PAUL FLETCHER
UNIVERSITY OF READING

The purpose of this paper is to report on a rather uncommon verb inflection over-generalisation in a British child learning English, and to explore some of the factors which appear to be relevant to its appearance, distribution and demise. The data reported comes from a study on the differentiation of past and present perfect in British English (henceforth BE). The immediate stimulus for this study was an analysis of verb-form data from 32 children, all aged 3;3, from the Bristol project (Fletcher 1981; see Wells 1981 for details of the Bristol project). This analysis indicated (a) that some of the children were using what looked like present perfect forms, with auxiliary have, though they tended to be lexically restricted, particularly to got; (b) other children were using past participles without auxiliaries, but did not seem to be using them in any way differently to past tenses. Both of these points seemed worth following up. The early appearance of 'present perfects' appeared to conflict with what was known from North American data (e.g. Cromer 1974). And the possibility of the child confusing past and present perfect was intriguing, especially in view of recent linguistic accounts which emphasise that the two forms are truth-functionally the same, in locating an event at some point prior to speech time (Inoue 1979, Smith 1981; see also McCawley 1981: 354). Such accounts attribute the undoubted meaning difference between the two to pragmatic factors which concern the different implication of the forms. Accordingly we began in November 1979 an intensive longitudinal study of a girl who was 2;4 at the time of the first recording. The study was planned to last for two years, and the recordings of the central subject's domestic life are supplemented by peer recordings at three-month intervals. Here we will only report data from Sally, the intensively recorded subject. This child is the youngest of three sisters, from a middle-class RP speaking family. Recordings of her conversations were made two to three times per week, for an hour at a time. The recordings were made at home, mainly with her mother, but also with her sisters, her father, and on one morning a week, two same-age friends. The MLU(m) value calculated from the first recording made was 2.48, which puts her squarely in Brown's Stage II. At the time of the first recording, in November 1979, when Sally was 2;4, most of her verbs were uninflected and unaccompanied by any auxiliary. She did however

Table 1: Regular and overgeneralised -en forms, one BE child, 2;5-3;5 (4.12.79-2.12.80)

Date	Form	Freq.	Date	Form	Freq.	Date	Form	Freq.
4.12	broken	8	17.3	letten	1	21.5	hiden	1
10.12	fallen	1	17.3	runnen	2	21.5	walken	1
10.12	broken	4	17.3	wasen	2	27.5	given	1
28.12	taken	1	17.3	putten	1	27.5	buyen	1
28.12	broken	1	20.3	touchen	1	29.5	closen	1
2.1	broken	4	20.3	putten	2	29.5	boughten	1
17.1	putten	1	20.3	haden	1	29.5	maken	1
2.2	fallen	1	20.3	getten	1	29.5	putten	1
2.2	putten	1	20.3	see-en	1	29.5	playen	1
12.2	given	1	20.3	rocken	1	14.6	taken	1
12.2	taken	1	24.3	fallen	1	14.6	seen	1
15.2	boughten	1	24.3	broken	2	14.6	putten	1
15.2	builden	1	24.3	given	3	18.6	fallen	1
19.2	eaten	1	24.3	maken	1	19.6	getten	2
19.2	riden	1	24.3	putten	2	19.6	haden	2
24.2	taken	1	24.3	helpen	1	21.6	given	1
24.2	getten	3	24.3	spoilen	1	21.6	bitten	1
26.2	given	1	31.3	taken	1	4.7	haden	1
26.2	cutten	1	31.1	maden	1	4.7	wearen	1
26.2	maden	1	31.1	maken	2	13.7	haden	1
29.2	wanten	1	31.3	tippen	1	14.7	broken	1
29.2	touchen	2	31.3	haven	1	14.7	leaven	1
4.3	taken	1	17.4	haden	3	14.7	haden	1
4.3	putten	1	18.4	taken	1	20.7	liken	1
4.3	haden	1	5.5	haden	1	20.7	haden	2
4.3	stepen	1	5.5	sitten	1	20.7	known	1
4.3	hurten	1	5.5	?caven	1	7.8	seen	1
6.3	leaven	1	5.5	grown	1	7.8	stayen	1
6.3	putten	1	8.5	given	6	7.8	haden	1
10.3	putten	1	8.5	haden	1	26.8	haden	1
10.3	bringen	1	8.5	sitten	2	11.9	haden	1
10.3	comen	1	8.5	letten	1	12.9	given	1
10.3	drawnen	1	8.5	wrappen	1	27.9	haden	1
11.3	hitten	3	8.5	putten	1	2.10	haden	1
11.3	maden	1	8.5	shoulden	1	2.10	given	2
11.3	putten	1	13.5	haden	2	2.10	seen	1
11.3	getten	2	18.5	haven	2	14.10	haden	4
11.3	taken	1	18.5	haden	1	14.11	haden	1
16.3	taken	1	21.5	given	1	2.12	forgotten	4
16.3	haden	1	21.5	given	1			
17.3	waken	1	21.5	haden	1			

use a few irregular pasts like made, got, found, had; some -ing forms - mending, falling; and the occasional can't, as in for example can't find, can't get. This of course fits a familiar pattern for early verb-forms. Over the next two months, though, there was a surprising development. First she started to use regular past participles like broken, fallen (without auxiliaries), and then very shortly after began applying the -en suffix inappropriately to a quite wide range of stems. She kept up this past participle overgeneralisation for most of 1980, though her most productive spell was in the first half of the year. A full list of regular and novel -en productions by the child is given in Table 1. While -en overgeneralisations are occasionally reported (see for example Zwicky 1970), there is nothing on this scale, and the data seemed worth closer scrutiny. Before trying to evaluate the significance of these forms in the child's development, though, we should first dispose of the most obvious question, which would ask whether these were -en forms at all, rather than misheard progressive forms. After all, the two are very similar in pronunciation in those accents of English which tend to use an alveolar instead of a velar nasal finally in the progressive. Fortunately, Sally's accent is RP, and she reliably differentiates progressive [ɪŋ] from past participle [ən]. So there is a reliable phonetic basis for the orthographic representations in Table 1.

How do we explain the data that appears in Table 1? At one level there is little problem. Overgeneralisation of inflections is a well-attested, cross-language phenomenon, which first appears at an early stage in the acquisition process. If the structure of their language provides them with regular and functionally transparent inflectional processes, then before they are three years old children will demonstrate recognition of the form-function mapping by application in novel instances. But in this case we cannot really leave it at that; there are a number of specific problems to be addressed if we are to fully evaluate the place of this period of overgeneralisations in the child's development of verb-forms. First, the -en suffix in English is not productive - it can be applied only to a small number of verbs, usually in the presence of an auxiliary. Why does the child latch on to it? Second, the child applies the suffix selectively - even though it is reasonably productive for the period it is used, not all available verbs are marked in this way. Is it possible to identify phonological or lexical factors which would account for this? Finally, we would like to know why the use of the -en suffix declines.

Not all of these questions can be answered directly, or fully. In what follows we will attempt to address as many as possible by examining grammatical, lexical and functional aspects of the data available. We will claim that (a) during the period of overgeneralisation the -en marker is a past time suffix, which coexists with other ways of marking past time; (b) that at least some of the selectivity apparent in its application is phonological; (c) that the demise of overgeneralised -en may be due to the child's eventual recognition of auxiliary distinctions and their functional relevance. But first, why this suffix? Unfortunately, some crucial data for this question is not available: the frequency and contexts of use of -en forms used to Sally in the months preceding our first sample. If the form was applied frequently in contexts that could be interpreted as past-referring, then (in the same way as is argued for -ing forms) its syllabicity and non-varying phonetic shape could facilitate segmentations the child would have to make as a basis for her later overgeneralisations. Whatever the input variables affecting her choice, all that can be said definitely is that by the time of the first overgeneralisation the child was using three correct -en participles: broken, fallen and taken. These exemplify two of the ways of forming past participles in English. One, with fall and take, adds the -en to the simple verb stem; the other, with break, adds the -en to the past tense form. Sally was to use both kinds of stems in her overgeneralised forms, though the fall, take type were more common.

We can now turn to the relationship between the forms in Table 1 and other potentially past referring forms. Table 2 lists the frequencies of these forms, along with -en overgeneralisations, for three periods of the first year or so of the study. The beginning of Period 2 coincides with the onset of -en overgeneralisations, and the end of Period 3 with their apparent disappearance. Periods 2 and 3 are equally divided by number of samples. From Table 2 it is apparent first that there are a range of forms used at the same time as overgeneralised -en which can serve to refer to past time. Two thirds of these are irregular pasts, as we might expect, but there are also -ed forms both regular and overgeneralised. If however we note that 80 of the 169 regular -ed forms appeared in (presumably) stereotypic utterances like what that called, or that called x, we can claim that -en suffixation is the most frequent lexical process.

Table 2: Incidence of past-referring inflections, one BE child, 2;5-3;5

	-en o/g	-en	Past Irreg	-ed	-ed o/g	Other PPartic.
Period 1 (23 Samples; 25.11-15.1)	0	21	180	29	1	34
Period 2 (40 samples; 17.1-3.6)	82	32	381	58	9	78
Period 3 (40 samples; 6;6-19.12)	27	15	426	82	16	21
TOTAL	109	68	987[a]	169[c]	26	133[b]
VERB-TYPES	36	10	30	38	19	6
TYPE-TOKEN RATIO	0.33	0.15	0.03	0.22	0.73	0.05

a got accounts for 40% of this total

b done and gone together make up 97% of this total

c called (as in what that called, or that called x) makes up 47% of this total

The second feature of Table 2 to note is the type-token ratios, recently rehabilitated (see Miller 1981: 42) as a measure of lexical diversity in spontaneous speech samples. If restricted, as here, to verbs, they can serve as a guide to productivity. TTRs for both -en overgeneralisations and -ed forms indicate, along with the number of verb-types, that these suffixes, taking Periods 1-3 as a whole, are reasonably productive. Before we leave Table 2, though, there is one other point we need to make; it appears that while the incidence of all -en forms, and indeed other past participles, is declining over the time covered by the Table, the use of past irregulars and -ed forms is increasing. We will return to this shortly.

We need now to turn to the question of the use of these forms in Table 2. Are all the forms listed in Table 2 used in similar ways? At this point in the child's development most past time references are to the immediate past, or the very recent past; some references do however go outside the here-and-now to earlier the same day, or less commonly to times rather more remote for the child, though usually salient - a birthday, or other significant family event. Table 3 lists some examples of past tense forms, and overgeneralised -en forms, with their temporal reference specified within an ad hoc scheme, keyed at the foot of the Table. The examples in Table 3, while representative, are not based on a complete analysis of the temporal reference of this data, which remains to be done. They do show however that both past tense and -en forms can refer to the immediate past, same day or previous day events, or more remote times.

Assuming that a complete analysis of the temporal reference of these forms holds up, we can now say that over the year covered by this data, the child has a number of grammatical choices for referring to the past; for other than irregular verbs, -en marking was initially more popular, but then declined, its place apparently being taken by -ed. Since some -ed forms were used from the beginning, however, can we identify any factors which, in Period 2 particularly, led to verbs being selected for -en marking? There are two avenues that might be worth exploring, one phonological and the other semantic. We know from Derwing's work on pluralisation (Derwing & Baker 1979) that an ordered acquisition of plural morphemes can be explained in terms of the phonological properties of stems. And recent work by Bloom and her associates has alerted us to the possibility that the aspectual character of verbs might affect the kinds of inflections applied to them (Bloom, Lifter & Hafitz 1980; see also Antinucci & Miller 1976). To deal with the latter possibility first: if we examine -en marked verbs we find no uniformity in their aspectual character. The suffix is attached to event verbs like forget, step or leave; to process verbs like hide, draw or rock; and to state verbs like want, like. The

Table 3: Temporal reference of past-referring forms: some examples from one BE child.

Date	Utterance	Past Time Category[a]
6.4	some milk dripped, dropped on the floor	IMM
6.4	probably me left that ahind a Zoes and Rory's	REC
6.4	you got the littlest	IMM
17.4	Annabel came play our house	REM
18.4	animal came in your room and my room	PAST
18.4	daddy sayed me that red jumper will fit me	PAST
13.5	me called it peanut butter	IMM
13.5	that cos me had it a lunch	REC
13.5	you already had pud	IMM
13.5	that Humpty lost one	VREM
29.5	found my letter	IMM
**		
31.3	me maden that	IMM
31.3	now me tippen that over	IMM
31.3	then maken, something maken a funny noise	REC
17.4	(Annabel came play our house) and her getten cold feet	REM
8.5	Mary given that when my birthday	VREM
13.5	me haden strawberries at lunchtime	REC
29.5	he closen it	IMM
31.5	(M. Who gave you that puzzle) nobody given it to me (M. how did you get it then?) me just buyen it	UNSPEC. UNSPEC.
17.6	in that shop where you getten my slides	PAST

a Category labels: IMM: up to five minutes prior to time of speaking; VREC: six minutes to one hour, or to beginning of sample; REC: prior to sample, same day; PAST: previous day; REM: up to one week; VREM: more than one week prior to time of sample; UNSPEC: unspecified past time - even time not identifiable from utterance or context.

semantic class to which verbs belong does not seem to be relevant to the application of the suffix.

Phonological factors do seem to be relevant, though. About one third of all the overgeneralised -en markings appear on monosyllabic CVC verbs ending in -t. That is, those irregular verbs which (with two exceptions) have no suffixation or vowel changes when used to refer to the past. The full list is put, get, cut, hurt, hit, let, sit, with get and sit the two morphological exceptions. If we also include CVC monosyllables with voiced alveolar stem-finals, then slightly more than half of the overgeneralised forms can be attributed to the phonological shape of the verbs they are applied to. Or rather, given the (presumably) temporary functional merger between present perfect and past for this child, the phonological shape of the verb will be relevant to whether or not it is -en marked. It is however only a sufficient condition for inclusion in the set of -en-marked verbs. There are verbs marked in this way which do not fit the phonological description (e.g. most of the regular verbs in Table 1), and other verbs which are -en-marked and have their usual irregular past form, in the same sample (see Kuczaj1977 for similar observations on overgeneralised -ed forms). We might assume that once the -en marking is introduced via verbs like put (if you look at Table 1 you will see that the first six overgeneralised forms meet the extended phonological condition described above), it becomes available to the child as a relatively productive process, and is available, for a time, to be attached to any verb. Variability results from the child having optional past markings.

Some added plausibility is attached to the overall argument by the child's behaviour with respect to one verb, got. In terms of frequency this is clearly an important form for the child. Its significance goes (I would suggest) much further than this. All the forms in Table 2 occur without auxiliaries, and it may have occurred to the reader to wonder what the child is doing with have auxiliaries, if indeed she has any, while all this is going on with her inflections. The data appears in Table 4. With the incidence and verb-type information given there it is clear that, at the period of maximum -en overgeneralisation, in Period 2, the child is using have auxiliaries, but only with got forms. At the same time, she has coined a form getten. Why? It has been pointed out (by Fodor & Smith 1978) that have got while formally a perfect, does not have the same meaning as other perfect forms. While perfect generally refers to a past event and emphasises its relevance for

Table 4: Incidence of Auxiliaries with past participles

	Frequency	Participle Types
PERIOD 1	6	got (4), lost, put
PERIOD 2	50	got (47), found (2), gone
PERIOD 3	96	got (64), gone (15), done (8), found (2), put (2), hurt (2), bought, throw, took
TOTAL	152[a]	

a Of this total, 50 are contracted auxiliaries ('ve or 's), 9 are of the type is you got, is her put, and the remainder involve has, hasn't, have or haven't

the current discourse context, have got constitutes an exception in referring to present possession or attribute states: have you got your shoes, I haven't got any pud, and so on. Sally appears to be giving witness to the exceptional status of have got by (a) making it her only have form during Period 2, and (b) coining a new form, getten, to refer to attribute states which are definitely in the past (as in Table 3 example, her getten cold feet, where we know that event time is three days prior to the time of speaking). It may seem far-fetched to introduce this one verb (if indeed it is appropriate to refer to it as one verb) as a relevant variable in the child's acquisition of grammar. But the child's treatment of these forms makes it very tempting. Quite how the child differentiates present perfect from past is still something of a mystery. But the decline of -en forms, the spreading of have auxiliaries across more verbs, and the rise of past do-support (summarised in Table 5) indicate that in the first half of her fourth year she is beginning to do so. Some light may be shed on this development by current work which is examining the spread of -ed, have and past do-support forms verb by verb, through and beyond Period 3.

Table 5: Incidence of past do-support

	Frequency of did/didn't	Verb-types	TTR
PERIOD 1	-	-	-
PERIOD 2	23	17	0.74
PERIOD 3	141	49	0.35

What is the relevance for language development studies of a temporary morphological overgeneralisation in a single English child? Any conclusions will be tentative. Nevertheless there are a number of points worth emphasising. First, the child's behaviour underlines the strength in the young child of this capacity to seek out regularities; in this case a very restricted process in the language serves as the basis for a productive marker. Second it shows how this capacity can interact with specific problem areas in the structure of a particular language - in this case the formal and functional similarity of past and present perfect in English - to produce novel forms. Third, it indicates that, in ways that we do not very well understand, the child can self-correct, apparently without any overt instruction, this particular false step in the long haul to language mastery. And finally, it suggests that for the analyst the investigation of lexis in development may be as heuristically important as the scrutiny of grammatical categories.

References

Antinucci, F. & Miller, R. (1976) How children talk about what happened. Journal of Child Language 3, 167-89.

Bloom, L., Lifter, K. & Hafitz, J. (1980) Semantics of verbs and development of inflections in child language. Language 56, 386-412.

Cromer, R.F. (1974) The development of language and cognition: the cognition hypothesis. In B. Foss (ed.) New perspectives in child development. Harmondsworth: Penguin Books.

Derwing, B.L. & Baker, W.J. (1979) Recent research on the acquisition of English morphology. In P. Fletcher & M. Garman (eds.) Language acquisition: studies in first language development. Cambridge, England: Cambridge University Press.

Fletcher, P. (1981) Description and explanation in the acquisition of verb-forms. Journal of Child Language 8, 93-108.

Fodor, J.D. & Smith, M.R. (1978) What kind of an exception is 'have got'? Linguistic Inquiry 9, 45-65.

Inoue, K. (1979) An analysis of the English present perfect. Linguistics 17, 561-89.

Kuczaj, S.A. II. (1977) The acquisition of regular and irregular past tense forms. Journal of Verbal Learning and Verbal Behavior 16, 589-690.

McCawley, J.D. (1981) Everything that linguists have always wanted to know about logic. Chicago: University of Chicago Press.

Miller, J. (1981) Assessing language production in children: experimental procedures. Baltimore: University Park Press.

Smith, N.V. (1981) Grammaticality, time and tense. Paper presented at the Royal Society/British Academy Meeting, 'The Psychological Mechanisms of Language', London, March.

Wells, C.G. (1981) Learning through interaction: the study of language development. Cambridge, England: Cambridge University Press.

Zwicky, A.M. (1974) A double regularity in the acquisition of English verb morphology. Papers in Linguistics 3, 411-18.

Avoiding repetitions:
Enough is enough

Lise Menn
Aphasia Research Center
Boston University School of Medicine
150 S. Huntington Ave.
Boston, MA 02130

Brian MacWhinney
Psychology Department
Carnegie-Mellon University
Pittsburgh, Pennsylvania 15213

Abstract: MacWhinney's (1978) psycholinguistic process model for the acquisition of morphophonology uses both rote-learned and rule-created affixed forms. Exploiting this duality, we can account for a variety of acquisitional phenomena concerning the under- and over-use of morphological markers, including 1) lateness of acquisition of "schwa-insert" affixes in English (and parallel phenomena in Hungarian and German); 2) reduced overregularization of English t/d final strong pasts (caughted compared to comed); 3) infrequency of inflectional back-formations; and 4) occasional affix repetition (duckses). This dual mechanism can also help to account for a morphological surface constraint in adult language: the absence of adjacent identical morphs representing different underlying morphemes, e.g. the absence of English adverbs in -ly from adjectives ending in -ly (*lovely-ly), the zero-plural marking of nouns ending in -Vs in Spanish, etc. Evidence is cited from English, Hungarian, Italian, Navajo, Ngarluma, Russian, Spanish, Swedish, and Turkish. We further justify an elaboration of MacWhinney's model with data from slips-of-the-tongue and theoretical perceptual considerations.

In this paper, we examine a very widespread linguistic tendency, one that might be called a universal if it did not have so many messy little exceptions. We will argue that a proper explanation of this phenomenon must be psycholinguistic, rather than purely linguistic; and we will draw crucially on language-acquisition data to build our psycholinguistic model.

The phenomenon being considered is the tendency of languages to avoid sequences of similar morphs when these morphs play distinct syntactic or semantic roles in a sentence: in other words, the avoidance of accidental repetition. For English speakers, one of the clearest examples of this phenomenon is the fact that we cannot generally make an adverb by adding -ly to an adjective if that adjective also ends in -ly. For example, we cannot form the adverb 'lovelyly' from the adjective 'lovely.' This illustration is given as example A1 in the Appendix. (For each of the examples we cite, the reader should consult the Appendix for the relevant details.)

Radford has called this phenomenon the 'like form' constraint; but a better term would be the accidental repetition constraint, for there is no constraint against deliberate repetition. On the contrary, reduplication is one of the major morphological devices of the world's languages. Sapir(1921) quotes examples of reduplication from, as he says, 'all parts of the globe.' We find it in some familiar Latin perfect stems, such as tetigi from tango, 'touch.' Illustrating this, Wilbur (1973) reports an example (A2 in the Appendix) from an Indian language spoken on Vancouver Island, in which the plural of the word for 'sea lion' has been formed by reduplicating the first syllable of the singular. It is clear that language is under no constraint to avoid reduplication per se; what it tries to avoid is accidental repetition.

This tendency to avoid accidental repetition cuts across syntax, derivational morphology, and inflectional morphology. Sometimes it applies to affixes that sound like stem beginnings or ends; sometimes it applies only to sequences of affix morphs; sometimes it applies to function words. Sometimes the tendency results in an absolute prohibition, sometimes in a strong but not absolute avoidance (example A1), and sometimes in a weak avoidance (example A3). There is evidence that the strength of the constraint can vary from person to person for a given morph. This variability has repeatedly frustrated grammarians in their attempt to construct a unified formal account of the constraint. This is most unfortunate, since it is intuitively clear that the phenomena involved here require a unified account.

What we have done is to construct an account which is unified psycholinguistically, not formally. We will first survey adult language data to support our claim that the accidental repetition constraint is formally intractable. Then we will describe the principal acquisition data that MacWhinney (1978) drew on for the construction of his model. Finally, we will show how that model accounts for the bulk of the cross-linguistic and acquisitional data. We will also discuss certain strategies for repetition avoidance that have become frozen into the grammar during the process of language change.

We speak to three audiences. To the formally-inclined, we suggest that the place to look for unity of messy phenomena may be in processing, rather than in grammar. To those who distrust grammar, we say that processing explanations will not do everything; grammar -- in this case, some kind of rule for choosing between allomorphs -- is also needed. To fellow developmentalists we say that child language data are vital to building models of language use in which grammar and processing interact, and that construction of such models in turn will give a deeper understanding of language acquisition.

First, let us consider a small cross-linguistic sample to display the variety of adult language phenomena. (A fuller catalog of examples will appear in an extended version of this paper now in preparation). In example B1 in the Appendix, we find that Swedish nouns ending in -Vn do not add the -en definite marker. Similarly, in Spanish and Portuguese, nouns in -Vs do not add another -es to parse their plural. So here we have the shape of the stem-end making an inflectional affix morph somehow unnecessary. Point B2 gives a pair of examples involving two identical affix morphs. In the Turkish example both morphs represent the plural morpheme. The plural morph -ler or -lar can mark either the plurality of the possessor, as in 'their book,' or the plurality of the item possessed, as in 'her books.' Alternatively, it can mark both types of plurality simultaneously: in 'their books' we still find only one -lar.

The familiar English example given in B2b shows how two distinct affix morphemes can merge when they look alike. Here the merger is between the possessive and the plural. This example also makes clear that the phenomenon we are studying must somehow take account of the surface shape of the morph, since the possessive and the plural both appear in words where the plural is not the regular sibilant, like 'men's' and 'women's.'

Under point B3 in the Appendix we repeat the 'gaps in the lexicon' phenomenon that we took as our first illustration: English has no '*lovelily' and no '*computerer.' This fact is dealt with in grammars by saying that -er attaches only to verb stems if they are 0-derived. But note that we also get blocking in some cases where a stem-end resembles a derivational affix -- one cannot derive Fisch-isch in either German or English. While we can always come up with 'fishy' or 'fishlike' if we need to, we can find ourselves stumbling over non-existent adverbs in real speech, as in: "He gave me an nasty look. I mean he really snarled uh- uh- it was an ugly snarl."

Up to this point, the various instances of the accidental repetition constraint have involved only deletion, merger, and blocking. All of these processes can be accomplished formally by output constraints--devices that look at output at some specified point in a derivation and decide whether it is 'good' or 'bad.' But now consider section B4 of the table. For these examples, the repeated-morph constraint can no longer be formally handled by output constraint devices. Instead, to borrow a legal term, these are cases of 'prior restraint,' and some type of true grammatical rule is necessary. Why necessary? Because here the allomorphic substitution which gets rid of a repeated morph occurs not just in the cases where repetition would have occurred, but also in other cases as well. In the Turkish example, the regular passive morpheme is -Vl; the alternative allomorph -Vn (which is the same as the reflective, incidentally) is used for the passive not only in cases where the stem ends in -l, but also in cases where the stem ends in a vowel. In this case Turkish is not waiting for trouble to start.

One final caution: this 'universal' is only a 'universal tendency.' There are clear cases where languages violate the constraint and allow accidental repetition anyway. For example, French permits forms like nous nous levons (= we wake ourselves up). Thus, whatever account we give for the avoidance of accidental repetition must also leave some room for the occasional acceptance of repeated morphs.

The major acquisitional phenomena we will consider are familiar: the late acquisition of regular inflectional endings on stems whose final sounds are similar to the regular ending (C1), the presence of markings in unanalysed forms before their appearance in analysed forms (C2), the tendency of partially regular forms to resist overregularization (C3), and the eventual appearance of accidental repetitions (C4). MacWhinney (1978) has reported on the occurrence of these phenomena in several languages; and MacWhinney (1979) also produced these effects in the context of a miniature artificial language experiment.

The fact that children demonstrate sensitivity to partial regularities indicates that they do not process morphs in a strictly one-morph-one-meaning fashion, but are able to perform analyses on words that leave incomplete or partial residues. In the C1 case, it was the children's failure to match the adult pattern that was surprising, because the adult pattern--adding plural markers to 'kiss' and 'box'--is regular and should be easy; in the C3 case, children's <u>success</u> at matching the adult pattern is the surprise, because the adult pattern is <u>irregular</u>. What these two cases have in common is that the form without the affix still somehow 'sounds marked.' In time English-speaking children do learn to add plural markers to sibilant-final words and past-tense markers to dental-final words. And eventually, as C4 states, over-markings and other overgeneralizations appear. Some of these, the double markings, are very peculiar objects. We have them both on regular stems, like 'duckses' and irregular ones, like 'broked.' They have to be accounted for.

The heart of our account for these phenomena involves the understanding of word formation as a real-time process which starts by <u>retrieving memorized affixed forms</u>. After a period of nonanalytic usage, the child acquires the ability to add affixes by rules, while still preferring to retrieve affixed forms from the lexicon. The play-off between these two processes of rote and combination is entirely dynamic. Because of this play-off, it can occur that sometimes both processes function, sometimes only one functions, and sometimes neither functions. Because of this dual mode of operation, the model needs an affix-checker: a device that looks to see whether a form about to be affixed by combination has already emerged as a rote form from the lexicon with its affix on it.

Many people are uncomfortable with the notion of inflectionally-marked forms in the lexicon; the longer the string of affixes, the less anyone likes it. But language after language tolerates irregular inflectional forms, so it is not unreasonable for inflectional markings to be entered in the lexicon at least some of the time. Moreover, there is evidence from slips-of-the-tongue indicating that attachment of inflectional affixes occurs on-line. Let's assume then that an affix-checker is part of that real-time process. To match the child's earliest productions we set up the most primitive or 'naive' version as in D1. It is designed to produce the missing affix effect noted in children, and it will also produce some of the patterns found in adult languages. The naive affix-checker operates like this: it looks superficially at an item that is supposed to bear a particular affix, and it sees if the end of that item matches the affix to be attached. For example: suppose the word is a Spanish word which is to be pluralized and if the word ends in -Vs. The naive affix-checker decides that it already has the plural marker on it, and dismisses it without adding anything. This mode of operation is correct for Spanish plurals and other cases where stem-end deletion is the rule. A child learning to make plurals in Spanish can stick with this naive version of the affix-checker and be correct her whole life.

Now consider what happens if this naive affix-checker operates on the English plural morpheme. Some things will be done correctly; a plural marker won't be added to a word that is already marked for plural with a sibilant. But the naive affix-checker will make two kinds of errors. It will add -z to irregular plurals, and it will fail to add -iz to sibilant final stems, like 'kiss.' Eventually, the English affix-checker must "get smarter." It must become able to tell whether a word-final sibilant belongs to a stem, as in 'kiss,' or to an affix as in 'ducks.' In the 'kiss' case, the affix must be added; in the 'ducks' case it must not. The version of the affix-checker which is capable of making such discriminations is listed as D2, a source-oriented checker.

Now, an erroneous plural like 'duckses' can be explained as the output of a naive affix-checker that is beginning to gain some experience (see D2). We think that the child producing 'duckses' has learned that English has such plurals as 'box-boxes.' At this stage -siz is included as a possible allomorph of the English plural. This allows 'duckses' to pass by the checker. However, this "smarter" checker now keeps track of whether the form-to-be-produced has already undergone combinatorial attachment of a plural suffix. If a form is produced by rote, it can still pass through this checker. Thus, the child can have 'ducks' as a rote plural and add a combinatorial plural to produce 'duckses.' This version of the checker still permits certain accidental reduplications. If combinatorial plurals are added to rote forms like 'boxes' and 'glasses,' the child will produce 'boxeses' and 'glasseses.' Such reduplications are rare, indicating that the D2 version of the checker quickly develops into the D3 version. When using this third version of the affix-checker, the child will conduct a more complete analysis. He will then block production of 'boxeses,' but if the plural 'ducks' is a rote form in the lexicon, the child can still produce 'duckses.'

To account for avoidance and gaps, like 'fishish' and 'heavenlily,' a truly sophisticated affix-checker is needed--one that keeps track of category labels not just on the incoming material but also on its own output. For example, suppose adverb-creation is taking place. The sophisticated affix-checker with -ly to add will not pass 'heavenly' as an acceptable adverb. Although it has a -ly at the end, the adult device will know that 'heavenly' is still only an adjective. Therefore, we suggest that derivational blocking requires the most sophisticated affix-checker, D4, for that is the version which has to deal with the greatest amount of information about the word being formed.

The final condition (D5) is the one which, as we said earlier, cannot be simulated by any output-checking device: the situation in which the speaker must choose among non-zero allomorphs. That is, in a sense, the standard situation - tacking on allomorphs without the notion of 'output constraint' ever being needed. But if choices among non-zero allomorphs do not involve morphological output constraints, then hasn't a generalization been lost? Consider the Turkish example in B4b. In the history of the language, the repeated morph constraint could have played a role at the time this allomorph was being created - individuals must then have had choices between the forms to use and those choices could have been in part motivated by the constraint (Menn, 1979).

In summary, then, the constraint against accidental repetition provides a good example of how aspects of language structure that are resistant to formal analysis can be illuminated by psycholinguistic accounts that view grammar as a set of strategies acquired over time. Moreover, we must realize that processing accounts involve much more than the translation of obligatory rules into variable or optional rules. Language processing involves a complex interplay between rote, combination, and analogy in lexicalization; it requires the coordination of a variety of ordering patterns that are compiled onto a linear output; and, finally, it involves monitoring and checking processes that undergo their own development during the course of language acquisition. Only by gaining a deeper understanding of these aspects of language processing can we reach a true understanding of the origins and nature of language structure.

Appendix

A. Repetition

A.1. Avoidance of Accidental Repetition

English: adjectival = adverbial /-ly/
divine	divinely
heavenly	*heavenlily
likely	*likelily
ugly	*uglily
surly	?surlily (Zwicky & Pullum)
silly	?sillily

A.2. Reduplication

Comox, Vancouver Island: kumaguin, 'sea lion,' pl. kumkumaguin

A.3. Euphony

English singular possessive: a rose's odor ? a narcissus' (s) odor

B. Crosslinguistic Evidence

B.I. Stem-end deletions

Swedish (Linell): nouns ending in /-Vn/ do not add the definite marker /-Vn/ (for a class of non-neuter nouns such as froeken).

B.2. Merger of successive identical morphs

a. Representing the same morpheme: Turkish (Lewis): plural markers ler/lar in possessive constructions: kitap, 'book'; kitabi, 'his/her/its book'; kitaplari, 'their book' kitaplar, 'books'; kitaplari, 'his/her/its books'; kitaplari, 'their books'; (not *kitaplarlari).

b. Representing different morphemes:
English: possessive = plural /s,z,ez/

sing.	gen. sing.	plur.
gen. plur.		
girl	girl/z/	girl/z/
girl/z/(not *girl/zez/)		
woman	woman's	women
women/z/		

B.3. Avoidance or blocking

In English the agentive -er cannot be added to the instrumental -er, as in *computerer (computer user; cf. hammerer) nor can one add the adjectival -isch to stems in -isch in German (*fisch-isch); the identical prohibition against ish-ish holds in English.

B.4. Substitution of a special allomorph

a. just where needed to avoid repeated morphs:

German (Radford) - (two function words): In the double comparative construction exemplified by Goethe ist bekannter als Schriftsteller denn als Naturwissenschaftler 'Goethe is better known as a writer than as a natural scientist,' denn is used uniquely to avoid a sequence of als als and is not permitted in other comparatives.

Tswana (Cole) - (stem-front and two affixes, given identical treatment): 1st singular concord marker on verbs is /ke-/, but is 'usually' replaced by /m-/ before the conditional mood marker /-ka-/ and before verb stems beginning in /k-/.

b. Substitute morpheme used in a well-defined and somewhat wider variety of cases than those which would result in successive identical or near-identical morphs.

Hungarian (stem-end): 2nd person sing. pres. indic./-asz,-esz,-sz/ has a set of suppletive allomorphs /-ol,-el,-ol/ used whenever the verb stem ends in a sibilant:
*masz- + -asz, replaced by masz- + -ol
*olvas- + -asz, replaced by olvas- + -ol.

Turkish (Lewis) - (stem-end): passive formed by adding /-Vl/ to all verb stems except those ending in /-l/ and those ending in vowels; in these cases, the passive is made by adding /-(V)n/.

Spanish: the well-known 'spurious se' rule (Perlmutter) by which *le lo da 'he gave it to him' is replaced by se lo da.

Exception: note that French tolerates a certain few identical pronoun sequences, as in: nous nous levons 'we get up' and vous vous levez 'you get up ' (Perlmutter).

Swahili and other Bantu languages tolerate some sequences of identical agreement markers: wa-wa-piga 'they beat them' (Clements).

c. 'Euphonic' changes: the definition of the cases in which the substitution occurs is fuzzy: Latin (Watkins) - (substitution said to be triggered by presence of /l/ as the most recent liquid in a word) use of adjectival form in /-aris/ instead of regular /-alis/: front-, frontalis along with radi-, radialis: but jugul-, jugularis; ulna-, ulnaris; however, an exception: aeraris, from aes, aeris 'copper, brass'

C. Language Acquisition Phenomena

C.1. Late acquisition of endings on certain stems

In English, on stems whose final sounds are similar to the sound of the plural, there is late acquisition of plural marking (Berko, Ervin-Tripp).

Hungarian, German: similar, e.g. late plural on Hammer, Glas, Pfeife.

C.2. Early plural not fully productive

In these cases as in all others, plural markings are found on real words before they can be added to nonce-words like Berko's 'tass,' 'niz.'

C.3. Acceptance of partial regularity

Over-regularization of verbs with t-final present and/or past, such as 'bought,' 'eat,' is less than in forms like 'comed,' 'ringed' (Kuczaj, Slobin & Bybee).

C.4. Overmarkings

Eventual overmarking of plural and past in English; children not only learn to say 'boxes' and 'batted' eventually, they also create 'duckses' (double regular plural) and 'broked' (irregular + regular past) and most other conceivable double-markings.

D. Operation of Affix-Checker

D.I. Naive version

Checker examines incoming item to see if its end matches (more or less) the affix to be attached. If the affix appears to be 'already there,' form is produced as is; otherwise, affix is attached. Effect: 1-type deletions (Spanish plural, Swedish definite) and 2-type mergers (English possessive plural,

Turkish plural possession); and children's early omission of affixes on words that 'sound like they are already marked.'

D.2. Source-oriented version

Checker examines incoming item to see if it was formed by productive attachment of an inflection. If so, it checks to see that it contains a permissible allomorph.

D.3. Exclusive use of permissible allomorphs

This checker operates like the previous one, but performs complete analyses.

D.4. Sophisticated version

This checker is sensitive to output syntactic category as well as to phonemic shape, boundaries, and input category. It looks 'back' to see if semantic-syntactic obligations have been discharged. It blocks derivation if they haven't been. Effect: gaps (*lovelily, *fishish)

D.5. Rules

Here, the processor must have access to grammatical information; it is no longer capable of being completely specified within a processing component. That is, a morpheme processor can only add the morpheme it has been told to add, pass the input form without adding anything, or block the derivation. When it is necessary to go and retrieve a special form, reference to the grammar in some form becomes necessary.

References

MacWhinney, B. The acquisition of morphophonology. *Monographs of the Society for Research in Child Development*, 1978, Vol. 43.

MacWhinney, B. Miniature linguistic systems as tests of universal operating principles. 1979. Paper presented at SRCD Biennial Meeting, San Francisco.

Menn, L. The repeated morph constraint. In R. Herbert (Ed.), *Applications of linguistics to the social sciences*. Michigan State University, 1979.

Sapir, E. *Language: An introduction to the study of speech*. New York: Harcourt, Brace & Co., 1921.

Wilbur, R. *Reduplication*. Doctoral dissertation, University of Illinois, 1973. distributed by the Indiana University Linguistics Club.

A CASE FOR LITERAL METAPHOR IN CHILD LANGUAGE*

Nancy Budwig, Michael Bamberg & Amy Strage
University of California, Berkeley

1 Introduction

Metaphor has become a lively topic of debate in recent discussions of child language development. It has been suggested that investigations of metaphor can shed light on the nature of both cognitive and semantic development. Crudely speaking, ongoing metaphor research can be divided into two camps. The first camp views metaphor as a secondary, derived result that is based on some more basic processes of perception and categorization. The second camp sees metaphor as the product of a direct, non-analytic process of perception and conceptualization.

The majority of research concerning metaphor in child language has drawn upon assumptions central to what is to be considered the derived process paradigm. Consequently, this kind of research has focused primarily on the question of when children begin to make use of and understand metaphoric utterances; and furthermore, what kind of cognitive and especially metalinguistic processes might be involved in children's understanding of metaphors at different stages of linguistic and cognitive development.

In this article we will discuss metaphor in child language within the framework of the direct process paradigm. Drawing upon longitudinal data of two 2-year-old girls we will suggest what the direct process model can contribute to a more general understanding of the relationship between growing linguistic and cognitive capacities in the child. More specifically, we will argue against a position central to those working within the derived process model, namely that children first learn a literal way to talk about the world before they "extend" or "bend" these literal meanings into non-literal, i.e. metaphoric ones. In arguing for literal metaphor, we exemplify how children's linguistic utterances reflect metaphoric conceptualizations in their ongoing process of constructing reality.

2 Toward a definition of metaphor

At first glance the notion of literal metaphor seems to involve a contradiction of terms. The notion of literal metaphor makes little sense according to the derived process model. Central to this model is the assumption that objects, events and classes have an existence more or less independent of how people conceive of and interact with them. The point is stressed by those working from the standpoint of the derived process model that there exists a literal way of conceiving of and talking about such objects, events and classes. Accordingly, metaphor is argued to be a deviant or non-literal way of talking about reality, often viewed as a stylistic or aesthetic device, or an embellishment to the literal ways of describing reality.

With regard to child language, proponents of the derived process model argue that children first go through a literal stage, where they learn to categorize the world according to the way "things are" and only then come to bend, extend, and transfer these conceptions in a more creative fashion. The distinction made between literal language and metaphor, and furthermore, the belief that metaphor must be viewed as a derived process, has left researchers working within the derived process paradigm with the question: When do children develop a metaphoric competence, and what does this kind of competence consist of? The answers to these questions are far from being settled: On the one hand, some researchers have suggested that metaphoric competence is based on the acquisition of formal operational skills (cf. Asch and Nerlove, 1960; Augst, 1978; Cometa and Eson, 1978). Others have tried to show that metaphoric competence is a much earlier developmental achievement (cf. Perkins, 1978; Verbrugge, 1979; Winner et al., 1980). In summary, those researchers working within the framework of the derived process model make a distinction between literal and figurative ways to conceive of and talk about reality. In developmental terms it is suggested that children go through the process of literal categorization before learning to extend meaning across category boundaries (Winner, 1979).

However, there exists a second paradigm within metaphor research - one which will be referred to here as the direct process model. This alternative framework has received little attention from researchers interested in developmental aspects of metaphor. The direct process model focuses on the interaction between individuals and their surroundings. Stressed is the individual's construction or creation of reality, as well as how people's conceptions of reality change. To the extent that metaphoric processes are believed to play an important role in organizing and reorganizing our understanding of reality, metaphor is viewed as neither deviant nor purely as an aesthetic tool.

Despite the fact that the direct process model has received little attention, the idea that the production and understanding of metaphor must proceed like that of any utterance is nothing new. The roots of this model can, in part, be found in Gestalt psychology (Köhler, 1929; Werner and Kaplan, 1963) as well as in the later writings of Wittgenstein (1953). More recent theoretical discussions in support of this model can be found in the work of Lakoff and Johnson (1980), Rumelhart (1979), Sadock (1979), and Searle (1978). Empirical findings (cf. Ortony et al., 1978; Pitts et al., in press; Pollio et al., 1981) suggest that processing metaphor does not require an initial stage of figuring out an utterance's 'literal meaning', but rather that - especially in ongoing communication - one "sees" one thing in terms of another as a direct experience that takes place all at once.

A consideration of this second processing model tosses up a variety of new research questions for researchers of metaphor in child language. Viewing metaphor as a direct, non-analytic process in adult language use, raises the question of whether this is also true for a developmental line of argument. In this paper, we will document how viewing metaphor as a direct, non-analytic process can contribute to a better understanding of child language development.

Within the two models of metaphor discussed above, there exists no agreed upon definitional stance towards metaphor. It seems that what is considered as metaphor is guided not only by the paradigm within which one chooses to work, but at the same time, by the methodology used and the experimental design employed. Metaphor in this paper will be viewed quite generally as a conceptual activity of SEEING AS. Wittgenstein describes SEEING AS as the "flashing of an aspect on us [which] seems half visual experience, half thought ... an amalgam of the two"; and further, "what I perceive in the dawning of an aspect is not a property of the object, but an internal relation between it and other objects" (Wittgenstein, 1953, pp. 197 & 212).

In the following discussion we will draw on interactional data from a year long longitudinal study of 2 white, middle-class girls. The children were video-taped in alternating homes with their mothers present. Though the mothers and daughters met one afternoon each week, we video-taped the play sessions at monthly intervals. The children were 2 years, 2 months and 2 years, 5 months at the beginning of the study, and the children were one year older at its completion. During the video-sessions a variety of activities took place including play with clay, storybook reading, craft tasks, puzzle making, and role play.

3 The notion of the SEEING AS CONTINUUM

Over the course of the study the children we observed produced an abundance of utterances that could be considered as instances of SEEING AS. The children continually focused on certain properties of objects they talked about and de-emphasized others, thereby expressing a particular understanding of the ongoing event or activity in which they were involved. Both within and across the various play sessions the children took a variety of perspectives on a given object, event, or activity. For example, a large cardboard container was called <u>a box</u> as well as <u>a mousetrap</u>, and the wireless microphones pinned to the children's clothing were referred to as <u>microphones</u>, <u>olives</u>, and <u>noses</u>.

We would like to suggest that the instances of SEEING AS uttered by the children are best viewed as falling along a continuum - with more conventional ways of SEEING AS falling toward one end, and more novel ways falling toward the other end. In appealing to the notion of a continuum we are attempting to highlight the direct and non-analytic aspect of metaphor. Rather than separating out and pitting against each other what previously has been called literal language and metaphoric language, we are suggesting that all instances of SEEING AS are best viewed as falling along <u>one</u> continuum. So to refer back to the examples previously mentioned, our claim is that namings such as <u>microphone</u> would fall more or less toward the conventional end of the continuum while naming the same object <u>an olive</u>, or <u>a nose</u> are more novel ways of viewing the wireless microphone.

It is our belief that past research on metaphor in child language all too often has been concerned with examples that fall mainly to either end of the continuum. Such cases present the clearest examples that highlight differences in ways of SEEING AS. Nevertheless, we have found several instances of SEEING AS which were rather difficult to segment into two distinct categories. Thus we appeal to the notion of a continuum not only to highlight the similarity in processes of SEEING AS, but also to better account for the full range of examples we have found in the children's speech.

To illustrate the full range of SEEING AS instances found in our data, we will start by focusing on one particular activity type that occurred in every session - namely play with clay. In conceiving of the clay the children displayed the ability to take a variety of perspectives of varying degrees of conventionality. In many of the sessions the children referred to the clay in fairly conventional ways, as for example: <u>I need some clay</u> or <u>I have play-dough</u>. Other somewhat conventional ways of viewing the clay were instances such as: <u>I making a pie</u>, <u>I'm rolling clay</u> and <u>I gonna put this in the oven</u>. While this second set of examples may seem different from the first, handling and viewing clay as dough seems to fit our conventional expectations of how to SEE clay.

Farther toward the middle of the SEEING AS continuum one can find instances where the clay was viewed by the children as a bridge: <u>Look</u> <u>at</u> <u>my</u> <u>bridge</u>; and a snowman: <u>Me</u> <u>gonna</u> <u>make</u> <u>a</u> <u>snowman</u>. Such examples, while perhaps to some extent less conventional, still do not seem particularly novel, since we tend to view play with clay in terms of making the clay substance <u>into</u> something. Thus focussing on the transformational quality of this substance is still relatively in line with our everyday expectations regarding children's activities with clay. However, there are also several instances in which the children viewed the clay in truly novel ways. One child referred to the bowl of clay as a bathtub, and in another session one child took the antenna of the wireless microphone and started to 'sew' through a wad of clay, announcing (just before the adult stopped this activity): <u>I'm</u> <u>threading</u> <u>clay</u>. A little later this child says to her peer: <u>I</u> <u>think</u> <u>you</u> <u>have</u> <u>a</u> <u>long</u> <u>thing</u> <u>I</u> <u>can</u> <u>sew</u>. These last few instances illustrate that already by the age of two the children are capable of viewing the clay along the full range of the SEEING AS continuum. Often the children constructed frames around multiple views of one and the same object or event (cf. Bamberg, 1981).

One could argue that the above instances of SEEING AS and the continuum along which they fall are 'by-products' of the sorts of activities that were chosen to highlight the point we have been claiming so far. We would agree that such activities as play with clay "play upon" exactly the notion of perspective seeing that we are developing here. The specific relationship between play and metaphor is investigated elsewhere by one of the authors of this paper (Bamberg, 1980, in press), therefore we will not review this line of argument here. Rather, we will briefly state our agreement that such play episodes are a frequent source of examples of all degrees of SEEING AS, but we must also emphasize that the examples of more or less conventional and novel ways of SEEING AS are by no means limited to the children's play activities, but can be found in many episodes of the study.

4 <u>Conventional</u> vs. <u>literal</u> ways of SEEING AS

In the preceeding section we have suggested that the ways of SEEING AS expressed by the children are best viewed as falling along a continuum. It is the aim of this section to document that the notion of a continuum with novel ways of SEEING

AS situated toward one side and conventional ways toward the other is not an attempt to restore the distinction between literal and metaphorical meaning in the gown of a continuum. In the following discussion of a few examples we think we can provide evidence that the notion of literal ways of SEEING AS inadequately accounts for our data. Let us turn to some examples from several interactions throughout our observations:[1]

(1) J: The sun is going down ... down in the mountains

(2) J: The sunset is coming up ... it's yellow

(3) J: Look at the fog is coming in . Michael

(4) J: [commenting on the sun] It gone down

(5) S: Where's the odder paper .. I need the odder paper .. where's that paper going

(6) J: [picking up canister of clay - looking at the clay] Does this one come out

(7)   [JM and J working on a puzzle]
    JM: You better help me ... are you tired
    J: Yes .. but I'll help you ... this go in .. goes in here

(8)   [S and J are blowing bubbles]
    S: [blowing extra hard] Nothing comes out ... nothing comes out .. I wonder why

    What these examples have in common is the perspective SEEING in terms of 'coming' and 'going'. In each example some object, entity or activity is viewed in terms of these actions. The question remains which of these utterances sound fairly novel. Perhaps the only example which appears novel is example (2), where one child views the sunset as 'coming up'. We will return to this example later, but for now we will question whether there is anything literal about the remaining examples. A good many of these examples refer to the sun as performing an activity at the end of the day - specifically, the sun is viewed as 'going down'. Adults too view the sun as 'coming' and 'going'; within our culture this seems to be a very conventional way of SEEING AS. Clearly though, everyone would admit that despite the fact that we've all "seen" a sunset, this is just a particular perspective and not in any sense 'literally' the way it is. We are claiming that such things as day, light, night, and darkness are viewed as SUBSTANCES which then can be conceptualized as 'coming' or 'going'.[2]

Looking back at example (2), the example in which Jennifer explains that the sunset is coming up, we would suggest that the child has selected a perspective on the sunset which, while rather novel, is nevertheless no more or less literal than the view of the sun as 'going down' or 'coming up'. The inadequacy of the notion of literal ways of SEEING AS becomes even more obvious when we take the point of view that is used for instance in the German speaking culture: In German it is quite conventional to say that 'the dusk' is coming up; a view that is not common to the English speaker. Would it be possible to argue that the child in the above example is taking a viewpoint towards the time and appearance of the day that is conventional to the German speaking culture; and not using the German word Abenddämmerung, she employs the word she knows, and that is sunset?

Turning away from the examples of the sun, we will examine the episode in which the children are playing with a bottle of bubbles (example 8). One child dips her stick into the bubble bottle several times and attempts to blow hard, but she is unable to transform the liquid into bubbles. Finally she utters: Nothing comes out. Again we would suggest this is one particular perspective that can be taken on the situation. That there is nothing inherently literal or non-literal about this view becomes clearer if we look at what happens further into this episode: Here, the child after much persistence is able to "produce" bubbles. After blowing a few, she watches them vanish, and announces: Mine popped. Note that she could have viewed the bubble's disappearance in terms of 'going', namely in the sense that at first bubbles 'come' and then they 'go'; but here she chose to focus on the "popping aspect" of the ongoing event.

What the above examples point up again is that there is nothing inherently literal about whether bubbles 'come', 'go' or 'pop', but rather that the use of specific lexical forms such as come or pop highlights or focuses on particular aspects of the activity frame. Within a particular culture we have a large pool of conventionalized ways of SEEING AS[3]. One might even want to argue that these forms of SEEING AS are conventions with which members of a culture are furnished in order to make sense of specific aspects of reality, and to negotiate these aspects meaningfully. However, each culture at the same time provides the basis on which novel ways of SEEING AS can be created and successfully negotiated.

What we have tried to highlight in this section is the notion that there exists at any given time a variety of perspectives that can be taken with regard to a given object or person, situation or event, and that within particular cultures there are many conventional ways of SEEING AS. However, to interpret the particular framing of or 'zooming in' on a given object, person or event in terms of literal vs. metaphoric ways of SEEING AS would impose inherent qualities or attributes on such objects or events which these objects all too often do not possess. Furthermore, this would disregard the cultural givenness of certain conventions. Whether light <u>comes</u> or <u>goes</u> is in the same way a matter of point of view as whether books <u>come</u> or <u>go</u> on a shelf (cf. footnoote 2); and the particular perspective that is taken toward such events can be more in line with conventional ways of interpreting them - or can be a rather novel way of SEEING AS. Having clarified these conceptual activities as ranging from rather conventional ways to more and more novel ways of SEEING AS along the metaphorization continuum, we can now proceed to present our case for literal metaphor.

5 Toward a case for literal metaphor

In juxtaposing the notion of <u>literal</u> with that of <u>metaphor</u> we are attempting to suggest the congruency of such notions. In keeping with the <u>direct</u> <u>process</u> <u>model</u> of metaphor, we want to highlight that metaphor is nothing special or derived from what has been considered more literal uses of language. We believe that an analysis of the children's more novel ways of SEEING AS can highlight the extent to which such utterances are neither deviant (a product of undeveloped categorization processes). nor purely random or whimsical. Rather, we want to illustrate in this section how the children attempt to make sense of reality, as well as express this sense by continually drawing on experiences with which they are familiar. One might want to argue that the use of ways of SEEING AS is not particularly productive for the child, but rather that the child is learning metaphors in the form of fixed expressions that have no motivation. Again we would want to argue that this view is misleading. In our video-sessions we have examples of particular instances of SEEING AS that give us good grounds to assume that the child starts out with rather unified ways of SEEING AS based on previous experiences that lay the groundwork for interpreting new and more complex experiences. We will turn now to a discussion of a few examples which illustrate how the children continually weave together past and fresh ways of SEEING AS in a way that reflects the children's productive achievements in their ongoing construction of reality.

In the following example the two children are reading a picturebook with one of the mothers. Jennifer and her mother have read this story several times during the preceding week and have brought it along to "tell" to Sarah. At the point of the following excerpt the child is telling the story to her peer with her mother's assistance:

(9)
  (a) JM: The owl is after the little boy .. isn't he .. and the boy climbs to the top of the rock .. now what does he hold onto?
  (b) J: deer ears
  (c) JM: deer ears?
  (d) J: deer horns
  (e) JM: OK .. then what happens

Two things are noteworthy about this passage. First, what the little boy in this story is holding onto is somewhat ambiguous. Upon reading the story the first time, one might guess that he is holding onto a branch of a tree, though on the subsequent page it becomes clear that the boy is actually holding onto a deer's antlers. So when Jennifer responds to her mother's question in line (9a) with deer ears, she is acknowledging that she has accepted a way of SEEING that picture that anticipates the events that follow. Her way of SEEING AS is part of a larger story framework. Nevertheless, and this is the second observation to be made about this example, the child responds in what can be considered a more or less non-conventional way in line (9b). What is interesting about this construction is that the child seems to make use of her understanding of other living creatures she is familiar with in arriving at her response. Jennifer knows that people and dogs and cats all have appendages on the same place of the body, all of which are called ears.

One might prefer to view the above example as an overextension in the sense that the child refers to all appendages located on this part of the body as ears (e.g. horns, antlers, antenna, etc.). This view would however presuppose a linguistic deficiency on the part of the child, i.e. that the child lacked the appropriate lexical term. Such a position is unable to account for the reason why this same child, when reading this story with her mother on previous occasions referred to the appendages as deer horns. We contend that example (9), like other examples that are not so easily subsumed under the heading of overextensions, are better viewed as a more general process of SEEING AS, a process in which children, as well as adults continually make use of their knowledge of past experiences in their ongoing interpretations of the world.

We will now turn to one more example in highlighting what we mean by literal metaphor. One could argue that the above example that we have offered, i.e. concerning deer ears, has very little to do with what is usually considered as metaphor. In the following example, the child's attempts to make sense of her surroundings perhaps seem to fit more closely with what one expects of a 'true metaphoric utterance'. Just as one of the researchers suggests a possible activity for the children to play, Jennifer interrupts by saying:

(10) J: Remember when those balls <u>runned</u> into the fireplace?

In this incident, Jennifer is referring to an episode that had occurred two months earlier. While involved in an art task of decorating white, circular objects (styrofoam balls) so that they looked liked the heads of 'Kings' and 'Queens', two of these objects fell off the table and 'rolled' into the fireplace. What is noteworthy about this example is the child's framing of the action of the balls in terms of <u>running</u>. Indeed this seems a fairly novel way to view this event, and we believe that it is a good example of a productive and novel way of SEEING AS. But we would also want to argue that a decision of what sorts of things can be viewed in terms of 'running' and what cannot, is more a matter of conventions than literalness. Consider the following examples: <u>The</u> <u>boy</u> <u>ran</u> <u>into</u> <u>the</u> <u>store</u>, <u>The</u> <u>girl</u> <u>ran</u> <u>around</u> <u>the</u> <u>track</u>, and <u>The</u> <u>dog</u> <u>ran</u> <u>to</u> <u>get</u> <u>the</u> <u>ball</u>. In these examples one might want to argue that the difference between example (10), i.e. a ball 'running', and a person or an animal 'running' is a matter of literalness. But what makes such a claim difficult to accept becomes clearer when we consider some other examples of the use of <u>run</u> by the children:

(11) J: Mommy my nose is <u>running</u>.

(12) SM: Do you have parsley in your garden?
     J: It died ... we <u>ran</u> out.

It becomes highly questionable that the child has to learn all such utterances as idiomatic or fixed expressions. Rather, such productive uses of utterances like that found in example (10) which the child might never have heard before in what can be considered her "linguistic input", can be taken as evidence that there is some basic experiential notion of 'running' that serves as the grounds from which all linguistic forms containing _running_ are generated. Under such a heading does not only fall 'running balls' but also 'running noses' and the notion of 'running out' of something. Later on the child might extend this basic experiential notion to incorporate new experiences of 'running' engines, juice that 'runs' all over the table when it is spilled, and so forth. Our point is that in talking about balls that _runned_, a _running_ nose, and a substance such as parsley that _ran_ _out_, the child does not necessarily reflect a literal understanding of the meaning of _run_. What makes example (10) for instance more or less novel has nothing to do with literalness, but with conventionality. Seeing noses as 'running', and viewing a substance that we once had, but no longer do, in terms of 'running out', within this culture seems fairly conventional. The child, in creating novel ways of viewing the ball in example (10) is making use of her experiences with running and suggesting that the swift action of the styrofoam balls should be viewed in a similar way.

What we are suggesting is that metaphoric thought is intrinsic to all processes of categorization - those that fall more toward the conventional end of the SEEING AS continuum, as well as those falling more toward the novel end. Our claim is that children do _not_ first come to learn some literal fashion of conceiving of the world before extending this metaphorically, as is suggested by the research carried out within the framework of the _derived_ _process_ _model_. Rather, from a quite early age (at least by the time they are two years old) the children take a perspective on objects, people and events which is metaphoric. Via a process of SEEING AS children come to make sense of reality by continually interpreting new experiences in terms of previous ones. To this extent, the children create new ways of understanding.

6 Concluding comments

Thus far this discussion has focused on the ability of SEEING AS as a purely cognitive operation. However, we are aware that conventional as well as non-conventional ways of SEEING AS are not purely the products of the imaginative monadic individual, but rather they are negotiated in communicative contexts (Bamberg, 1981, in press). As we have attempted to illustrate, the child is not acquiring a prefabricated view of the world, nor in learning to speak is the child purely or solely imitating those around him or her. The process of the creation of meaning, as Halliday (1978) suggests, is interactive: "The exchange takes place in the context of and interpretation with the reality that is 'out there;' but what is 'out there' is a social construct..." (p. 92).

In this paper, metaphor in child language has been discussed from the standpoint of the direct process model. It has been suggested that the view of metaphor as a direct, non-analytic process has not yet received much attention in developmental studies of metaphor. In keeping with the direct process model, metaphor has been viewed generally as a conceptual activity of SEEING AS. We have emphasized that ways of SEEING AS are best viewed as falling along one continuum - with more conventional ways of SEEING AS falling toward one end and more novel ways toward the other. It has been our contention that the continuum is better viewed as ranging from conventional to novel ways of SEEING AS, rather than from literal to novel ways. Through the use of examples, we have pointed out that there is often nothing 'literal' about conventional ways of SEEING AS and also that there is nothing particularly 'nonliteral' about many of our creative ways of perceiving of the world. Conventional as well as novel ways of SEEING AS are based on the same processes of meaningfully interpreting new experiences. Viewing metaphor as a process of SEEING AS has stressed the similarities between metaphor and all processes of categorization involved in children's productive language use. This though is not to imply that there are no differences between conventional ways of SEEING AS and more creative ones. As our work concerning shared ways of SEEING AS suggests, young children seem to be sensitive to the distinctions between using conventional and novel utterances.

We have claimed that the study of metaphor can help us clarify how children make use of their current knowledge of the world in their continuous processes of making sense of reality; and in this sense, metaphor is central to all problems of human understanding. Within this framework, the study of metaphor promises more than an understanding of the poetic use of language, whereby 'poetic' is understood as a special or derived faculty. It is our contention that developmental investigations of metaphor based on the direct process model can enrich our understanding of metaphor, as well as the issue of child language development. The sort of position developed in this paper can be applied to several areas within the field of language acquisition. For example, insight into the nature of lexical development may be enhanced by an analysis of the more novel ways of SEEING AS. A second avenue of research relates to the study of whether ways of SEEING AS may motivate syntactic development. The work of Lakoff & Johnson (1980) and those developing the notion of Space Grammar (cf. Langacker 1979, 1982) suggests that this may be the case with adult grammar. We are just beginning to look at the children's use of prepositions, i.e. how the children over the course of the study developed different conceptualizations which are reflected in the varying use of prepositional particles. Finally, an important area of study seems to be how children arrive at a shared understanding of a communicative activity despite differences in their conceptual systems.

These are just some of the areas we believe child metaphor studies can and should address. It is our contention that the time has come to put aside the question of whether children do or do not have metaphoric competence. The results of such studies, which have dominated the work within the derived process model, have left us only with the conclusion that the answer to such a question is less of an empirical fact and more a consequence of what one takes the notion of metaphor to be, and how one can test for such a concept. Taking the notion of literal metaphor as a starting point generates new research questions that remain open to future empirical investigations.

Footnotes

* The term <u>literal metaphor</u> was originally coined by George Lakoff and Mark Johnson in 1978. This notion as well as their subsequent work on metaphor has inspired a great deal of the ideas that went into this paper. We would also like to express our thanks to Sarah and Jennifer for their productive input; and the families for their efforts and cooperative spirit that made this study possible. This research was supported by National Institutes of Health National Research Service Award HD07181 from the National Institute of Child Health and Human Development.

1 In the examples that follow the children are referred to as J (Jennifer) and S (Sarah), their mothers as JM and SM, and the researchers as R. Horizontal periods (...) indicate pauses, and contextual explanations are added in square brackets.

2 Turning to languages that have slightly different conceptualizations of 'coming' and 'going' highlights the same point from a different perspective: Consider for instance the new

conceptualization a native speaker of English arrives at when he/she finds out in the process of learning German that books do not go on a shelf (that book doesn't go on the shelf), but rather come on a shelf (das Buch KOMMT auf's Regal).

3 See for a similar argument Johnson & Lakoff (1981).

References

Asch, S. & Nerlove, H. The development of the double-function terms in children: An exploratory investigation. In: B. Kaplan & S. Wapner (Eds.), Perspectives in psychological theory. Essays in honor of Heinz Werner. New York: International Universities Press, 1960.

Augst, G. Zur Ontogenese des Metaphernerwerbs - eine empirische Pilotstudie. In: G. Augst (Ed.), Spracherwerb von 6 bis 16. Düsseldorf: Pädagogischer Verlag Schwann, 1978.

Bamberg, M. What is in a metaphor of a four year old child? Unpublished manuscript, 1980.

Bamberg, M. The communicative functions of metaphor in young children. Paper presented at the Annual Meeting of the American Psychological Association. Los Angeles, August 1981.

Bamberg, M. Metaphor and play-interaction in young children. In: F.E. Manning (Ed.), The world of play. New York: Leisure Press, in press.

Cometa, M. & Eson, M. Logical operations and metaphor interpretation: A Piagetian model. Child Development, 1978, 49, 649-659.

Halliday, M.A.K. Meaning and the construction of reality in early childhood. In: H.L. Pick & E. Saltzman (Eds.), Modes of perceiving and processing information. Hillsdale, N.J.: Lawrence Erlbaum Associates, 1978.

Johnson, M. & Lakoff, G. Metaphor and communication. Unpublished manuscript, 1981.

Köhler, W. Gestalt psychology. New York: Liveright, 1929.

Lakoff, G. & Johnson, M. Metaphors we live by. Chicago: University of Chicago Press, 1980.

Langacker, R.W. Grammar as image. Linguistic Notes from La Jolla, 1979, 6, 88-126.

Langacker, R.W. Space grammar, analysability, and the English passive. Language, 1982, 58(1), 22-80.

Ortony, A., Reynolds, R. & Arter, J. Metaphor: Theoretical and empirical research. Psychological Bulletin, 1978, 85, 919-943.

Perkins, D. Metaphorical perception. In: E. Eisner (Ed.), Reading, the arts, and the creation of meaning. Reston, Va.: National Art Education Association, 1978.

Pitts, M.K., Smith, M.K. & Pollio, H.R. An evaluation of three different theories of metaphor production through the use of an intentional category mistake procedure. Journal of Psycholinguistic Research, in press.

Pollio, H.R., Fabrizi, M.S., Sills, A. & Smith, M.K. Is metaphoric comprehension a derived process? Unpublished manuscript, 1981.

Rumelhart, D.E. Some problems with the notion of literal meanings. In A. Ortony (Ed.), Metaphor and thought. Cambridge: Cambridge University Press, 1979.

Sadock, J.M. Figurative speech and linguistics. In: A. Ortony, (Ed.), Metaphor and thought. Cambridge: Cambridge University Press, 1979.

Searle, J.R. Literal meaning. Erkenntnis, 1978, 13, 207-224.

Verbrugge, R.R. The primacy of metaphor in development. In: E. Winner & H. Gardner (Eds.), Fact, fiction, and fantasy in childhood.- New directions in child development. Vol. 6. San Francisco: Jossey-Bass Inc., 1979.

Werner, H. & Kaplan, B. Symbol formation. New York: Wiley, 1963.

Winner, E. New names for old things: The emergence of metaphoric language. Journal of Child Language, 1979, 6, 469-491.

Winner, E., McCarthy, M. & Gardner, H. The ontogenesis of metaphor. In R.P. Honeck & R.R. Hoffman (Eds.), Cognition and figurative language. Hillsdale, N.J.: Lawrence Erlbaum Associates, 1980.

Wittgenstein, L. Philosophical investigations. Oxford: Basil Blackwell, 1953.

THE WORD-CONTEXT PRODUCTION STRATEGY IN THE EARLY ACQUISITION OF MEANING[1]

ESTHER DROMI

Most contemporary investigations into the acquisition of word meaning presuppose that during the very early phases of lexical development children learn to recognize and to distinguish between underlying components of meaning (e.g., Bowerman, 1978, 1980; Carey, 1978; Clark, 1973, 1975; Nelson, 1974, 1979). Thus Rescorla (1980) for instance, argues that the child's knowledge about the formal, functional, and action properties of objects, and her[2] affective responses to objects and events become the meaning components of the word she associates with that object or event. Such components, the underlying semantic features of a given word, are often identified by looking at the basis for extension of that word to a number of different referents. These components are taken to constitute the primitive base in terms of which the child initially defines the meaning of a new word she acquires (Carey, in press).

In the investigation reported here diary descriptions of the contexts in which one subject produced the same words over time were examined in order to determine the extensional behaviors of early words. It was found that 11 out of the child's first 55 words manifested a pattern of extension that is hard to explain by means of a compositional model of meaning. Below I argue that these words were applied by my subject as cover terms for whole situations, and were thus extended to objects, actions, and relations not sharing any identifiable semantic components either with each other or with a prototypical referent.

1. <u>Three Categorical Models of Meaning</u>

Despite certain differences in their respective conceptions of early word meaning, the notion of underlying components is central to the models proposed by Clark (1973, 1975), Nelson (1974, 1978), and Bowerman (1978, 1980). Thus, according to Clark's "Semantic Feature Hypothesis", the initial representation of a word is viewed as incomplete, and as including only a subset of the semantic components that are associated with the same word in adult usage. Since the initial definition of a new word is incomplete, the child makes many referential errors in using it. The number of criterial features in the child's definition of a word increases until its meaning is complete, or in other words, conventional. The "Semantic Feature Hypothesis" predicts that during the early phases of production many words will be applied to referents that share one or more perceptual attributes. For example, the word dog may initially be extended not only to different types of dogs, but also to other (four legged), (furry), or (small sized) animals.

Nelson (1974) provides a critique of the "Semantic Feature Hypothesis". In Nelson's alternative model of meaning, the "Functional Core Hypothesis", the process of learning the meaning of words is viewed as inseparable from the establishment of early concepts. Nelson questions whether, in general, young children are capable of carrying out detailed semantic feature analyses of the referents they encounter. She claims that children assign objects to categories on the basis of their functional properties, and then label the category by a word. In the functional core construct, objects are organized hierarchically, with one object, which is the functional core of that category, located at the top. Thus, in that model the meaning of a new word is initially represented by a set of stable functional components, and it is assumed that the child will apply a new word to referents which have common functional properties. The word ball, for example, may be used for a set of various objects that (can be rolled), (are bounced), etc.

An underlying assumption in both these models of word meaning is that children extend words to a number of referents only if these referents share at least one perceptual or functional attribute with each other. Bowerman (1978, 1980) was the first to question the generality of this claim. She noted that some early words show a "complexive" pattern of extension very similar to what Vygotsky (1962) described as an associative complex. According to Bowerman, a word that shows complexive behaviors is initially identified with one referent or a group of closely related referents, that constitute a "best exemplar" for that word. After a period in which the word is applied restrictively to a single referent (or a set of such), it is extended to other referents which share one or more features with the original "best exemplar".

The "Prototype" model of meaning as adapted by Bowerman to child language predicts a quite complicated pattern of extension for a new word. It attributes to the child the mental capacity to carry out detailed, systematic analyses of meaning. The child is taken to perform decomposition and novel recomposition of semantic features that she has extracted from her underlying representation of the best exemplar. The model presupposes that children are capable of conducting such analyses of underlying components of meaning from at least somewhere close to the onset of speech.

2. The Data-Base for this Study

The present investigation is a diary study (see Braunwald & Brislin, 1979) based on a continuous handwritten record and periodic audio - and video - recorded speech samples. The subject of the study is my daughter Keren, acquiring Hebrew as her first and only language. Keren was ten months and twelve days, represented here as 10(12), at the beginning of data collection. On that particular day, I identified her first comprehensible verbalization haw, said in meaningful context (she said the word when pointing to a small white dog that was barking at us). On the last day of data collection, Keren was seventeen months and twenty three days old (17(23)). By this cut-off point, in the course of 30 minutes of audio-recordings, Keren had produced 279 utterances, 36% of which were novel multi-word expressions.

During the eight months of data collection, I noted down most of my daughter's comprehensible utterances, together with extensive information about their contexts of use. I kept the record myself, and collected data at all times and whenever I could observe and immediately inscribe the linguistic behavior of my subject[3]. In the present analysis I refer to the information gathered on the different uses of the child's first 55 words. The number of data points on each word varied depending on the number of entries in the child's diary, and the frequency of occurrence of a word in the audio-tapes. This number ranged from at least 3 to a total of 163 different context descriptions for use of a given word.

3. Predicted and Unpredicted Extensional Patterns

Each of the child's first 55 words was assigned to one of the following two classes:
(a) those manifesting predicted extension behaviors; and (b) those manifesting unpredicted extension behaviors.

Predicted extension behavior was defined as: The application of a word to a number of referents (objects or actions) that share one or more components with each other or with an identifiable best exemplar.

Eleven out of the first fifty five words in Keren's productive lexicon were assigned to the second category. Table 1 below lists these words, their number in the cumulative lexicon, the child's age on date of acquisition, and English glosses of each word. The English glosses give the sense of the word in colloquial Hebrew. When the child's word is non-conventional in Hebrew, comments indicating the most typical use of the word/sound in the language addressed to the child are given in parentheses instead of English glosses. In table 2 short summaries of consistent contexts for using some of class b words are presented. These summaries are in some cases suggestive as to the referent of the word for the child.

TABLE 1: Early Words Manifesting Unpredicted Extensional Behaviors

Child's Word	Word's Number	Age of Acquisition	English Translations
haw[4]	01	10(12)	'bow-wow'
ham	04	11(18)	(said when being fed)
pipi	09	12(13)	'urine'
haita	10	12(16)	(said when going out for a walk)
tik tak	12	12(18)	'tick-tock' (the sound of a clock)
hupa	14	12(20)	'upsi' (said when jumping or when balls are bounced)
dio	15	12(23)	'giddy-up'
nad-ned	23	12(28)	(said to accompany the motion of swinging)
niyar	50	14(5)	'paper'

TABLE 1 continued

Child's Word	Word's Number	Age of Acquisition	English Translation
dod	51	14(7)	'(an) uncle' or 'any unfamiliar man'
iga (rega)	52	14(13)	'(a) moment'

TABLE 2: Summaries of the Contexts for a Sample of "Class b" Words

Child's Word	Consistent Contexts for Use	
ham	pointing to:	foods, snacks, and drinks; animals playing on carpet or in the yard; bibs; empty dishes; bottles.
	When, shortly before or immediately after:	being taken to the kitchen; being put in highchair; wearing her bib; playing with own hands and mouth; inserting small objects in mouth.
pipi	pointing to:	her potty; wet diapers, undressed parts of body; the toilet door.
	When, shortly before or immediately after:	taking off clothes; playing with undressed dolls; revealing parent's uncovered body part; hearing water dripping from faucets or seeing wet toys.
haita	pointing to:	hats; strollers; small objects that can be picked in hands.
	while:	holding in hands small objects (e.g. her hat, a purse, boxes, and empty bottle) and moving them back and forth.

TABLE 2: continued

Child's Words	Consistent Contexts for Use	
	When, shortly before or immediately after:	climbing steps, waking up from afternoon nap, when somebody is about to leave the house or has just left it.
hupa	pointing to:	balls; balloons; small round objects
	When:	observing objects irregularly located in space; or sudden contact between an object and the floor.
	Shortly before or immediately after:	jumping; touching the floor; walking down the steps; throwing a ball; or falling down.
dio	pointing to:	riding horses; pictures of horses; any bouncing repetitive movements.
	When, shortly before or immediately after:	riding a horse in the playground, sitting on parent's lap, or on the heater with two legs apart.
iga (rega)	When pointing to:	a diaper; an undressed doll; Keren's teddy bear.
	When, shortly before or immediately after:	the action of diapering; trying to cover toys with a piece of cloth; trying to wrap a rubberband around the honey jar.

Not only were the words listed in Tables 1 and 2 above extended to several referents that did not share attributes with each other, but it was in many cases impossible to determine from the contexts of use what the "meaning" of the word was for the child. In some cases, a word might be uttered in a more or less appropriate context, but it was in no way obvious that the child was referring to some specific action or object (for instance, <u>hupa</u> said either to the ball or to the action of jumping). In other cases, it seemed that the same word was, in fact, used for both the action and the object. Table 3 below presents descriptions of some contexts in which the word <u>niyar</u> was recorded. Throughout the period of study it was never clear to me whether this word referred to pencils, papers, the action of writing and/or drawing, or the product itself. In retrospect, I believe that Keren used this word as a coverterm for <u>all</u> of these referents.

TABLE 3: Descriptions of Several Contexts in Which Keren Said the Word <u>Niyar</u> 'Paper'

(1) 14(5): In the kitchen; M is writing notes in K's diary; K observes M. Suddenly she starts to yell repeatedly <u>niyar/x/x/</u> 'paper'. M gives K a piece of paper. K continues to whine. She says again and again <u>niyar/x/x/</u> 'paper' and tries to catch M's hand. M gives K a pencil. K takes it happily. She sits down and draws on her piece of paper.
(2) 14(7): In the living room; M is writing in her diary. K pulls M's pencil, looks at it and says <u>niyar</u> 'paper'. (K's tone is quite emphatic, I don't think that she meant to verbally request the pencil; rather, I think that she named it).
(3) 14(10): In the kitchen; M is writing notes on a piece of paper which is attached to the refrigerator. K is sitting in her highchair; she says <u>niyar</u> 'paper'. I confirm her utterance, saying <u>ken ani kotevat al niyar</u>, 'yes, I write on a piece of paper'. K seems satisfied.
(4) 15(7): In K's room; K is lying down on her back sucking her thumb. M enters the room. K gets up, picks up her little pillow, and shows it to M. She points to the applique of two birds on the cover of the pillow and says <u>niyar</u> 'paper'.

(5) 15(17): Outside; M and K are walking on the sidewalk. Suddenly K stops, points to the painting of an arrow on the sidewalk (a chalk drawing from a children's game), and says niyar 'paper'. M is very surprised. She says ze ciyur 'it is a painting'. Later on when we pass another arrow M stops, points at it and asks K: ma ze? 'what (is) this?' K says confidently niyar 'paper'.
(6) 16(4): In the study; K takes out of my bag a pen, hands it to me and says niyar 'paper'.
(7) 16(4): In the living room; K is playing with an empty plastic container of food. She sees a sticker on it with the name of the product. K gives the container to me and says with rising intonation niyar? 'paper'?

One might argue that the unpredicted contexts for using the word niyar and some other early words by Keren do not reflect shifting referential behaviors of these words. Rather, it could be said that these productions resulted from the child's developing linguistic ability to use words associatively rather than referentially (Greenfield & Smith, 1976). That is, the word was learned by the child as the name of a specific referent, and was later uttered in the absence of that referent to indicate some relationship between the stable referent and the entity indicated (e.g., a child saying 'daddy' when pointing to the father's hat to encode the relationship of possession between hat and father).

Keren's consistent uses of the word dod '(an) uncle' for unfamiliar people and for sounds coming from outside is a good example of a case where it is quite difficult to determine whether the child uses a word referentially or associatively. The two earliest recorded uses of dod occurred in imitation. Subsequent occurrences were noted for unfamiliar faces and for all kinds of noises. When Keren said dod on hearing a noise, I could not determine whether she was naming the sounds in question (i.e. a referential use of the word) or the people who may have initiated these noises (i.e. an associative use of the word).

From very early on in her production of the word dod Keren would say it in the absence of any person, and without any attempt to look for a possible source of the noise. Hence, I suspect that the word referred to the sound itself.

Consider the following conversation, audiorecorded when Keren was 16(1).

> In K's room; Keren and Mother are playing on the rug. Mother hears the sound of a lawnmower coming from outside.
> K: dod/
> '(an) uncle'
> M: dod, ken dod ose ra?aš, ra?aš, naxon?/
> '(an) uncle, yes uncle is making (a) noise, noise, right?'
> K: dod/
> '(an) uncle' (she starts to whine).
> M: at roca lexapes et ?adod?/
> '(do) you want to look for the uncle?'
> K: dod/
> '(an) uncle'
> (Mother opens the window and looks outside, Keren does not come closer to the window, she sits on the rug and whines).

In the early phases of producing a new word, Keren very rarely uttered this word when its referent was absent in the immediate context. Associative uses of words always lagged behind referential ones, and started to be productive for most words more or less at the same time - towards the second half of the one word stage.

On these two grounds, I conclude that during the early phase of production the word dod manifested shifting referential behaviors and served as Keren's double purpose word for unfamiliar people and for noises coming from outside. I suggest that among the first 55 words acquired by my daughter, eleven can be grouped together as showing shifting referential behaviors. These words are termed here: "situational words".

4. Generality of the Class of "Situational Words"

The question arises as to whether the use of some early words as cover-terms for entire situations is an idiosyncratic characteristic of my particular subject, or whether, the Hebrew findings are in fact compatible with those described by other researchers. The contexts in which Keren produced her word dod are remarkably similar to contexts in which Laura, Braunwald's (1978) daughter, produced her early word 'bow-wow'. Braunwald argued that 'bow-wow' was "a multi purpose word referring to the sound of barking, bird chirping, car and airplane engines or any noise audible in the house from outside as well as to the sight of dogs and cars" (1978: 520).

The unusual extension of the word 'bow-wow' was explained by the author as a semantic mismatch. The child failed to identify the intended adult referent for the word, and subsequently matched the word with separate visual or auditory schemes that were based on her overall experiences with this word in repeated situational contexts. I find Braunwald's explanation very appealing. I hypothesize that Keren's unclear definition of the word dod resulted too from a semantic mismatch. Keren frequently heard this word during our walks outside. It happened often that I stopped for a short conversation with people whom I knew and she did not know. In these contexts I used to tell Keren: ze haya dod? at lo makira oto 'this was somebody (an uncle) that you don't know'. Such a context for learning a new word is vague, and therefore it may explain why my daughter produced the same word for unfamiliar people and for various sounds she heard.

Ferrier's (1978) descriptions of her child's uses of the word 'phew' are strikingly similar to my observation of Keren's early productions of her situational word pipi. The utterance 'phew' was an exclamation of the mother in reaction to the unpleasant odor of wet diapers. Ferrier's subject extended the word to several referents that were in some way connected to the routine of nappy changing. The word 'phew' was her name for diapers-both clean and dirty - and for her diaper pail.

Bowerman's comprehensive records of the early linguistic development of her two daughters contain several examples that can be taken to reflect a tendency on the child's part to use the same word for several aspects of one situational context (Bowerman, 1978, 1980, and personal communication)[5]. Eva's early uses of 'gi' for 'giddy up' read like direct translations of my Hebrew examples of Keren's word dio used for 'horse' and 'riding'.

Some of my subject's early uses of situational words were similar to the early production of certain words by Estonian - speaking children (Valsiner & Lasn n.d.). These researchers report that some subjects used words for 'thank you', 'food' and 'out to the yard' with a multiplicity of meanings. The authors argued that the initial meanings of these words are reflected by the fuzzy set of contexts in which they were used. In their analysis the child gradually restricts the number of contexts in which she utters the word. Eventually the word is uttered only in contexts which are acceptable in terms of adult speech.

The parallel between my Hebrew records and the data of other investigators clearly indicates that some early words show extensional behaviors that cannot be explained by a categorical or featural model of meaning. In the section that follows I conclude this paper by outlining an alternative model of meaning which may be more suitable for representing the underlying meaning of situational words.

5. The Word-Context Production Strategy

The extension of a word to various objects and actions which do not share perceptual or functional features is clearly incompatible with the theoretical proposals of Clark and of Nelson. One could, however, argue that shifting referential behavior is in line with Bowerman's "complexive" explanation. Bowerman, in fact, provides a very plausible explanation for the shifting behaviors she noted in words. Yet my subject's early uses of situational words were not pure complexive overextensions, and therefore the 'prototype' model does not provide a satisfactory explanation for their early extensional behaviors.

My subject's situational words were never used either by her or her parents to label a prototypical referent (i.e. a specific object or action). There is no evidence in my data that the child associated these words with one referent (the "best exemplar"), and that she only later extended the word to other referents. It is interesting to note that the situational words were always applied to referents connected to the same situational context. H<u>am</u>, for instance, was used for food, eating, inserting objects into the mouth, empty dishes, bibs, the high chair, etc. All of these referents comprise the situation of a child being fed. This observation leads me to believe that a situational word is associated by the child with the underlying representation of a "scene", "frame" or "scheme". If my hypothesis is correct, then a situational word is uttered whenever the child encounters any object or action that is identified with the situational context in which the word was learned.

Scholars working on different topics that are related to the cognitive organization of information have recently suggested that one of the basic and earlier forms of organized knowledge revolves around "script-like" episodes (e.g. Fillmore 1975, 1978; Nelson, in press; Mandler, 1979, in press; Schank and Abelson, 1977). Fillmore, for instance, has argued that the cognitive notion of a "frame" is closely related to people's linguistic processing abilities, thus: "particular words or speech formulas, or particular grammatical choices are associated in memory with particular frames, in such a way that exposure to the linguistic form in an appropriate context activates in the perceiver's mind the particular frame" (1978: 8).

I propose that situational words are uttered by children before they carry out any detailed analysis of their meanings. It is knowledge of appropriate contexts for saying a word which elicits the word at particular times. What I am calling a context-based production strategy may operate in the child for quite some time, and is clearly noted for the words classifed here as situational words.

More research is needed in order to fully understand why some words are learned by the child as cover terms for whole situations while others are not. Cross-linguistic comparisons may provide important clues to the question of which contents are likely to be represented schematically by children. Another open question is how long the child uses situational words as well as how their meanings change over time. Finally, it seems worthwhile to carry out systematic examinations of the contexts in which words are being learned. Such investigations may help us to understand why different words follow different paths to adult meaning.

Notes.
1. I am indebted to Dr. Melissa Bowerman for detailed discussions invaluable to the issues considered here, and

to Dr. Ruth Berman for her comments and criticisms of an earlier draft of this paper.
2. Feminine pronouns are used throughout this paper for the sake of grammatical uniformity.
3. For a detailed description of the methods of collection, transcription, and organization of data, as well as of five different measures for evaluating the reliability and validity of procedures, see Dromi, 1982.
4. Throughout this manuscript Hebrew words and sentences are given in phonetic transcription and are all underlined. A Hebrew word in parentheses indicates the adult equivalent for a child's approximation.
5. Some of Bowerman's examples are reported in her publications of 1978 and 1980. These examples are cited to support the claim that some early words show complexive extension behaviors that can only be explained by the "prototype" model of meaning.

REFERENCES

Bowerman, M. (1978) The acquisition of word meaning: An investigation into some current conflicts. In N. Waterson and C. Snow (Eds.) Development of Communication. New York: John Wiley & Sons.

Bowerman, M. (1980) The structure and origin of semantic categories in the language learning child. In M. Foster and S. Brandes (Eds.), Symbol as Sense. New York: Academic Press.

Braunwald, S.R. (1978) Context, word and meaning: Towards a communicational analysis of lexical acquisition. In A. Lock (Ed.), Action, Gesture and Symbol: The emergence of language. London: Academic Press.

Braunwald, S.R. and Brislin, R.W. (1979) The diary method updated. In E. Ochs and B.B. Schieffelin (Eds.), Developmental Pragmatics. New York; Academic Press.

Carey, S. (1978) The child as word learner. In M. Halle, J. Bresnan and G. Miller (Eds.), Linguistic Theory and Psychological Reality. Cambridge

Mass: MIT Press.

Carey, S. (1982) Semantics and development: State of the art. In L. Gleitman and E. Wanner (Eds.), Language Acquisition: The State of the Art. Cambridge, England: Cambridge University Press.

Clark, E.V. (1973) What's in a word?: On the child's acquisition of meaning. In T.E. Moore (Ed.), Cognitive Development and the Acquisition of Language. New York: Academic Press.

Clark, E.V. (1975) Knowledge, context and strategy in the acquisition of meaning. In D. Dato (Ed.) Twenty Sixth Annual Georgetown University Round Table on Languages and Linguistics. Washington, D.C.: Georgetown University Press.

Dromi, E. (1982) In pursuit of meaningful words: A case study analysis of early lexical development. Ph.D. dissertation, University of Kansas.

Ferrier, L.J. (1978) Some observations of error in context. In N. Waterson and C. Snow (Eds.), The Development of Communication. New York: John Wiley & Sons.

Fillmore, C.J. (1975) Frame semantics and the nature of language. Presented at the Conference on the Origins and Evolution of Language and Speech. New York.

Fillmore, C.J. (1978) On the organization of semantic information in the lexicon. In D. Farkas, W.M. Jacobson, and K.W. Todrys (Eds.), Papers from the Parasession on the Lexicon, Chicago Linguistic Society. Chicago: University of Chicago Press.

Greenfield, P.M. and Smith, J.H. (1976). The Structure of Communication in Early Language Development. New York: Academic Press.

Mandler, J.M. (1979) Categorical and schematic organization in memory. In C.R. Puff (Ed.), Memory, Organization and Structure. New York: Academic Press.

Mandler, J.M. (In press) Representation. To appear in J.H. Flavell and E.M. Markman (Eds.), Cognitive Development. Vol. 2, of P. Mussen (Ed.), Manual of Child Psychology. New York: John Wiley & Sons.

Nelson, K. (1974) Concept, word, and sentence: Interrelations in acquisition and development. Psychological Review, 81, 267-285.

Nelson, K. (1978) Explorations in the development of a functional semantic system. In W. Collins (Ed.), Children's Language and Communication: The 1977 Minnesota Symposium on Child Psychology. Hillsdale, New Jersey: Lawrence Erlbaum.

Nelson, K. (In press) The syntagmatics and paradigmatics of conceptual development. In: S. Kuczaj (Ed.) Language, Vol. 2: Language, Thought and Culture. Hillsdale, New Jersey: Lawrence Erlbaum.

Rescorla, L.A. (1980) Overextension in early language development. Journal of Child Language, 7, 321-335.

Schank, R.C. and Abelson, R.P. (1977) Scripts, Plans, Goals and Understanding: An inquiry into human knowledge structure. Hillsdale, New Jersey: Lawrence Erlbaum.

Valsiner, J. and Lasn, M. (n.d.) Contextual differentiation: The development of first word meanings in children.

Vygotsky, L.S. (1962) Thought and Language. Cambridge, Mass: MIT Press.

COMPLEMENTARITY, ANTONYMY, AND SEMANTIC DEVELOPMENT: A METHOD AND SOME DATA.

Michael J. Evans

Anglistisches Seminar,
Universitaet Heidelberg, D-6900, West Germany

In the last few years there has been a considerable upsurge of interest both in linguistic semantics and in the study of semantic development in child language. One of the areas of particularly intense activity in the second field has been concerned with how children comprehend and use gradable antonyms[1] like little, big, small, long, tall and short that describe fairly concrete aspects of their environment.

Although there had been some activity in this field before 1967 (e.g. Bruner, 1964; Donaldson, 1963), in that year two publications gave a special impetus to research in this area of language: in linguistics, Bierwisch's (1967) paper attempted to apply techniques of componential analysis to parts of the lexical field concerned; and in psycholinguistics, Sinclair-de Zwart (1967) examined some of the relationships between children's language usage and the transition from the preoperational to the concrete operational stages of intellectual development that are described in Piagetian psychological theory.

After this, it seemed that on both sides of the Atlantic this area of study quickened.[2] Eve Clark's (1973a) formulation of the Semantic Feature Hypothesis, which later became well-known, was derived directly from proposals made by Bierwisch (1967), but there was no shortage of alternatives (e.g. the British work by Wales and Campbell, 1970; and Donaldson and Wales, 1970; as well as the increasingly prominent theoretical developments in North

America, such as Nelson, 1976, and Rosch, 1978). The number of hypotheses has kept pace with the increase in the amount of new data, but it seems rare for them to be mutually reinforcing.

Now it is not my purpose to say very much about these hypotheses. What I wish to do instead, having just acknowledged the intellectual parentage of my own work, is to add a new dimension, or perhaps - more modestly - to resuscitate an old one, in the study of the semantics of gradable antonymy in child language. I shall start with some general observations on what seems to have been a typical investigative paradigm in this field, then briefly outline some theoretical considerations which seem to have been neglected recently. I shall then describe an investigative method which might make good the neglect, and present the analysis of some data collected with an imperfect, earlier version of the method.[3] Finally, I hope to show that the results have novel implications for our interpretation of semantic development.

To start with, three general observations can be made. Firstly, much of the research into gradable antonym development has concentrated on the first seven years of life, and many studies have focused on comprehension rather than production. This is particularly true of experimental work reported in the journals. In a typical experiment, each child subject is shown an array of three or possibly four objects, and asked either to indicate or to hand to the investigator an object from the array that is <u>taller than</u>, <u>shorter than</u>, or <u>longer than</u> a certain source object, which may or may not be in the array. Alternatively, the child may be asked to respond suitably to instructions containing the uninflected adjective forms: for example, <u>Show me the tall one</u>. If the child can respond to this sort of instruction, the investigator duly concludes that the, or an, adult meaning for the adjective has been acquired.[4]

Secondly, with one or two notable exceptions (e.g. Donaldson and Wales, 1970), little attention is paid to whether the instruction is formulated using a base form of the adjective or using a comparative or superlative inflected form, although where children's own usage has been observed, as in Sinclair-de Zwart's original (1967) study, it has been found that comparative structures appear only after operational conservation is achieved by the child, and that children in the pre-operational stage most frequently use base adjectives rather than comparatives. Thence comparatives have been inferred to be linguistic indicators of a more advanced stage of intellectual development in children.

Thirdly, it is assumed in the Semantic Feature approach that "size adjectives" can be arranged in order of conceptual difficulty. A recent writer (Rice, 1980:156)[5] put it like this: "the relationship between non-linguistic concepts and the meaning of spatial adjectives involves a hierarchic ordering, such that the more general conceptual information (the comparative core) is mapped first into words that have a broad range of reference. As the conceptual information becomes more differentiated, with greater awareness of perceptual (dimensional) differences, new word meanings appear to map the new distinctions". It is generally accepted that the meanings of the gradable antonyms big/little or big/small are acquired first, and deep and shallow last. Children are said to initially interpret other size adjectives in terms of big and little, respecting the polarity feature[6], which is taken to be simplex, i.e. not analysable further. Polarity is said to be the first feature learned, presumably in a once-and-for-all fashion.

After making these three observations, I wish to argue: (a) that we cannot conclude from the comprehension data that children who use the relevant gradable antonyms in a way appropriate to an adult therefore have the same semantic system; (b) that far from representing a more primitive stage in cognition, base-forms of gradable antonyms are associated with cognitive complexity in terms of both their internal semantic organisation and their full range of appropriate uses; and (c) that polarity is not a simple semantic feature, but has a number of components only one of which we might wish to recognise as being in any sense acquired at an early stage of child language development. Support for these arguments is found by considering firstly the problem of <u>extension</u> versus <u>intension</u>, and secondly the extensional difference between <u>complementarity</u> and <u>antonymy</u>.

For anyone not familiar with the first problem, I refer to Carnap (1955).[7] In linguistic semantic terms, intension encompasses relations of sense, and extension encompasses denotation and possibly reference (See Lyons, 1977, ch.7). Carnap (1955) points out that two or more people may be in total agreement on the <u>extension</u> of a predicate without sharing the same <u>intension</u> for that predicate. To give a simple example: we may agree that each of a certain group of animals in a field is to be called <u>a cow</u>. Thus we agree on the extension of the predicate <u>be a cow</u>. If a further animal appears, we may still agree to call it a cow, but your basis for doing so might be that the animal has horns, whereas mine might be that it has an udder. It would need the fortuitous arrival of either a hornless or an udderless cow - but not one with both defects - for us to realise that we had a different intension for the predicate <u>be a cow</u>.

If we now try to apply this insight to a typical comprehension study of gradable dimensional adjectives, we find that the adult investigator quite often constructs an array of comparison objects in such a way as to discourage the accidental discovery of disparity between his and his child subjects' intension for a predicate. In the case of an adjective like <u>tall</u>, for example, there may be too few objects in the array for more than one of them to be appropriately called <u>tall</u>.[8] It should not be concluded that the children who pick out the object that the investigator would label as <u>tall</u> operate with the same intension for this predicate; or in more familiar terminology, that they share the adult's semantic features for the adjective. They may do so, of course, but this has not been proved.

Now let us consider how we can perhaps get round this difficulty by taking an extensional view of antonymy and distinguishing it from complementarity. Although big and small are here used to exemplify the various semantic structural relations involved in antonymy, the analysis is intended to apply generally to other pairs of gradable antonyms also.

Complementarity is a type of semantic relation with a relatively simple, binary character, as illustrated in Figure 1 by the complementary adjective pair (a)live and dead. The rectangle represents a universe of discourse, the circle any set of entities of which the adjective terms could be predicated in that universe. For such a set, the members

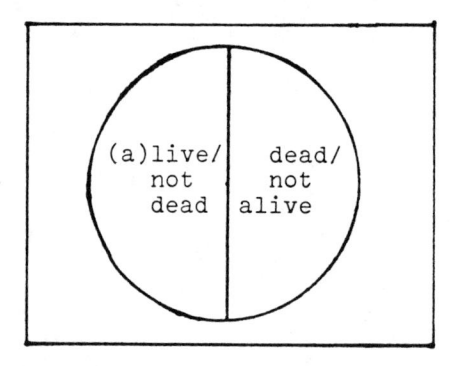

[Figure: a rectangle containing a circle divided into two halves labeled "(a)live/ not dead" and "dead/ not alive"]

Figure 1: complementary categorization.

of the (a)live category will be identical to those in the category not dead. Similarly, the category dead and not alive will contain identical members. The categories (a)live and dead will absorb the set without remainder, as will the categories not alive and not dead together. In each pair of opposed categories, no entity will appear more than once. The facts can be represented more formally as six Conditions of Complementarity, as listed below:

1. (a)live and not alive are contiguous categories and together exhaustive (thus complementary).
2. dead and not dead similarly.
3. (a)live and dead similarly.
4. not alive and not dead similarly.
5. (a)live and not dead are isomorphic (i.e. identical) categories.
6. dead and not alive are isomorphic (identical) categories.

However, in antonymy, exemplified by big and small, only Conditions 1 and 2 apply. Conditions 3 - 6 are radically altered. The categories for big and small will not inevitably exhaust a set of entities, since there will be an intermediate, "norm" category belonging to neither, but represented by the intersection of their complements: both not big and not small (or, equivalently, neither big nor small).We can superimpose one half of Figure 2 on the other to represent a universe of discourse for "ideal", or purely logical, categorization of (as I shall call it) antonymic type. Such categorization can then be specified as the conjunction of the following six Conditions of Antonymy for any appropriate set of entities:

1A. big and not big are contiguous categories and together exhaustive (thus complementary).
2A. small and not small similarly.
3A. big and small are non-contiguous, separate, non-exhaustive categories (mnemonic:"gapped")
4A. not big and not small overlap (i.e. share some members) and are together exhaustive.
5A. big is properly included within not small, so it is non-isomorphic and they are together non-exhaustive.
6A. small is properly included in not big, so it is non-isomorphic and they are non-exhaustive.

(We could replace big and small by the terms x and y and use the more technical terminology of set theory to generally characterize the necessary logical "competence" underlying the appropriate use of all pairs of gradable antonyms, but I shall not do

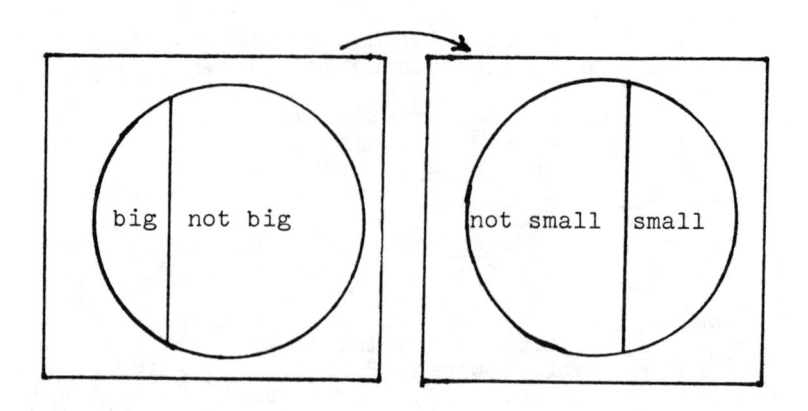

Figure 2: antonymic categorization.

that here.) Importantly, in a variety of "performance" situations, pragmatic variables will force a relaxation of some of the six antonymy conditions. The source of these variables is: (a) the nature of the set of actual entities graded; (b) the cultural knowledge possessed by the grader; (c) the contents of his or her memory store.

To understand this, we need to differentiate between the set of entities universally available for categorization, call it the background set, and the ones categorized on a particular occasion, which we can call a focus set. A focus set is almost always a proper subset of the background set. In everyday experience with grading, we are confronted with focus sets rather than background sets, and we learn the characteristics of the background set in one or both of the following ways: firstly by accumulating personal experience of various focus sets, storing it in memory; secondly, by informing ourselves as to the relevant background set from other, more experienced, members of our cultural community, either by observing their grading behaviour or by inquiry.

Although in optimal circumstances a focus set is a fair sample of the background set, two types of distortion can occur: it may either lack a whole category or disproportionately represent one or more categories found in the background set. To illustrate the first distortion: if the background set is <u>horses</u>, antonymically categorizable as <u>big</u>, <u>medium-sized</u> and <u>small</u>, a focus set may contain only some Welsh and Shetland ponies. To grade this focus set we then face a choice: either we use our knowledge of the background set in categorization, or we ignore it completely and treat the focus set as a representative sample. The first approach dichotomizes the focus set into, let us say, <u>small</u> and <u>medium-sized</u> horses, whereas the second yields three categories, <u>big</u>, <u>medium-sized</u> and <u>small</u>, the extension of which does not, however, match up with that of their namesakes in the background set.

The second distortion involves category size, as whatever the category-distribution of <u>big</u>, <u>medium-sized</u> and <u>small</u> in the background set, one or more categories may be under- or over-represented in a particular focus set. Here too, consulting knowledge of the background set will make a difference to how the focus set is graded. Antonymic categorization by reference to the background set in both kinds of circumstances will be termed <u>absolute grading</u>, and antonymic categorization that ignores the background set will be termed <u>contingent grading</u> here.

As far as gradable antonyms related to size are concerned, the background/focus notions certainly apply to naturally occurring objects but perhaps not to all human artefacts, since these may have a background set whose categories are unstable or indeterminate for a community. It is difficult to establish the extension of <u>medium-sized</u> for blocks of quarried stone, for instance, or how big a factory must be to be categorized <u>big</u>. On the other hand, this problem is reduced for artefacts that are strongly associated with naturally occurring kinds. For example, the range of sizes for <u>horses' saddles</u> is somehow dependent on the range of sizes for <u>horses</u>; similarly, it should be possible to establish a background set for <u>gloves</u> if we have one for <u>people</u>.

If we now consider the problems the child faces in developing a semantic system for gradable antonyms, we find two complexes. The first consists of establishing the six conditions of antonymy, in particular those four that differentiate antonymy from complementarity, and the second consists of establishing what the background sets of entities are, where this is relevant. Neither of these tasks is an easy one. Note, moreover, that knowledge of antonymic structure in terms of the six conditions of antonymy may be achieved even in the absence of knowledge of relevant background sets.

To investigate the extent of the child's semantic knowledge, we must present one or more focus sets, preferably of a natural kind, which systematically misrepresent the background set in one or more of the ways already described. By asking the child to indicate the extensions (s)he has for the categories designated by a pair of gradable antonyms and their complementaries (e.g. big, small, not big, not small), and by asking a number of adults from the same community to do this also, we can first establish what the so-called category-widths[10] are for each category, and then observe how these interrelate, comparing the child's behaviour with the adults'.

The results I am going to present to illustrate this method were obtained using focus sets not of actual natural kinds, but of pictorial representations of them. There are certain problems with pictures which I cannot go into here; in retrospect I consider use of pictures to have been a possible flaw in procedure, but I have not yet checked on this by doing further studies.

This study used two focus sets, one consisting of eleven ants and the other of thirteen butterflies.[11] For absolute grading, the focus set for ants both over-represented and exaggerated the category big, whereas that for butterflies under-represented big and over-represented small. Ants and butterflies were chosen for the focus sets because children would be likely to have experienced them in real life.

Each focus set appeared in two visual displays, as shown in the Appendix (64% of size actually used): Form A, ants, versions 1 and 2, and Form B, butterflies, versions 1 and 2. The subjects participated in two judgement sessions spaced twenty-four hours apart. Each display was seen once per session on an A4 sheet of paper. The presentation sequence was A1, B1, A2, B2, and subjects were asked each time to imagine that the ants or butterflies were really of the size portrayed. They were then asked to cross out the ones they judged as belonging to a certain size category. Over the two sessions they crossed out for big, small, not big and not small. In a single session the big-small categories were elicited for one focus set while the not big - not small categories were elicited for the other. Subjects were 130 British schoolchildren from 8-13 years of age in two schools, and 15 naive British adults, many of whom had been educated to tertiary level. Subjects were grouped by age as in Table 1: although there were differences in the female/male subgroups' data, nothing will be said about these here.

Table 1: Number of Subjects Grouped according to Age and Sex

	Group No.	Age Range (yrs; mths)	Mean Age (yrs; mths)	Females	Males	Total
children	1	8;1 - 9;2	8;08	19	13	32
	2	9;3 - 10;1	9;09	12	10	22
	3	10;2 - 11;2	10;07	11	11	22
	4	11;0 - 12;7	11;10	13	19	32
	5	12;7 - 13;7	13;00	9	13	22
				64	66	130
adults	6	19;0 - 33;0	22;03	12	3	15

Three different types of analysis were performed on the data: (a) category widths, (b) category relations, and (c) category relation combinations, all by age group. Most of the following remarks will be on the first two analyses. For (a), subjects' judgements of the extensions of the four categories in the two focus sets were tabulated. Significant differences in extension were found related to age, consistent with the hypothesis that the youngest children were grading contingently while subjects in the oldest child group had some ability to grade absolutely. The results have been tabulated (In simplified form) in quartiles in the histograms of Figure 3. The letters identifying the drawings in Focus Sets A and B have been ordered from left to right to represent the ranked sizes of the drawings from biggest to smallest. The frequency with which each group allocated a particular drawing to a category is shown by the numbers 1, for 1-25% agreement, 2 for 26-50% agreement, 3 for 51-75%, and 4 for 76-100%. In addition, the solid black line in the fourth quartile marks off the area of total agreement for a category allocation. The overlapping of categories found in the youngest group tends to decrease in older groups, though not consistently. The bias of the focus sets was not recognized by the youngest ones,

```
Focus Set:  A (Ants)                    B (Butterflies)
Category: big.
          Pictures:                     Pictures:
          |T S E F C G B J K L M|       |U Q X V D I W A H R O N P|
Group: 1  |4 4 4 3 1            |       |4 4 4 4 3 1 1 1 1        |
       2  |4 4 4 4 1 1          |       |4 4 4 4 4 3 1 1 1        |
       3  |4 4 4 4              |       |4 4 4 4 4 3 1 1 1        |
       4  |4 4 4 4 1            |       |4 4 4 4 3 2 1            |
       5  |4 4 4 4 2 1          |       |4 4 3 3 2 2              |
       6  |4 4 4 4 4 3 1 1 1    |       |4 3 3 3                  |

Category: small.
          |T S E F C G B J K L M|       |U Q X V D I W A H R O N P|
Group: 1  |        1 1 4 4 4 4 4 4|     |1   1 2 2 4 4 4 4 4 4 4  |
       2  |          4 4 4 4 4 4 4|     |      1 1 3 4 4 4 4 4 4  |
       3  |          4 4 4 4 4 4 4|     |      2 2 4 4 4 4 4 4 4  |
       4  |        3 4 4 4 4 4 4  |     |      1 1 4 4 4 4 4 4 4  |
       5  |      1 2 3 3 3 3 4 4  |     |          1 4 4 4 4 4 4 4|
       6  |        1 2 2 3 4 4 4  |     |      2 2 3 4 4 4 4 4 4  |

Category: not small.
          |T S E F C G B J K L M|       |U Q X V D I W A H R O N P|
Group: 1  |4 4 4 4 1 1   1 1 1  |       |4 4 4 4 3 2 1            |
       2  |4 4 4 4 2            |       |4 4 4 4 3 3 2 1          |
       3  |4 4 4 4 2 1 1        |       |4 4 4 4 3 3 1 1 1        |
       4  |4 4 4 4 2 1          |       |4 4 4 4 3 2 1 1          |
       5  |4 4 4 4 3 2 1        |       |4 4 4 4 3 3 1 1          |
       6  |4 4 4 4 4 3 2 2 1 1  |       |4 4 4 4 2 1              |

Category: not big.
          |T S E F C G B J K L M|       |U Q X V D I W A H R O N P|
Group: 1  |  1 4 4 4 4 4 4 4    |       |      1 1 1 4 4 4 4 4 4 4|
       2  |      4 4 4 4 4 4 4  |       |      1 1 1 4 4 4 4 4 4 4|
       3  |      4 4 4 4 4 4 4  |       |  1 1 1 1 4 4 4 4 4 4 4  |
       4  |  1 3 4 4 4 4 4 4    |       |      1 1 4 4 4 4 4 4 4  |
       5  |      2 2 4 4 4 4 4  |       |          1 4 4 4 4 4 4 4|
       6  |      2 2 4 4 4 4 4  |       |  1 2 3 3 4 4 4 4 4 4 4  |
```

Figure 3: Age-related differences in Category Width.

but to some extent was by the older groups, and there was an
increase in this tendency with age.

In the second analysis, six category relations were examined by cross-matching each of the category extensions with the other three. These six relations have already been alluded to above in the Conditions of Antonymy, but the latter represent only a selection of the types of extensional structure that occur when members of a focus set are variously categorized. There were in fact six types of extensional structure for the paired categories brought into relation in the data. They are described in Table 2, where they are also allocated value labels consisting of a short mnemonic and a letter prefix for later use in the text below.

Table 2: Six Category Relations and their Extensional Structure

Category Relation value	Extensional structure
a. "gapped"	Neither category shares a member with the other. In addition there is at least one member of the set in neither category.
b. "contiguous"	Neither category shares a member with the other. There are no set members outside both categories.
c. "overlapping"	The categories intersect, sharing at least one member.
d. "included"	An adjective category is properly included in the category formed by the complement of the antonym of that adjective.
e. "isomorphic"	There is a one-to-one correspondence between members of an adjective category and the members of the category formed by the complement of that adjective's antonym.
f. "reversed"	The category formed by an adjective properly includes the members of the category formed by the complement of that adjective's antonym.

Overall, no paired relation yielded more than three of these values. The first three values, a-c, were found for the relations small-not small, big-not big, big-small and not big-not small. The values d-f were found in the relations small-not big and big-not small. For groups 2 and 3 in the sample, the first four category relations have a majority of b values, and the last two relations have a majority of e values. These values are consistent with the conditions of complementarity rather than antonymy, and the analysis of category relations revealed few people categorizing with an antonymic scheme in the first three groups (For antonymy, the small-not small and big-not big relations have value b, big-small has value a, not big-not small value c, while both big-not small and small-not big have value d). Indeed, a composite of the analysis of the six relations in the two focus sets shows this quite clearly (See Figure 4). The only values above chance happen to be those characteristic of complementarity. Only in Groups 4 and 5 do other relations begin to assume values associated with antonymy. These data suggest that for the six category relations antonymic structure is established gradually in the sequence shown in Figure 5.

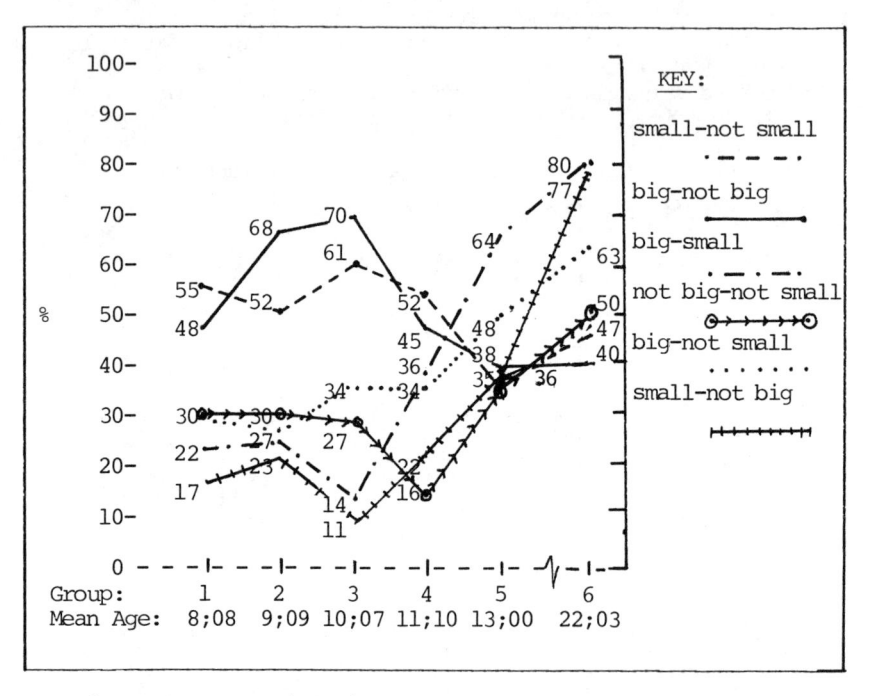

Figure 4: Composite histogram: Percentage frequencies of Category Relation values typical of antonymy, related to the age groups sampled.

The third type of analysis considered together the third and fourth category relations, big -small and not big-not small (see Conditions of Antonymy 3A and 4A), and examined their combined values to search out the "core" characteristics of complementarity vs. antonymy, with value combinations b/b and a/d respectively. These are plotted in Figure 6 and it can be seen that while the frequencies of both value combinations are higher for Focus Set A than for B, the essence of the previous analysis is not radically altered. There is no time, unfortunately, to detail other manipulations of the data, but in the age range studied,

Structure	relation	children 8;08　9;09　10;07　11;10　13;00	adult 22;03
contiguous	small-not small		
contiguous	big - not big		
included	big - not small		
gapped	big - small		
included	small - not big		
overlapping	not big - not small		

Key: minimum 50% frequency:
minimum 33.3% frequency: - - - - - -

Figure 5: Antonymic structure development according to two criteria percentage frequencies and related to the age groups.

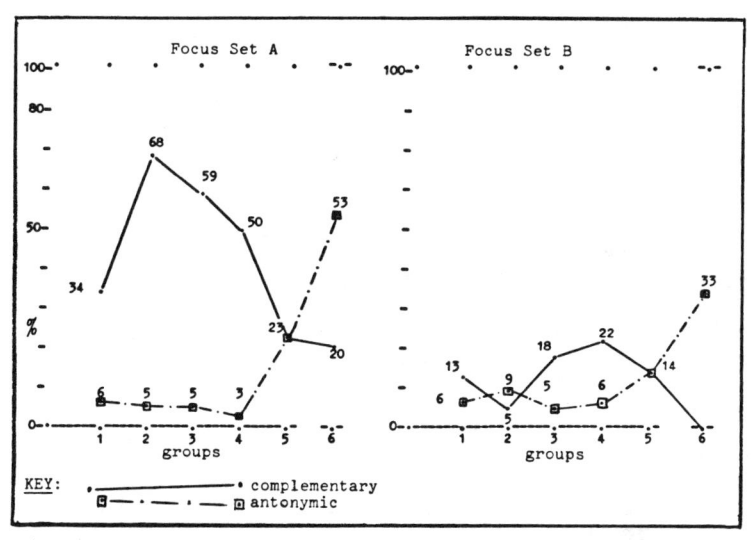

Figure 6: Percentage frequency for complementary and antonymic characteristics in extensions for Category Relations 3 (big-small) and 4 (not big-not small) by age group.

four stages can be discerned in the development of antonymic structure.
In Stage One: There is a lack of structural definition, producing inconsistency in category relations.
In Stage Two: Category relations become organized on the basis of complementarity.
In Stage Three: Complementarity structure is destabilized, possibly as ability in absolute grading grows.
In Stage Four: The structural relations characteristic of antonymy develop and become stabilized.

There are certainly sub-stages in this development, but more data are needed before anything can be said about these. However, if the ages of the present sample are the least bit characteristic, then it seems the development for complete semantic structure for antonymy comes relatively late in childhood. It is therefore unrealistic to claim that children acquire complete adult meanings for antonyms before they go to school.

Notes:

1. Kempson (1977:84). Various other terms are used, such as relative adjectives (Bierwisch, 1970b), polar antonyms (Donaldson and Wales, 1970:225), and dimensional polar terms (Ehri, 1976: 369).

2. Cf. for instance Baron (1973); Bartlett (1976); E. Clark (1972, 1973a, 1973b, 1974, 1975, 1977a, 1977b); Donaldson and Wales (1970); Ehri (1976); Eilers, Oller and Ellington (1974); Keil and Carroll (1980); Kuczaj and Lederberg (1977); Lumsden and Poteat (1968); Maratsos (1973); Nelson (1976); Townsend (1976); Wales (1971); Rice (1980); and Rosch and Lloyd (1978).

3. There is not space to present all the data here. Interested readers are referred to my Ph.D. thesis (Evans, 1979) for further details.

4. See, for example, Bartlett (1976:214), who claims that "adult meanings of terms which describe overall size" were acquired by children who were in some cases less than three-and-a-half years old.

5. Rice gives a general updated summary of the broad theoretical position as follows (Rice, 1980:155-156): "Two aspects of lexical meaning are encoded in spatial adjectives. The first is a core comparative structure requiring a dimension of comparison (height for 'tall'), a standard of comparisons (what is usual for 'tall') and a direction from the standard (greater than or less than)...The second aspect of lexical meaning for spatial adjectives is that of dimensional features that differ-

entiate the pairs, such as height (tall/short) or width (wide/narrow), or length (long/short)."

6. So that wide is always interpreted as big, never as small or little, for example. Similarly, narrow is interpreted in terms of small/little.

7. Carnap (1955) uses the term intension to apply to the cognitive designative component of meaning for a given predicate. Cognitive meaning "may be roughly characterized as that meaning component which is relevant for the determination of truth" (Carnap, 1956:237). The complementary term to intension is extension, and this is connected with denotative aspects of meaning.

8. This is often apparent in the investigator's instruction: "Give/Show me the tall one" is used rather than "Give/Show me a tall one." See, for example, Rice (1980:156).

9. We might wish to postulate that for naturally occurring kinds, such as horses, each category big, medium-sized and small would contain an equal number of members of the background set. There is no reason why this should be so, however, since the six conditions of antonymy will be met provided that each category contains at least one member not in the others. Presumably the interests of the community are instrumental in deciding what the membership of each category is to be.

10. This technique is a modification of the approach used in personality studies and cognitive psychology (Cf. Pettigrew, 1958; Tajfel, Richardson and Everstine, 1964; Wallach and Caron, 1959).

11. To reveal extensional discrepancies, relatively large focus sets are preferable to the arrays of three or four objects more generally used. This is not a new idea: Sinclair-de-Zwart's (1967) study involved sets of nine sticks, and was quite successful in revealing antonymic grading, though she does not appear to have paid much attention to this (op.cit.: 104-108).

References

Baron, Jonathan (1973). Semantic components and conceptual development. Cognition, 2, No. 3, 299-317.
Bartlett, Elsa Jaffe (1976). Sizing things up: the acquisition of the meaning of dimensional adjectives. Journal of Child

Language, 3. 205-219.

Bierwisch, Manfred (1967). Some semantic universals of German adjectivals. Foundations of Language, 3. 1-36.

Bierwisch, Manfred (1970). Semantics. In Lyons (1970:166-184).

Bruner, Jerome S. (1964). The course of cognitive growth. American Psychologist, 19. 1-15.

Carnap, Rudolf (1955). Meaning and Necessity. A Study in Semantics and Modal Logic. 2nd edition. Chicago: University of Chicago Press.

Clark, Eve V. (1972). On the child's acquisition of antonyms in two semantic fields. Journal of Verbal Learning and Verbal Behavior, 11. 750-758.

Clark, Eve V. (1973a). What's in a word? On the child's acquisition of semantics in his first language. In Moore (1973: 65-111).

Clark, Eve V. (1973b). Non-linguistic strategies and the acquisition of word meanings. Cognition, 2, No. 2. 161-182.

Clark, Eve V. (1974). Some aspects for the conceptual basis for first language acquisition. In Schiefelbusch and Lloyd (1974: 105-128). First published in Papers and Reports in Child Language Development, 007 April 1974 (Committee on Linguistics, Stanford University, California).

Clark, Eve V. (1975). Knowledge, context and strategy in the acquisition of meaning. In Dato (1975:77-98).

Clark, Eve V. (1977a). First language acquisition. In Morton and Marshall (1977:1-72).

Clark, Eve V. (1977b). Strategies and the mapping problem in first language acquisition. In Macnamara (1977:147-168).

Dato, Daniel P., ed. (1975). Developmental Psycholinguistics: Theory and Applications. Georgetown University Round Table on Language and Linguistics 1975. Washington, D.C.: Georgetown University Press.

Donaldson, Margaret (1963). A Study of Children's Thinking. London: Tavistock.

Donaldson, Margaret and Roger Wales (1970). On the acquisition of some relational terms. In Hayes (1970:235-267).

Ehri, Linnea C. (1976). Comprehension and production of adjectives and seriation. Journal of Child Language, 3. 369-384.

Eilers, Rebecca E., D. Kimbrough Oller and Judy Ellington (1974).

The acquisition of word meaning for dimensional adjectives: the long and the short of it. Journal of Child Language, 1. 195-204.

Evans, Michael J. (1979). A psycholinguistic study of some aspects of gradability, with special reference to child language. Edinburgh University: unpublished Ph.D. thesis. Additional copy at each of Universitaet Bamberg, Teilbibliothek 4+5, 8600 Bamberg, and Bibliothek des Anglishtischen Seminars, Kettengasse 12, 6900 Heidelberg; both West Germany.

Flores d'Arcais, Giovanni B. and Willem J.M.Levelt, eds. (1970). Advances in Psycholinguistics. London, Amsterdam: North Holland Publishing Company.

Hayes, John R., ed. (1970). Cognition and the Development of Language. New York: Wiley.

Keil, Frank and John J. Carroll (1980). The child's acquisition of "tall": implications for an alternative view of semantic development. Paper presented at the 12th Annual Child Language Research Forum, Stanford University, California, March 1980.

Kempson, Ruth (1977). Semantic Theory. Cambridge: Cambridge University Press.

Kuczaj, Stan A. II, and Amy R. Lederberg (1977). Height, age and function: differing influences on children's comprehension of 'younger' and 'older'. Journal of Child Language, 4, No. 3. 395-416.

Lumsden, E.A., and B.W.S. Poteat (1968). The salience of the vertical dimension in the concept of 'bigger' in five and six-year-olds. Journal of Verbal Learning and Verbal Behavior, 7. 404-408.

Lyons, John, ed. (1970). New Horizons in Linguistics. Harmondsworth, Pelican.

Lyons, John (1977). Semantics 1. Cambridge: Cambridge University Press.

Macnamara, John, ed. (1977). Language Learning and Thought. New York: Academic Press.

Maratsos, Michael P. (1973). Decrease in the understanding of the word "big" in preschool children. Child Development, 44. 747-752.

Moore, Timothy E., ed. (1973). Cognitive Development and the Acquisition of Language. New York: Academic Press.

Morton, John, ed. (1971). Biological and Social Factors in Psycholinguistics. MRC Applied Psychology Unit, Cambridge:Logos Press Ltd.

Morton, John and John C. Marshall, eds. (1977). Psycholinguistics Series -1. Developmental and Pathological. London: Elek Science.

Nelson, Katherine (1976). Some attributes of adjectives used by young children. Cognition, 4. 13-30.

Pettigrew, Thomas F. (1958). The measurement and correlates of category width as a cognitive variable. Journal of Personality, 26. 532-544.

Rice, Mable (1980). Cognition to Language. Categories, Word Meanings, and Training. Baltimore: University Park Press.

Rosch, Eleanor (1978). Principles of categorization. In Rosch and Lloyd (1978:27-48).

Schiefelbusch, Richard L. and Lyle L. Lloyd, eds. (1974). Language Perspectives - Acquisition, Retardation and Intervention. London: Macmillan.

Sinclair-de Zwart, Hermina (1967). Acquisition du langage et developpement de la pensée. Paris: Dunod.

Tajfel, Henri, Alan Richardson and Louis Everstine (1964). Individual consistencies in categorizing. Journal of Personality, 32, 90-108.

Townsend, David J. (1976). Do children interpret 'marked' comparative adjectives as their opposites? Journal of Child Language, 3. 385-396.

Wales, Roger (1971). Comparing and contrasting. In Morton (1971: 61-81).

Wales, Roger and Robin Campbell (1970). On the development of comparison and the comparison of development. In Flores d'Arcais and Levelt (1970: 373-396).

Wallach, Michael A. and A.J. Caron (1959). Attribute criteriality and sex-linked conservatism as determinants of psychological similarity. Journal of Abnormal and Social Psychology, 59. 43-50.

APPENDIX

Form A Version 1

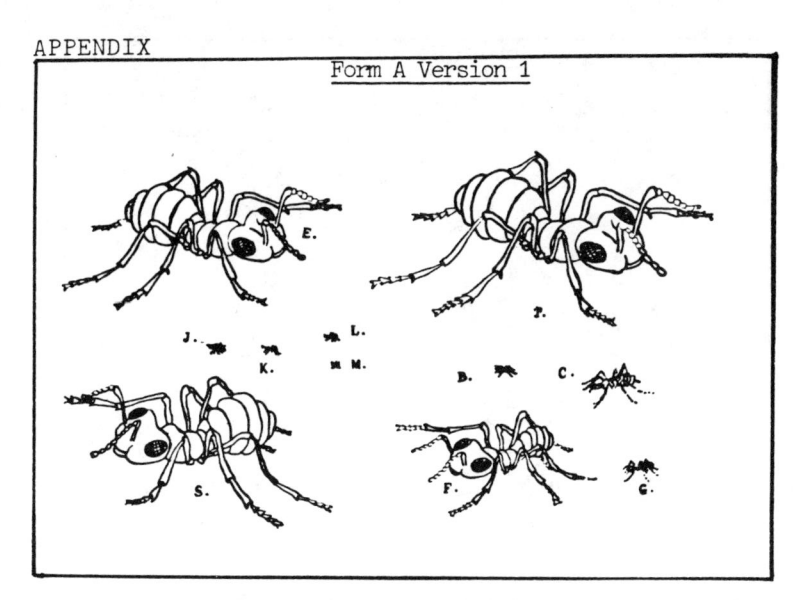

Form A Version 2

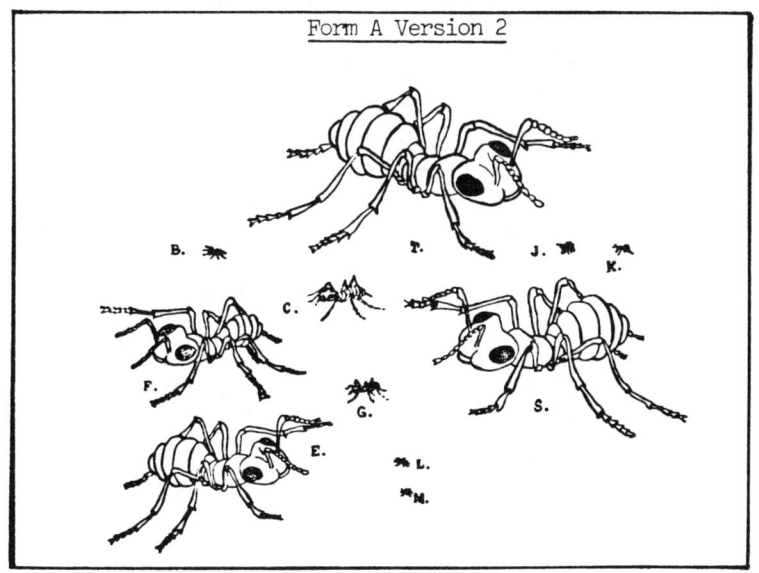

161

Form B Version 1

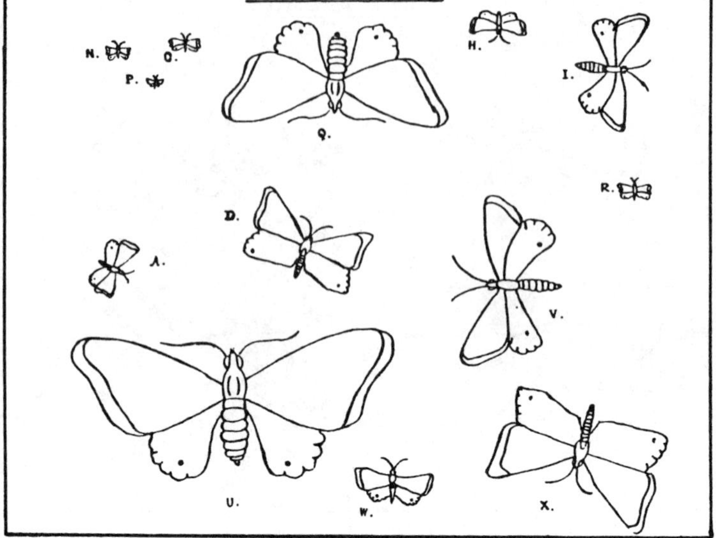

Form B Version 2

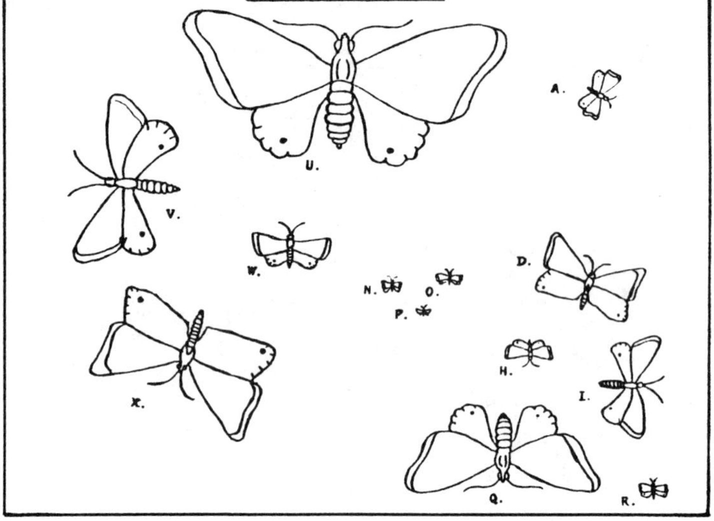

"Gone" and the Concept of the Object*

Alison Gopnik

The Ontario Institute for Studies in Education

252 Bloor Street West

Toronto, Ontario

Abstract

The use of gone by nine children from 15-24 months old was studied. Children used gone when they turned away from objects or placed objects behind them, when objects moved behind or inside other objects, when containers were emptied, and when the children searched for invisibly displaced objects and "hypothetical" objects. These uses of gone are related to Bower's (1974) account of the development of the object concept. It is argued that from birth to 18 months they generalize across these rules and this allows them to deal with new types of disappearance. It is argued that the early gone encodes this generalization. It is suggested that the infant's interest in the problem of disappearance motivates his acquisition of gone and that the acquisition of gone could facilitate the development of the 18-month-old object concept.

*A version of this paper was presented at the Second International Congress for the Study of Child Language. It is based on work undertaken for a University of Oxford doctoral dissertation. I am grateful to Andy Meltzoff and David Olson for helpful discussions and criticism.

"Gone" and the Concept of the Object

"Gone" is one of the most frequently used early words, despite the fact that it plays a complex syntactic and semantic role in the adult language and it has no obvious social significance. A number of writers (Bloom, 1973; Brown, 1975) have suggested that the early use of "gone" might have something to do with the child's cognitive development, particularly his development of the concept of the object. However, no one has spelled out exactly how the meaning of "gone" and the object are related. Moreover, psycholinguists have simply accepted Piaget's account of the development of the object concept, although more recent work suggests that this account must be modified.

In this paper, I will begin by describing how nine children used "gone" in the one-word stage. I will argue that "gone" encodes the fact that the child does not presently perceive an object. I will then briefly review some recent research and present a "neo-Piagetian" account of the development of the object concept based on that work. I will argue that the concept encoded by "gone" is only developed after the child is approximately 18 months old. Finally, I will suggest that the word "gone" is developed at about the same time as the concept it encodes, and that the development of "gone" might actually facilitate the development of the object concept.

Methodology

I recorded the spontaneous speech of nine children as part of a wider study of the development of early non-nominal expressions (Gopnik, 1981). Three of the children were 12 months old when recording began and were audio-taped for one hour in their homes bi-weekly until they had reached the two-word stage. Three children were 15 months old when recording began and were videotaped for one half-hour monthly for six months. Finally, three more children were videotaped monthly in their homes for six months from the time they were 18 months old.

A total of 378 utterances of "gone" were recorded. Each of the nine children used "gone" at one time or another. I examined the contexts in which children used "gone", in order to determine what concept "gone" encoded.

Results

Almost all (94%) of the utterances of "gone" took place in one of four contexts. Children said "gone" when they saw an object and then the object disappeared, when they searched for missing objects, when they commented on empty containers, and when objects were suddenly transformed.

Disappearance

153 of the utterances (40%) occurred when the children saw an object and the object disappeared. All nine children used "gone" in this way. The disappearance could take many forms. Children said "gone" when they turned away from an object so that they could no longer see it. They said "gone" when they moved an object to one side of them or behind them. They said "gone" when an object moved behind a screen or a screen moved in front of an object, in peek-a-boo games, for example. They also said "gone" when an object moved underneath or inside another object, for instance, when they pushed blocks into a toy posting box. In all of these cases it was clear that the children expected the object to reappear. Usually, the children made the object disappear and then made it reappear, by turning back towards it, or removing the screen or cover. These hiding and finding games could go on ad nauseam.

In the vast majority of these "disappearance" contexts (121 of 154) the children made the object disappear themselves. They turned away from the object or hid it behind or underneath another object. Perhaps more strikingly, all the children used "gone" when they made objects disappear before they used "gone" to comment on disappearances they did not cause. (See Table 1.)

Search

The children said "gone" a total of 113 times (30%) when they searched for a missing object. All nine children used "gone" in this way. In most of these cases, the children had not actually seen the object disappear. One child said "gone" when I surreptitiously hid a jigsaw puzzle piece under my skirt; he searched in various locations and finally figured out where it was. Children also said "gone" as they searched for "hypothetical" objects, objects they had never actually

Table 1

Order of Appearance of Types of Disappearance Uses of "Gone"

Group I

Jonathan	Rachel	Henry
Self-Initiated	Self-Initiated	Self-Initiated
Other Initiated	Other Initiated	Position Change
		Movement Away/ Other Initiated

Group II

John	Christian	Harriet
Movement Away/ Self-Initiated	Movement Away/ Self-Initiated	Self-Initiated
Position Change	Position Change	Position Change/ Movement Away
		Other Initiated

Group III

Paul	Hannah	Anna
Position Change	Self-Initiated	Self-Initiated
Self-Initiated	Other Initiated	Other Initiated

seen but whose existence they had deduced. One child nests a set of beakers, but there is still a space left in the smallest beaker; she says "gone" as she searches for another, smaller beaker to put in the space, even though there is no such beaker. The children clearly believed that these objects existed somewhere; otherwise their search would have had no point.

Emptiness

"Gone" was used 75 times (20%) in contexts that involved containers. Eight of the children used "gone" in this way. Sometimes, children said "gone" as they emptied containers. These contexts were similar to the contexts in which the child placed an object out of sight. The children looked into the container, saw the object and then placed it where they could not see it, to one side of the container.

Children also said "gone" when they commented on empty containers. The children seemed to expect that containers should have objects in them. When they opened a container and found that it was empty they were surprised and said "gone". Bower (1974) has remarked that when children of this age see an object removed from a container, they will pick up the container, examine it and shake it, as if expecting objects to pop out: "The cup is seen as a cornucopia rather than as a container, something that objects can emerge from without first having to go into." The children in this study seemed to have a similar view of cups. When they did not see the expected object they said "gone". These contexts are similar to the contexts in which children searched for hypothetical objects. In both cases, the children comment on the fact that they do not see an object they expected to see.

Transformation

Five of the children used "gone" when stable configurations unexpectedly broke up, when a tower of blocks fell down or an ironing board suddenly collapsed. However, only 15 such uses (4%) were recorded. These uses of "gone" are rather difficult to interpret. In these contexts the child sees an object and then stops seeing it, as he does in the "disappearance" contexts. However, it is not clear whether, in these contexts, the child believes that the object still continues to exist or recognizes that it has been destroyed. In any case, these uses of "gone" only appeared in the earliest sessions. (See Table 2.) Children stopped using "gone" in this way in the later sessions.

The Meaning of "Gone"

What is the meaning of "gone" for these children? Clearly, "gone" doesn't encode a feature of objects, or a relationship between objects. Any object may disappear in any way. On the other hand, it doesn't encode a type of action or a social relationship or an emotional state. Instead, "gone" encodes a relationship between the child and objects.

This relationship is not easy to characterize. Perhaps the best way of describing it is to say that the children comment on the fact that they do not perceive an object. However, the children seemed to believe in the existence of the object, or at least to believe that the object would reappear, at least in the later sessions after they stopped using "gone" in "transformation" contexts. "Gone" marked this contrast between the children's perceptions and their beliefs.

This relationship has a number of interesting characteristics. First, it has an egocentric quality; the children used "gone" when they did not see an object regardless of whether the object was visible to others. It is also a very abstract relationship; it involves a very general conflict between belief and perception. Finally, it is not a relationship that plays an important role in the semantics of the adult language. In fact, there is no one word or syntactic structure that encodes this concept in adult English.

Discussion

The Development of the Object Concept

It seems that we are most likely to find an explanation for the early use of "gone" by looking at the 18-month-old's conception of the world. Clearly, the concept encoded by "gone" is related to the child's understanding of the appearances and disappearances of objects. Fortunately, this area of cognitive development has been extensively studied. Unfortunately, both the experimental results, and the interpretations of those results can be confusing and contradictory.

Table 2
Uses of "Gone" in Different Contexts

Session No.	Search	Disappearance	Emptiness	Transformation	Other
	Rachel				
9	1	1			
10	1			7	1
11	5				
12		4			
13	2	5			
	Jonathan				
21		1	3		
23			2		1
24			1	1	
25	3	2	1		
26		2			
	Henry				
11				1	
13	1		2		1
14		1	5		
15			2		
16			4	1	
17		20			
18	9	14	4		
19	3	3	3		
20	4	2	2		1
21	1	3			
22	2	2	2		1
23	3	4	6		1
24	21	14	5		2
	John				
1	4	5	9	1	
2	1	3	6		
3		3			
4	1	10			
	Christian				
3	3	3	3	4	1
4	4	10	1		1
5	1				

Piaget's original account (Piaget 1954) has had to be modified in the light of more recent studies. In addition to studying the ways in which infants retrieve hidden objects, researchers have studied the infant's eye movements and their reactions to unusual disappearances. This new evidence has led to new interpretations of the old Piagetian problem. While Piaget argued that the problem was that the infant could not represent an object if it was out of sight, Bower (1974) argues that the problem is really a spatial one, and Moore and Meltzoff (1978) argue that it is a problem of identity. In addition to these differences in interpretation, these authors also make different empirical predictions. For example, Piaget predicts that a nine-month-old can only find an object under a cup, if he has found it there before, since, for Piaget, the infant believes that his actions actually recreate the object. Bower, on the other hand, suggests that the nine-month-old will look for the object, even if he never acted on the object at all. Similarly, Moore and Meltzoff claim that at about twelve months, children can't find an object when it moves behind a screen, but can find it when the screen moves in front of it, which would not be predicted by Piaget's theory or Bower's theory. Bower claims that the crucial factor is whether the object is hidden behind or inside another object, which neither Piaget nor Moore and Meltzoff would predict.

However, all these theorists, and others who believe that object permanence is a genuine problem, agree about some things. They agree that during the period from birth to 18 months, children do sometimes predict that an object that disappears will reappear, and they agree that children make more predictions of this kind as they grow older. They also agree that the children don't always make these predictions; at each stage of development up to 18 months they can't deal with some types of disappearance. They agree that during this period of development the children sometimes make contradictory predictions. Finally, they agree that after 18 months the children predict that, in general, objects will reappear when they disappear, and they become able to deduce the location of missing objects.

Even very young infants sometimes predict that an object that disappears will reappear. For example, when they turn away from an object, they expect that the object will reappear when they turn back to it (Piaget, 1954).

Somewhat older infants can retrieve an object when they place it to one side of them (Piaget, 1954). There is also some evidence suggesting that after 3 months, infants predict that an object will reappear when it moves behind another object. Infants are surprised when a screen moves in front of an object, and the object does not reappear when the screen moves back up (Charlesworth, 1966). Similarly, if a moving object disappears behind a screen, 6-month-olds will look towards the far edge of the screen as if they expect the object to emerge there (Bower, Broughton and Moore, 1979).

Despite this, 6-month-olds won't search for an object when it disappears underneath or inside another object, and they show no surprise when a cup moves over an object and the object is not there when the cup is removed (Gratch, 1976). It is clear that 6-month-olds do not predict that an object will reappear when it disappears inside a container.

At about 9 months, the infant does begin to predict that the object will reappear in these cases but these predictions seem to be the result of rather specific ad hoc rules. Bower has argued that the 9-month-old has two rules. One is "The object will reappear where it disappeared"; the other is "The object will reappear where it appeared before." Each of these predictions will be confirmed fairly often, especially if the child has tidy parents and a toy box. However, the rules may actually conflict in certain circumstances. When the 9-month-old sees an object appear several times at a location, he will search there even if the object is placed at another location -- the A not B error.

In addition, these specific rules will not allow the child to deal with all types of disappearance. If the child does not actually see the object disappear at a location and the object has not appeared there before, these rules are useless. For example, 9-month-olds cannot find an object if it is hidden under a cup which is placed beside another cup and the two cups are transposed. Moore and Meltzoff (1978) have suggested that there are a number of important substages in the development of the object concept between 9 and 18 months. At each point, the infant can deal with some types of disappearances but not others. The fact that the infant does not generalize his predictions and the fact that he is willing to entertain contradictory predictions, suggest

171

that up to 18 months he is gradually accumulating more and more information about the disappearances and reappearances of objects, and constructing more and more specific rules that allow him to predict when and where objects will reappear.

Sometime between 15 and 24 months, during Piaget's stage 6, all this changes. Infants begin to search for objects at a location even if they have not seen them disappear at that location. They can solve the transposed cup task, eventually, and even more difficult tasks. For example, if an object is placed in a cup, the cup is placed under a series of covers and the object is left behind under one of the covers, the infant can deduce the location of the object at the end of stage 6.

Even more significantly, the children seem to be able to make intelligent guesses about the location of an object that has disappeared, even if they cannot deduce the exact location of the object. Gratch (1976) reports that when 18-month-olds see a box come down over an object, and then find that the box is empty, they are extremely surprised, and they search for the object in other parts of the room or under a washcloth on the table, even though they have neither seen the object disappear there, nor seen it appear there before.

What causes these changes? Piaget, Bower and Moore & Meltzoff all suggest in different ways, that 18-month-olds construct a general model, which replaces the specific rules they have gradually accumulated. With these rules, children will be able to deal with almost all the disappearances they come across. In a wide variety of situations they will be able to predict that an object that disappears will reappear. While previously all these predictions have the same form, they are the result of separate unrelated rules; at about 18 months, the child seems to ask, "Are all these disappearances and reappearances the result of the same underlying process?"

The answer to this question may be found in the child's developing concept of space. All these disappearances are due to movement, either the child's own movements, or the movements of objects. The 18-month-old develops a model of observers, or rather a single observer, the child himself, and objects moving in the same spatial framework. The appearances and disappearances of objects are a result of changing spatial relationships.

This model allows the child to make all the specific predictions that the specific rules allowed him to make. When you move away from an object or place an object behind you, or when an object moves behind or under another object, the spatial relationship between you and the objects around you has changed.

This model also allows children to make predictions that were not possible with the specific rules. It allows them to deduce or guess the location of objects, even when they haven't actually seen the objects disappear. As Bower puts it, "Deduction becomes possible after all the information gathered during the course of development is organized in a coherent whole with general principles which can be coordinated and applied in specific situations" (Bower, 1974, p. 230). Before 18 months, infants seem to think, "An object that disappears is gone for good unless one of my specific rules applies." After 18 months they interpret all disappearances in terms of their model of moving objects. If an object disappears they try to figure out what possible changes in the spatial relationship of the objects around could have led to that disappearance.

This change appears to be part of a more general change at about 18 months. Before 18 months, children do seem to be able to represent an object even when they do not actually see it (Bower, 1974; Meltzoff, 1981). However, they do this only in specific circumstances that are perceptually defined. They predict that the object will reappear only if they see it disappear in a particular way. After 18 months, their belief in the existence of the object does not depend on any particular perceptual experience, or sequence of experiences. They seem to believe that the object is there even if they have not seen it disappear, in fact even if they have not seen it at all. This liberation of belief from perception is also apparent in other ways. For example, after 18 months, children begin to be able to pretend that objects exist (Piaget, 1962).

The development of the 18-month-old's theory of the object is rather like the development of a scientific theory. Before 18 months, the infant is rather like Tycho Brahe or a celestial navigator; he looks at the behavior of objects around him and constructs specific rules that allow him to predict when and where objects will appear. After 18 months the infant is more like Galileo. He has a general theory of the objects he sees. This theory subsumes all the specific rules that have been constructed earlier and it allows him to make new predictions, predictions that he could not have made simply by observing the object's behavior.

Object Permanence and the Meaning of "Gone"

How are these developments related to the child's early use of "gone"? "Gone" was applied to all the different types of disappearances that should lead to reappearance according to the infant specific rules. "Gone" was used when children turned away from an object or moved it out of sight, and when the object moved behind another object. Even a 6-month-old should be able to deal with these types of disappearance. "Gone" was also applied to more difficult types of disappearance; it was used when objects disappeared inside other objects. However, a 1-year-old should also predict that the object will reappear in these cases.

But children also used "gone" in more difficult situations. When children said "gone" as they searched for missing objects, especially when they searched for hypothetical objects, they had not actually seen the object disappear. Nevertheless, they clearly expected the object to appear at some location, and they searched at locations where they had not seen the object appear before. This sort of behavior requires the 18-month-old's theory of the object. This theory also seems to operate when children say "gone" as they look into empty containers. The children believe that an object should be in the container, even though they have not seen the object in the container.

There are two important points to make about these uses of "gone". First, they involve a generalization about all the many different types of situations in which an object disappears. In order to use "gone" in this way, infants must recognize some similarity between all these events. But, more significantly, children also use "gone" when they do not see an object disappear, but they believe that an object exists in a location. We saw that one of the most important characteristics of the 18-month-old theory was precisely that it allows this sort of generalization; it allows a general explanation of all the specific types of disappearances that were covered by specific rules and it also explains other situations in which the child does not perceive an object. The general concept encoded by "gone", a concept of existence that is independent of perception, is one of the concepts that is central to the 18-month-old's understanding of the world.

The Relationship Between Conceptual and Semantic Development

Unfortunately, there was no way of telling exactly what stage of cognitive development the children had reached when they began to use "gone". However, we do know how old the children were when their first uses of "gone" were recorded. "Gone" was first recorded between 15 and 24 months (the mean was 18.8 months). Since recordings only lasted an hour and were done at intervals, and since the three 18-month-olds already used "gone" at the start of the study, it is likely that the children actually began using "gone" at an even earlier age. This suggests the possibility that children began to use "gone" when they were in the midst of developing the 18-month-old theory of the object. If "gone" encodes a concept that is an important part of that theory, then children used "gone" to encode a new and problematic concept rather than an old and well-established one. Some additional support for this hypothesis may be found in a recent study by Nicholich (1981), who reports that children began to use "gone" when they had barely reached the first sub-level of stage 6. The children only reached the end of stage 6 after they had been using the terms for some time. Corrigan (1978) reported a slightly later appearance of "gone". Her children used "gone" for the first time in the same session in which they solved the most difficult object permanence task -- that is, at the end of stage 6. Both Nicholich's and Corrigan's results, however, are consistent with the hypothesis that "gone" and the stage 6 object concept develop simultaneously. There doesn't seem to be a delay between the acquisition of the concept, and the acquisition of the linguistic encoding of that concept.

Most theories of the relationship of cognition and early language have assumed that linguistic expressions can only be developed after the concepts they encode are developed. However, in some circumstances the acquisition of words and the acquisition of concepts go hand in hand. When we learn a science, for example, we seem to learn the terms of the science and learn the concepts those terms encode simultaneously. We can't say that we learn what "entropy" means first and they learn what entropy is or vice-versa. I am suggesting that when children learn "gone" they are not simply translating a term of their cognitive language into English. Instead, like the physics students, they are developing a new term and a new concept.

This might help to explain why children used "gone" most frequently when they made objects disappear and reappear. When they face difficult problems, children often experiment. They try to create the events they are trying to understand. If "gone" refers to a problematic type of context, we might expect the children to attempt to create those contexts. The child's behavior might be analogous to the behavior of an adult who tries to solve a difficult problem. He experiments and he simultaneously talks through the problem.

More generally, the fact that "gone" encodes a problematic context might actually motivate the child to acquire "gone". Children are more likely to pay attention to phenomena that are at the frontiers of their cognitive competence than they are to phenomena that are familiar or to phenomena that are way beyond them. If 18-month-olds are trying to figure out the phenomena of disappearance, they should pay special attention to the disappearance of objects and they might also pay special attention to the words they hear when objects disappear. Similarly, children might be more likely to hypothesize that a word has a new interesting meaning, rather than a familiar well-established one.

It is even possible that the development of the word "gone" actually helps the children to develop the 18-month-old theory of the object. We saw that one of the most important steps in this development came when the child began to realize the similarities between many different kinds of disappearance. The fact that adults say the same word, "gone", when objects disappear in all sorts of ways, might lead the child to consider whether these events are similar.

I have argued then that "gone" encodes a concept that is characteristic of the theory of objects that infants develop between 18 and 24 months. I have also argued that children begin to use the word "gone" when they are in the midst of developing this concept. Elsewhere (Gopnik, 1982),

I have argued that there is a similar relationship between the development of other early expressions such as "no", "there", "oh dear" and "more" and the development of the child's plans. These expressions also seem to encode concepts the child is in the course of developing, though these concepts are more concerned with actions than objects. It is clear that linguistic developments can facilitate conceptual development for adults, and this may also be true for older children. It would be interesting if linguistic and conceptual development are this intimately related from the time the child produces his first words.

References

Bloom, L. One word at a time: The use of single-word utterances before syntax. The Hague: Mouton, 1973.

Bower, T.G.R. Development in infancy. San Francisco: W.H. Freeman, 1974.

Bower, T.G.R., Broughton, J.M. and Moore, M.K. Development of the object concept as manifested by changes in the tracking behavior of infants between seven and twenty weeks of age. Journal of Experimental Child Psychology, 1971, 11(2), 182-192.

Brown, R. A first language: The early stages. Cambridge, Mass.: Harvard University Press, 1973.

Charlesworth, W.R. Persistence of orienting and attending behavior in infants as a function of stimulus-locus uncertainty. Child Development, 1966, 37, 473-491.

Corrigan, R. Language development as related to stage 6 object permanence development. Journal of Child Language, 1978, 5(2), 173-189.

Gopnik, A. The development of non-nominal expressions in 12-24-month olds. In P. Dale and D. Ingram (Eds.) Child language: An international perspective, Baltimore: University Park Press, 1981, 93-104.

Gopnik, A. Words and plans: Early language and the development of intelligent action. Journal of Child Language, 1982, 9(2), 303-318.

Gratch, G. On levels of awareness of objects in infants and students thereof. Merrill-Palmer Quarterly, 1976, 22(3), 157-176.

Meltzoff, A. Imitation, inter-model matching and representation in early infancy. In G. Butterworth (Ed.) Infancy and epistemology. London: Harvester Press, 1981.

Moore, M.K. and Meltzoff, A. Imitation, object permanence and language development in infancy. In F. Minifiel and L. Lloyd, Communicative and cognitive abilities: Early behavior assessment. Baltimore: University Park Press, 1978.

Nicholich, L. The cognitive bases of relational words in the single-word period. Journal of Child Language, 1981, 8(1), 15-34.

MEANING AND FUNCTION OF COMMON, PROPER AND NICK NAMES: HOW SCHOOLCHILDREN VIEW THE RELATION BETWEEN WORDS AND THEIR REFERENTS

Hannelore Grimm & Werner Kany

University of Heidelberg

More than 5o years ago, Piaget (198o; first ed. 1926) had already shown by the technique of clinical interviews that, for a long time, children have difficulties understanding the nature of the relation between words and their referents. He explained this with the theory that children have not yet developed the cognitive competence of decentering and, therefore, regard the words as parts or attributes of the objects.
While it may be correct that smaller children believe that words are consubstantial with things, it is very unlikely that 1o-year old children still follow this nominal realism. Markman (1976) and Papandropoulou and Sinclair (1974), therefore, suggest a semantic explanation for the fact that older children fail to differentiate between words and their referents. Markman argues that second graders incorrectly answer questions referring to the existence and to the meaning of words, once their referent is no longer present, because they have developed a naive version of a referential theory of meaning, according to which words are merely labels or names of things. Similarly, Papandropoulou and Sinclair suggest that children do not regard pronouns and articles as words because they do not have fixed referential objects. Thus, these authors each assume that children believe that words are non-existent when they are not bound to an object.

The advantage of this *semantic explanation* is that it establishes a relationship between the children's answers to questions referring to the differentiation of words and their referents and their conception of the meaning of words. The disadvantage of this explanation, however, is that it is primarily a structuralist approach, like Piaget's *cognitive explanation*, since only the aspect of the semantic meaning is taken into account, whereas the fact that speakers perform acts by means of words is not explicitly considered. This functional meaning of words is the core of our *pragmatic explanation: Children do not reject the existence and the meaning of words simply because the objects labeled by the words no longer exist, but because the absence of objects restricts the possibility of using words in speech acts.* In our opinion, the children do not follow a naive version of a referential theory of meaning but a *simplified speech-act theory*.

In the studies of Markman (1976) and Papandropoulou and Sinclair (1974), the act of reference is regarded as an isolated one. They neglect the fact that a speaker, when he/she uses a word to refer to an object, at the same time, also states something about this object. Searle (1969, p. 118) describes the referential act as an incomplete and nonautonomous act of the superior propositional act which necessarily has to be supplemented by the predicative act.

Central to our argument is the view that it is the meaningfulness of the words that determines the extent to which a propositional act implies not only reference but predication as well. The referential act prevails if the meaning of the word is very restricted; the predicative act prevails if the words carry more meaning.

From this relationship it can be derived that children are much more likely to reject the existence of words with little meaning than those with a lot of meaning, because words with more meaning are not only linked to an external object, but also to an internal concept. This means that even in the absence of external objects these words can still be used in a nonreferential manner.

If one also considers that, through the predicative act, a statement is made about the object referred to and that one can rightly be asked to prove the correctness of this statement, it can further be derived that for children it is more difficult to realize the arbitrariness of the relationship between words and their referents when words that have a lot of meaning are used than when words which have less meaning are used. In other words: *It is difficult for children to accept the exchangeability of words with lots of meanings because they believe that they make a wrong statement when exchanging the words.*

According to Johnson's findings (1976, p. 39) second graders at an average age of 8;9 years do indeed accept the exchangeability of proper names whereas they do not accept the exchangeability of common names. This finding suggests that the postulated relationship between the type of word meaning and the understanding of the arbitrary nature of the relation between words and their referents in fact exists. A good example of this can also be found in Piaget's study (1980, p. 76): The child is asked: "Do you have a brother?" - "Gilbert" - "Could Gilbert have been given the name Jules?" - "Yes" - "Well then, could the sun have been called moon?" - "No" - "Why not?" - "Because the sun cannot change, it cannot become smaller". Piaget does not pursue the difference underlying these answers any further, but rather, exclusively discusses the common names. This makes clear that he did not realize the dependence of the understanding of the arbitrary relationship between words and their referents on the type of words.

To summarize: We argue that it depends upon the functional linkage, and not just upon the object linkage of words, whether children, once the object is removed, reject the existence and the meaning of the name of the object and whether they recognize the arbitrary relationship between words and their referents.

To examine this assumption further, we chose proper names, nick names, and common names as words with different degrees of meaning. Proper names have a restricted meaning and, therefore, a primarily referential function. In contrast, common names have more meaning so that they can fulfil both the referential and the predicative function. Nick names should take an intermediate position because of their special status: They can be used as proper names, common names, or both. However, the ability to differentiate between these aspects would presuppose highly developed metalinguistic skills.

In this study, we proceeded as follows:
A. First, the children were asked in two questions to define the proper, common, and nick names given. We expect
   - that second grade pupils differentiate to a less extent between them than fourth grade pupils,
   - that there is a relationship between the exactness of differentiation and the answering of the following questions:
B. The children were asked three questions concerning the differentiation between words and their referents.
   If our assumptions are correct, then the existence of the proper names was to be rejected more often than the existence of the common names once the referential object was removed. The nick names would take an intermediate position.
C. Three questions were also asked concerning the exchangeability of the words. We expect a tendency for the younger children to accept the exchangeability of proper names and to reject the exchangeability of common names. The nick names again are expected to be in the intermediate position.

The first name of each child and two other first names (*Klaus, Inge*) were chosen as proper names. *Dog* and *Cat* were the common names, *Bean-Pole* and *Chicken* were used as nick names: The dominant physical character of Bean-Pole is tallness, the dominant psychological characteristic of Chicken is fear (the German name for Chicken is "Angsthase", literally translated "anxious person" thus stressing the psychological characteristic of fear inherent in the word itself).

As table 1 shows, the study was carried out with 2o second-grade pupils, averaging age 8, and with 25 fourth graders, averaging age 1o.

Table 1   Children Participating in the Study

Grade	N	Boys	Girls	Mean age
2	2o	13	7	8;06
4	25	14	11	1o;o4

Following Piaget (198o), we used the technique of clinical interviews. The main questions and the side-questions, however, were pre-set as Flavell (1963, p. 431) has suggested. Some of the questions were those formulated by Piaget or Markman, and some questions were new.
This experiment is a part of a comprehensive study which also deals with the following aspects: origin and function of the names, productive use of nick names, and the relationship between nicknaming and the social structure of the group.

A. First let us look at the result of the two different types of questions concerning the definition of meaning (Table 2, 3).
   First, the children were given the following questions of type 1:
   - Proper name (child's first name) = PN
     - "What do you think? Does the name PN mean anything?" -
   - Nick name *Bohnenstange* (Bean-Pole)/*Angsthase* (Chicken) = NN1/NN2
     - "Does the nick name NN1/NN2 mean anything?"
   - Common name *Dog* = CN
     - "Do you know what the word CN means?"
The answers were categorized in the following way: a) I don't know; b) The word has no meaning; c) referential meaning: This category includes all answers emphasizing the referential

function of the word in question. For example: "A proper name means that you call someone by it". "It's the name of a person"; d) semantic meaning: Answers stressing meaning aspects of the word. For example: "My name means that I'm a boy". "Dog means an animal that barks".

Table 2   Children's Definitions of the Meaning of Three Types of Words

| | | Second Graders | | | | Fourth Graders | | |
Type of Word	PN	NN1	NN2	CN	PN	NN1	NN2	CN
a	1	1	-	-	1	-	-	-
b	9⁺	9	4	2⁺	18⁺⁺	4	1	3⁺⁺
c	6	-	-	9ˣ	6	1	-	-ˣ
d	4]⁺	1o	16	9ˣ]⁺	-]⁺⁺	2o	24	22ˣ]⁺⁺
N =		20				25		

⁺X^2 = 6.175; df = 1; p < .o5; ⁺⁺X^2 = 19.822; df = 1; p < .oo1.
ˣ Fisher-Test; p < o.oo1

As expected, the children defined the names differently. Table 2 shows that all children differentiate between the proper names and the common names in such a way that they much more often do not attribute a meaning to the proper name (Chi-Square Test). However - and this is also in line with our expectations - only the fourth graders differentiate semantically between the proper name and the common name (Fisher-Test): Without exception they explain the common name semantically, whereas 9 of the younger children only stress its referential meaning.

Contrary to our assumption, the nick names do not take an intermediate position: With only one exception, the children explain their meanings by naming their prominent features, and do not refer to their referential functions.
It is not clear why as many as 9 second graders do not attribute a meaning to the nick name *Bean-Pole*. A possible explanation could be that

they have not understood the metaphorical usage
of the name.

Second, four questions of type 2 were asked:
PN/CN: "And what would you tell a kindergart-
ner who asks you whether the name/word
PN/CN means anything?"
NN1/NN2: "And what would you tell a friend who
asks you whether the nick name NN1/NN2
means anything?"
The answers were categorized as above.

Table 3   Children's Definitions of the Meaning of
Three types of Words

| Type of Word | Second Graders | | | | Fourth Graders | | | |
	PN	NN1	NN2	CN	PN	NN1	NN2	CN
a	1	3	3	3	4	3	1	3
b	3	5	-	-	10	-	-	-
c	10	2	-	8	10	1	-	2
d	6	10	17	9	1	21	24	20
N =		20				25		

The results are interesting in-as-much as the
children characterize the proper name as meaningless less frequently than before, when they
were asked to explain the meaning of the proper
name to an imaginary kindergarten child (questions type 1 vs. type 2: second graders: x^2_2 =
4.068; df = 1; p <.05; fourth graders: x^2 = 3.572;
df = 1; p = n.s.). Rather, they are now eager
to explain the name by indicating its referential function. This makes clear that even second
graders are able to decenter and to put themselves in the place of others.

B. Three different types of questions concerning
the differentiation between words and their referents were asked (Tables 4, 5, 6).

Questions of type 1:
PN/NN1/NN2: "Suppose the people with the name
PN/NN1/NN2 have disappeared. Not
one of them is left in the whole

CN: world. Now that all the people are gone, can there still be the name PN/NN1/NN2?"
"Suppose all the dogs have disappeared. Not one of them is left in the whole world. Now that all the dogs are gone, can there still be the word CN?"

Table 4 Number of Children Affirming versus Denying the Existence of Words, Given the Nonexistence of Referents

| | Second Graders | | | | Fourth Graders | | | |
Type of Word	PN	NN1	NN2	CN	PN	NN1	NN2	CN
yes	11	11	8	13	16	17	18	19
no	9	9	11	6	9	8	7	6
no answer	-	-	1	1	-	-	-	-
N =		20				25		

As Table 4 shows, the assumption - that the children more often believe that the word disappears once the referential object has disappeared when the word is a proper name as compared to a common name - is only confirmed as a general tendency. But the fact that children spontaneously restrict their correct answer to accept only the existence of a name once the referential object has disappeared when it is possible to use the name in another way, suggests that even these children follow a simplified speech-act theory in the sense defined here. Thus, they require a new referential object for the proper name. For example: "The name *Stefan* still exists if you want to have a baby that can also be called *Stefan*." With regard to the common name, the possibility of metaphorical usage is also stressed by the fourth graders. For example: "The word *Dog* still exists if a person says "You dog" as a swear word". In the spontaneous comments of the children who give incorrect answers, comparable indications of the linkage of the words to their usage can be found.

The following answer illustrates the fact that this linkage is more important than the simple 1:1 relationship of the semantic explanation: "The name still exists, merely the people who have this name no longer exist. But actually, the name does no longer exist because it is no longer used, nobody says it any longer". The statement that children do not follow a simple 1:1 relationship suggests at the same time that they do not believe that words are consubstantial with things, the basis of Piaget's theory. The results of Tables 5 and 6 corroborate this statement. Table 5 summarizes the answers to the questions of type 2:

PN/NN1/NN2/CN: "Suppose nobody in the whole word is using the name/word PN/NN1/NN2/CN anymore. Therefore the name/word PN/NN1/NN2/CN does not exist anymore. Have *you/Hans/Juergen*/the *dog* changed, if the name/word PN/NN1/NN2/CN does no longer exist?"

Table 5   Number of Children Affirming versus Denying that Nonexistence of Names Entails Changing Properties of the Referent

Type of Word	Second Graders PN	NN1	NN2	CN	Fourth Graders PN	NN1	NN2	CN
yes	2	1	3	2	2	2	3	-
no	18	19	17	18	23	23	22	25
N =		20				25		

Table 6 summarizes the answers to the questions of type 3:

PN/NN1/NN2: "Now that all the people with the name PN/NN1/NN2 have disappeared, what would you tell a kindergartner/friend who asks you whether the name PN/NN1/NN2 means anything?"

CN: "Now that all the dogs have disappeared, what would you tell a kindergartner who asks you what the word CN means?"

Table 6   Number of Children Affirming versus Denying that Words Would Have Meaning Given the Absence of Referents

| Type of Word | Second Graders | | | | Fourth Graders | | | |
	PN	NN1	NN2	CN	PN	NN1	NN2	CN
yes	7	1o	12	1o	4	16	15	14
no more	1	1	1	1	-	-	1	-
none at all	6	1	2	-	8	1	1	-
no answer	6	8	5	9	13	8	8	11
N =		2o				25		

With very few exceptions the children are sure that the disappearance of a name does not imply a change of the referential object (type 2). And the reverse question, whether the meaning of a name changes once the referential object has disappeared, is also correctly rejected (type 3). However, some children did not answer this question because it might have been too difficult for them.

C. The questions regarding the exchangeability of words were:

Type 1:
Same sex first name = PN1; opposite sex first name = PN2.
PN1/PN2: "Instead of PN could you have been named PN1/PN2?"
NN1/NN2: "Instead of NN1/NN2 could *Hans/Juergen* have been given a different nick name?"
CN: "Suppose that we all agree to call the dog *Cat* and the cat *Dog*. All we want to do is to change their names. Could we do this if we wanted to?"

Type 2:
Common name *Dog* = CN1; Common name *Cat* = CN2.
CN1/CN2: "Suppose we agreed to change their names. Dogs and cats now have a different name. What does the word CN1/CN2 mean now?"

Type 3:
PN: "Do you know the reason why you have a name at all?"
NN1/NN2: "What do you think? Why has *Hans/Juergen* a nick name like NN1/NN2 besides his PN?"
CN: "Do you know why the dog and the cat have names like *Dog* and *Cat*?"

The answers with respect to type 3 were categorized in the following way:
a = functional explanation: This category includes answers stressing the function of the word. For example: "My name is for calling me"; "Dog and cat are called 'dog' and 'cat' to tell them apart". b = attributional explanation: Answers emphasizing a natural correspondence between words and their objects. For example: "Dog and cat are given these names because they fit to them". c = no answer.
The results are shown in Tables 7, 8 and 8 respectively. Three points have to be emphasized.

Table 7   Number of Children Affirming versus Denying the Arbitrariness of Names

Type of Word	Second Graders					Fourth Graders				
	PN1	PN2	NN1	NN2	CN	PN1	PN2	NN1	NN2	CN
yes	17^x	1	19	18	10^{+x}	20	2	23	22	21^+
no	3^x	19	1	2	10^{+x}	1	23	1	2	4^+
other answer	-	-	-	-	-	4	-	1	1	-
N =	20					25				

$+\chi^2 = 5.993$; df = 1; $p < .05$; $^x\chi^2 = 5.584$; df = 1; $p < .05$.

First, the assumption is confirmed that the second graders more often accept the exchangeability in the case of proper names than in the case of common names. Along with the fourth graders, however, they refuse to accept a girl's name for their own boy's name and vice versa. The characteristics of sex is so dominant for them that they are not able to abstract from it.
Table 7 also shows that the assumption could not be confirmed that nick names take an intermediate position between the proper names and the common

names; rather, they are treated like the proper names.

Table 8   Number of Children Affirming versus Denying Change of Meaning with Change of Referent

Type of Word	Second Graders CN1	CN2	Fourth Graders CN1	CN2
yes	4+	5x	14+	15x
no	10+	8x	4+	4x
no answer	6	7	7	6
N =	20		25	

$+\chi^2 = 7.748$; df = 1; p < .05; $^x\chi^2 = 5.398$; df = 1; p < .05.

Second, the fourth graders have basically understood the arbitrary relationship between words and their referents. As Table 8 shows, this is corroborated by the fact that they accept the exchangeability of the common names and also draw the right conclusion from it: It is clear to them that when a dog is called *Cat* the word *Cat* must have the original semantic meaning of the word *Dog*.
If one compares this result with the children's answers to the questions concerning the differentiation between words and their referents, it is obvious that children find it easier to recognize the arbitrary nature of the relationship between a word and its referent than to understand that words can exist independently from their referents. This is a direct contradiction of Piaget's (1980) so far undisputed assumption that overcoming "ontological realism" is the necessary prerequisite for overcoming "logical realism". According to our assumption that children follow a simplified speech-act theory, the present sequence of acquiring both abilities was to be expected because the removal of a referential object restricts possibilities of using words more than does the exchange of words.

Table 9   Children's Answers to Questions about the Reasons of Names

Type of Word	Second Graders				Fourth Graders			
	PN	NN1	NN2	CN	PN	NN1	NN2	CN
a	19	11	4	12	23	13	7	21
b	-	4	14	1	-	1o	16	-
c	1	5	2	7	2	2	2	4
N =			2o				25	

Third, how important the functionality of the words is for children can also be demonstrated by the answers to the question why referents have names at all. As shown in Table 9, the reasoning that the name serves as a means of indication or identification is much more frequent than the reasoning that the name is well suited to the characteristics of the referent. Such functional motivations are also contained in Piaget's report (198o). He may not have recognized them because he was more concerned with the proposition that children regard words as consubstantial with things.

Finally, it remains to be demonstrated that there is a relationship between the types of definitions of meaning and the answers to the questions concerning the differentiation between words and their referents and arbitrariness. In detail, we expect:
first, that children who define meaning in a purely referential manner more often reject the continued existence of a word once the referential object has disappeared - for without an object, the word becomes functionless;
second, that children who stress the predicative aspect of words have greater difficulties in
realizing the arbitrary nature of the relationship between words and their referents.
The first expectation is confirmed: With regard to the proper names, 9o% of the children who had given referential definitions gave wrong answers - with regard to the common names, 67% of the children gave incorrect answers.

The second expectation cannot be tested because the second graders did not give enough semantic definitions and the fourth graders were already able to abstract words as signs from concrete speech acts. It is, however, striking that half of the second graders reject the exchangeability with regard to the common names. As far as questions referring to arbitrariness are concerned, obviously not only the predicative aspect comes into play but also the referential aspect which implies the danger of an incorrect indication.

One final remark has to be made concerning the choice of nick names. The assumption that questions with nick names are answered incorrectly more often than questions with proper names and less often than questions with common names proved to be wrong. But it turned out that nick names do take an intermediate position insofar as they are treated like proper names concerning questions referring to the relationship between words and their referents and, like common names, with regard to questions referring to the meaning of words.

In conclusion, this study deals with what can be described as a naive theory of language children have and thus represents a contribution to the expanding research on the growth of metalinguistic awareness.
   Even though not all assumptions have been confirmed, the results support our basic theoretical argument that children follow a primitive version of a speech-act theory when reasoning on the word-referent relationship.
Still unanswered are the questions how children come to develop such a speech-act theory and in which way is it modified during development. These questions should be investigated longitudinally.

References

Flavell, J.H. The developmental psychology of Jean Piaget. Princeton, N.J.: Van Nostrand, 1963.
Johnson, C.N. Children's reflections on the nature of names. Unpublished doctoral dissertation, University of Michigan, Ann Arbor, 1976.
Markman, E. Children's difficulty with word-referent differentiation. Child Development, 1976, 47, 742 - 749.
Papandropoulou, I., & Sinclair, H. What is a word? Human Development, 1974, 17, 241 - 258.
Piaget, J. Das Weltbild des Kindes. Frankfurt/M.: Ullstein Taschenbuch Verlag, 1980 (First ed. 1926).
Searle, J.R. Speech acts. Cambridge, Mass.: Cambridge University Press, 1969.

Development of the Kinship Term
Semantic System in English Speaking Children

Stan A. Kuczaj II

Southern Methodist University

The research in the present paper was intended to add to the growing literature on children's acquisition of the meaning of kinship terms (Benson and Anglin, 1981; Chambers and Tavuchis, 1976; Danzinger, 1957; Haviland and Clark, 1974). Previous research has demonstrated that children both overextend and underextend kinship terms, and that certain terms are acquired before others, but has not determined the basis for these developmental patterns. The present research was intended to test one hypothesis about the type of knowledge responsible for the development of kinship terms. This hypothesis will be called the "moving ego" hypothesis, following H. Clark's (1973) use of the "moving ego" metaphor to describe temporal experience. In Clark's discussion, the "moving ego" metaphor was used to describe an individual's sense of moving through time, from the past into the future. The "moving ego" hypothesis proposed here is rather different, referring to the ability to consider the relation of others based on a basic relation which focuses on the self. The hypothesized basic relation is "child of" and is suggested to be quite influential in children's learning of kinship relations and thereby children's creation of meaning for kinship terms. This hypothesis has been hinted at by previous researchers in explanations of their findings about kinship term meaning acquisition. Haviland and Clark (1974) suggested that "the child's own roles may play a part in the acquisition process" (p. 45), but focused on semantic complexity (defined by criteria established by E. Clark, 1973) as a more important variable. Benson and Anglin (1981) found that an "ego" reference point was most common in the definitions provided by children and adults. Thus, <u>aunt</u>

might be defined as "your mother or father's sister" rather than as "a female who has nieces or nephews" (the latter being a reciprocal definition and supposedly more advanced). Although the "ego" reference point is compatible with the "moving ego" hypothesis proposed here, Benson and Anglin did not focus on the "child of" relation as central.

Based on the notion that the "child of" relation is of critical importance for the acquisition of the meaning of kinship terms, the following hypotheses were advanced: (1) kinship terms for which children do not need to move their ego to establish the correct relation (e.g., son, mother) will be acquired first. (2) Terms for which the "child of" relation must refer to someone other than the child (e.g., brother, grandmother, aunt) will be acquired later because the child must employ the "moving ego" strategy to successfully determine the meaning of such terms. These two hypotheses rest on the assumption that the child first establishes the meanings of kinship terms using the "child of" relation, using himself as the focal point of the relation. Later the child becomes able to employ the "moving ego" strategy and so use the basic "child of" relation to establish the meaning of terms in which the child's own ego is not a focal reference point. Thus, semantic complexity in the context of kinship terms is determined by how central the "child of" relation is for the meaning of a given term and by whether the child's own ego is an essential aspect of the term's meaning. For example, son may be represented as "X child of Y" where the child is male and X. Mommy may also be described as "X child of Y" where the child is X and the mother is Y. Sister has a slightly more complex description ("X child of Y", "Z child of Y", "Z is female"), and so should be acquired later than son or mother (for male children). Of course, with development these factors gain generality. However, even at their most general level, the factors rest on the child's relation to others and the child's ability to generalize on the basis of these learned self-other relations.

Method

Subjects. One hundred children ranging in age from 3;1 (years; months) to 7;9 participated in the present investigation. There were 20 children (ten males and ten females) in each of five age groups. The characteristics of each group were as follows: Group I - age range 3;1 to 3;10, $\bar{X}$ age = 3;7; Group II - age range 4;2 - 4;11, $\bar{X}$ age = 4;8; Group III - age range 5;0 to 5;11, $\bar{X}$ age = 5;6; Group IV - age range = 6;0 to 6;10, $\bar{X}$ age = 6;7; and Group V - age range = 7;1 to 7;10, $\bar{X}$ age = 7;6.

Procedure. Each child, tested individually, was given two tasks: (1) an interview task and (2) a comprehension task. The order of presentation of the two tasks was counterbalanced across sex and age.

Interview Task. The interview task focused on 28 kinship terms: mother, father, son, daughter, sister, brother, uncle, aunt, cousin, nephew, niece, step-brother, step-sister, step-mother, step-father, mother-in-law, father-in-law, sister-in-law, brother-in-law, grandmother, grandfather, great-grandmother, great-grandfather, great-aunt, great-uncle, parents, wife, and husband. For each term, the child was asked: (1) Do you have a _____?, and (2) What is a _____? The order of presentation of the 26 pairs of questions was random for each child.

At the conclusion of the interview, children were asked about the kinship relations of their parents and siblings. We were particularly interested in determining if children realized that an individual could hold more than one kinship relationship (e.g., that a father could also be a brother, that a son could also be a brother). These questions were scored independently of the other interview questions.

Comprehension Task. The comprehension task involved a set of dolls, a set of statements about the dolls, and the target question. The questions were designed to assess children's knowledge of each term. There were 224 target questions (112 with <u>yes</u> as the correct response, and 112 with <u>no</u> as the correct response. Examples of the statements and target questions are given below:

Target Term	Statement Set
1. Mother	X is Y's daughter.
2. Brother	X is Y's daughter.
	Z is Y's son.
3. Great-grandfather	X is Y's son.
	Z is X's son.
	Q is Z's son.
4. Mother	X is Y's sister.
5. Brother	X is Y's daughter.
	Z is Y's brother.
6. Great-grandfather	X is Y's son.
	Y is Z's son.

Target Question

1. Is Y X's mother?   (Yes)
2. Is Z X's brother?   (Yes)
3. Is Y Q's grandfather? (Yes)
4. Is Y X's mother?   (No)
5. Is Z X's brother?   (No)
6. Is Z X's great-grandfather? (No)

Note: The dolls varied along the dimensions of age and sex in order to ascertain the significance of these factors in children's understanding of kinship terms.

Results and Discussion

Interview Task. The results of the interview task will be considered first. Table 1 shows the percentage of <u>yes</u> responses to the "do you have a _____?" questions.

Table 1

Percentage of Yes responses to
"Do you have a _____?"

Age	Percentage
3	33.4
4	48.1
5	42.9
6	47.3
7	48.9

The difference in yes responses between the three-year-olds and four-year-olds most likely reflects the four-year-olds' greater knowledge of the target terms. The general strategy by the children seemed to be to respond "no" to the questions which contained terms which they found unfamiliar. Each child's parents were also surveyed in order to better determine the accuracy of the children's responses to the "do you have" questions. The results of this survey are shown in Table 2.

Table 2

Percentage of children's parents
who stated that their child
had a _____ (e.g., mother).

Percentage of Children	Term(s)
100	mother, father
75-99	grandmother, grandfather, parents
50-74	sister, brother, aunt uncle, cousin
25-49	great-grandmother
0-24	daughter, son, mother-in-law, father-in-law, nephew, niece, stepbrother, stepsister, stepmother, stepfather,

Percentage of Children	Term(s)
	sister-in-law, brother-in-law, great grandfather, great uncle, wife, husband.

The correlation between the parent's and the children's responses was rather small, r = .41. In general, the relation between parent and child responses increased with age.

Table 3 shows the percentage of correct responses each age group gave to the "what is a ____?" questions. As expected, performance improved with increasing age.

Table 3

Percentage of Correct Responses to "What is a ____?"

Age	Percentage
3	1.9
4	9.0
5	23.9
6	30.7
7	42.1

Based on their responses to the "What is a ____?" questions, children seemed to acquire the meaning of terms in four main steps: (1) mother, father, son, daughter, (2) brother, sister, (3) grandmother, grandfather, grandson, granddaughter, wife, husband, parent and (4) aunt, uncle, nephew, niece, cousin. The remaining terms did not appear to be acquired in any consistent fashion, most likely because the children were too young to evidence knowledge of the meanings of concern.

The correlation between "having a ____" and being able to correctly define a ____ was quite small, r = .14. Not only were children in many instances unable to define a term for which they said they had an instance, but there were also instances in which children were able to define a term for which they stated they did not have an instance.

Comprehension Task. The results from the comprehension task support those of the interview task in that the terms most likely to be responded to correctly in the interview task were also most likely to be responded to correctly in the comprehension task. Surprisingly, some of the children who gave correct definitions in the interview task did not consistently respond correctly in the comprehension task for the same term(s), suggesting that the comprehension task was more difficult than the interview task. The results from the comprehension task are given in Table 4.

Table 4

Percentage of correct responses to the questions in the comprehension task.

Age	Percentage
3	38.4
4	52.2
5	62.1
6	69.2
7	75.0

In addition to the above patterns of correct responses to the interview and comprehension tasks, the following error-patterns were observed: (1) young children are likely to treat both son and daughter as son (or both as daughter), depending on the child's sex. Children who are daughters are likely to treat both terms as daughter whereas those who are sons are most likely to treat both terms as son. (2) Depending on the sex of the children's siblings, young children are likely to treat brother and sister as brother (for those who have brothers) or as <u>sister</u> (for those who have sisters). This relation is also influenced by the sex of the child. Young children who are brothers seem most likely to treat the two terms as <u>brother</u>, but those who are sisters seem most likely to treat both terms as <u>sister</u>. (3) Both males and females are treated as <u>aunt</u> or <u>uncle</u>. This error does not depend on whether children have primarily aunts or uncles. Instead of being based on individual experience as in the case of <u>son</u>/<u>daughter</u> and <u>brother</u>/<u>sister</u>, this error seems to reflect a more general lack of awareness of the importance of sex in the definition of kinship terms. (Note: the error of equating male and female opposites for a given kinship relation did not extend to parents or grandparents. No child equated <u>mother</u> and <u>father</u> or <u>grandmother</u> and <u>grandfather</u>. (4) Children commonly restricted terms inappropriately. The most common error involved age. For example, adults were inappropriately excluded from being brothers or sons. Other errors involved sex. For example, several children thought that only boys could be cousins. (5) Initially, children did not understand that they or their nuclear family members could be part of more than one kinship relation. For example, many children failed to recognize that one individual can be both a father and a son. Nor did they recognize that an individual can be both a son and a brother. Children appear to learn that they may be more than one relation (e.g., a brother and a son) before doing so for other members of their family.

Conclusion

The data support the notion that the acquisition of the kinship term semantic system is based on the "child of" relation, reflecting children's centration on their own relations to others. The kinship term system expands as children become able to use a "moving ego" comparison point. Initially, then, terms in which "X is child of Y" and X is the child are acquired. Next come terms in which X is someone other than the child. Terms which involve multiple relations (e.g., sister = "X child of Y" and "Z child of Y" and X is female) are acquired later than those with fewer relations. Few of the children understand concepts such as step-mother and mother-in-law, reflecting their lack of understanding of kinship relations based on legal rather than blood relations. For legally determined terms, the first to be acquired are husband and wife.

These results and speculations fit well, albeit not perfectly, with the findings of previous investigators (see Benson and Anglin, 1981; Chambers and Tavuchis, 1976; Haviland and Clark, 1974). Moreover, the hypothesis concerning the importance of the "child of" relation has a historical precursor in Baldwin's (1911) suggestion that the concepts of self and other develop in mutual interdependence (see also Bretherton and Beeghly, in press). Baldwin's view may be roughly restated as follows: the concept of self depends on the concept of others (or another). Regarding kinship relations, the child must comprehend both self and other, and correctly relate the two. The child must also learn to use the "moving ego" strategy, which allows others to be substituted for the self in kinship relations and thereby expand the kinship semantic system. In order to use the "moving ego" strategy, the child must free himself from his centration on the self. The development of the semantic system rests on a number of factors: (1) the child's developing concepts of self and others, (2) the child's centration on the "child of" relation, this reflecting the child's centration on the self, and (3) the child's decentration and learning to employ the "moving ego" strategy.

References

Baldwin, J.M. The individual and society. Boston: Goreham Press, 1911.

Bretherton, I., & Beeghly, M. Talking about internal states: the acquisition of an explicit theory of mind. *Developmental Psychology*, in press.

Benson, N.J., & Anglin, J.M. The child's knowledge of English kin terms. Paper presented at the Biennial Meeting of the Society for Research in Child Development, Boston, April, 1981.

Clark. H.H. Space, time, semantics, and the child. In T. Moore (Ed.), *Cognitive development and the acquisition of language*. New York: Academic Press, 1973.

Chambers, J.C., & Tavuchis, N. Kids and kin: Children's understanding of American kin terms. *Journal of Child Language*, 1976, $\underline{3}$, 63-80.

Haviland, S.E., & Clark, E.V. 'This man's father is my father's son': A study of the acquisition of English kin terms. *Journal of Child Language*, 1974, $\underline{1}$, 23-48.

SEMANTICS OF MODAL AUXILIARY VERB USES BY PRESCHOOL CHILDREN

Roy D. Pea
Bank Street College and Clark University,
Heinz Werner Institute for Developmental Psychology

& Ronald Mawby
Clark University

Modal auxiliaries are a dominant verb phrase form in the language of preschoolers (Fletcher, 1979; Wells, 1979), and a major means for expressing the modal aspects of thought so central to human mentality (e.g. Johnson-Laird, 1978; Lyons, 1977; Miller, 1977; Pieraut-Le Bonniec, 1980), yet the study of the semantics of modal and quasi-modal auxiliaries has been generally neglected. This is not altogether surprising, since modals in adult language are notoriously complex (e.g. Lyons, 1977; Palmer, 1979), expressing a variety of modalities and interacting in surprising ways with negation (e.g. Miller & Kwilosz-Lyons, 1980; Wertheimer, 1972). Nonetheless, we believe it is important to provide a preliminary characterization of an early period in the ontogenesis of modal semantics, which we will then discuss from the geneticdramatistic perspective on lexical development (Pea & Kaplan, 1981). We will confine our attention here to modal and quasi-modal auxiliary verbs (see Table 1), primarily because, unlike modal adverbs such as "perhaps", modal adjectives such as "necessary" or

---
(Insert Table 1 here)

"possible", and modal inflections such as "-able", they occupy the most central position among modal linguistic forms in the current grammatical structure of English (Lyons, 1977, p. 802).

Our goals for this initial inquiry into early modal semantics were: (1) to characterize which modals and quasi-modals preschool children use, in a range of settings representative for the talk of preschoolers; (2) to develop a system of semantic categories for the analysis of uses of such expressions, informed by work in modal logic by linguists and philosophers; (3) concurrent with the second goal, to characterize the general bodies of knowledge, or modalities, which appear to be invoked in preschoolers' uses of such expressions, and the extent to which affirmative versus negative values of such modalities are utilized in their talk; and (4) to characterize, insofar as possible given the brevity of this paper, the interconnections of the semantics of modal auxiliary development with their pragmatic and synactic aspects, and the complexities of children's lives. To these ends, we chose to study a corpus of children's utterances taking place in a wide range of activities and over an extended period of interactions with agents of different status. The talk of preschoolers in a nursery, between peers and with their teacher, satisfied these requirements. Had our purpose been to "assess" what any individual child does with modals, our research strategies would have been quite different.

Six children, three boys and three girls, from white professional families attended a nursery at Rockefeller University[1] for two hours a day, four days a week, over a period of seven months, and were regularly videotaped in a variety of contexts, such as free play, snack time, arts and crafts, and cleaning-up. The children ranged in age from 28 to 34 months when the nursery recordings began. Utterances and aspects of the environmental context were transcribed and entered onto computer tapes for subsequent analysis. Seven videotaped sessions across the seven months of recording with a total length of nine hours were selected for analysis. The total number of child utterances during these nine hours of nursery activity was 4027.

Four principal modalities have been distinguished by linguists and philosophers in their discussions of modal logics and their relationships to natural language expressions of modal concepts. These modalities appear to be necessary for the characterization of modal auxiliary semantics for adult English. Schematic definitions of the four modalities, or bodies of knowledge which may be invoked in the use of natural language modal expressions, are presented in Table 2.

205

(Insert Table 2 here)

The PRAGMATIC modality is comprised of two distinguishable but related modalities, the DYNAMIC and the DEONTIC. The DYNAMIC modality is concerned with the <u>logic of actions</u>, and such questions as whether or not an agent has the ability to accomplish an act, or whether it is necessary that the agent do X in order to accomplish an act. The DEONTIC modality is concerned with such questions as whether or not an agent has <u>permission</u> or is <u>obligated</u> to do some act. The deontic modality is related to the dynamic in ways such as the following: if one is unable to do X, one cannot be obligated to do X. The EPISTEMIC modality is concerned with the <u>logic of knowledge or belief claims</u>, such as whether or not some event is necessary or possible, given inferences from factual knowledge. The ALETHIC modality was the first studied extensively by philosophers, and is concerned with whether propositions expressed in utterances are or are not <u>logically necessary or possible</u> (hence unconcerned with 'fact').

One point of interest for the developmental study of modals is that the interdefinability of possibility and necessity cross-cuts all four modalities. For example, as shown in Table 3, p is necessary if and only if it is

----
(Insert Table 3 here)
----

not possible that p is not the case. This interdefinability of modals by means of negation has the consequence that systematic logical relationships, such as contradiction and contrariety, are expressible with modal auxiliaries, and may be exploited in conversational inferences. Also note that negation may, across all modalities, modify modals in two different ways, either <u>de dicto</u> (- , -), which includes the modal operator, as in "it is not permissible for you to leave", or <u>de re</u> (-, -), in which the negation modifies only the clause and not the modal, as in "it is possible for you to not go outside".

RESULTS

A general summary of results provides some indication of the predominent features of preschoolers' uses of modals and quasi-modals in nursery settings. Of the 4027 child utterances, 395 of them (10%)[2] used at least one modal or quasi-modal auxiliary verb[2], for a total of 418 of such terms. Two or more such terms were used in only 21 of the 395 utterances (5%). Further, of all of the modals used, 89% (373) were categorizable, 8% were incompleted utterances or inaudible, and 3% were ambiguous between modalities. Our semantic analyses made extensive use of the discourse context, including prior topics and subsequent responses to and elaborations of the specific modal utterance being analysed, as well as details of the environmental context. Two experienced coders working independently concurred on 91% of the total set of assignments to modal semantic categories.

Table 4 summarizes these findings by modality and by modal values. Four principle groups of modals may be
----
(Insert Table 4 here)
----
distinguished. The epistemic modality value of possibility was extremely common in the children's utterances, a finding due in large part to the predominance of volitional[3] statements such as "I'll give you a little tiny fork" (170 of the 217 epistemic modality cases: 78%), or 46% of all occurrences of modals. The second group are the modals of the dynamic modality, or 24% of the total. The third group are the modals of the deontic modality, or 18% of the total, with the fourth group, the remaining epistemics, accounting for 13% of the total. Examples of each of these categories are presented in Table 5.

(Insert Table 5 here)

Next, one may ask which modal values are predominant in the children's uses of modals, irrespective of the particular modality concerned. It is very striking that the modals which convey the affirmative modal values of necessity and possibility together represent 91% of all the modals the children used. Negatives occurred only once in every twelve uses of modals by the preschoolers. Several notable gaps occurred in negative modal values. For the DEONTIC modality, children did not express either the permission to not do, or non-obligation, as in "I don't have to do that". For the DYNAMIC modality, the practical possibility of not doing some act was also not expressed. In fact, almost all of the negative modals either expressed constraints on action or an unwillingness to act AT THE TIME OF SPEAKING. In other words, there was little spatiotemporal distance between the negative modal symbolic act and the event to which it referred.

Similarly prominent is the absence of modal uses for the alethic modality. Such young children did not discuss the logical possibility or necessity of propositions expressed in utterances, just as we might expect given the great difficulty with such conceptions for much older children revealed in Osherson & Markman's (1974/1975) work.

Many of the most fascinating findings concern the frequencies and modal values for the individual modals used (see Table 6), which we may but briefly refer to

---

(Insert Table 6 here)

---

here. The children's choices of modals were selective, and many affirmative terms were used without negative counterparts. MAY, MUST, OUGHT (TO), and SHALL were never used; MIGHT, SHOULD, and WOULD were rarely used. Only a few terms, such as CAN, CAN'T, COULD, and HAVE TO were used to convey the three remaining modalities; others such as GONNA were restricted to a single modality.

From the holistic framework for lexical development of Genetic-Dramatism outlined earlier in this session (Pea & Kaplan, 1982), we may view the modal terms used as INSTRUMENTALITIES which embody the ACTION an AGENT engages in for a PURPOSE, taking place with respect to a SCENE, which may be either a concrete environmental context, or at some symbolic remove from the current physical setting (e.g., next year; Easter; in a fairy tale). We have observed several prototypic features of the uses of modals in this corpus, which may be compared to lexical developmental goals:

(1) the scenes of modality are almost always current environmental or discourse contexts, rather than symbolic scenes at some temporal or spatial distance from modal speech acts; even announcements of intentions to act are with reference to plans just about to be enacted. The "distancing" (Werner & Kaplan, 1963) of modal speech acts from their referential events is thus a critical development rarely manifested in the preschoolers' modal talk.

(2) the actions of modal purpose are most frequently self-oriented and volitional or wishful in nature (e.g. permission requests, action requests, internal reports) rather than world or other-oriented (e.g. attributions) and predictive or explanatory. The will-do is thus much more basic to the children's talk than the will-happen.

(3) different agent-statuses may be taken on by the preschoolers in pretend play scenes, but generally are a reflection of family roles. The modalities in such scenes were predominantly DEONTIC and "authority"-based, e.g. "You will be the grownup" as the child assigns a make-believe status role to another child.

(4) the purposes of modality are remarkably diverse, from soliciting help in order to accomplish subgoals of higher-order goals, to obtaining permission, to taking power in toy-possession negotiations, to soliciting attention by proudly asserting new achievements or physical abilities. The same purpose (e.g. conveying the modal concept of epistemic possibility) was often achieved by different instrumentalities (e.g., "can", "could"), but some lexical terms serve a greater diversity of purposes in adult English than in the children's talk, such as "will" for promises, and "need to" for stating obligations.

In conclusion, we probably do not need to state that we have but scratched the surface of child modality. But at least we have manned the shovels. We must confess that one goal for our paper was left unstated - our wish that you might also be enticed to engage in the study of modal semantic development. The great riches of human intelligence, creativity, and sociality are perhaps nowhere more apparent than in modal language. Locked within the expression and understanding of modals throughout childhood and adulthood lie, we believe, many mysteries: of moral development, of the development of planning, of the understanding of power and status, of scientific and aesthetic understanding, of the construction of a theory of mind. What remains is the necessity of their study.

FOOTNOTES

[1] Laboratory staff, facilities, data collection, transcription, and proof-editing were supported by a grant from the Grant Foundation to Professor George A. Miller. Some of the analyses in this paper were supported by NIMH Traineeship #15125 to the first author while at Rockefeller University.

[2] For purposes of exposition, we will refer to these collectively as "modals" throughout the remainder of this paper. In addition, but not a focus of analysis here, the children used "want to/wanna" 241 times and "don't want to/don't wanna" 18 times. The complexities of "want" (e.g. Wilensky, 1977) warrant a separate study, now in progress. "I want X" is often, though not always, used to accomplish the same ends as "Can I have X?"

[3] Ninety-three percent of 115 uses of "gonna", and 87% of 55 uses of "will" (as well as 100% of the 259 uses of affirmative and negative forms of "want to") expressed volition, and of these, most sentence subjects were first person (80%, 81%, and 95%, respectively, for the different terms). Relatively few predictive uses of such terms occurred for non-volitional events or even volitional events of other persons than the child.

REFERENCES

Fletcher, P. The development of the verb phrase. In P. Fletcher & M.Garman (Eds.), Language Acquisition: Studies in First Language Development. Cambridge: Cambridge University Press, 1979.

Hintikka, J. Knowledge and Belief. Ithaca, N.Y.: Cornell University Press, 1962.

Johnson-Laird, P.N. The meaning of modality. Cognitive Science, 1978, 2, 17-26.

Lewis, C.I. & Langford, C.H. Symbolic Logic. New York: Dover, 1932.

Lyons, J. Semantics. (2 vols.) Cambridge: Cambridge University Press, 1977.

McCawley, J.D. Everything that Linguists have Always Wanted to Know about Logic* :*but were ashamed to ask. Chicago: University of Chicago Press, 1981.

Miller, G.A. How people think about modal verbs. Colloquium paper presented at University of Minnesota, April 4, 1977.

Miller, G.A. & Kwilosz-Lyons, D.M. Interactions of modality and negation in English. In A. Yoshi, B. Nash-Webber & I. Sag (Eds.), Elements of Discourse Understanding. Cambridge: Cambridge University Press, 1981.

Osherson, D. & Markman, E. Language and the ability to evaluate contradictions and tautologies. Cognition, 1974-75, 3, 213-226.

Palmer, F.R. Modality and the English Modals. London: Longman, 1979.

Pea, R.D. & Kaplan, B. Lexical development from the perspective of genetic-dramatism. In C.E. Johnson & C.L. Thew (Eds.), Proceedings of the Second International Congress for the Study of Child Language, Vol. I. Washington, D.C.: University Press of America, 1982,

294-311.

Pieraut-Le Bonniec, G. The Development of Modal Reasoning: Genesis of Necessity and Possibility Notions. New York: Academic Press, 1980.

Rescher, N. The Logic of Commands. London: Routledge & Kegan Paul, 1966.

Wells, C.G. Learning and using the auxiliary verb in English. In V. Lee (Ed.), Cognitive Development: Language and Thinking from Birth to Adolescence. London: Croom Helm, 1979.

Werner, H. & Kaplan, B. Symbol Formation. New York: John Wiley, 1963.

Wertheimer, R. The Significance of Sense: Meaning, Modality, and Morality. Ithaca, N.Y.: Cornell University Press, 1972.

Wilensky, R. A conceptual analysis of the verbs "need" and "want". Cognitive Science, 1977, $\underline{1}$.

Wright, G.H. von An Essay in Deontic Logic and the General Theory of Action. (Acta Philosophica Fennica, 21). Amsterdam: North-Holland, 1968.

Wright, G.H. von An Essay in Modal Logic. Amsterdam: North-Holland, 1951.

Wright, G.H. von Norm and Action. London: Routledge & Kegan Paul, 1963.

Table 1. Modal and quasi-modal auxiliary verbs[a]

MODALS	QUASI-MODALS
*can	going to/ *gonna
*cannot/*can't/can not	*not going to/ *not gonna
*could	*got to/ *gotta
could not/couldn't	don't got to/don't gotta
may	*had better
may not	had better not
must	*have to
must not	*have to not/*not have to
*need	ought to
need not/*not need	ought to not/ought not to
*might	*supposed to
might not	supposed to not/not supposed to
shall	
shall not/shan't	
*should	
should not	
*will	
will not/*won't	
*would	
would not/wouldn't	

([a] Words or phrases marked by an asterisk occurred at least once in the corpus non-imitatively)

Table 2. Four Modalities for Modal and Quasi-Modal Auxiliaries

(Note: the coding categories for the semantics of modal and quasi-modal auxiliary verbs are derived from a survey of the substantial philosophical and linguistic literature on the various modalities; sources to which we owe substantial debts are cited in the descriptions of the various categories. Table 5 provides examples of children's utterances expressing these modalities.)

Four principle modalities are distinguished: DEONTIC, DYNAMIC, EPISTEMIC, and ALETHIC, the first two subsumed under the PRAGMATIC generic modality, since they each concern the conditions of action.

DEONTIC

This modality is concerned with the possibility (permission) or necessity (obligation) of acts performed by agents, which derives from some source or cause (e.g. another agent allows permission, or obligates one; or one obligates another by command; see Lyons, 1977; von Wright, 1951, 1968; Rescher, 1966).
   e.g. It is necessary that I pay my income tax by April 15th.

DYNAMIC

This modality is concerned with the logic of actions basic to deontic logic, such as whether an agent has the ability to accomplish an act (von Wright, 1963), or whether it is necessary to do X/have X to accomplish an act.
   e.g. It is necessary that I use the screwdriver to open the safe.

EPISTEMIC

This modality is concerned with the logical structure of statements which assert or imply that a (set) of proposition(s) is known or believed (Hintikka, 1962; Lyons, 1977, p. 793; McCawley, 1981). The factuality of the proposition(s) for knowers/believers is at issue here.
   e.g. It is necessary that Ronald Reagan is President of the United States.

ALETHIC

This modality is concerned with the truth of propositions. The distinction between necessary and possible (contingent) truth is one made in the alethic modality (Lyons, 1977; Pieraut-Le Bonniec, 1980; von Wright, 1951).
   e.g. It is necessary that you are either reading or not reading this sentence.

Table 3. Modalities and Modal Values[a]

Symbolic Representation	DYNAMIC	DEONTIC	EPISTEMIC	ALETHIC
☐ p	necessary to do	obligated to do	necessary	necessary
◇ p	possible to do	permitted to do	possible	possible
☐ -p	necessary to not do	obligated to not do	necessary not	necessary not
-◇ p	impossible to do	not permitted to do	impossible	impossible
-☐ p	not necessary to do	not obligated to do	not necessary	not necessary
◇ -p	possible to not do	permitted to not do	possible not	possible not

MODAL INTERDEFINABILITY: Either necessity or possibility may be treated as primitive, and the other term defined in terms of the primitive and negation. So, for **necessity**:

☐ p = -◇-p   (p is necessary if and only if it is not possible that p is not the case)

and for **possibility**:

◇ p = -☐-p   (p is possible if and only if it is not necessary that p is not the case)

---

[a]The semantic categories which are common to all of the modalities in their logical form conform to a variant of the Aristotelian logical square which incorporates de re and de dicto negations, i.e., those of both narrow and wide scope (Pieraut-Le Bonniec, 1980). Traditionally, de re categories of the modalities have been neglected, but negations of different scope do have different logical status. Many natural language statements which involve scope of negation and modal value are ambiguous between two interpretations, even within a specific modality, such as "I can't go to the movie", which may mean either OBLIGATED TO NOT GO or NOT PERMITTED TO GO (de re necessity and de dicto possibility, respectively). The semantic category modal values may be symbolically represented in the same way, regardless of the modality. We have used the standard Lewis & Langford (1932) notation. KEY: "☐" = necessary; "◇" = possible; " - " = negation; "p" = any proposition.

Table 4. The Frequencies of Modal Values Expressed in Preschoolers' Uses of Modals and Quasi-Modals

	DYNAMIC	DEONTIC	EPISTEMIC	ALETHIC	TOTALS
necessary	64	17	4	0	85
possible	10	42	201	0	253
necessary not	1			0	1
	----------	(8)[a] -----	(5) ----------		(13) --
impossible	11			0	11
not necessary	3	0		0	3
			(6) ----------		(6) --
possible not	0	0		0	0
TOTALS PER MODALITY	89	67	217[b]	0	373[b]
PERCENT PER MODALITY OF TOTAL CODABLE[c] TERMS	24%	18%	58%	0%	100%

[a] Numbers within parentheses for negative modal or quasi-modal uses refer to cases which are ambiguous between two different modal values within a modality.

[b] One miscellaneous case is included in these column totals, ambiguous between de re and de dicto possibility (◊-p and -◊p).

[c] Twelve cases occurred which were ambiguous across modalities, and 33 cases were either incompleted utterances or inaudible.

Table 5. Examples of modal and quasi-modal child utterances expressing the modal values of affirmative(+) and negative(-) possibility and necessity for the dynamic, deontic, and epistemic modalities[a]

DYNAMIC MODALITY[b]

	Possibility	Necessity
(+)	I can wash. I can flush the toilet too.	I nee...,I need a cup. (while holding milk carton)
(-)	I can't reach. I'm not big enough to reach. (light switch)	I don' need it. (rejecting offer of tissue)

DEONTIC MODALITY

	Possibility (Permission)	Necessity (Obligation)
(+)	Now could I have it?	Have to go wash your hands! (pretend mother at dinner)
(-)	You can't come to my house[c].	

EPISTEMIC MODALITY

	Possibility	Necessity
(+)	Sue, if you didn't want that other pretzel, I would eat it.	And now I turn off the light. This way, uhm, then then if this is in then, that thing in, in that will have to go to bed. (re: turning off plant box light; teacher has told them it makes the plants "sleep")
(-)	It can't fit, it won't fit on top of it.	

[a] Space constraints do not allow the inclusion of all discourse and environmental context utilized in the semantic categorization of these utterances. The modal which is the focus of the example is underscored.

[b] The various modalities are defined in Table 2.

[c] Note for the deontic and epistemic modalities that the negative examples are ambiguous between necessary not (□-p) and not possible (-◇p) interpretations. Other cases are ambiguous between not necessary (-□p) and possible not (◇-p) interpretations, but are not included here for ease of exposition.

217

Table 6. Frequency distribution of modal and quasi-modal auxiliary verb uses by modal semantic category and modal value

Lexical term(s)	Total#	Semantic modality (modal value)[a]	Frequency	% of total #[b]
(1) CAN	(48)	deontic permission	29	60
		epistemic possibility	6	13
		dynamic possibility	5	10
		incomplete/inaudible	5	10
		cross-modally ambiguous	3	6
(2) CAN'T	(30)	dynamic possibility	10	33
		deontic (obligated not/ not permitted)	7	23
		incomplete/inaudible	7	23
		epistemic (necessary not/ not possible)	4	13
		dynamic (necessary not)	1	3
		epistemic (not possible/ possible not)	1	3
(3) COULD	(30)	deontic permission	12	40
		epistemic possibility	9	30
		dynamic possibility	5	17
		cross-modally ambiguous	2	7
		dynamic (not possible)	1	3
		incomplete/inaudible	1	3
(4) GONNA	(124)	epistemic possibility	123	99
		incomplete/inaudible	1	1
(5) NOT GONNA	(2)	epistemic (not necessary/ possible not)	1	50
		incomplete/inaudible	1	50
(6) GOT TO	(4)	deontic obligation	2	50
		dynamic necessity	1	25
		cross-modally ambiguous	1	25
(7) HAD BETTER	(1)	dynamic necessity	1	100
(8) HAVE TO	(54)	dynamic necessity	24	44
		deontic necessity	14	26
		incomplete/inaudible	8	15
		cross-modally ambiguous	6	11
		epistemic necessity	2	4

[a] Within-modality ambiguities with negation are noted by the listing of both negative modal values.

[b] Total percentages per lexical term may not equal 100% due to rounding.

Table 6 (continued)

Lexical term(s)	Total#	Semantic modality (modal value)	Frequency	% of total #
(9) NOT HAVE TO/	(2)	deontic (obligated not/not permitted)	1	50
		incomplete/inaudible	1	50
(10) MIGHT	(1)	epistemic possibility	1	100
(11) NEED (TO)	(42)	dynamic necessity	38	90
		incomplete/inaudible	4	10
(12) DON'T NEED	(3)	dynamic (not necessary)	3	100
(13) SHOULD	(2)	epistemic necessity	1	50
		deontic permission	1	50
(14) SUPPOSED TO	(1)	epistemic necessity	1	100
(15) NOT SUPPOSED	(1)	incomplete	1	100
(16) WILL	(59)	epistemic possibility	54	92
		incomplete/inaudible	4	7
		deontic obligation	1	2
(17) WON'T	(6)	epistemic (not necessary/ possible not)	5	83
		epistemic (necessary not/ not possible)	1	17
(18) WOULD	(8)	epistemic possibility	8	100

LANGUAGE AND THE COGNITIVE BREAKTHROUGH AT AGE SIX

H. Stephen Straight

State University of New York at Binghamton

In recent years many challenges have been posed to the Piagetian outline of cognitive development, on both theoretical and empirical grounds. Of course, none of these challenges has attempted to deny the evidence for profound cognitive differences between the typical school-age child ("7-year-old") and the typical preschool child ("5-year-old"). The standard Piaget-type argument, though, is controversial: Sevens and fives are said to perceive and act in fundamentally different ways because of major *qualitative* differences between them resulting from essentially *maturational* changes in thought processes that occur between the ages of five and seven. But even if these differences were shown to result from purely *quantitative* rather than qualitative changes (increases in attention and memory spans, for example), or from changes in *environment* rather than from maturational factors (entry into school, for example), the cognitive differences would still be there to be explained. And even if they were to prove to be highly variable from culture to culture and susceptible to acceleration or reordering through instructional means, a theory of mental growth must in some way account for the systematic differences between 5-year-olds and 7-year-olds with regard to many dimensions of learning, perception, and language.

My aim today will therefore *not* be to demonstrate the "age six" timing of a "cognitive breakthrough", though I do believe that a sweeping change in linguistic and non-linguistic functioning at about this age is supported by the evidence.

Unfortunately, this evidence is so extensive and diverse, and controversial, that even a cursory review of it would take several hours longer than I have to talk to you today. Moreover, I could speak for days and convince you merely that a multitude of cognitive differences separates the typical 5-year-old from the typical 7-year-old. Neither you nor I would be likely in the process to achieve an understanding of how such cognitive differences derive from specific physiological or social or other causes. It is bound to be difficult to integrate such findings as the following (from White, 1965, except for item 5):

1. Seven-year-olds can transpose learned discriminations of relative size to examples presented both nearer and farther than the training presentation, but five-year-olds transpose only to the nearer examples (Kuenne, 1946).

2. Seven-year-olds prefer visual exploring, but five-year-olds prefer the tactual mode (Schopler, 1964).

3. Seven-year-olds can tell their left from their right side, but five-year-olds cannot (Piaget, 1959).

4. Seven-year-olds report sensation on both face and hand when the two are touched simultaneously, but five-year-olds report only the touch to the face (Fink and Bender, 1953).

5. Seven-year-olds ignore differences in angle of view in face-matching tests, but five-year-olds overdiscriminate (Saltz and Sigel, 1967).

6. Seven-year-olds exhibit the adult pattern of speech distortion when auditory feedback is delayed, but five-year-olds are typically immune to this effect (Chase et al., 1961).

If I were to go beyond this ever-lengthening recitation of American research results to review the cross-cultural evidence, our collective bewilderment would no doubt reach paralytic proportions. The possible effective variables are quite consistently intertwined: Nutrition, neurophysiological maturation rate, early socialization practices, genetic background, and numerous other factors have been implicated, but no single study takes them all into account.

I will therefore limit myself in this short presentation to just a few of the *linguistic* aspects of the age-six cognitive breakthrough, though in a work currently in preparation I hope to present a fuller treatment of the phenomenon along with some empirical research comparing five-year-olds with seven-year-olds with regard to some potentially critical linguistic functions. The linguistic examples I will focus on here lie in the area of semantics, and a bit of syntax, but phonological and pragmatic, and other syntactic, changes do occur in conjunction with these.

Perhaps the best-known example of a linguistic change that occurs at about age six is the shift from so-called *syntagmatic* to so-called *paradigmatic* responses in word-association tests:

Stimulus	Paradigmatic Response	Syntagmatic Response
BIG	little	house
RED	black	truck
TALL	high	man
TREE	bush	green
WALK	run	fast
DUCK	goose	rubber

The 7-year-old tends to give many instances of antonymous, synonymous, and other coordinate associates which are typically members of the same word class (hence, "paradigmatic"), but the five-year-old tends to respond with words that could combine ("syntagmatically") with the stimulus word in clausal constructions. In her 1977 survey of this topic, Katherine Nelson concluded that the factors behind this shift are numerous. A key element, though, is some sort of reorganization of the information the child has available for the comprehension and production of individual words, or--if not a reorganization of this information--at least a change in the way this information is manipulated during the word-association task. That is, 7-year-olds respond with words that 5-year-olds recognize and use, but they do so in a way that can be related to the stimulus by processes of selective retention of the meaning of the stimulus to yield a response close in meaning to it. Five-year-olds, in contrast, more often give associates that are relatable to the stimulus only by means of particular imagined instances of co-occurrence of the concepts labelled by the two words (see examples above).

In addition to the syntagmatic-paradigmatic shift, a number of other related changes can be discerned in children's ways of dealing with words during the five-to-seven period. A sampling of these may be suggestive:

1. Emergence of semantically-based, as opposed to phonetically-based, generalization in operant conditioning (Naroditskaya, 1956). For example, response to <u>tall</u> may generalize to <u>high</u> for 7-year-olds but to <u>ball</u> (on the basis of rhyming) for 5-year-olds.

2. Achievement of adult-like judgments of word similarity (Flavell and Stedman, 1961), including similarities in emotive meaning as measured by the semantic differential test (Maltz, 1963; DiVesta, 1966).

3. Ability to give synonyms in word definition tasks (Werner and Kaplan, 1952).

4. Ability to interpret and produce so-called "syncategorimatic" adjectives, such as <u>good</u>, which are variable in their import--and truth value--according to what description of an object they are modifying. Five-year-olds have difficulty understanding that a <u>good baseball player</u> who plays the violin is not necessarily a <u>good violinist</u>. Similarly, a <u>big ant</u> is not necessarily a <u>big insect</u>.

5. Sharp increase in appropriate understanding and varied use of causal connectives such as <u>since</u> and <u>because</u>, or logical connectives such as <u>but</u> and <u>then</u> (from Piaget, after White, 1965: 211).

What I propose as a way to account for these and many other related phenomena is a shift at about age six away from words as the central unit in the organization of semantic and syntactic information. In place of words, the seven-year-old begins to employ more abstract features of meaning as the minimal units to be manipulated during the comprehension and production of linguistic forms. Furthermore, I hypothesize that the ways in which these minimal units are organized after age six are modelled on the ways in which words are organized in sentences. That is, the meanings of clauses as wholes come to be relatable to each other in hierarchical ways by means of such abstract features as CAUSATION or CONTRADICTION or TEMPORAL PRIORITY (or even SUBORDINATE--cf. Ingram, 1975, and previously cited examples of causal and logical connectives). And the meanings of individual words come to be clausal in form, so that <u>butcher</u>, for example, becomes decomposable into some such hierarchical nominal construction as 'person who cuts meat for a living'. Furthermore, this reorganization of the information in the lexicon depends upon syntax not only for its structure but probably also for its very emergence: The syntactic features that young children clearly employ in the comprehension and production of clausal constructions (for example, agents, objects, actions, states, instruments, locations, and so on) are among the earliest aspects of the componential structure of words. At the same time, the earlier, more holistic conceptions of word meaning do not simply go away but are rather refined into the "prototypic representations" that we find operative in older children and adults.

What I am arguing, then, is that the 5-year-old has, for the most part, singulary, global representations of word meanings while the 7-year-old has, to a great extent, two rather different but coexisting ways of representing meanings:

EARLIER	LATER
holistic	componential
core-conceptual	featural
prototypical	criterial
experiential	logical
Gestaltic	decompositional
episodic	hierarchical
global	analytic
spatial-geometric	linear-algebraic
iconic	symbolic
concrete	abstract

The newer mode of semantic organization is in terms of features of a logical sort derived from continuing dissection of the commonalities of meaning among all the words in the child's vocabulary and arranged in the form of propositional constructions built up on the model of sentences and of the aspects of word meaning that necessarily depend upon propositional structures even at an early age (Macnamara, Baker, and Olson, 1976). But the older way, that continues to develop after age six, is in terms of sensorimotor categories that define the prototypical instances of the objects, events, or attributes labelled by words (Rosch et al., 1976). This representation provides access to idealized scenarios in which the concepts labelled by the words occur (Anderson, 1976) and also to episodic memories of experienced instances of those concepts (Tulving, 1972).

It is tantalizing to suggest, first, that these two radically different modes of semantic organization may develop out of the single earlier mode through the differentiation of analytic, linear mental processes and global, spatial processes associated with the lateralization of brain functions by about age five (Krashen and Harshman, 1972). Recent neurolinguistic research (Bub and Whitaker, 1981) suggests that some sort of "visual coding" of word meanings may be specific to the right hemisphere of the brain, while the more componential coding occurs in the left hemisphere. This line of explanation would treat the five-year-old's system as an undifferentiated but variegated coding that is neither fully "global" nor fully "analytic".

A second possible line of explanation would be to suppose that the accumulation of non-componentialized representations of word meanings prior to age six becomes burdensome. Perhaps this mode of information storage and manipulation simply grows to its limit, or at least to some cognitively critical level, and then triggers the new modes of differentiation and integration of meanings as a move toward "cognitive economy". This line of causation would allow for a great deal of cultural relativity, as environments may differ in their experiential-cognitive complexity.

Yet a third possibility is that, for reasons that are not at all specific to language, arising from a general development of decentration (cf. Braunwald,1981), the child begins to reflect upon its own output during the five-to-seven period. (Remember, also, the change toward susceptibility to delayed auditory feedback, mentioned earlier, and Louise Cherry Wilkinson's observations at this congress on metalinguistic awareness.) Such self-consciousness, which would most probably be linked importantly to the change in importance of inhibitory neural pathways cited in Sheldon White's 1965 review of the age-six shift, would necessarily result in recognition of various mismatches between the productive and the interpretive linguistic mechanisms of the child (Straight, 1976, 1980). These mismatches could only be alleviated by close attentiveness to the often rather small differences in the conceptual representations that are associated, on the one hand, with words as input to interpretive processes and, on the other hand, with words as output from formulative processes (cf. Goldin-Meadow et al., 1976). The child who notices that its own description of a tennis ball as "furry" sounds funny is in a good position to sort out the semantic differences that separate furry from fuzzy. This line of causation would allow for a great deal of influence from specific instruction, which typically includes enhanced--even *enforced*--self-consciousness.

Whatever the mechanism or mechanisms whereby the change takes place, and all three of the above factors might contribute to it simultaneously, what emerges from this examination of language and the cognitive breakthrough is that at about age six children shift from (1) a predominance of Gestaltic, imagistic word meanings in a linguistic system that componentializes meanings only to the extent demanded in the processes of *clause* formation and interpretation to (2) a predominance of analytic, logical features of meaning that are abstracted from the meanings of particular words and phrases and then used to construct complex ideas that may be bigger than, smaller than, or different from extant linguistic forms. It is the 7-year-old who will say, "I've forgotten: What's a baby aardvark called?", by separating out the babyhood feature from words like puppy, calf, kitten, etc. and recombining it with the constellation that underlies aardvark to create a possible lexical item for which there is, to my knowledge, no phonological form. The older child's gradually emerging ability to comprehend and create metaphoric and other "analogical" uses of words and sentences, without losing the ability to recognize and use them in their usual sense, reveals the most obvious examples of this post-six separability and manipulability of features of word meaning (cf. Gardner et al., 1978). This increasing flexibility in the language of children can, according to the view presented here, be seen as late effects of a basic and far-reaching reorganization of the semantic system that occurs at about age six.

Acknowledgments

The approach taken to semantic development in this paper has grown out of an essay on "Syntax, Semantics, and Cognitive Development" presented in partial fulfillment of the requirements for the master's degree in the Department of Linguistics at the University of Chicago in 1970. Wilbur Hass and Carol Feldman, my teachers in developmental psycholinguistics, provided essential encouragement and criticism in the development of these ideas both before and after that date. Also, Robert A. Rubinstein and Nancy Wakeman, two students at SUNY-Binghamton, deserve thanks for their efforts, on two separate occasions, in helping me bring my bibliography on this topic up to date.

References

Anderson, J.R. 1976. Language, memory and thought. Lawrence Earlbaum.

Braunwald, Susan R. 1981. Egocentric speech reconsidered - III. Paper presented at the Second International Congress for the Study of Child Language, Vancouver, Canada.

Bub, D.B., and Whitaker, H.A. 1981. Lexical access and imagery: Would the right hemisphere please stand up? *Cognition and Brain Theory*, 4, 61-68.

Chase, R.A., Sutton, S., First, D., and Zubin, J. 1961. A developmental study of changes in behavior under delayed auditory feedback. *Journal of Genetic Psychology*, 99, 101-112.

DiVesta, F. 1966. A developmental study of the semantic structures of children. *Journal of Verbal Learning and Verbal Behavior*, 5, 249-259.

Fink, M., and Bender, M.B. 1953. Perception of simultaneous tactile stimuli in normal children. *Neurology*, 3, 27-34.

Flavell, J.H., and Stedman, D.J. 1961. A developmental study of judgments of semantic similarity. *Journal of Genetic Psychology*, 98, 279-293.

Gardner, H., Winner, E., Bechhofer, R., and Wolf, D. 1978. The development of figurative language. In *Children's language, Volume 1*, ed. by K.E. Nelson, Gardner Press, 1-38.

Goldin-Meadow, S., Seligman, M.E.P., and Gelman, R. 1976. Language in the two-year-old. *Cognition*, 4, 189-202.

Ingram, D. 1975. If and when transformations are acquired by children. In *Georgetown University Round Table on Languages and Linguistics 1975*, ed. by D.P. Dato, Georgetown University Press, 99-127.

Krashen, S., and Harshman, R. 1972. Lateralization and the critical period. *UCLA Working Papers in Phonetics*, 23, 13-21.

Kuenne, M.R. 1946. Experimental investigation of the relation of language to transposition behavior in young children. *Journal of Experimental Psychology*, 36, 471-490.

Macnamara, J., Baker, E., and Olson, C.L. 1976. Four-year-olds' understanding of *pretend*, *forget*, and *know*: evidence for propositional operations. *Child Development*, 47, 62-70.

Maltz, H. 1963. Ontogenetic change in the meaning of concepts as measured by the semantic differential. *Child Development*, 34, 667-674.

Naroditskaya, G.D. 1956. A study of the question of the phenomenon of the so-called secondary excitation in the cerebral cortex of children. In *Works of the Institute on Higher Nervous Activity, Pathophysiological Series, Volume 2*, ed. by Ivanov-Smolenskii, National Science Foundation, 131-139. (Cited in Ervin, S.M., and Miller, W.R., 1963, Language development, *NSSE Yearbook, Part 1*, University of Chicago Press, 108-143.)

Nelson, K. 1977. The syntagmatic-paradigmatic shift revisited: a review of research and theory. *Psychological Bulletin*, 84, 93-116.

Piaget, J. 1959. *Judgment and reasoning in the child*. Littlefield, Adams.

Rosch, E., Mervis, C.B., Gray, W., Johnston, D., and Boyes-Braem, P. 1976. Basic objects in natural categories. *Cognitive Psychology*, 8, 382-439.

Saltz, E., and Sigel, I.E. 1967. Concept overdiscrimination in children. *Journal of Experimental Psychology*, 73, 1-8.

Schopler, E. 1964. *Visual and tactual receptor preference in normal and schizophrenic children.* Unpublished doctoral dissertation, University of Chicago. (Cited in White, 1965.)

Straight, H.S. 1976. Comprehension versus production in linguistic theory. *Foundations of Language,* 14, 525-540.

Straight, H.S. 1980. Auditory versus articulatory phonological processes and their development in children. In *Child phonology, Volume 1: Production,* ed. by G. H. Yeni-Komshian, J.F. Kavanagh, and C.A. Ferguson, Academic Press, 43-71.

Tulving, E. 1972. Episodic and semantic memory. In *Organization of memory,* ed. by E. Tulving and W. Donaldson, Academic Press, 381-403.

Werner, H., and Kaplan, E. 1952. The acquisition of word meaning: a developmental study. *SRCD Monographs, Volume 15, Number 51.*

White, S.H. 1965. Evidence for hierarchical arrangement of learning processes. In *Advances in child development and behavior, Volume 2,* ed. by L.P. Lipsitt and C.C. Spiker, Academic Press, 187-220.

Wilkinson, Louise Cherry and Saywitz, Karen. 1981. Developmental differences in metalinguistic awareness. Paper presented at the Second International Congress for the Study of Child Language, Vancouver, Canada.

THE RELATION OF REASONING, MEMORY AND VERBAL ABILITY OF CHILDREN

Shizuko Amaiwa
(Iwaki Junior College)

Both memory and verbal ability seem to be fundamental to solving reasoning tasks. Trabasso (1975) reported that 4-year-olds performed well on tasks of transitive inference in cases when they could memorize the premises sufficiently. He concluded that young children's failure on similar tasks in other experiments was not proof of the lack of their inference ability, rather only a consequence of insufficient and inaccurate memory. Case (1978a, b, c, 1980) claimed that the levels of tasks which children could solve were determined by their range of working memory and argued that it is important to devise ways to minimize the burden of working memory when giving such tasks to children.

As to verbal ability, some studies found a correlation between levels of understanding of relational terms, e.g. "more", "less" and "same", and performance on transitive inference reasoning tasks. These reports showed that comprehension of relational terms is needed for solving inference tasks.

Through the above experiments, it is not clear exactly how three abilities--reasoning, memory and verbal ability--are integrated, what aspect of each ability is related, or how one ability is influenced by another. In this research I want to try to clarify the relationships among reasoning, memory and verbal ability of children.

Method

In this study, six tasks were given to 203 kindergarten children--114 boys and 89 girls classified into a 4-year-old-group (with a mean age of 4;8) or into a 5-year-old-group (with a mean age of 5;6). (See Table 1 for the composition of the subjects.)

There were two transitivity tasks, two memory tasks, two relational terms tasks and one weight judgment task.

To measure reasoning ability, I prepared tasks of concrete transitivity and formal transitivity. In

Table 1

Composition of subjects

	M	F	Total	$\overline{M}$
4-year-olds	47	56	103	4;8
5-year-olds	67	33	100	5;6
Total	114	89	203	

Figure 1

Tasks of concrete transitivity

	A	B	C
1	○	= ◊	> △
2	○ <	◊ <	△
3	◊	> △	> ○
4	◊ <	△ =	○
5	△ =	○ <	◊
6	△ >	○ >	◊

Table 3

Forward digit span	Backward digit span
(1) 5-8 7-2	(1) 2-5 6-3
(2) 3-8-6 6-1-2	(2) 5-7-4 2-5-9
(3) 3-4-1-7 6-1-5-8	(3) 7-2-9-6 8-4-9-3
(4) 8-4-2-3-9 5-2-1-8-6	(4) 4-1-3-5-7 9-7-8-5-2
(5) 3-8-9-1-7-4 7-9-6-4-8-3	(5) 1-6-5-2-9-8 3-6-7-1-9-4
(6) 5-1-7-4-2-3-8 9-8-5-2-1-6-3	(6) 8-5-9-2-3-4-2 4-5-7-9-2-8-1
(7) 1-6-4-5-9-7-6-3 2-9-7-6-3-1-5-4	

general, transitivity is the type of reasoning used to infer the relationship of A and C, when the three elements A, B and C are arranged in order, for example, A is larger than B and B is larger than C. In the case of concrete transitivity, children were asked to compare concrete objects--a ball, a sausage and a triangle made with clay (Figure 1)--and in the case of formal transitivity, the problems were given to the children only verbally (Table 2).

Table 2 Tasks of formal transitivity
1. blue box > white box, white box > red box
2. Blue box < red box, blue box = white box
3. red box > white box, red box < blue box
4. blue box = white box, white box < red box

To measure memory, the tasks of forward digit span and backward digit span shown in Table 3 were prepared, and for verbal ability, levels of understanding of relational terms were determined by children's descriptions comparing two or three different sized circles.

The weight judgment task was given to the children verbally, to examine whether or not they understood the relational terms. The children were asked to answer two questions: 1. Is an apple heavier than a pear? 2. Is Taro lighter than Yoshio? (Taro and Yoshio are popular boys' names in Japan.)

After the execution of these tasks, some tasks concerning relational terms were given to the children to determine the degree of improvement in understanding relational terms due to the experience provided by the experimental tasks.

Results

Table 4 shows the mean scores on seven tasks. The significant differences between the two age groups on the tasks of forward digit span, backward digit span, weight judgment and formal transitivity are indicated with asterisks. The scores on the backward digit span task increase remarkably with an increase in age.

Table 4

Mean Values of tasks

		4 yrs.	5 yrs.	T	Total
1	Relational terms	3.26	2.89		3.08
2	Forward digit span	3.88	4.28	*	4.08
3	Backward digit span	0.57	2.10	***	1.33
4	Concrete transitivity	2.86	3.15		3.01
5	Weight judgment	0.85	1.05	*	0.95
6	Formal transitivity	1.34	1.73	*	1.53
7	2nd. relational terms	4.19	3.75		3.98

*** $p < .005$ * $p < .05$

Table 5 uses totalled scores for both age groups. It shows significant correlations (p < .005) between the first and second relational terms task scores, between the forward and backward digit span tasks scores, and between the concrete and formal transitivity task scores. Considering the relation of the three abilities, understanding of relational terms (as shown in both first and second tasks) correlates significantly with the forward digit span task (p < .05) but does not correlate with the reasoning tasks. Both digit span tasks correlate highly with formal transitivity scores (p < .005). The forward digit span task correlates with the weight judgment task (p < .05).

Table 6 provides intercorrelations of the scores for the seven variables for the two age groups. Highly significant correlations (p < .005) again appear between the first and second relational terms task scores, and between the forward and backward digit span task scores. Differences between the two age groups indicate that some relationships of the three abilities may alter with age: for the 4-year-old group only there are significant correlations (p < .005) between the first and second relational term scores and the forward digit span scores.

Table 7 shows the numbers and percentages of subjects at each level of understanding relational terms. The levels are determined according to the points gained by the subjects. Table 8 shows the results of T-tests between different levels of relational terms

Table 5

Intercorrelations of variables (Total)

	0	1	2	3	4	5	6	7
0 Age		-.026	.134*	.536***	.137	.125*	.125*	-.069
1 Relational terms			.148*	.076	-.004	-.017	.039	.659***
2 Forward digit span				.459***	.036	.139*	.214***	.141*
3 Backward digit span					.114	.088	.307***	.034
4 Concrete transitivity						.041	.211***	.003
5 Weight judgment							.068	.028
6 Formal transitivity								.083
7 2nd. relational terms								

*** p<.005   * p<.05

Table 6

Intercorrelations of variables (upper: 4 yrs. under: 5 yrs.)

	0	1	2	3	4	5	6	7
0 Age		-.073	-.089	.138	.194*	-.010	-.058	-.190*
1 Relational terms	.115		.029	.057	-.028	-.024	.130	.622***
2 Forward digit span	.080	.327***		.443***	-.003	.028	.252***	.045
3 Backward digit span	.248***	.176*	.451***		-.010	-.060	.276***	-.030
4 Concrete transitivity	.010	.031	.056	.172*		.018	.174*	-.041
5 Weight judgment	.037	.002	.224*	.071	.040		.001	.023
6 Formal transitivity	-.019	-.029	.111	.233**	.228*	.081		.133
7 2nd. relational terms	.085	.693***	.294***	.162	.062	.047	.054	

*** $p<.005$ ** $p<.01$ * $p<.05$

understanding. Significant differences are seen clearly in forward digit span in the 5-year-old group of level 3/1 as well as level 2/3.

Table 7   Numbers of each level of relational terms

	level 1 (0)		level 2 (1-7)		level 3 (8-12)	
	N	%	N	%	N	%
4 yrs.	54	(52.4)	25	(24.3)	24	(23.3)
5 yrs.	58	(58.0)	19	(19.0)	23	(23.0)
Total	112	(55.2)	44	(21.7)	47	(23.2)

Table 9 shows the numbers and percentages of subjects at each level of performance on the backward digit span task. Table 10 shows the results of the T-test between the different levels of the backward digit span task. Level 1/3 in the 4-year-old group and levels 1/3 and 4/0 in both groups show clearly the significant differences in formal transitivity. Level 2/3 in the 5-year-old group for relational terms is also significantly different.

Table 9   Numbers of each level of backward digit span

	Level 1 (0)		Level 2 (2)		Level 3 (3)		Level 4 (4)	
	N	%	N	%	N	%	N	%
4 yrs.	81	(78.6)	8	(7.8)	13	(12.6)	1	(1.0)
5 yrs.	21	(21.0)	38	(38.0)	30	(30.0)	11	(11.0)
Total	102	(50.2)	46	(22.7)	43	(21.2)	12	(5.9)

Conclusions

1. There are significant increases in performance between the 4- and 5-year-old groups on the two digit span, the weight judgment, and the formal transitivity tasks.

Table 8

Results of the T-test between the different
levels of relational terms

		levels of relational terms		
		1 2	2 3	3 1
4 yrs.	1 Forward digit span 2 Backward digit span 3 Concrete transitivity 4 Weight judgment 5 Formal transitivity 6 2nd. relational terms			
		***	*	***
5 yrs.	1 Forward digit span 2 Backward digit span 3 Concrete transitivity 4 Weight judgment 5 Formal transitivity 6 2nd. relational terms		* * *	*** *
		***	**	***
Total	1 Forward digit span 2 Backward digit span 3 Concrete transitivity 4 Weight judgment 5 Formal transitivity 6 2nd. relational terms			
		***	***	***

*** p<.005   * p<.5

239

Table 10

Results of the T-test between the different levels of backward digit span

		1-2	2-3	3-4	1-3	2-4	4-0
4 yrs.	1 Relational terms						
	2 Concrete transitivity						
	3 Weight judgment		*		***		
	4 Formal transitivity	*	*				
	5 2nd. relational terms						
5 yrs.	1 Relational terms		***		*		
	2 Concrete transitivity						
	3 Weight judgment		*			*	*
	4 Formal transitivity					*	*
	5 2nd. relational terms				*		
Total	1 Relational terms		*		*		
	2 Concrete transitivity		*				
	3 Weight judgment				***	*	***
	4 Formal transitivity					*	
	5 2nd. relational terms						

*** $p<.005$ ** $p<.01$ * $p<.05$

240

2. The verbal ability tasks (first and second relational terms tasks) are related to each other as are the two memory tasks (the forward and backward digit span tasks).

3. The two reasoning tasks are related because the correlation is high between the concrete and formal transitivity scores for the totalled scores and the correlations are reasonably high ($p < .05$) when the two age groups' scores are considered separately.

4. The correlations between the two digit span task scores and the formal transitivity task scores are highly significant when the scores for the two age groups are totalled. But only the relationship between the backward digit span tasks and the formal transitivity task is confirmed when the scores for the two age groups are considered separately.

5. The correlations between the two relationship tasks and the forward digit span task scores are highly significant when the scores for the two age groups are totalled. But only the relationship between the relational terms tasks and the forward digit span task is confirmed for the five-year-old group when the scores for the two age groups are considered separately.

Regarding the relationship among reasoning, memory and verbal ability:

We can confirm a general relationship between memory and reasoning given the connections between backward digit span task and formal transitivity scores.

We can confirm a weak relationship between verbal ability and memory given the connections between the two relational terms task scores and the forward digit span task scores for the 5-year-old group.

We also acknowledge the importance of knowing the contents and structures of each task when investigating the relationships among reasoning, memory and verbal ability.

References

Case, R. (1978a) Piaget and beyond: Toward a developmentally based theory and technology of instruction. In Glaser, R. (ed.) Advances in instructional psychology. Vol. 1, LEA.

Case, R. (1978b) Intellectual development from birth to adulthood: A neo-Piagetian interpretation. In Siegler, R.S. (ed.) Children's thinking: What develops?. LEA.

Case, R. (1978c) A developmentally based theory and technology of instruction. Review of Educational Research, 48, 3, 439-463.

Case, R. (1980) Intellectual development: A systematic reinterpretation. In Farley, F.H. & Gordon, N.J. (eds.) New perspectives in educational psychology. National Society for the Study of Education.

Trabasso, T. (1975) Representation, memory, and reasoning: How do we make transitive inferences? Minnesota Symposia on Child Psychology, 9, 135-172.

TALKING BACKWARD: SPEECH PLAY IN LATE CHILDHOOD

Nelson Cowan and Lewis A. Leavitt

University of Wisconsin, Madison

Of the many types of play in which children take part, one of the most facinating is the type in which the object of play is the child's native language. This type of play may yield information about the <u>cognitive prerequisites</u> of linguistic behaviors. We have been fortunate enough to find two children, 9 and 10 years of age, with remarkable and apparently self-taught abilities to reverse the order of linguistic units within words; that is, to "talk backwards." We also have transcripts and retrospective reports from a number of adults and teens with similar although more fluent talents with backward speech, all of whom reported beginning this game spontaneously in childhood or early adolescence.

To tell our story chronologically, our first subject, A.L., was a very fluent <u>adult</u> backward talker whom we studied with the help of Dominic Massaro and Raymond Kent (Cowan, Leavitt, Massaro, & Kent, 1982). This subject, upon hearing an English sentence for the first time, could rapidly produce each word with the order of phonemes reversed, while leaving the words themselves in the original order. No written aids were used. This process at least matched the speed one observes for the expert "simultaneous translation" of one natural language to another. Of course, A.L.'s reversed speech is much different from what one would get by playing an English recording backward. The basis of this difference is that in backward speech, unlike a reversed recording, the acoustic pattern within each phoneme remains in forward order rather than being reversed.

One important aspect of this phoneme-by-phoneme reversal of speech is that it allowed us to discover the phonemic units into which our subject divides words. We must first explain how we knew that A.L.'s reversed forms were based upon sound rather than spelling. Many critical probe stimulus words gave us this information. For example, the word "though" was reversed as [oð], in direct contrast to what one would expect if the written form for the same word were scanned backward (e.g., [hɔgu'ahət]). As another example, homographs (such as [bow] vs. [baʊ]) were very clearly distinguished in the reversals (that is, [ob] vs. [aʊb]), and were unlike the single form one would expect on the basis of spelling (that is, [wab]). This was true even of differing pronunciations of letters within a word, such as the "g's" representing /g/ vs. /ʒ/ in the word "garage," which was reversed as [ʒarag]. Furthermore, silent letters such as the "s" within "island" were not pronounced in the reversals.

Once we knew that sound rather than spelling was the basis of A.L.'s representation directly underlying backward speech, we had yet to determine exactly what the form of sound representation was. For example, the diphthongs [aɪ], [ɔɪ], and [aʊ] are complex sounds composed of two elements, but linguists generally consider each diphthong to be a single phoneme. Similarly, the affricates [dʒ] and [tʃ] are complex phonemes each consisting of two consonant sounds. Our transcripts indicated that A.L. consistently preserved the structure within these complex phonemes. For example, the word "choice" was consistently reversed as [sɔɪtʃ], rather than as one would expect if complex phonemes were broken down into more elementary phonic units: [sɪɔʃt].

This issue of the mental representation of phonemes becomes especially interesting when one considers that in recent years, linguistic work has thrown into question the degree of abstractness of speakers' phonemic representations. According to the predominant generative phonological theories, inspired primarily by Chomsky and Halle's <u>Sound Pattern of English</u> (1968), there is a highly abstract underlying representation that takes into account the etymological relationship between words, and no other level of representation before the narrow phonetic description of speech as a bundle of distinctive features. For example, consider the words "serene" and "serenity," in which the pronunciation of the second "e" changes with the addition of the "-ity" ending. In the Chomsky and Halle system, there is a single underlying abstract vowel phoneme common to both words, and low level phonetic processes are said to adjust the pronunciation both with and without the addition of the suffix. Now, suppose our backward talker represented phonemes in this abstract manner. Then in reversing the words "serene" and "serenity," the same sound should have been used for the second vowel of both words. Instead, however, the distinction between vowels was always maintained in cases such as these. There was no evidence that A.L. was using a phonemic representation as abstract as Chomsky and Halle have formulated (Cowan & Leavitt, in press a).

On the other hand, there was evidence that the representations may be abstract to a degree proposed by earlier linguists, most notably by Sapir (1933/1968). For example, in English the distinction between the phonemes /d/ and /t/ is often neutralized to an alveolar flap in word-medial position. Thus, the words "latter" and "ladder" have identical pronunciations. Nevertheless, these words were represented differently by A.L., as Sapir would have expected. "Latter" was reversed as ['rətæl] , whereas "ladder" was reversed as ['rədæl] . This and a number of similar considerations lead us to suggest that A.L. reverses speech by representing each word as a sequence of phonemes, reversing the order of phonemes, and transforming the reversed sequence of phonemes to speech.

To our surprise, when A.L. made public media appearances, he was contacted by over 30 English speakers who claimed to be able to talk backward. We interviewed 27 of them, including 16 males and

11 females. Interestingly, 63% of the subjects estimated that they began talking backward at an age within the range of 7-11 years, and most of these estimates fell within an 8-10 year old range. No subject reported having started talking backward earlier than 7 years or later than 15 years of age. All enjoyed reading, had high verbal abilities, and had no known mental defects. However, none of the fluent backward talkers were linguists or understood their skill linguistically. Proficiency varied, but most of these subjects appeared to possess impressive, better-than-normal abilities to reverse speech. A set of spoken sentences and diagnostic words were administered to all subjects, and these stimuli revealed that although no two subjects reversed the words identically, their methods of speech reversal were neatly divided into two distinct types: About half reversed speech on the basis of the phonemic representation of sounds, and about half on the basis of an orthographic representation. We were impressed by the fact that subjects within the phonemic group were remarkably similar to A.L. in their manner of speech reversal. For example, with one possible exception, all of these subjects consistently produced the diphthongs [aɪ], [ɔɪ], and [aʊ] and the affricates [dʒ] and [tʃ] in the forward order within the reversed forms.

Our two youngest subjects were representative of the others, in that one reversed speech phonemically and the other as if scanning the written representation in reverse. We asked the two children to translate over 100 words and several sentences into backward speech to obtain a better linguistic understanding of their unusual skills (Cowan & Leavitt, in press b).

One subject, B.W., was 8; 10 at the time of testing, and an only child. A digit span test revealed that B.W.'s memory was considerably above the norm on backward digit recital, but only at the norm on forward recital. He also did exceptionally well on tests of verbal skills and vocabulary. He likes math and is recognized by teachers as bright, although sometimes uninterested in school work. He lives with his father, a math teacher, and his mother, a social worker. Neither his parents nor his friends are able to talk backward. Not only were diphthongs, affricates, and most other phonemes preserved within his backward speech, as in the older subjects, but the transcriptions generally revealed a fascinating sophistication of phonemic representation. To illustrate this, B.W. preserved the final velar nasal sound in his reversals, unlike some of the <u>adult</u> backward talkers. For example, B.W. reversed the word "ring" as [ŋɪr]. In contrast, some adults with basically phonemic reversal methods reversed "ring" as [gənɪr], perhaps due to orthographic contamination of the phonemic representation. B.W.'s reversals also contained evidence of more abstract phonemic classifications, such as the preservation of /d/ and /t/ phonemes in word-medial position. However, it was not possible to test him with words sophisticated enough to address the level of abstractness proposed by Chomsky and Halle.

Our other young backward talker, D.R., was 9; 11 at the time of testing, and is a good student who likes reading and social sciences. He is one of eight children, and lives in a rural community with his father, an English professor, his mother, a well-educated homemaker, and a younger sister, none of whom can talk backward. His forward and backward memory spans were <u>not</u> above the age norms, but tests of <u>verbal skills</u> revealed exceptional abilities.

Given that D.R.'s "backward" language is orthographically based and cannot reveal his representation of phonemic units, does that mean that his skill is useless to us? We think not. In order to pronounce letter sequences in reverse in an orderly manner, one must draw upon a set of rules for letter-to-sound conversion. D.R.'s reversals are indeed orderly. A useful framework for analyzing these productions is Venezky's (1970) work, The structure of English orthography. In it are summarized the regular pronunciations of different letters within specific letter contexts. For example, the letters "g" and "c" are usually pronounced as [g] and [k] respectively, unless followed by an "e," "i," or "y" within the same morpheme, in which case they are usually pronounced as [dʒ] and [s]. Similarly, vowel letters generally are pronounced as short vowels when followed by two consonant units or by a word-final consonant, and as long vowels otherwise. In his reversals, D.R. usually selected pronunciations of both consonant and vowel letters that were contextually appropriate given the rules that Venezky described.

In addition to revealing phonemic representations and letter-to-sound rules in children's thought, the backward speech game may help us to understand the relationship between linguistic skills and cognitive development. Recall that subjects in our adult sample reported beginning their unusual pastime at the minimum age of 7 years and a median age of 8-10 years. It is possible that the ability to talk backward depends, concretely enough, upon the mastery of Piagetian "reversible operations." The child might need to understand that the ordering of linguistic units within speech is an act that can be redirected under conscious control if desired.

A second explanation for the minimum age of talking backward is that reading instruction may be required. Consistent with that interpretation, recent research suggests that the ability to analyze speech into phonemes may depend not merely upon the attainment of a minimum cognitive level, but also upon an exposure to written language. For example, Morais, Cary, Alegria, and Bertelson (1979) found that illiteracy prevented adults from performing phonetic segmentation tasks, although illiteracy apparently did not interfere with syllabic segmentation.

Finally, there are interesting similarities and differences between these spontaneously invented backward language forms and established, culturally-transmitted secret languages (see Kirshenblatt-Gimblett, 1976). Forms of "talking backward" have been reported in the last century in England and France as secret jargons used by groups of peddlers and criminals, and in cultures as diverse as Thailand, the Philippines, France, and Panama as childhood language games. The minimum ages of children participating in these games remains largely undocumented. The games consist of learned vocabularies along with productive use of reversal rules only for very short words. In contrast, many of our subjects can reverse almost any known word rapidly. It is also interesting to note that secret languages of children are quite similar in form cross-culturally, and include many games that require the division of words into <u>syllables</u> instead of (or in addition to) phonemes. In striking contrast, out of the 27 subjects whom we have contacted, <u>only one</u> had developed a syllabic form of backward speech. Thus, the relationship of the spontaneous invention of a private language in childhood to culturally transmitted language games remains undetermined. It may well be the literacy of our subjects that stimulates the phonemic rather than syllabic basis for language games.

References

Chomsky, N., & Halle, M. The sound pattern of English. New York: Harper & Row, 1968.

Cowan, N., & Leavitt, L.A. Juggling acts with linguistic units. In M.F. Miller, C.S. Masek, & R.A. Hendrick (Eds.), Proceedings from the parasession on language and behavior. Chicago: Chicago Linguistic Society, in press. (a)

Cowan, N., & Leavitt, L.A. Talking backward: exceptional speech play in late childhood. Journal of Child Language, 1982, 9 (2), 481-495. (b)

Cowan, N., Leavitt, L.A., Massaro, D.W., & Kent, R.D. A fluent backward talker. Journal of Speech and Hearing Research, 1982, 25, 48-53.

Kirshenblatt-Gimblett, B. (Ed.) Speech play. Philadelphia: University of Pennsylvania Press, 1976.

Morais, J., Cary, L., Alegria, J., & Bertelson, P. Does awareness of speech as a sequence of phones arise spontaneously? Cognition, 1979, 7, 323-331.

Sapir, E. The psychological reality of phonemes. (Original article 1933). In D.G. Mandelbaum (Ed.), The selected writings of Edward Sapir in language, culture, and personality. Berkeley: University of California Press, 1968.

Venezky, R.L. The structure of English orthography. Mouton: The Hague, 1970.

Some Problems for the Cognitivist Approach to Language
Kim Plunkett & Anna Trosborg

Introduction

In recent years, the role of general cognitive development in language acquisition has been stressed, in particular by the Geneva school (Sinclair, 1973). This emphasis on cognitive development was a reaction against a previous view of language learning, in which it was held that mere exposure to language was a sufficient condition for its acquisition (Bloom, 1970; McNeill, 1969). Linguistic universals were regarded as innate, and language learning was treated as if it occurred independently of cognitive development. This one-sided approach has been "corrected" by the cognitivists. McNeill's claim (1970, p. 2)[1] that "The facts of language acquisition would not be as they are unless the conception of a sentence is available to children at the start of their learning", has been substituted by a more credible claim (Bruner, 1976, p.6) that "The facts of language acquisition could not be as they are unless fundamental concepts about action and attention are available to children at the beginning of learning".

Several researchers (e.g. Brown, 1973; Bloom, 1973; Greenfield & Smith, 1976) have shown that as far as the two- to three-year-old child is concerned, the child's cognitive development and desire to express himself is clearly in advance of his linguistic means to do so. His two word utterances express relations such as location and possession, e.g. 'sweater chair', 'mummy sock' (Brown, 1973, p. 136) which are meaningful within the given context, although the child does not have at his command the correct linguistic form. The acquisition of the concepts involved in location and possession thus precedes the acquisition of their grammatical marking.

The cognitive perspective on the relation between linguistic and cognitive development also finds support beyond the domain of developmental studies. During the past decade, anthropologists, linguists and psychologists have searched for similarities among the languages of the world. Their endeavours have uncovered a fairly large set of linguistic universals. Generally, these universals would appear to have a cognitive or social basis. That is, one can point to aspects of the speaker's extra-linguistic

---

[1] McNeill no longer agrees with this claim. See McNeill (1974).

251

experience which correspond to the distinctions he realises in his language. For example, Berlin and Kay's (1969) demonstration that all languages select their basic colour terms from just 11 possibilities corresponds well with what is known about the physiology of human colour vision, (McDaniel, 1974). Basic category names (e.g. 'horse, flower, apple, walk') also appear to be universal. In nature, properties go together to form categories with which the human perceptual apparatus is specifically geared to deal (Rosch, 1977). Other examples of universals include shape, names, spatial terms, number, negation, time, cause and effect (see Greenberg, 1966; Clark, 1977). In the social domain, regularities have been found in the kinship terms used by different languages. For example, all languages distinguish at least three characteristics in relatives: generation, blood relationship, and sex.

In sum, there is good reason to believe that a large number of linguistic distinctions are universal and that they have a cognitive or social basis. Indeed, such findings as these would appear to justify developmental psychologists going beyond the claim that cognitive development is a prerequisite of linguistic development (Cromer, 1974). Cognitive development might be considered an explanation of linguistic development. The distinctions realised in a language are a mere reflection of the distinctions realised on a cognitive plane of representation which are wholly attained through extra-linguistic experience. Schlesinger (1977) has called this viewpoint cognitive determinism.

This approach, however, suffers certain important inadequacies. Clearly, only the underlying structures which are the bearers of meaning can possibly be acquired through cognitive development. However, there are linguistic concepts such as gender in some languages, which are uncorrelated or only very imperfectly related with semantic concepts. For example, in Danish, unlike English, all common nouns are assigned one of two genders - common or neuter. Thus we have 'en bog' for 'a book' vs. 'et hus' for 'a house' in the case of the indefinite article. For the definite article, gender is realised either as an analytic construction on modified nouns, e.g. 'den røde bog' for 'the red book' vs. 'det røde hus' for 'the red house', or as an inflection on unmodified nouns, e.g. 'bogen' for 'the book', vs. 'huset' for 'the house'. There are no linguistic rules that enable the Danish child or anyone else to assign gender to nouns in a productive manner. Neither is there a cognitive basis for the distinction, common noun vs. neuter noun. On the other hand, the linguistic rule described above does enable the child to decide which position the definite article must occupy. If the noun is unmodified, the definite article is formed by adding the indefinite article as a suffix to the noun. If the noun is modified, the 'den' or 'det' form is used before the modifier. However, it is not possible to identify any cognitive basis for these distinct forms of the definite article. There is nothing in the child's extra-linguistic experience that could lead him to expect that 'den røde bog' is correct whereas 'rød bogen' is wrong.

In addition, many grammatical rules such as agreement phenomena are such that communication would not be impaired by their non-observance; the loss of subject/verb agreement in certain English creoles does not hinder communication between native speakers of the creole (Todd, 1974). There are then complexities in language beyond those required for expressing the concepts and relations attained by cognitive development. These are surface phenomena which must depend entirely on linguistic input for acquisition.

Arguments like these convince us that cognitive determinism cannot adequately explain the process of language learning. However, a weaker version of cognitive determinism is still permissible, namely that, apart from those linguistic distinctions which   are purely artificial, linguistic distinctions that do refer to the real world are cognitively determined. That is, language has little, if any, effect on the way the world of experience is categorised. But even this position is open to attack. Consider the linguistic distinction between common and proper nouns (e.g. chair vs. John and Fido). Macnamara (1972) and Katz, Baker & Macnamara (1974) hold that the child's extra-linguistic experience makes him aware that persons and dogs are individuals in a way that chairs and toy blocks, for instance, are not. It is this experience which enables him to learn the distinction between common and proper nouns. In contrast, Quine (1960) argues that the child observes how the different nouns are treated linguistically. Notably, common and proper nouns differ in respect of their use of articles (a boy vs. John). Again, the distinction may rely entirely on this surface phenomenon for its acquisition. Neither can we rule out the possibility that the child might be told about the difference and thus benefit from direct instruction.

In short, there are equally strong arguments for the hypothesis that the child's linguistic development has to be determined by his experience with language. Indeed, some researchers claim that linguistic input is fundamental to intellectual development as well as linguistic development. "By naming objects, and so defining their connections and relations, the adult creates new forms of reflection of reality in the child, incomparably deeper and more complex than those which he could have formed through individual experience ... The word has a basic function ..." (Luria and Yudovich, 1971, p. 22-23).

And so the argument goes on. We may summarise it thus: There are sets of linguistic distinctions (e.g. gender) which quite clearly have no basis in extra-linguistic experience. These are the <u>artificial</u> categories of language. They also include various inflections which are redundant as far as meaning is concerned yet heighten linguistic complexity. The artificial categories of language also force on the speaker an abstract categorisation which has no basis in extra-linguistic experience. That is not to say that the artificial category is useless. Although it may be redundant, it often provides a source for disambiguating the meaning of complex utterances. On the other hand, most linguistic distinctions are concerned with dissecting the real world. These are the <u>natural</u> categories of language. Controversy centres upon this latter category with the cognitivists claiming that the natural linguistic categories are acquired as a result of extra-linguistic experience whilst their opponents stress the role of linguistic input.

<u>Division of Categories</u>

We shall draw the outlines of our argument by reference to the domain of colour perception. During the past 30 years, this area of human experience has come under close scrutiny from cross-cultural researchers. Much of the work was re-evaluated in the light of Berlin & Kay's (1969) study (see Brown, 1976 for a comprehensive review). Berlin & Kay's most celebrated discovery is that given the number of generic colour terms in a language, one can predict the colours to which those terms will refer. For example, any language possessing five basic colour terms will have the equivalent of the English - "black", "white", "red", "yellow", and "green". Terms are equivalent in so far as the best example of any equivalent term is the same, no matter which language is considered. Furthermore, no language may have more than 11 basic colour terms. All colour vocabularies are drawn from the same set of 11 possibilities.

On the basis of such evidence, Berlin & Kay make a strong claim for an internal colour representation based on the 11 focal colours; the colour domain divides naturally into categories determined by the physiology of the human visual system. However, the mapping of linguistic symbols onto this core structure varies in its degree of differentiation. For example, languages differ in the number of basic colour terms realised in their colour vocabularies. Languages possess as many as 11 basic colour terms and as few as 2. Yet, in each case, the colour vocabulary dissects the whole of the colour space. This yields a variation in the extension of basic colour terms from one language to the next. Language with relatively small colour vocabularies attach broader meanings to individual colour terms. We shall refer to this type of variation as <u>core differentiation</u>. Ultimately, the degree of core differentiation is culturally motivated. However, core differentiation is possible because of an inherent structuring of the conceptual domain whether this is a result of a structured environment or through the individual's cognitive interpretation of the environment.

Apart from identifying a universal core of colour terms, Berlin & Kay's observations showed considerable variation in the placement of boundaries between colour terms from one language to the next. Variation appeared not only between languages which differed in their number of basic colour terms, but also between languages which encoded the same focal colours. For example, two languages may possess colour terms for red and blue, but not for purple. Yet one language may categorise purple as 'red' whilst the other refers to it as 'blue'. In such cases, it is difficult to identify any cognitive basis for the placement of the boundary. The physiology of the human visual system provides no clues. It is true that social factors may play a role. Yet these are difficult to identify, especially when individuals within a culture may vary in their placement of the boundary.

Notice that we are not arguing that the language determines the cognitive core. The language of basic colour terms only reflects a pre-established set of focal colours. This is the domain of cognitive determinism. But the language can and does influence the setting of boundaries between the focal cores. Cognitive determinism cannot account for this variability in categorising the natural world of colour. It seems more plausible that the language itself helps individuals decide how to categorise hues that fall outside the focal colour space of any particular language. Purple may be called 'blue' or 'red' not because of any unique cognitive property of purple but simply because the language chooses to name it so.

The mapping of linguistic symbols onto the internal representation of the colour spectrum varies from one language to the next for several reasons. First, languages may set the boundaries between the core categories of focal colours in different positions. We shall call this second source of cross-language variation, boundary variation. Very often the specific positioning of the boundary is completely arbitrary. We shall argue that the cognitivist approach is inadequate for explaining the basis of linguistic distinctions realised as a consequence of core differentiation or boundary variation. Our claim is that the language itself motivates many of the categorisations observed, especially when there are no clear cut extra-linguistic reasons for classifying an example of a concept in one category or another.

Core Differentiation

In the above discussion, we have treated the cognitive core as though it were a relatively well-defined entity. We tend to assume that cognitive representations are constructed out of a large but limited set of core concepts (Miller & Johnson-Laird, 1976). Different languages differentiate between these cores to varying degrees. Basic colour vocabularies are a particularly clear example of varying core differentiation.

The vocabularies of kinship terminology also adopt distinctions which may often be predicted on extra -linguistic grounds. However, languages still differ in the particular distinctions they choose to realise. Consider the following differences between English and Danish.

grandfather	farfar	(father's father)
	morfar	(mother's father)
grandmother	farmor	(father's mother)
	mormor	(mother's mother)
cousin	fætter	(male cousin)
	kusine	(female cousin)

The higher degree of differentiation of Danish follows a pattern which is justifiable on extra-linguistic grounds (sex). This distinction is observed in many other languages of the world, and could, of course, be made explicit in the English language as well, cf. 'maternal/paternal grandfather' etc. In contrast, there are conceptual domains which English differentiates to a greater degree than Danish. Consider the way Danish and English encode certain actions involving location and possession. In English, the verbs 'to take' and 'to bring' are used to describe the same action but from different points of view. Briefly, if the goal of the action is towards the speaker then 'bring' is used. Clearly, there are extra-linguistic grounds for deciding which is the appropriate term to use. However, even though Danish also has two different terms 'at bringe' and 'at tage', the grounds for distinguishing between the two terms are other than deictic. In Danish you can 'take things with you', whether the destination is 'towards' or 'away from' the speaker, but the Danish grocer will 'bring' goods out to his customer. In the case of 'borrow' and 'lend', the English distinction is unrealised in Danish, which uses the single term 'at låne', rather like the term 'loan' found in some English dialects. Examples of lexical distinctions in English not necessarily occurring in Danish include:

bring)	tage	look)	se	(kikke)
take)		see)		
borrow)	låne	listen)	høre	(lytte)
lend)		hear)		
teach)	lære (undervise)	touch)	føle	(røre)
learn)		feel)		

Given the close relation between location and possession, Danish would appear to be less deictic than English. That is not to say that Danes are unable to understand the distinctions which are realised in English; they would soon become confused as to the ownership of an object if they could not perceive the distinction between borrowing and lending! In the cases of teach, look, listen, touch, Danish does have possible means of expressing the distinction in question, namely through the respective lexical items undervise, kikke, lytte, røre. Although these words are almost equivalent in meaning to the English, the distinction is not obligatory in Danish, and more often than not it is not made. The point is that different languages may or may not realise a distinction which has a cognitive base.

The cognitive basis of a distinction is not always so easy to identify. Consider the set of objects that in English we label by the term 'brush'. The concept 'brush' includes objects as diverse as toothbrush, pastry brush and shoe brush. In Danish, the same set of objects is divided into 3 categories - 'pensel', 'børste' and 'skrubbe'. Examples of these categories are given below:

Pensel	Børste	Skrubbe
Paintbrush	Toothbrush	Floorbrush
Pastrybrush	Shoebrush	
	Clothesbrush	
	Hairbrush	

Danes have a larger choice of words as a means of classifying 'brushing' objects, and, unlike the English, they are not bound to scrub their floors with a brush.

At first glance, there seems no more reason to classify toothbrush under 'børste' than to classify it under 'pensel'. Toothbrushes no more resemble hairbrushes than they resemble paintbrushes, i.e. there are no obvious perceptual criteria for distinguishing the class of brushes. However, closer examination reveals a functional distinction between the 2 categories. 'Pensler' are used to apply or smear objects (usually liquid) over a surface, whilst 'børster', although not exclusively, are used to remove objects from surface. However, 'skrubber' are also used for this purpose. It is assumed here that toothbrushes and shoebrushes were classified as "børste" before toothpaste or shoepolish came along. Thus the criteria for classification is by no means easy to define.

Many conceptual domains are susceptible to alternative functional divisions. In the case of brushes, the criteria for classification could have been based on whether the tool was used for tending to personal belongings and bodyparts rather than external objects. A conceptual domain may be subdivided in any manner of ways when the distinction is based on functional criteria. There is nothing necessary about the way Danish distinguishes between brushes. Yet, it chooses to do so.

Boundary Variations

We now turn to the source of linguistic variation which is perhaps the most problematic for the cognitivist approach to categorising the natural world. It also turns out that linguistic

theory itself has difficulty in accounting for the degree of
variation found between languages as a result of boundary variation. We introduced boundary variations through a consideration of Berlin & Kay's (1969) study of basic colour terms. There
are, however, other examples of lexical differentiation which are
by no means straightforward. At the generic level (see Berlin et
al., 1973) English normally distinguishes between 2 types of
sitting object - the chair and the stool. Danish divides this
domain into 3 categories - 'stol' (chair), 'taburet' (approx.
stool) and 'skammel' (approx. stool/footrest). Yet the subsequent
differences between English and Danish are not merely a result of
this varying differentiation. For example, a barstool is called a
'barstol' (barchair) in Danish. Such variations may be historical
in origin. The result is a changing of the boundary between a
given distinction (back/no back) which the language learner could
not know beforehand. We shall now argue that this type of variation
is widespread not only as far as lexical items are concerned
but also as regards grammatical categories. We shall consider 3
such categories: transitivity, possession, and count/mass nouns.
We will demonstrate that variations are often so arbitrary as to
defy linguistic or cognitive explanations.

Transitivity:

In discussing the acquisition of transitive verbs, Macnamara
(1972) argues that the child must perceive that something happens
to the object; the object is affected by the action denoted by
the verb. But how affected does it have to be? Both in English
and Danish we have the patient category as in "John hit the
wall" but the locative as in "John sat on the bed". Schlesinger
contrasts these 2 examples, pointing out that the wall, though
little affected by the action, is generally considered a patient
whereas the bed newly made, may be considerably ruffled by the
action and yet only considered a locative.

Further examples show that English and Danish do not always agree
on the extension of the category of transitive verb. In English
sit, lie etc. can be considered intransitive verbs (with corresponding transitive versions set, lay, etc.). So also might wash,
shave, dress, etc. be considered: Every morning he washes, shaves,
and dresses, before he sits down to have breakfast.

In Danish, however, reflexivisation is obligatory in such instances;
Han vasker sig, barberer sig, klæder sig på, før han sætter sig
....

The problem seems to be the categorization of the self as an object. When an action is performed and the agent is also the patient, Danish tends to use reflexivization and thus a transitive verb. This is also the case for the Danish versions of the English He sits down, lies down on the bed, etc., where Danish uses a transitive verb even though it has the intransitive sidde and ligge corresponding to the English lie and sit. English on the other hand, can conceptualise these instances as intransitive.

Here we are concerned with a boundary variation, which in one language must be realised as transitive, in another can be realised as either. Furthermore, in examples such as hit the wall/sit on a bed it is the linguistic form of expression that determines the extension of transitivity. Thus linguistic input is necessary to learn the extent of the patient category so that it results only in grammatically correct utterances.

Possession

English has two ways of expressing the genitive: The s-genitive and the of-genitive. Generally speaking the s-genitive is favoured by the classes that are highest on the gender scale, e.g. persons and animals with gender characteristics ("John's arm", but "the roof of the house"). Semantically, it is congruent with the notion of ownership. For example, the possessive, John's hat, probably has a straightforward mapping onto the semantic notion of ownership. However, here also we get into problems. Not only does the concept include such diverse semantic relationships as e.g. John's hat (alienable possession), John's arm (inalienable possession), John's victory (subjective genitive), John's defeat (objective genitive), which clearly shows that lack of core differentiation is an obvious feature of the English way of marking the genitive, but the distinction between inanimate and animate is by no means clear-cut. We find instances of inanimate nouns marked by an 's construction as well as instances of animate nouns marked by an 's construction, where possession is not involved. Consider the following examples:

    a) a butcher's knife   en slagterkniv
    b) a man's shirt   en herreskjorte
    c) a boat's length   en bådlængde
    d) a stone's throw   et stenkast
    e) an hour and a half's talk halvanden times samtale

A butcher's knife might not belong to a butcher. Neither does a man's shirt necessarily belong to a man. Boat, stone, and hour are inanimate nouns and we might expect an of-construction.

Danish has only one genitive construction, which can be extended to most of the English uses of s- and of-genitives and is in this respect even less differentiated than English. However, in the case of a), b), c), and d) Danish has no such construction, but makes use of compounding. This seems logical enough, in that possession is not involved, but then there seems little logic in realising the genitive in e). Similarly, English is inconsistent in its choice of the genitive form: It also makes use of compounding. While a doorhandle is perfectly grammatical, a chairarm is less likely to be used as a compound noun in English and the phrase "the arm of a chair" used in its place.

We have thus seen the diversity of meanings to which both the s- and the of-genitive can be extended, and how they vary from one language to another. Exposure to the full range of linguistic variation is necessary to acquire complete control of the structures in question, not only in first language acquisition, but also for the second language learner, who on the one hand cannot transfer his notion of what counts as the genitive and on the other has to cope with different forms of construction.

Count/Mass Nouns

In the domain of common nouns, a fundamental cognitive distinction is   concerned with whether an entity is countable or not. Thus flowers are countable (one flower, two flowers, many flowers), in that it is possible to distinguish these as separable entities, while sugar is not. As the term mass implies, the notion of countability (of "one" as opposed to "more than one") does not apply to mass nouns, which are seen as continuous entities (much sugar, *one sugar, *few sugar). These substances or concepts are regarded as having no natural bounds, and they are subject to division only by means of certain "gradability expressions" (a bowl of sugar) (Arndt, Preisler & Østergaard, 1977; Quirk, Greenbaum, Leech & Svartvik, 1972; Steller & Sørensen, 1966).

The distinction according to countability in count and mass nouns is basic in both English and Danish, and both languages have various means of signalling this distinction. For example, many/ few flowers vs. much/ little sugar.

Yet, the division of concepts into countables and non-countables is not always a straightforward matter. With respect to the concept of number (singular or plural), mass nouns do not fall "naturally" into one or the other class. Still, mass nouns generally do have a singular, although it would be more accurate to say that they are invariable and lack number contrast:

    Music is   )
    *Musics are   ) my favourite hobby

For concepts such as water, sand, gravel, and air there is no clear association with either singularity or plurality. Of course, it is possible to talk about a certain amount of sand and thus associate it with the singular. On the other hand, sand consists of a large number of tiny stones (grains of sand) and thus it becomes possible to associate it with the plural. In itself, sand is neither singular, nor plural, but as English and Danish (and many other languages as well) have only the two possibilities, a choice must be made. This choice is linguistically determined as conceptually the nouns in question belong in neither category. In many cases English and Danish make the same choice, as in the above mentioned examples, which both languages treat as being singular.

However, a number of English mass nouns have corresponding countables in Danish, e.g. business, advice, evidence, information, interest, money, nerve, progress, furniture, lightning, news, etc. While the Englishman may have much money, but not *many monies, a Dane, on the other hand, can have mange penge (even without feeling himself the richer). A Dane can talk about 'en god nyhed' where in English one must refer to a piece of good news. Thus, while Danish nouns for these concepts occur in both the singular and the plural, the English nouns are singular and can only occur as count nouns by means of partitives. Notice, however, that although a Dane may refer to mange gode nyheder, an Englishman is unlikely to refer to many pieces of good news. He is more likely to refer to a lot of good news where a lot of is unspecified as to the singularity/plurality distinction. It must also be mentioned that apart from furniture, lightning, and news, which are restricted to the singular non-countable category, there is often a possibility of reclassification for these nouns. This countability becomes possible in English but only together with a change in meaning.

    He is in the wool business./He has a business of his own.

It appears that in the case of the assignment of boundary examples, English favours the singular (non-countable) category against the Danish choice of countability. This is not the case. English has a number of nouns which only occur in the plural and which in Danish can be conceived of as singular nouns:

English plural	Danish singular	Plural
alms	almisse	almisser
arms	våben	våben
ashes	aske	aske
goods	vare	varer
oats	havre	havre
proceeds	udbytte	udbytte
riches	rigdom	rigdomme
thanks	tak	tak
tidings	efter-retning	efter-retninger
wages	løn	(lønninger)
pains	umage	umage

As it appears, the English plural nouns correspond to either a mass noun or nouns which take both the singular and the plural.

The two languages also differ in their ways of naming tools and articles of dress. Those tools which consist of the joining of two equal parts, Danish treats as constituting summation plurals: denne saks/disse sakse (singular/plural), the corresponding English expressions are *not*: this scissor/these scissors, as would have been the case for e.g. flowers, but instead: this scissors/ these scissors. Only when subject to partitivity can such items be counted in English.

Further complexity is added by such nouns as *gasworks* and *headquarters*, which morphologically resemble plurality, but are the forms used for both the singular and the plural, and by nouns which relate conceptually to both the singular and the plural by means of a singular form, e.g. *aircraft*, *counsel*. (This gasworks is out of date / Two aircraft took off for Copenhagen). Irregularities in one language may or may not correspond with irregularities in the other (e.g. one sheep, two sheep / et får, to får, but one egg, two eggs / et æg, to æg).

263

The particular realisation of the count/mass distinction is
unpredictable in both English and Danish. The languages are
neither consistent with each other, nor are they consistent
within themselves. A wide and fuzzy no-mansland separates the
countables from the non-countables. Cognitive criteria are unable
to predict the categorisation of substances and concepts according to the count/mass distinction in the borderline region. Even
the language itself may be ambiguous to classification. Indeed,
one wonders how the language learner ever gets it right!

Extension of Categories

There are a set of linguistic distinctions which are not always
predictable on the basis of the extra-linguistic evidence to
which they refer but which, nevertheless, have a cognitive basis.
Consider the concepts of alienable and inalienable possession.
Normally, the expression 'my hand' constitutes an example of inalienable possession whereas 'my glove' constitutes an example
of alienable possession. In English, no linguistic distinction is
made between these two forms of possession even though we can
understand the distinction quite readily. However, there are
languages (see Fillmore, 1968) where a linguistic distinction is
realised for the two forms of possession. The core concept of
possession may be more or less differentiated from one language
to the next. Often core differentiation occurs in a predictable
manner (as in the Berlin & Kay, 1969 study). Sometimes, however,
core distinctions are extended in a rather unusual way. For
example, Fillmore (1968) cites a language where the term for left
hand is treated as inalienable whereas the term for hand is
treated as alienable, and the language of the Arapaho in which
lice are treated as inalienable. Such extensions of the core
categories are almost certainly not arbitrary. For example, lice
probably play a very special role in the Arapaho culture and the
left hand may have religious significance in some cultures!
However, these unusual extensions could not be predicted on the
basis of extra-linguistic experience alone. It is more plausible
that a child discovers that his left hand differs in alienability
from his right through the medium of language itself; unless, of
course he lives in a culture where he is continually exposed to
members having their right hand amputated. The <u>parasitic extension</u>
extends a core distinction beyond the domain to which it is
normally applied.

Metaphors, Idioms and Abstraction

The metaphorical use of language is essentially parasitic in nature. Here, language is used in a non-obvious way but nevertheless draws in meaning from its normal interpretation. For example, body parts are a favourite source of metaphor in English: Miller & Johnson-Laird (1976) offer a sample list:

"body" : of water, of an airplane, of people, of knowledge
"head" : of a page, of a committee, of a cabbage, of a pin
"arm" : of a coat, of the sea, of a chair, of government
"leg" : of a race, of a table, of a pair of trousers
"foot" : of a mountain, of a bed, of a stocking, 12 inches

Danish, however, does not seem so keen on body parts. For example, one cannot have "the arm of a coat" nor the "leg of a race". Nevertheless, because metaphors are parasitic on core distinctions it is often possible to decipher their meanings. Thus English speakers can decipher the Danish metaphor 'to fall over a discovery'.
In contrast, idioms have no predictable basis for interpretation. When we are told someone has 'kicked the bucket', we cannot infer from the individual word meanings that he has died. We must simply know the meaning of the whole expression. In this respect, idioms are 'twice arbitrary'. Combinations of existing, arbitrary, linguistic symbols are further interpreted in an arbitrary manner. Just as a language learner must learn the meaning of linguistic symbols, so must he learn to substitute new meanings for old conventions. Not so with metaphors. New metaphors are created daily in most languages. If we had to learn their meanings then for general communicative purposes they would be useless. The parasitic relation between language, thought, and reality is a crucial source of creativity.

Unlike the core categories, which are based on universal conceptual cores, the parasitic function of language enables us to go beyond the given relations of reality to create new, though abstract, relations. Bruner has succinctly characterised our claim:

> Once language is applied, then it is possible, by using language as an instrument, to scale to higher levels. In essence, once we have coded experience in language, we can (but not necessarily do) read surplus meaning into the experience by pursuing the built-in implications of the rules of language. (Bruner, Olver, & Greenfield, 1966, p. 51).

But this property of language does not exist in a vacuum. We can 'read surplus meaning' into our experience because language is already endowed with meaning in relation to the core categories. Surplus meaning is not arbitrary but a differentiation or parasitic extension of the distinctions already realised in the language. Through parasitic extensions, language is used to go beyond the given reality to create new abstract realities.

Conclusion

The task of deciphering whether a linguistic distinction is meaningful or not must be daunting for both the first and second language learner. But even when this problem is solved, he still has to discover the details of the linguistic dissection of the natural world. We have argued in this paper that the detailed linguistic dissection of the natural world is a complex and often arbitrary process. Language relates to cognition in diverse ways which we have outlined above. Some of these relationships are amenable to theoretical analyses, albeit mutually exclusive. Others defy linguistic or cognitive analysis.

The controversy between cognitive determinism and the linguistic input hypothesis is misconceived. In categorising the natural world, the language learner must possess both a cognitive representation and a device for dissecting that representation. Neither of these in themselves are a sufficient account of the mapping of linguistic categories onto concepts. However, both would appear to be necessary components of any adequate theory. Often the representation itself motivates the form of the dissection. However, linguistic devices may vary in their action on the representation. Language may not only draw attention to the dissection but also determine where the boundaries are drawn.

References

Arndt, H., Preisler, B. & Østergaard, F. (1977). *Kompendium i Engelsk Grammatik*. Copenhagen. Akademisk Forlag.

Berlin, B. & Kay, P. (1969). *Basic colour terms. Their universality and evolution*. Berkeley and Los Angeles: University of California Press.

Berlin, B., Breedlove, D.E. & Raven, P.H. (1973). Covert categories and folk taxonomies. *American Anthropologist* 75. 214-242.

Bloom, L.M. (1970). *Language development: Form and function in emerging grammars*. Cambridge, Mass.: M.I.T. Press.

Bloom, L.M. (1973). *One word at a time: The use of single word utterances before syntax*. The Hague, Mouton Publishers.

Brown, R. (1973). *A first language: The early stages*. Cambridge, Mass.: Harvard University Press.

Brown, R. (1976). In memorial tribute to Eric Lenneberg. *Cognition*. 4. 125-153.

Bruner, J.S., Olver, R.R. & Greenfield, P.M. (eds.) (1966). *Studies in cognitive growth*. New York: Wiley.

Bruner, J.S. (1975). The ontogenesis of speech acts. *Journal of Child Language*. 2. 1-19

Clark, H.H. & Clark, E.V. (1977). *Psychology and Language*. New York. Harcourt Brace Jovanovich.

Cromer, R.F. (1974). The development of language and cognition: The cognition hypothesis. In B. Foss (ed). *New perspectives in child development*. Harmondsworth, Middx: Penguin Books.

Fillmore, C.J. (1968). The case for case. In E. Bach & R.T. Harms (eds.). *Universals of linguistic theory*. New York, Holt, Rinehart and Winston.

Greenberg, J.H. (1966). *Language universals*. The Hague: Mouton Publishers.

Greenfield, P.M. & Smith, J.H. (1976). *The structure of communication in early language development*. New York: Academic Press.

Katz, N., Baker, E. & Macnamara, J. (1974). What's in a name? a study of how children learn common and proper names. *Child Development* 45. 469-473.

Luria, A.R. & Yudovich, Ia. (1959). *Speech and the development of mental processes of the child*. London: Staples Press.

Macnamara, J. (1972). Cognitive basis of language learning in infants. *Psychological Review*. 79. 1-13.

Macnamara, J. (1977). On the relation between language learning and thought. In J. Macnamara (ed). *Language learning and thought*. New York: Academic Press.

McDaniel, C.K. (1974). Basic color terms: Their neurophysiological bases. Paper presented at the Annual Meeting of the American Antropological Association, Mexico City, November 1974.

McNeill, D. (1969). Explaining linguistic universals. Paper presented at the XIXth International Congress of Psycholinguistics.

McNeill, D. (1970). The acquisition of language: The study of developmental psycholinguistics. New York: Harper & Row.

McNeill, D. (1974). Semiotic extension. Paper presented at the Loyola Symposium on Cognition, Chicago. April.

Miller, G.A. & Johnson-Laird, P.N. (1976). Language and perception. Cambridge, Mass.: Harvard University Press.

Quine, W. (1960). Word and object. New York: Wiley.

Quirk, R., Greenbaum, S., Leech, G. & Svartvik, J.A. (1972). A grammar of contemporary English. London: Longman.

Rosch, E. (1977). Human categorization. In N. Warren (ed). Advances in cross-cultural psychology (Vol. 1). London Academic Press.

Schlesinger, I.M. (1977). The role of cognitive development and linguistic input in language acquisition. Journal of Child Language. 4. 153-69.

Sinclair, H. (1973). Language acquisition and cognitive development. In T. Moore (ed). Cognitive development and the acquisition of language. New York: Academic Press.

Steller, P. & Sørensen, K. (1966). Engelsk grammatik. Copenhagen: Munksgaard.

Todd, L. (1974). Pidgins & Creoles. London: Routledge & Kegan Paul.

THE INTERRELATIONS BETWEEN COGNITIVE AND COMMUNICATIVE DEVELOPMENT: SOME IMPLICATIONS FROM THE STUDY OF A MUTE AUTISTIC ADOLESCENT

Adriana L. Schuler
Graduate School of Education
University of California
Santa Barbara, CA.

Christiane Bormann
Max Planck Institute for Child Psychiatry
Munich, West Germany

Introduction

The interrelations between communicative, cognitive and linguistic development have for long been subject to much speculation and controversy. For instance, the position that linguistic development is an immediate reflection and spin-off of overall cognitive development has been opposed by the notion that linguistic development stands by itself, is unique and not accurately predicted by cognitive achievement in other domains.

This paper presents a synopsis of an extensive series of non-verbal investigations of the mental capacities of an autistic adolescent with minimal communication skills and an extremely uneven developmental profile. The findings reported suggest that differentiations should be made between a range of mental abilities which are commonly lumped as "cognitive." Certain dimensions of cognitive development may be completely independent of linguistic or even communicative development in its broadest sense, while other dimensions may be closely interwoven. The extreme developmental discontinuity presented in this case study is of immediate relevance to current thinking about the interrelationships beweeen thought, language and social interaction (for a detailed discussion of the issues, see Curtiss, Kempler and Yamada, 1981) as the discrepancies reported serve to seriously question those theories which assume close parallels across developmental domains.

Subject Description

The subject reported in this study was a nineteen year old male, the first born of an identical twin. Both twins had been diagnosed repeatedly as suffering from early childhood autism, complicated by severe retardation. Inspection of the case histories revealed that despite early enrollment in intensive intervention programs the twins were institutionalized at age six, requiring intensive care, as they had only developed minimal self-help, communication and social interaction skills, and were almost continuously engaged in various forms of self-stimulatory behavior.

The first born twin, hereafter referred to as S, is the focus of this study, since he presented the most extreme discrepancies in development. S's lack of communicative speech was contrasted by rather high rates of self-stimulatory vocalizations, and some approximations of single one or two syllable words, apparently of a delayed echolalic nature. They did not seem to serve a communicative function, as they were not accompanied by other non-verbal communicative signals, such as changes in body orientation, gaze shifts, gestures, etc. Rather, they were memorized in context, and apparently triggered by a need to re-enact established routines. Also, some of them were embedded in his motor actions, and may have served some regulatory function (Prizant and Duchan, 1981; Prizant and Rydell, 1981). The paucity of S's communicative development may be best captured by the almost complete absence of the types of non-verbal precursors of speech that can be readily observed in normal pre-verbal children (Bates, 1979). In fact, speech production skills surpassed communicative intentions, suggesting an overall breakdown within the realm of social interaction, not of linguistic skills per se.

While S's speech comprehension skills were believed to be superior to his expressive speech, extensive testing revealed that his speech comprehension skills were minimal when no redundant cues were presented. S's ability to "read" contextual cues and his memorization of routines allowed him to handle everyday instructions; apparently S had developed some compensatory skills, allowing the "translation" of speech into a visual and possibly motor cue system. While S was able to imitate some gross motor movements when instructed to do so, this seemed the result of extensive training; spontaneously he didn't imitate other's actions. Furthermore, it was found that he was much more cued in to location than to sequences of actions over time. For instance, he failed to discriminate a single from a repeated pounding motion despite extensive training. Differentiation was only obtained when the repeated motions were associated with two different locations.

In marked contrast to S's communicative deficiencies, he demonstrated great skill in putting together puzzles, sorting and matching on the basis of perceptual attributes, such as size, and shape, as well as other tasks requiring visuo-spatial discrimination skills. In fact, when engaged in such tasks S took on a near-normal appearance.

In summary, extremely limited development in the domains of communication, imitation, and symbolic development was contrasted by some remarkable skills within the visuo-spatial domain that waited to be further elucidated. So far, standard assessment practices which rely on at least rudimentary communication and/or social interaction skills and are not specifically designed to investigate learning processes, had failed to clarify S's intellectual capacities and level of development. The following series of experiments were thus designed to clarify these matters.

A further investigation of conceptual, representational and referential abilities; an experimental approach

S' discrepancies in skill development, his lack of responsiveness to more traditional forms of assessment paired with the remarkable ease with which he learned certain tasks set the occasion for further inquiry into his knowledge of the world, his problem solving strategies and his thinking abilities in general. His severe limitations in communication in its broadest sense rather than a more formal language system are of particular interest to those who study the interrelationship between linguistic, social, and cognitive development. Nevertheless, limitations in social and linguistic development which were of primary interest, imposed a methodological problem; how to bypass the need to understand instructions, to imitate, to cooperate, and how to provide for an unbiased response mode. For instance, standard Piagetian assessments examine the communication of judgements, surprise, newly acquired knowledge, etc. to the examiner. Even a rather suitable test, as the Leiter (the only IQ test on which S proved testable) introduces a bias, i.e., a left-right progression in expressing sequential judgements. S's observed performance on this test suggested that he was apt to generate visual symmetry (or visual closure) rather than an open ended left-right sequence.

An attempt was made to provide for a mode of operation in which spatial location would be a prime consideration; objects were to be placed in a carefully delineated position rather than handed to the examiner. Specific training, utilizing differential reinforcement, was to take the place of instructions and to provide for the motivation to perform. The experiments carried out were too extensive to be fully incorporated into this report. However, the main findings regarding conceptual and representational abilities are reported in the next section. A following section summarizes S's ability to acquire labels through non-speech as compared to speech modes.

A. Conceptual and Representational Abilities

The following series of experiments were designed to determine the extent to which S was able to discriminate on tests of representational and conceptual rather than perceptual criteria. A systematic training and generalization testing paradigm was used in place of verbal or gestural instructions. Furthermore, a spatial task layout, common objects, and geometrical configurations were adopted, congruent with S's demonstrated discrimination skills and everyday experiences.

The first series of experiments examined the ability to make cross-modal associations, as such skills have repeatedly been linked with language and abstract forms of representation (for a discussion, see Premack, 1976). S's performance on a variety of cross-modal association tasks, such as, the ability to form visual representations of tactile stimulus input were examined. An extensive series of experiments showed S capable of making such associations. Also S did orient himself toward anyone giving instructions. Hence, no detailed reports are supplied in this section. Because conceptual knowledge about objects and people's actions seems so closely intertwined with the acquisition of language the following series of experimental analyses were carried out.

1) Associating objects on the basis of conceptual rather than perceptual attributes

In order to evaluate the extent to which S was able to move from purely perceptual to more conceptual and functional judgements, a series of matching tasks of increasing conceptual complexity were designed. More specifically, the following matching tasks were presented:

Subtest:

1. matching of identical objects; e.g. two identical metal spoons

2. matching of similar objects; e.g., a metal spoon with a differently shaped plastic spoon

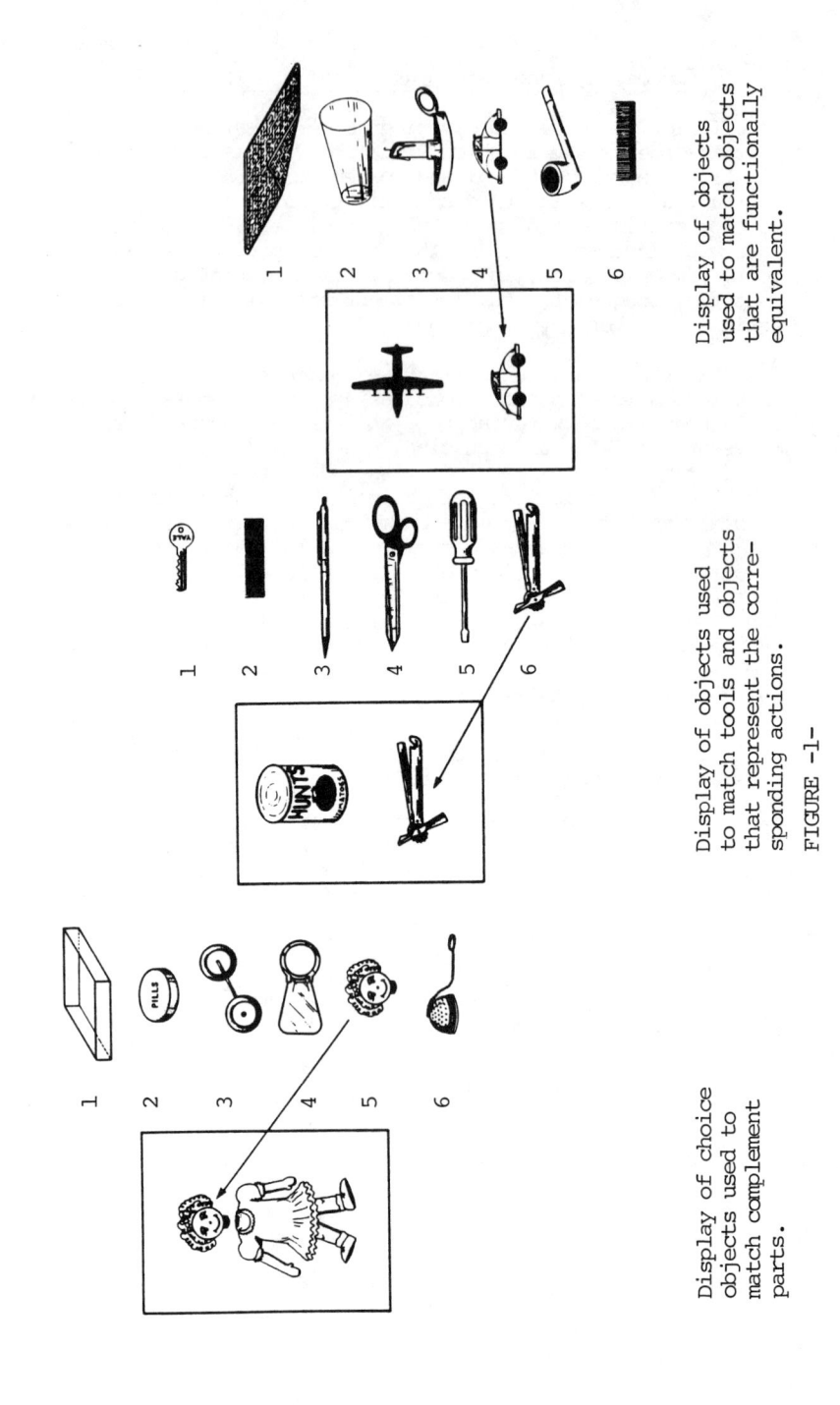

Display of objects used to match objects that are functionally equivalent.

Display of objects used to match tools and objects that represent the corresponding actions.

FIGURE -1-

Display of choice objects used to match complement parts.

274

3. matching of broken and whole objects; e.g., the broken spoon and a whole spoon
4. matching of complement parts; e.g., the glass bottom of a jar and its metal top. (See Figure 1.)
5. matching of tools and their complements; e.g., a pen with a piece of scribbled paper. (See Figure 1.)
6. matching of functional equivalents; e.g., a baby bottle and a cup. (See Figure 1.)

Experimental procedures

A "match to sample" paradigm was adopted; S was to respond by placing the closest matching object next to the sample object. Every subtest was introduced by a series of training trials during which S was prompted to select the matching object out of two choice objects upon presentation of a sample object placed upon a response pedestal (see Figure 1). Using differential reinforcement of correct responses, training trials were continued until a criterion of five consecutive correct unprompted responses. At that point six untrained generalization items (see Figure 1) were presented which served as the actual test of conceptualization since comprehension of the underlying matching rule can be inferred on the basis of continued correct responses.

Results

S performed as follows: all items correct on subtests 1, 2, and 3; four out of six correct on subtest 4, one out of six on subtest 5, and no correct selections on the last subtest. Nevertheless, in all cases S reached criterion on all training trials without ever making any errors. An error analysis revealed an interesting tendency. S at all times matched in reference to the most suitable perceptual criterion. For instance when unable to match jar bottom and top, S would select the doll's body, similar in color and size. Furthermore, the matching rules were flexibly altered dependent on the available choice objects. In other words, S seemed to find the best fitting match (either shape or size or mass or shine, etc.) for every sample object which suggests that he was able to postulate, test, and alter hypotheses regarding physical properties of objects. However, S was apparently unable to apply such cognitive operations in reference to the functional properties of the same objects.

The next series of experiments served to further explore S's abilities to make abstractions about physical attributes.

2) Abstracting rules regarding physical attributes

As S demonstrated a marked ability to make refined visuospatial discriminations, the nature of these abilities was further investigated. The experiments described in this section examined S's ability to make inferences on the basis of his observations and to isolate single features within a stimulus complex.

Experimental procedures

Again, a discrimination training and subsequent generalization testing paradigm was used to assess S's understanding of the following concepts: "big vs small," "more vs less," "some vs different," "centered vs off-centered," "rotated vs non-rotated," and "translated vs non-translated." The latter concept will be used to illustrate the experimental procedures.

S was presented with the first two stimulus cards depicted in Figure 2. On the first trial S was prompted to select the figure on the right (mirror-imaged pair). Prompts were gradually eliminated on subsequent trials while the position of the cars was systematically altered. Once the target card was consistently selected, the second pair depicting the same conceptual distinction was presented. If needed, training was supplied until the mirror-imaged card was again consistently selected. At that point the third set of cards was presented, followed by up to twenty additional illustrations of the same

1a. "Translated" 1b. "Reflected"

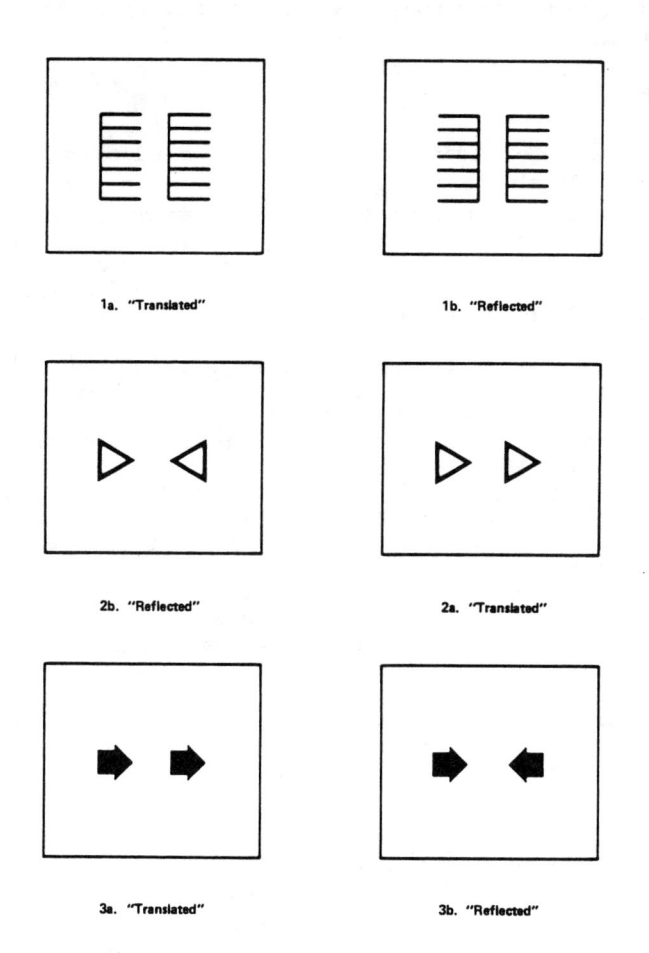

2b. "Reflected" 2a. "Translated"

3a. "Translated" 3b. "Reflected"

FIGURE -2- Display of stimulus cards used to test the ability to make abstractions about geometric properties.

concept. The series was stopped when clear evidence of generalization occurred, that is, when the correct card was continuously selected upon first presentation nine out of ten times.

Results

Evidence of generalization was supplied for all concepts assessed. In all cases no more than twelve sets of cards need to be presented to reach generalization criterion. In addition, evidence of number conservation (skills for numbers one through five) was inferred on the basis of S's ability to match on the basis of number only, and to disregard irrelevant perceptual attributes.

The experiments reported so far all suggest that S's skills within the visuo-spatial realm cannot be simply discarded as due to memory, inadvertent cueing or some other artifact. Rather, S was able to single out particular stimulus features, and to classify stimuli according to such features. In other words, S was able to make abstractions about physical realities, implying some mental analogue of predicative statements. Nevertheless, the process which underlies S's responses remains elusive. The remarkable speed with which he operated suggests that regularities within the overall spatial configuration are analyzed rather than component parts. In other words, a different non-language mode of thinking may be involved.

To further elucidate S's mode of thinking the next series of experiments were carried out focusing on the cognitive operations involved in acquiring labels for objects and their attributes.

B. Referential abilities; the acquisition of labels through different modes

The following series of experiments were designed to investigate whether S's linguistic and communicative breakdown might be a function of the stimulus properties of the conventional coding systems, such as, speech and gesture. In addition, if some principles of language could be taught through an alternative mode, this would allow for an investigation of the conceptual limitations involved.

A comparison between the acquisition of spoken, signed and written word labels

Before systematic training was provided some quantitative baseline measures of S's understanding of spoken, signed and written labels was obtained. For this purpose S was presented with ten common objects out of his everyday environment. Separate calculations of percentage of correct responses to spoken, signed, and written word labels were made on the basis of the repeated presentation of all labels involved in randomized order. In all cases S responded at or below chance levels. A program to teach receptive responses to pairs of spoken, signed, and written word labels was then started at three different times of the day. The teaching program was designed in such a way that additional pairs of labels would be added as soon as discriminative responses to the first pair of labels were similar in design to allow for unbiased comparisons, and a failure criterion of 500 teaching trials without any signs of progress was built in.

S learned the first pair of written word labels, within 180 trials, that is, within the minimal number of trials possible at that point on the program (for a more detailed description of the program, see La Vigna, 1977). However, the two training programs designed to teach speech or signs were terminated after 500 trials.

Additional pairs of written word discriminations were then taught with increasing ease (twenty trials; through use of differential reinforcement only). However, extensive efforts to use the learned written word discriminations as an aid in the acquisition of the equivalent spoken and signed labels failed when all written word cues were eliminated. At one point S was cued by differences as subtle as those between a laminated and non-laminated blank card. The systematic prompt fading program was terminated, because a shift in stimulus control could not be established.

The acquisition of more abstract labels

Given S's ability to acquire written word labels for concrete objects, attempts were made to determine whether he would be able to acquire labels for more abstract notions. Given S's understanding of number and other physical attributes, written labels were taught for the numbers one through five as well as for the distinction "big vs little." While S readily acquired these labels, extensive efforts to combine them into three word combinations, such as, "three big cups" vs "two little cups" failed. Observation of S's performance on this task suggested that it was difficult for him to incorporate two separate judgements into a serial order. Imposing elements of grammar onto an otherwise straightforward act of labeling may have been the stumbling block.

Use of written words permitted the probe for yet another cognitive operation. Would S be able to infer equivalence on the basis of indirect associations? After S had learned the label "cup" for that object, he was taught that the label equaled "tumbler." At that point it was tested whether S could associate "tumbler" with the original referent object. S was able to do so, indicating a comprehension of logic of the type: a=b; b=c; therefore, a=c.

Conclusions and discussion

The various studies reported are cumulative in terms of their findings, as the results of the various studies support each other. Apparently, S's cognitive deficiencies did not cut across all developmental domains. Rather, they seemed specific to the nature of the stimulus input. S was able to learn and solve problems when only non-transient stimuli were involved. However, he was not able to do so when dealing with more transient stimuli, such as speech, signs, or object-related action sequences. In addition, the observed cognitive disparities are congruent with other investigations of the mental capacities of non-communicative, autistic or otherwise disordered individuals. For instance, Curcio (1978) in his investigations of the sensorimotor abilities of twelve mute autistic individuals reported that minimal verbal or non-verbal communication skills were consistently associated with poor performance on means-end scales. However, performance on the object permanence scales was generally higher. S's inability to match on the basis of object use also suggests poor understanding of means-end relations. In addition, observation of S in his everyday environment further supports this notion. S's extreme reliance on memorized action sequences suggests limitations in the ability to conceptualize the impact of his own actions. This may be best illustrated by S's need to open the kitchen cabinet, get a cup, and fill it whenever thirsty, and his inability to re-use that same cup. In other words, when wanting to drink water, S will keep taking out new cups without emptying out or refilling old cups.

S's knowledge of where various objects are or should be located in space, and his ability to match on the basis of object attributes are congruent with the higher object permanence scores reported by Curcio. However, the disparities exhibited in this study are of greater magnitude, because of the formal thinking abilities demonstrated. This suggests that certain dimensions of cognitive development may develop independently of communicative/linguistic development.

Interestingly, the longitudinal investigations of sensorimotor and communicative abilities in normal children by Bates and her co-workers (Bates et al., 1979) also suggest that imitation, symbolization, communication and social tool use may develop independently from object related and spatial thinking. As far as the causation of the reported developmental disparity is concerned, one can only speculate.

On the one end, the problem could be primarily a perceptual one. An inability to discriminate and/or store transient stimulus input would interfere with social development, and account for the developmental profile described. On the other end, the problems observed could also be attributed primarily to severe limitations within the realm of social interaction. The extent to which engagement in social interaction alters human perception remains to be clarified. Making sense out of transient stimulus input may be rooted within the transience of early social interactions. Human thinking may be greatly influenced by the medium of early social interaction and role taking (for a more extensive discussion of these matters, see Wolf and Gardner, 1981). In providing a perspective on cognitive development without the constraints of early socialization and communication, studies as the one reported here may ultimately help to unravel the mysteries surrounding the ontogeny of human thinking.

References

Bates, E., Benigni, L., Bretherton, I., Camaioni, L., and Volterra, V. 1979. The Emergence of Symbols: Cognition and Communication in Infancy Academic Press, New York

Curcio, F., 1978. Sensorimotor functioning and communication in mute autistic children Journal of Autism and Childhood Schizophrenia, 3, 281-292

Curtiss, S., Kempler, D., and Yamada, J. 1981. The relationship betwen language and cognition in development: Theoretical framework and research design UCLA Working Papers in Cognitive Linguistics, 3, 1-61

La Vigna, G.W. 1977. Communication training in mute autistic adolescents using the written word Journal of Autism and Childhood Schizophrenia, 7, 135-149

Premack, D. 1976. Language and intelligence in ape and man American Scientist, 64, 674-683

Prizant, B. and Duchan, J.F. 1981. The functions of delayed echolalia in autistic children Journal of Speech and Hearing Disorders, 46, 241-249

Prizant, B. and Rydell, P. 1981. A functional analysis of delayed echolalia of autistic children. Paper presented to the Annual Meeting of the American Speech and Hearing Association, Los Angeles

Wolf, D. and Gardner, H. 1981. On the structure of early symbolization, in R. Schiefelbusch and D. Bricker (eds.) Early Language: Acquisition and Intervention University Park Press, Baltimore, Maryland

The Acquisition of Linguistic Structures
and Cognitive Development

by
Gisela E. Speidel

Kamehameha Educational Research Institute
and University of Hawaii

Piaget at the Cornell conference made a very strong claim: "Words are probably no short-cut to better understanding. The level of understanding seems to modify the language that is used, rather than vice versa.... Mainly language serves to translate what is already understood; or else language may even present a danger if used to introduce an idea which is not yet accessible" (Piaget, in Ripple & Rockcastle,1964, p.5).

Piaget, himself, however, "has never paid as much attention to the acquisition of language as to other aspects of human knowledge" (Inhelder, 1978, p. 226). Hermine Sinclair is the Genevan who has concerned herself the most with relating Piagetian cognitive development theory to language acquisition. She has conducted numerous studies on this issue and draws such conclusions as "Intellectual development is possible without language, but language acquisition is bound to the elaboration of cognitive structures in general" (Sinclair, 1975, p. 225). The cognitive structures she believes to be the basis of language acquisition are those postulated by Piaget: a coherent set of mental operations, "universal in their form if not in their content" (p. 224).

The actual research to support such a conclusion about the dependency of language acquisition on general cognitive structures is weak. Sinclair's research has never shown a direct effect of the hypothesized cognitive structures on language; her conclusions are based on data that are at best correlational, showing increased competence in both the linguistic and in the cognitive domain with age. For instance, in one of her frequently cited studies (Sinclair-de Zwart, 1967) she grouped children age 4½ to 8 years together and found that most conservers used more mature language structures, while most of the non-conservers still used the simple linguistic forms. From this finding she concludes that the more mature linguistic forms cannot be acquired without the cognitive structures leading to conservation.

Some reflection will show that such a conclusion is totally unwarranted. The finding may simply indicate a well known fact that older children are more competent on most any skill than younger children. For instance, I would not be surprised if at age 5 we would find a large correspondence between inability to ride a bicyle and inability to produce passive sentences, and at age 8 a large correspondence between ability to ride a bicycle and mastery of the passive. Using Sinclair's reasoning we would then conclude that bicycle riding is a necessary condition for learning the passive. However, we realize that such correspondence could be due to many factors that are related to age. Such correlational data provide no evidence for the primacy of Piagetian cognitive structures in the development of certain linguistic structures, and the observed correspondence could even come about if language were a necessary condition for conservation to develop.

In other Piagetian psycholinguistic studies the actual level of cognitive development was not even assessed, and the argument rested merely on drawing similarities between the changes and errors found in the acquisition of certain linguistic structures and in the performance of certain Piagetian tasks (Sinclair, Sinclair & Marcellus, 1971; Sinclair, 1971; Sinclair, 1975).

For example, Sinclair, Sinclair, and Marcellus (1971) conducted a study on the comprehension and production of the passive voice in children 4 to 10 years of age. They found that younger children had much more difficulty comprehending and producing the passive than older children. Only the 8 to 10 year-olds were able to produce the passive readily. In characterizing the development of comprehension and production of the passive, they described similarities between problems young children have with the passive voice and with conservation tasks: Both, they argued, reflect the difficulty younger children have in viewing an event from two different points of view. This type of difficulty was observed in children speaking either French, German or English. Even though the performance of the children was never assessed on any Piagetian cognitive tasks, Sinclair et al. concluded, "Acquisition of the passive voice, in the sense of correct understanding and production of reversible passive sentences....can only start when the child's general cognitive development has progressed to the level where the child is capable of considering an event from two different points of view, or in Piagetian terminology, the beginning of logical decentration."

The very obvious need to take appropriate cognitive measures simultaneously with the language measures in order to provide any support for such a conclusion was rectified in two subsequent studies by Beilin (1975) and Moore and Harris (1978). Beilin, using level of reversibility as his cognitive measure, found a positive correlation between reversibility level and comprehension and production of the passive. From this "general correlation between these developments", Beilin concludes that "Our findings support the general claim that language development occurs as a consequence of and in association with the development of cognitive structures and functions" (p. 83). As we have argued above (and as Beilin himself concedes) such correlations are very likely mediated by age and therefore say very little about any causal relationship between "cognitive structures of reversibility and comprehension and production of the passive voice."

Moore and Harris used acquisition of conservation as measured by the Goldschmid-Bentler test as their cognitive measure in mapping comprehension and production of the passive to operational thought. Their analysis is an improvement over previous studies in this area, in that they test a specific hypothesis implied in the Piagetian position. "If correct use of the passive structure is dependent upon proper presence of reversibility operations, as measured by conservation tasks, then. . . . there should be no evidence of facility with passives, in the absence of conservation skills" (p. 143). They proceeded to look at the performance of children who were nonconservers on the Goldschmid-Bentler test and found a single child who was a nonconserver but fully competent in both the comprehension and production of the passive. A few other nonconserving children showed partial knowledge of the passive. From this data, Moore and Harris concluded that there was "evidence for the appearance of logical operations in language prior to their emergence in cognitive non-verbal activity" (p.144). This is a strange twist to the initial hypothesis they wanted to test.

For purposes of this discussion, the results of the

Moore and Harris study do not constitute very stong evidence against the Piagetian cognitive primacy hypothesis, since only one child clearly contradicted the Piagetian prediction.

The present study is a further attempt to test Sinclair et al.'s (1971) implication that concrete operational thought is necessary for the full mastery of the passive. It is therefore a partial replication of the Sinclair et al. study, but includes the necessary simultaneous assessment of the Piagetian cognitive structures assumed to underlie mastery of the passive. Following Moore and Harris' example, performance on conservation tasks constituted the measure of the children's nonverbal cognitive level. The relationship between conservation and mastery of the passive is implied in the theorizing of Sinclair et al. In the passive transformation of an active sentence, several operations are required, among them the reversal of subject and object in sentence position. Conserving meaning while performing these transformations is presumed to require the same cognitive operations as are required by conservation tasks: a realization of the reversibility of an action and that essential characteristics remain the same when transformations occur on irrelevant dimensions.

An environmental variable was included in the present study. Two different socioeconomic groups of children were studied: a middle/upper middle class group speaking standard English (upper SES group) and a lower socioeconomic group (lower SES group) speaking Hawaiian English which is a dialect of English. Although there is no information on the relative frequencies of passive voice usage by the two populations from which these children are drawn, one might expect that the lower SES group of children has less exposure and is less familiar with the passive voice than the upper SES group. Performance differences between the two groups would suggest the influence of environmental factors in the acquisition of cognitive and linguistic structures.

Before describing the present study, a major difficulty needs to be pointed out in Piagetian theorizing pertaining to the assessment of particular cognitive structures hypothesized to underlie particular language structures. These cognitive structures are initially content-bound, emerging at different times in different content. This results in indistinct, fuzzy criteria for deciding when a particular cognitive structure (or language structure) has been acquired. This in turn makes the hypothesis that certain cognitive structures are necessary for the mastery of certain linguistic structures virtually impossible to test, impossible to verify, and impossible to reject. Whatever level of cognitive development is used to investigate the primacy of cognitive structures in linguistic development, someone may argue that it was not the intended, the implied level. We have attempted to address this difficulty by analyzing the data in two ways: one reflecting the continuous development of concrete operational thought, and the other reflecting presence or absence of the cognitive operations. Not everyone may be in agreement with the manner in which we have attempted to map cognitive structures, as reflected in performance on the conservation tasks, to the mastery of the passive. Yet, it should be emphasized that in order for a theory to be scientifically useful, it must yield testable hypotheses. The present study has translated a major assumption of the Piagetian psycholinguistic position into a testable hypothesis, trying to retain as much as possible Piagetian assumptions about learning.

Method

Subjects. Eighty children participated in the study, 20 at each grade level from kindergarten to third grade. Half of the children at each grade were from low-income, dialect speaking, Hawaiian families. The other half of the children spoke standard English and were enrolled in a private parochial school with a large ethnic and racial mix. Within each sub-group, there was an equal number of boys and girls.

Procedure. Level of cognitive functioning was assessed on the Goldschmid-Bentler conservation tasks, which consist of the conservation of space, number, mass, weight, continuous and discontinuous quantity.

Acquisition of the passive voice was studied using a procedure modelled after the one used by Sinclair et al. There were four phases: two comprehension and two production, presented alternately. In the comprehension phases the experimenter said a sentence and asked the child to act out with toys what had been said. In the production phases the experimenter acted out some activity and asked the child to describe what had happened. For example, the experimenter might have a toy doll wash a spoon and ask the child, "What is happening here?" If the child described the action in the active voice, the experimenter would try to elicit the passive by prompting in the manner described by Sinclair et al., "Tell me the same thing but begin with the spoon (patient)." If the child did not respond with the full passive, the experimenter gave a series of other predetermined prompts.

The actions used for the comprehension and production tasks were those used by Sinclair et al. For the comprehension task, five irreversible, five reversible, and two nonsense actions were employed. For the production task, five irreversible and five reversible actions were used. (E. g., An irreversible action would be "girl washes spoon; a reversible action would be "girl washes boy"). There were different sets of subject-verb-object combinations so that a child never had the same combination for production and comprehension.

Results

Comprehension. Since comprehension of the passive voice is more advanced than production (e.g. Sinclair et al., 1971; Beilin, 1975), the more critical test for the dependence of correct usage of the passive on concrete operational thought is found in relating ability to conserve to the production of the passive. Therefore, I will only briefly mention that (a) by second grade the children essentially comprehended the passive sentences; (b) the upper SES group had a slight, non-significant edge over the dialect speakers; and (c) irreversible sentences were slightly easier than the reversible sentences.

Production. Several different analyses were conducted with the passive production data, each highlighting a different perspective. The intention is to show that the different forms of analyses all point to the same conclusion: no evidence supporting the Piagetian psycholinguistic position.

A very stringent criterion for production of the passive was used. A child was only credited with mastery of an item if he responded with the full passive to the very first passive eliciting prompt. No points were credited for truncated passives, or for full passives given after the first minimal prompt. Since the reversible passive was no more difficult than the irreversible passive for the present groups of children, performance on

reversible and irreversible passives was combined. A child
was classified as having predominant use of the passive if
on eight out of the ten trials he responded with the full
passive to the first prompt. Such a stringent measure was
used so that a child classified as using the passive
predominantly would be seen as a child who had mastery of
the passive in the full sense imposed by Sinclair et al.
Criteria for classifying a child on the conservation
measure varied with the different analyses performed.

The percentages of children who mastered the passive
and who conserved are shown in Figure 1. For this analysis
a child was classified as a conserver, if he had a score of
10 or more out of the possible 12 points on the Goldschmid-
Bentler. Aside from some irregularities, the number of
children who achieved success on the two behaviors
increased from kindergarten to third grade in both SES
groups.

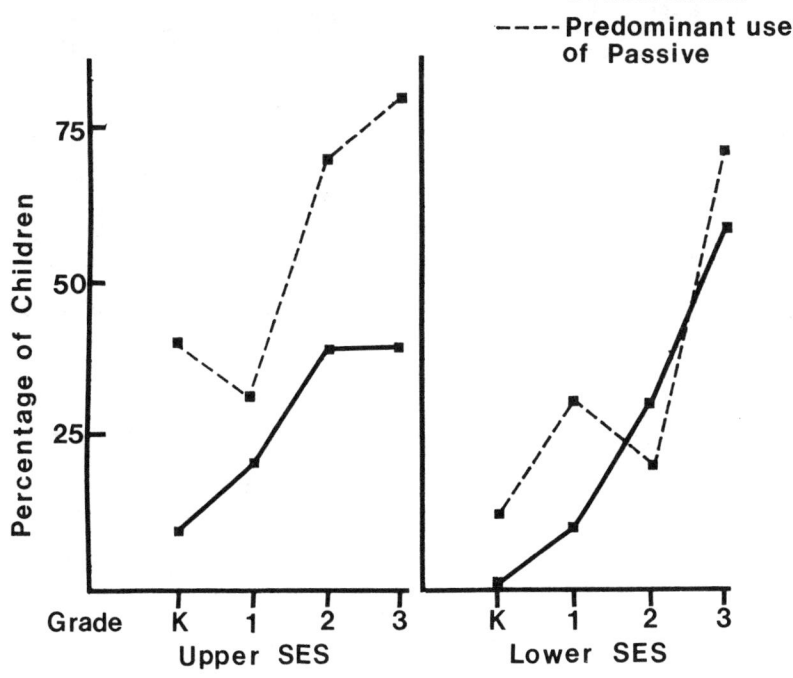

Figure 1. Conservation and predominant use of passive.

There are several issues to discuss regarding the findings shown in these figures.

1. The curves, showing simultaneous increase in conservation and in mastery of the passive with age, point out how readily such curves, and correlational data in general, can be misinterpreted as reflecting a causative link between the behaviors.

2. In this case, acquisition of the passive appears to lead acquisition of conservation at least with the upper SES group. However, some reflection will reveal that the exact relationship between these curves is a function of the point at which each of the behaviors is considered as acquired. For example, if the criterion for conserving is shifted downward on the Goldschmid-Bentler, the advance noted in the production of the passive would be eliminated.

Actually, both conservation and production of the passive appear to be acquired gradually as reflected in the finding of individual records which yielded the whole range of scores on both the language and the non-verbal tasks. If both conservation and production of the passive increase gradually with time (with increasing number of learning experiences), it is practically impossible to test the influence of one cognitive domain on the other without experimental manipulations. Such gradual increases in performances also suggest the artificiality of the analyses that will be presented below. However, to test the hypothesis that universal cognitive structures exhibited in the concrete operations are necessary for the acquisition of the passive voice by using Sinclair et al.'s non-experimental method, specific mapping of the performance of the passive and level of conservation is required.

3. With regard to the SES variable, when the results are grouped across age levels, we find there is virtually no difference in number of children conserving in the two groups; in the low SES group there are ten children, in the upper SES group there are 11 out of 40. However, with respect to predominant use of the passive the different social/linguistic backgrounds appear to create differences. Nearly twice as many children in the upper SES group (22 out of 40) have predominant use of the passive than in the lower SES group (13 out of 40). This finding suggests a strong environmental component to the age of acquisition of the passive.

4. There is a dip in the performance of the passive in both groups of children. The responses of the children have not yet been analyzed to see whether this dip is attributable to a particular type of error or strategy which could perhaps be related to the dip observed to occur in the comprehension of the passive in children between the ages of three and four (Maratsos, 1974).

According to the implied Piagetian psycholinguistic hypothesis, all children who have mastered the passive should theoretically be at the level of concrete operational thought, should be conserving, while none should still be at the nonconserving level. Table 1 describes where children who have mastered the passive tend to be in terms of their acquisition of the concrete operations. For this table, the criterion for mastery of the passive remains the same as above, eight or more correct productions of the full passive. The categorization of the children in levels of conservation was performed on the basis of scores obtained on the Goldschmid-Bentler test: conservers, 10 or more; high intermediates, 6-9; low intermediates, 3-5; and nonconservers, 0-2. The table clearly shows that if younger children, at the kindergarten and first grade level, have mastered the passive they tend not to be conservers. In second and third grade we see greater correspondence between conserving and use of the passive.

Table 1. Percentage of children at the different levels of conservation for children who have mastered the passive.

	Grade	Conservation Level				
		NC	Lo I	Hi I	C	(N)
Lower SES						
	K	–	100	–	–	1
	1	66.7	–	33.3	–	3
	2	–	–	50.0	50.0	2
	3	–	–	42.9	57.1	7
Upper SES	K	50.0	–	25.0	25.0	4
	1	–	33.3	33.3	33.3	3
	2	14.3	14.3	14.3	57.0	7
	3	–	25.0	25.0	50.0	8

Note: Lo I = low intermediate; Hi I = high intermediate; C = conserver; NC = non-conserver.

However, by third grade most of the children are either high intermediate conservers or conservers anyway, so that by chance alone there is a high probability that a child who has mastered the passive is also a conserver.

The above analysis makes it clear that children who master both the passive and who conserve, as well as children who have not yet begun to acquire either skill, do not yield any evidence for or against the primacy of cognitive structures in the acquisition of the passive. Rather it is children who show a discernible discrepancy in their development of concrete operational thought and acquisition of the passive that can throw light on the

Piagetian hypothesis. For the following analysis only children who were at the extreme ends in their mastery of the two tasks were studied: children who showed virtually no competence in the production of the passive (scoring only 0-2 on the passive production task), but who had mastered the conservation tasks (scoring 10-12 on the Goldschmid-Bentler), and children who had mastery of the passive (scoring 8-10 on the passive production task) but no conservation (scoring 0-2 on the Goldschmid-Bentler). There were seven such children, nearly 10% of the total sample. Five of these had mastered the passive and were nonconserving; for only two children the reverse was the case. Therefore, when looking at the sequence of acquisition of the two skills in children who show a discrepancy in their development, there were more children who contradicted than supported the Piagetian hypothesis.

A similar analysis was performed using different criteria for inclusion into the "developmental discrepancy" sample. A child was characterized in his development of conservation in terms of his performance on the liquids conservation task (a typical task used by Piagetians for assessing a child's level of conservation). He was classified as a conserver if he gave a conservation response and a logical explanation, as an intermediate conserver if he gave a conservation response unsupported by a logical explanation, and as a non-conserver if he did not give a conservation response. A child was classified as mastering the passive in the previous manner, 8 or more full passive responses on the passive production task, and as not mastering the passive if he produced between 0-7 full passives. Only children were studied for this analysis who had mastered the passive, but were nonconserving or vice versa. There were 25 such children, 32% of the total sample.

Table 2 shows the sequences in which the two skills are acquired among these 25 children. The results clearly indicate that there is no particular sequence of acquisition. There are at least as many children who have full mastery of the passive but are still nonconservers, as there are children who conserve, but have not acquired the passive. The Piagetian hypothesis of cognitive primacy for certain linguistic structures is once again not substantiated.

Table 2. Percentage of children mastering the language and conservation tasks at different points in time (N=25).

Grade	Mastery of the Passive Before Conserving	(N)	Conserving Before Mastering the Passive	(N)
Lower SES				
K + 1	60%	(3)	40%	(2)
2 + 3	25%	(2)	75%	(6)
Upper SES				
K + 1	50%	(4)	50%	(4)
2 + 3	75%	(3)	25%	(1)

Conclusion

The present study replicated the Sinclair et al. study on the passive, but included assessment of acquisition of the concrete operations. The results do not support the assertion that the passive cannot be acquired before the beginning of logical decentration, if the beginning of logical decentration is defined as possessing the cognitive structures underlying conservation. Even though an extremely stringent criterion for the production of the passive was used, among the young children who have mastered the passive, most were not conservers. It was only at second and third grade that a correspondence between conservation and mastery of the passive was found. At that point, a very high proportion of children were conservers, so that by chance alone most children who had mastered the passive would also conserve. Furthermore, looking only at children who showed a distinct lag in the mastery of one of the two behaviors, the predicted earlier appearance of the cognitive structures in conservation was not found: The passive voice was mastered before conservation just as frequently as conservation was acquired before the passive.

It is possible to argue, as Moore and Harris have suggested, that logical operations underlying conservation can first become manifest in the linguistic domain. In other words, the concept of decalage (the manifestation of the same cognitive structure at different ages with different content) could be invoked to explain the different levels of cognitive development observed sometimes between the verbal and the non-verbal domain. If the concept of decalage, however, is introduced to account after the fact for the finding that some children can produce the passive voice reliably before they conserve, then the Piagetian psycholinguistic stance about the necessity of universal cognitive structures for the acquisition of such lingusitic structures as the passive voice becomes meaningless. Without ability to prove the existence of the cognitive structure before its appearance in the related lingistic structure, the theory cannot be proven or disproven.

Although we did not investigate the differences in the age of acquisition of the passive in the two SES groups in any detail, there were significantly fewer lower SES than upper SES children who had mastered the passive. It seems, therefore, that experience and exposure to language models of the passive form is a more critical determinant for age of acquisition of the passive than being able to conserve. Recently, two researchers of the Genevan school, Karmiloff-Smith and Bronckardt, have independently of each other begun to question the unidirectional influence between cognitive structures and language. Karmiloff-Smith writes: "In analyzing psychological phenomena, Piaget has unjustly relegated language to a secondary role and thereby underestimated the importance of language as a constructive factor in development" (1979, p. 2).

I do not wish to imply that certain cognitive, non-verbal understanding may not be necessary for the acquisition of certain verbal concepts, or linguistic structures. It is very clear that many concepts, concepts such as those of time--tomorrow, yesterday, minutes--develop through experiences many of which are non-verbal. Also, I do not wish to imply that the learning processes underlying language need to be different from learning processes underlying other intellectual activities. What I do wish to argue is that the data upon which the Piagetians have rested their claims about the primacy of universal cognitive structures for the acquisition of certain language structures is extremely weak, and that one of the few testable hypotheses was not supported in the present study. The theory of universal, global mental structures influencing all intellectual behavior was not supported.

References

Beilin, H. *Studies in the cognitive basis of language development*. New York: Academic Press, 1975.

Inhelder, B. Language and thought: Some remarks on Chomsky and Piaget, *Journal of Psycholinguistic Research*, 1978, 7.

Karmiloff-Smith, A. *A functional approach to child language: A study of determiners and reference*. New York: Cambridge University Press, 1979.

Maratsos, M. P. Children who get worse at understanding the passive: A replication of Bever. *Journal of Psycholinguistic Research*, 1974, 3.

Moore, T. E. and Harris, A. E. Language and thought in Piagetian theory. In Linda S. Siegel and Charles, J. Brainerd (Eds.) *Alternatives to Piaget: Critical essays on the theory*. New York: Academic Press, Inc., 1978.

Ripple, R. E. and Rockcastle, N. N. (Eds.) *Piaget rediscovered*, 1964.

Sinclair A., Sinclair H., & Marcellus, O. Young children's comprehension and production of passive sentences. *Archives de Psychologie*, 1971, 41, 1-22.

Sinclair, H. Sensorimotor action patterns as a condition for the acquisition of syntax. In R. Huxley & E. Ingram (Eds.) *Language acquisition: Models and methods*. New York: Academic Press, 1971.

Sinclair, H. The role of cognitive structures in language acquisition. In Lenneberg, E. H. and Lenneberg, E. (Eds.) *Foundations of language development*. New York: Academic Press, 1975.

Sinclair-de Zwart H. *Acquisition du language et développement dela pensée*. Paris: Dunod, 1967.

Sinclair-de Zwart, H. Language acquisition and cognitive development. In T. E. Moore, (Ed.) *Cognitive development and the acquisition of language*, New York: Academic Press, 1973.

On the Relationship Between Language and Cognition:
Evidence from a Hyperlinguistic Retarded Adolescent

Jeni E. Yamada
Department of Linguistics, UCLA

Introduction:

This paper discusses aspects of my work to date with "Marta," an eighteen year old moderately retarded young woman who appears to be what I will call "hyperlinguistic." Marta can be termed hyperlinguistic in that she presents a performance profile of extremely advanced linguistic abilities alongside markedly depressed nonlinguistic cognitive abilities, with a testable IQ in the low 40s. This discrepant profile is provocative because it indicates that language can develop in the absence of many nonlinguistic cognitive abilities; in particular, those which have been theorized to be prerequisite to language or to reflect underlying principles in common with language.

This type of high language/low cognition profile is not predicted by theoretical models stating that language can be largely accounted for by nonlinguistic capacities. In one view language is seen as emerging out of cognitive development (Piaget, 1980; Sinclair, 1971, 1973, 1975) while in another related view, language and cognition are seen as linked by a set of common underlying organizing principles (Piaget, 1977; Bates, 1979; Beilin, 1980). While there is no doubt that language interacts with cognition, Marta's case and others like it (Curtiss and Yamada, 1981; Yamada and Curtiss, 1981) support the contention that language cannot be accounted for on the basis of nonlanguage abilities identified to date. Such cases provide empirical evidence for a model of language development that sees aspects of language as independent of other cognitive systems, governed by learning systems unique to language (Chomsky, 1980a, 1980b). Indeed, if it is possible for an individual to develop language in the absence of putatively prerequisite or commonly governed abilities, it can be seriously questioned whether and to what extent language is dependent upon or linked to those other abilities.

Documentation of selectively impaired individuals is important in the attempt to understand the relationship between language and other mental functions. Such individuals provide us with real-life means of testing our theoretical hypotheses.

The selectively impaired individual provides the opportunity to observe to what extent it is possible for particular abilities to emerge, develop, and function in isolation of other abilities and thus also discover the dependencies which do exist.

Evidence that language, or at least aspects of language, may develop independently of nonlinguistic cognition has already been indicated by studies of individuals with Turner's syndrome, with hydrocephaly, and with mental retardation. Subsets of these groups show relatively intact linguistic ability alongside substantial cognitive deficits (Money, 1964; Money and Alexander, 1966; Garron, 1970; Silbert, Wolff, and Lilienthal, 1977; Schwartz, 1974; Swisher and Pinsker, 1971; Yamada and Curtiss, 1981; Curtiss and Yamada, 1981; Yamada, 1981).

The case discussed here is unique in several respects. First, Marta's linguistic ability appears to be more advanced than that of many previous subjects studied, especially relative to her nonlinguistic ability. Thus, the discrepancy between her linguistic and nonlinguistic capacities is especially marked. In addition, Marta at age eighteen, is no longer making significant changes developmentally in either language or nonlanguage domains, making it possible to examine just how far language can potentially develop in the face of severe cognitive deficits.

Case History:

Marta was born on September 12, 1963, the fourth and last daughter of professionals. She was 16 at the outset of study and 18 at this writing. According to her parents, Marta was an easy, quiet baby, but within the first year they noticed developmental delays, becoming concerned when she was not yet sitting alone at 9 to 10 months. At about one year Marta was diagnosed by a pediatrician as mentally retarded (with etiology unknown). Diary notes by Marta's mother dating from when Marta was 1½ to nearly 8 and extensive medical and educational records document well Marta's early development.

Marta's developmental milestones were delayed. She sat alone at 15 months, stood at 20 months, and walked at about 2 years. Toilet training was completed when she was about 4. In addition, language was delayed. At 1½ Marta understood only a few words and was not yet talking. At 3½ Marta was using only about twenty words regularly and about fifty words total. By four and a half she was talking in sentences, using some inflectional morphology and pronominal forms. In school records Marta's tendency to be verbal was frequently noted, with echolalia and excessive, incessant talking (often irrelevant to the topic at hand) noted as characteristic. Throughout development verbal ability was noted to be her strongest area, while abstract reasoning, number concepts, and visuo-motor skills were among her weakest. Marta's performance on past WISC-R tests reflects the discrepant profile which still persists.

	Verbal IQ	Performance IQ	Full Scale IQ
6/11/75 (age 11½)	58	0	44
6/9/78 (age 14½)	52	32	41

In a report written when Marta was 8:5 her mother is said to have indicated that Marta "has difficulty thinking with her language in the sense that she gives the impression that she knows and thinks more than she really does. This is so because she often repeats what she has heard without understanding the substance of what has been stated..." Indeed, Marta's enhanced language has confused educators as to the proper course of action to take with regard to her schooling. In an educational system that often correlates linguistic sophistication with intelligence and academic competence, Marta never fit neatly into any particular category.

Marta had one EEG at age 9 which revealed some abnormalities. An EEG done in May 1980 showed spikes in the right temporal region and an additional EEG obtained in June 1980 was also mildly abnormal due to "generalized slowing of the record during the waking stage." However, Marta's most recent EEG in September 1980 was normal and a non-contrast CT scan done in July 1980 was also normal.

Marta lived at home with her family until she was fifteen years old, thus benefitting from the loving and stimulating environment provided by her parents and three older sisters. She is currently living in a residential setting and attends a special school.

Assessment:

Marta's language and nonlanguage abilities were evaluated through formal testing and informal observation and interaction.

Language Assessment: Marta's language knowledge was tapped in a variety of ways. First, formal language tests developed by Susan Curtiss and the author were administered (Curtiss and Yamada). The Curtiss-Yamada Comprehensive Language Evaluation (CYCLE) focuses on specific structures and features of English in the areas of syntax, morphology, semantics, and phonology. The test contains a receptive battery, an elicitation battery, and a spontaneous speech analysis protocol. The receptive battery (CYCLE-R) covers many structures and features in the various language components. The elicitation battery (CYCLE-E) parallels, in form and content, the receptive language tests but also includes other areas, e.g. conditionals and modals. For a description of the CYCLE and the methodology used, refer to Curtiss, Kempler, and Yamada, 1981.

For the spontaneous speech analysis, language samples were taken from transcriptions of audio tape recordings of sessions and informal conversation. Marta's use of many structures, including those tapped in formal testing, were analysed with particular attention being paid to the range of structures used, their degree of complexity, and their appropriateness in context. For purposes of additional comparison with normal children, a portion of Marta's language sample was analysed according to the Laura Lee Developmental Sentence Scoring method (Lee and Canter, 1971; Lee, 1974). In addition, a Peabody Picture Vocabulary Test-Revised was administered. Sentence repetition tasks were also administered. Sentences presented were either phonemically, syntactically, or semantically anomalous. Some items were taken from Whitaker (1976) while others were designed by the author. Only a subset of the language data will be presented here.

Nonlanguage Assessment: Marta's nonlinguistic functioning was assessed by administration of a broad range of tests and tasks tapping specific areas of cognition. The tests were selected for a variety of reasons. Abilities which show clear developmental trends like drawing, memory, number concepts, and hierarchical construction, as well as various Piagetian abilities characteristic of the sensorimotor and concrete-operational period, were assessed in order to determine Marta's developmental stage. In addition, particular tasks were given because they tap abilities which are claimed to be prerequisite to or otherwise linked to language.

Sensorimotor abilities for example, have been described as prerequisite to at least the earliest stages of language acquisition, and concrete operational abilities, to later, more advanced linguistic attainments such as the emergence of complex sentences (Ingram, 1975). Certain specific features associated with language have been claimed to exist in other domains as well. For example, representational ability has been claimed to underlie copying, drawing, and symbolic play, as well as language (Piaget and Inhelder, 1969). Hierarchical organization has been claimed to be embodied in visuo-constructive tasks (Greenfield and Schneider, 1977; Greenfield, 1978) and classification (Inhelder and Piaget, 1964), in addition to language. Also, rule abduction has been said to exist in nonlinguistic (Neimark, 1970, cited in Flavell, 1977) and in linguistic domains (Maratsos and Chalkey, 1980). In addition, while the precise relationship between language and memory has not been established, a correlation between memory span and language ability has been noted (Graham, 1968; Masland and Case, 1968; Menyuk, 1964).

Table 1 lists some of the specific language tests which were given to Marta. On some tests Marta's task on a given item was to listen to a sentence read by the examiner and to point to the picture (in an array containing 2 to 4 pictures) corresponding to the test sentence. On other tests she was to act out the sentence using small toys. Still other tests required her to follow particular instructions (e.g. Before you touch your eye, touch your ear). Her age level of performance for each test was established by comparing her results to those of children in a normative sample consisting of about 150 children.

Table 2 lists some of the nonlanguage tests and tasks administered.

Classification: In order to analyse her classification abilities Marta was given circles and squares of different colors (red and blue) and sizes (large and small) and was asked to sort the items into two piles (Inhelder and Piaget, 1964). In addition, tasks developed by Sugarman (1979) for assessing classification ability in the pre-operational child were given. Marta was also asked to sort pictures which could be sorted on the basis of particular conceptual features (male-female), features which are also coded linguistically in English (gender).

Conservation: Marta was given standard Piagetian tasks for conservation of length, solid, and liquid quantity (Lovell et al. 1962; Elkind, 1961; Wallach et al., 1967; Beard, 1963; Uzgiris, 1964).

Seriation: She was also given a seriation task requiring her to seriate colored sticks of varying lengths (Inhelder and Piaget, 1964).

Hierarchical organization: To examine hierarchical constructive abilities Marta was asked to copy stick models and block models of increasing complexity, ranging from simple rows to complex, hierarchical structures. Some models used were taken from Greenfield, 1978 and Greenfield and Schneider, 1977.

Number concepts: Number concepts were assessed by a task in which Marta was asked to count increasing larger arrays of items (Gelman and Gallistel, 1978; Gelman, 1972).

Drawings: Marta's spontaneous drawings were analysed and compared to developmental norms described by Kellogg (1970), DiLeo (1973), and Selfe (1977).

Copying: To assess copying ability Marta was asked to copy a series of 21 geometric figures designed by Piaget and Inhelder (1967).

Rule abduction: Rule abduction abilities were assessed through administration of a series of tests modeled after Furth (1966) and through administration of a subtest of the Muma Assessment Program (Muma and Muma, 1979) entitled Rule/Nonrule Governed Learning.

Auditory short term memory: Auditory memory span was assessed through administration of the Wepman Auditory Memory Span (1973) and the Auditory Sequential Memory subtest of the Illinois Test of Psycholinguistic Abilities (ITPA) (Kirk, McCarthy, and Kirk, 1968).

Results:

Results of language and nonlanguage testing are given in Tables 1 and 2 respectively.

Language: In general Marta appears to be more advanced in linguistic as compared to nonlinguistic areas. Analysis of her spontaneous language indicates that she is capable of producing complex forms and structures. Moreover, Marta's developmental sentence score of 16.3 places her above the 6.11 age level, the ceiling of the test.

Table 1: Marta's Language Test Results

Test	% correct	Marta's performance age level	*age of mastery/ normals
Receptive Language Tests:			
Active Voice Word Order			
(The boy is pulling the girl)	63	3	4
Passive Voice Word Order II			
(The girl is being pulled by the boy)	0	<2	5
Subject Relativization			
(The girl who is smiling is pushing the boy)	60	2	4
Object Relativization			
(The boy is pushing the girl who is smiling)	40	2	8
WH Questioning of Subject			
(Who is pushing the girl?)	60	2	4
WH Questioning of Object			
(Who is the girl pushing?)	20	<2	5
Double Embedding I			
(The clown that is big has the balloon that is blue.)	80	4	4
Double Embedding II			
(The clown that is chasing the girl that is little is big.)	20	3	7
Pluralization (Auxiliary)			
singular (The deer is eating.)	80	4	5
plural (The deer are eating.)	40	<2	5
Pluralization (Main Verb)			
singular (The deer eats.)	20	<2	5
plural (The deer eat.)	40	2	over 8
Pluralization (Noun)			
singular (cat)	33	2	
plural (cats)	75	2	4
Comparative (bigger)	100	4	4
Superlative (biggest)	0	2	4

Prepositions (for/with) (carrying groceries for/with mom)	100	8**	7
Prepositions (to/from) (a picture to/from the girl)	80	5	5
Negation (Complex) (The book that is on the table is not red)	40	2	4
Negation (Simple) (The boy is/is not riding)	100	3-4**	2
Lexicon-Description II	40	<2	2-3
Lexicon-Description III	80	3**	3
Before and After	could not do		
Tense and Aspect			
finish	40	<2	2
gonna	0	<2	7
-ing	80	5	5
will	20	2	7
-ed	40	2	6
Simple Declaratives (The woman is running.)	63	<2	2
Possessive ('s) (The baby's bear vs. the baby bear)	50	4	7
Quantifiers			
one	40	2	4
many	20	<2	5
none	40	2.5	4
Curtiss-Yamada Comprehensive Language Evaluation-Elicitation	Marta produced forms that are also evident in her spontaneous speech.		
Sentence Repetition Tasks:	Marta spontaneously corrected sentences which were semantically, syntactically, or phonemically anomalous.		
Peabody Picture Vocabulary Test	40 (MA 3-11)		
Laura Lee Developmental Sentence Scoring	Marta scored higher than Lee's highest scoring 6:6 to 6:11 year olds. Marta's DSS = 16.3 (ages 6:5-6:11 DSS = 13.71)		

*age of mastery = 80% of children at this age scored 80% or better on this test.
**ceiling performance; lowest age group of children who performed at this age level

Table 2: Marta's Nonlanguage Test Results

Conservation	Does not conserve for length, solid, or liquid quantity. Pre-operational level.
Classification	Could sort by color when explicitly instructed—could not shift tasks. Sugarman tasks (1979)—could attend to two classes (24-36 month level).
Rule abduction	Did not exhibit rule-governed learning. (Muma and Muma, 1979). Learned "same" rule only after 70 trials (Furth, 1966).
Seriation	Could not seriate colored rods Stage I; pre-school level
Number concepts	Can rote count; lacks true counting concepts; lacks knowledge of 1-1 and cardinal principles in counting. 3 year level at best.
Play	Tends not to explore objects. Symbolic play noted on one occasion.
Drawing	Repetitious and perseverative. Preschool level.
Copying	Stage IB-IIA; age level 3:6-4:0
Hierarchical construction	
blocks	Could only do simple bridge.
sticks	Could only do stack and row (not simple bridge). At or below 3 year level.
Memory (Auditory)	
Auditory Sequential Memory (ITPA)	Could do some 3 digit spans.
Wepman-Morency Auditory Memory Span	Could do some 3 word spans (Score = 6; below level of adequacy).

She is capable of producing a wide range of rather complex forms, forms which she does not necessarily have a grasp of receptively (as indicated by formal testing).

For example, while she did not do well on the receptive Passive test (see her response in example 1) Marta uses passives, full passives, in her own speech (examples 2 and 3).

1. (Marta's task was to act out the test sentence with small toys.) (test sentence) The cow was pushed down by the girl. Marta's response: moves cow.

2. (re crocodiles at the zoo) I don't want to get eaten by one.

3. Last year at <u>name of school</u> when I first went there three tickets were gave out by a police last year.

Marta also did poorly on formal comprehension tests for relative clauses but often uses such forms in her own speech. While relative clause-like forms begin emerging fairly early (around age three according to Limber, 1973), the earliest forms do not include Wh relative pronouns and are generally object relatives. Marta produces relativized sentences (including subject relatives) with relative pronouns, and double relatives (where the relativized noun plays a different role in the relative clause as opposed to the matrix sentence), reflecting her sophisticated level in this area of the grammar.

4. She, does paintings, this really good friend of the kids who <u>I went to school with last year and really loved</u>.

5. ...a really nice guy <u>who I went to</u> and I really loved him after awhile.

6. The cook <u>who does it</u>, um sometimes give us these good enchiladas an' oh, they're so good!

Marta also uses a variety of other subordinating conjunctions, further indicating the complexity of her syntax.

7. I'm waiting until my hair grows out.

8. It makes me feel sad because they had to leave.

9. It was hard for me to do, but I did it.

Modal and auxiliary forms are also present in Marta's speech.

10. I should've brought it back.

11. And I didn't know how much the bank would let me take out of my account.

In addition to the above, Marta has demonstrated the capacity to use many other forms including negatives (in simple sentences), plural marking (both on the noun and on the verb), possessives, pronominals, case-marking prepositions, Wh and yes-no questions, quantifiers, comparatives, and tense/aspect forms (see examples 12-14).

12. I'm not sure we're gonna let her fly.
13. They're speaking Spanish, can you hear it?
14. My granddad used to watch it (a particular TV show).

In addition, she is able to use elliptical utterances quite appropriately, indicating that she has learned the rules regarding when it is appropriate and preferable to delete parts of the utterance.

15. Yeah, my dad was all upset and so was I.

Marta then, has learned numerous syntactic and morphological rules.

Marta appears to have a fairly well-developed lexicon although she did poorly on a recent PPVT, scoring at age level 3:11. Indeed, while many of the words she uses seem advanced, she does not always seem to understand (or perhaps attend to) the meanings of the words she uses.

16. Yeah. I started livin' wi' my parents 'n they took me out of the home,___ be better if I had a little respite an' ...
17. (M. is shown a picture of a bear) Polar bear, like in the word kodak (i.e. kodiak?).

This problem is also evident in Marta's use of numerical terms. Marta frequently uses numerical terms to modify, particularly the cardinal terms two or three, and ordinal terms second and third. In many cases, while the term she uses is syntactically correct and certainly semantically plausible, it is factually incorrect. For instance, with regard to example 18, Marta is actually one of four, not three children.

18. I have three kids in my family.[1]
19. 'cause this is like, my third home.

While Marta knows when a numerical term is appropriate, she does not always have a grasp of the meanings involved, as shown in 20 and 21.

20. J: How many nights did you stay there (at a hotel with the family)?
    M: Oh, about 4 out of 1.
21. I was sixteen last year and now I'm nineteen this year.

Marta's selection of inappropriate lexical items in other cases such as in 22 also reflects her tendency to use words she does not fully understand.

22. It was broken, <u>desperately</u> broken. (re her watch)

Some utterances are difficult, if not impossible to interpret.

23. He won't even recognize until you see his bangs are cut.
24. She was thinking that it's no regular school, it's just plain old no buses.

Marta's failure to repair utterances is yet another indication that she uses structures or items she has little or no grasp of semantically.

25. M: Oh. That's where I got the account out of my money. Oh, that's where..
    J: (Repeating the utterance, confused as to what M. meant.) That's where you got the account out of your money.
    M: Oh, the account out of the money.

The phrase "account out of the/my money" appears to derive from "money out of the/my account". Apparently she has heard the phrase, but since she does not understand its meaning she has inadvertently transposed the nouns. If the error were merely a production error, Marta probably would have "repaired" or corrected the phrase when she repeated it. Since she did not, this interchange serves as a good example of production exceeding comprehension.

In addition, it appears that Marta does not understand the meaning of some of the temporal phrases she uses. For example, while her use of various temporal forms is often appropriate, at other times she uses adverbial phrases that do not match the tense of the verb.

       (future adverbial)
26. It's <u>a week from Saturday</u> and J. an' Mom, my dad...I
       (past tns)
    think I <u>brought</u> my camera with me that week.

Thus, while Marta uses a wide range of complex utterances, there is a marked discrepancy between her syntactic and her semantic levels.

<u>Pragmatic knowledge</u>: There also seems to be quite a discrepancy between her syntactic and pragmatic knowledge. Marta can use her language communicatively as well as referentially to the extent that she is able to obtain and give out information. Nonetheless she is still quite deficient pragmatically. While she exhibits an awareness of communicative devices that contribute to a pragmatically appropriate interchange, she often fails to use them. She cannot tell a coherent story regarding a past event, and is often unaware of the needs of the listener, sometimes neglecting to establish and maintain topics and referents or provide necessary background information. This is a characteristic evident at certain stages in normal children. However, unlike normal children, Marta sometimes seems unconcerned as to whether anyone is listening to her or understanding what she is saying. In many ways she is less aware socially than the normal child who is otherwise functioning at her syntactic level. There is a discrepancy then, between Marta's knowledge of language and her use of language.

27. (excerpt from a dialogue)
    J: M., did you have a Halloween Party this year at all?
    M: Yeah, they had one.
    J: At school here?
    M: Yeah.
    J: What happened?
    M: They had,___I didn't dress up as anything, I just went as my regular self. (chuckles)
    J: (laughs)
    S: Just went to school as my regular self, and, what did they do to celebrate Halloween?
    M: Well people in <u>name of city</u> um, in the five school districts, there are no buses there are only cars. <u>unintell.</u> I hear a bus, yes I thought there was school, but there was Sunday School.
    S: Sunday School?
    M: Yeah, an' I was part right. She was thinking that it's no regular school, it's just plain old no buses, 'n she heard...
    J: Who's "she"?
    M: This counselor that I, was talkin' to, you gotta shape up, and she did behave in the <u>house...unintell.</u>
    S: Was this at Halloween?
    M: No, this was last night, <u>unintell.</u> kept quiet all the time.

Productivity:

It is clear that Marta has achieved a certain degree of linguistic proficiency. Is her language truly productive or primarily formulaic and stereotypic?

The issue of formulaic vs. spontaneous speech is a complex one. It has been argued that normal speakers incorporate a certain amount of routines and automatic phrases in their conversational speech (Pawley, 1980; Kempler, 1977). Such routinization, seems to enable us to speak with fluency and rapidity, so that we do not have to formulate 'from scratch' every structure we use. However, the claim that normal individuals utilize such a strategy in discourse does not preclude the fact that they can and do produce creative and productive language. Given that people may use stereotyped forms obviously does not account for their capacity to produce and understand novel utterances or propositional speech. While Marta does use many stereotypic phrases, she can and does produce novel utterances. Many of Marta's sentences are unlikely to be utterances she has heard others use, as indicated by their unusual form and/or content.

28. I ate slow 'n went to the beach.
29. You, see, so that's where they been, the mother's accent spits right out the mouth...

In addition, Marta makes errors which indicate that she has learned linguistic rules and that she, like the normal language-learning child, sometimes overextends them.

30. I don't know how I catch<u>ed</u> it.
31. The parents of her, are, from Peru.

Marta's ability to productively use morphological markers to create novel forms also attests to the creative nature of her language.

32. Father: What about the problem of you and cussing, M.?
     M: Well, big upsetness!
33. We went car-looking.

Admittedly, Marta can be somewhat perseverative linguistically. However, she is not like the high-level autistic child who replays identical "tapes" (i.e. repeats himself or herself word for word) on different occasions. While she has favorite themes she does not necessarily use the exact same sentences to discuss them. Her use of stereotyped utterances then, may be more a function of cognitive than linguistic limitations.

As mentioned above, Marta's expressive language abilities seem to exceed her receptive language abilities. While she is able to use a wide range of complex structures and features expressively, on many of the receptive language tests she did quite poorly, performing at or below the two to three year level. She did well on some tests for which the age of mastery is much higher. For example, she scored 100% on a case-marking prepositions test for which the age of mastery is seven years of age.

Her poor performance on many receptive language tests may be due in part, to her immature test taking capacity. For example, Marta had difficulty attending to arrays involving four pictures and in picture interpretation, characteristics noted in only the very youngest children (ages two and under) in our normative population. Thus, her poor performance on some of the receptive language tests may have been due to nonlinguistic as well as linguistic limitations. However, the fact that she was able to do well on at least some tests indicates that the nonlinguistic task demands were not necessarily beyond her conceptual capacity, and in turn indicates that her production indeed exceeds her comprehension.

Nonlanguage performance:

In contrast to her spontaneous language performance, Marta's performance in nonlinguistic areas is quite poor.

Classification: When presented with items or shapes to sort, Marta had a great deal of difficulty and for the most part could not perform the tasks. When given a stack of pictures of males and of females and asked to "make two piles of things that go together or are the same," Marta did not sort on the basis of gender, but invariably made two seemingly random piles. Normal three to four year olds are able to do this task. Significantly, Marta could name the elements of the set (e.g. man, woman, boy, girl) and the superordinate category (people). Thus, her difficulty did not reflect a lack of knowledge of the categories involved, but rather a failure to abduce a rule. This failure is interesting in view of her apparent ability to extract rules in the linguistic domain.

Rule abduction: Marta also failed to demonstrate rule governed learning on the Muma Assessment Program subtest, and when given a simple rule acquisition task (inspired by Furth, 1966) learned the rule only after 70 trials.

Conservation: Marta failed the standard Piagetian tasks for conservation of solid and liquid quantity. On several occasions she gave conserving responses to tasks for conservation of length but subsequent re-testing has revealed that she does not conserve for length.

Seriation: When given seriation tasks using rods of varying lengths Marta was unable to anticipate how the rods would look in serial order and was unable to seriate the rods. Her performance was thus at Stage I or preschool level.

Number concepts: Marta's number concepts are also limited. Even when attempting to count small sets she does not consistently demonstrate knowledge of the one-to-one principle involved in counting. In addition, she lacks knowledge of the cardinal principle; even when she counts items "correctly," she cannot then tell you how many items are in the array. Marta does not know her own age, cannot tell time, and has no concept of money values.

Drawing: Marta's drawing is quite primitive and perseverative, placing her within the preschool level. She generally draws the same thing over and over, even when specifically asked to draw something else. Generally she draws humans consisting of a head with legs.

Copying: Her ability to copy geometric figures is at the preschool level (Stage IB-IIA). At this stage in copying, curved lines begin to be distinguished from straight-sided lines, but the square and triangle are still indistinguishable.

Hierarchical organization: Marta was very poor at constructing hierarchical models of sticks and of blocks. When attempting to copy models of stick configurations she could not copy a simple bridge (⊓), and when attempting to copy block models she could not construct anything more complex than the simple bridge. Vereecken (1961) notes that children are able to construct a simple bridge by 2:9 and 2:10.

Auditory memory span: Marta's memory span is surprisingly limited given the length and complexity of her utterances. On the Wepman-Morency Memory Span and the ITPA digit span she could do spans of 1-2 items in length, but the 3-item spans only occasionally. Marta's rote memory abilities also seem limited; she has difficulty reciting numbers, letters, days of the week, months, and performing other such rote-learned tasks.

Discussion:

While Marta is functioning well beyond the preschool level linguistically in certain respects, nonlinguistically she is still within the pre-operational (pre-school) stage. There is a marked discrepancy between Marta's linguistic and nonlinguistic abilities. Thus, certain connections proposed to exist between language and nonlanguage cognition are not substantiated by Marta's profile.

Some of the non-linguistic tasks tested (i.e. those in the action domain) have been described as reflections of abilities which contribute to a cognitive base for language (Greenfield, Nelson, and Saltzman, 1972). It is revealing then, that Marta had difficulty with many of these tasks. Ingram (1975) has hypothesized that a true, productive capacity to formulate complex linguistic structures does not develop until a more advanced cognitive level has been attained, i.e. the concrete operational level. Abilities associated with the concrete operational period (e.g. reversibility) have been tied to the child's capacity to use transformational rules of language to create complex sentences.

Thus, it is significant that Marta, who is functioning at a pre-operational level, is able to produce complex sentences in a clearly productive fashion. Her cognitive deficits are reflected in her language and render it abnormal in certain respects. These deficits however, have not arrested language development. Marta's language, particularly in the area of syntax, seems to have progressed to quite a sophisticated level.

If, as Bates and her colleagues have suggested (Bates et al., 1976; Bates, 1979) language and nonlanguage abilities are linked by some third, shared underlying principle or principles, this would be reflected by the existence of formal parallels across domains. That is, organizing principles in one area should also be apparent in another. For example, hierarchical organization and rule abduction are two features that seem to exist in both linguistic and nonlinguistic domains. It is significant then, that Marta did so poorly on classification and rule abduction tasks compared to her apparent capacity to learn or construct linguistic rules. Also, whereas Marta is able to produce hierarchically complex linguistic structures, in the visuo-constructive domain she could not make anything more than a simple bridge. The discrepancy between Marta's capacity to use rule abducting strategies and to produce hierarchically complex structures in language vs. nonlanguage domains may not prove, but does suggest that the same constraints and principles are not operating in both areas. While both language and nonlanguage cognitive abilities involve hierarchical complexity, the similarities across domains do not imply that they are mutually dependent, or derive from some more general capacity.

While much research is yet to be done with regard to exploring formal parallels across domains, inherent differences in the constraints upon the physical as opposed to linguistic domain are already evident. Limitations in the visuo-constructive domain are very much linked to the laws of physics. For example, a hierarchically complex block structure must be fairly symmetrical in height in order to stand. Such purely physical considerations do not however, constrain embedded structures in language. Even those who have argued in favor of the existence of formal parallels (e.g. Greenfield and Schneider, 1977) caution against carrying the analogy across domains too far. Indeed, the analogy is a more general one. All that can be said with regard to language and action for example, is that hierarchical organization (and degree of interruptedness) increase with development. The analogy is thus not very revealing. It is doubtful that simply indentifying hierarchical structure in various systems and domains is going to tell us much about language. It must be shown that the constraints and limitations operating across domains are also similar in nature.

One might argue that Marta demonstrates difficulty in the nonlinguistic area due to superficial blockage such as emotional or physical problems. For example, her difficulty in building block models may reflect a fear of engaging in visuo-constructive tasks, limited visuo-perceptual abilities, or a motor apraxis. One or all of these problems could result in the absence of an ability in one domain even though the more general underlying governing mechanism exists. In Marta's case however, none of the above problems account for her deficits. While Marta was not able to build the more complex hierarchical models, she was able to reproduce simpler structures (a stack, row, and simple bridge) as well as a tall tower composed of numerous blocks. If Marta had a fear of manipulating the blocks, a serious visuo-perceptual problem, or an apraxia, we would not expect the problem to apply only to the construction of models beyond certain level of complexity. A deficiency due to channel-specific blockage would affect all performance in a given area; the fact that she built a tall tower indicates a willingness to manipulate the materials and an adequate degree of visual acuity and coordination to properly place and balance the blocks. Given that positing blockage problems cannot be used to account for her poor performance in the constructional domain, it is likely that Marta indeed lacks the nonlinguistic cognitive capacities underlying the tasks given.

Marta's nonlinguistic deficits have a differential effect on the various aspects of her language. As previous studies have shown (Curtiss, Fromkin, and Yamada, 1979; Curtiss, Kempler, and Yamada, 1981; Curtiss, 1981) the semantics system seems more closely linked to general cognitive development than does syntax. Marta's performance indicates that she is functioning at a preschool level semantically and cognitively, while syntactically she is beyond the preschool level. (This is not to imply that semantics is simply a mirror of conceptual development. Marta's capacity to deal with classes and categories seems better in the linguistic as opposed to nonlinguistic areas. While Marta seems to have mastered the pronominal system for example, she has trouble on simple sorting tasks. Marta's strength truly seems to be a linguistic one; one which is evident in all areas of language to some degree. Thus, while her capacity to deal with semantic features may be poorer than her ability to deal with syntactic structures, her semantic ability still seems relatively better than her nonlinguistic abilities.)

Is syntax correlated with any nonlanguage abilities at all? Earlier studies of isolated language ability have found that auditory memory span correlates with syntactic ability (Curtiss, Fromkin, and Yamada, 1979; Curtiss and Yamada, 1981). While correlations do not prove causal or dependency relationships, this correlation has caused some speculation regarding the relationship of language to specific cognitive abilities. It is surprising then, that there is no correlation between Marta's syntactic ability and her auditory memory span. Of course it is still possible that syntax is linked to other specific nonlinguistic capacities which have not yet been identified. However, Marta's syntax is not correlated with any nonlanguage ability examined to date.

In Marta then, we see an isolated syntactic capacity; isolated from semantics (to some degree), from concrete-operational abilities, from visuo-constructive abilities, and from auditory short-term memory. Marta has somehow achieved an advanced syntactic level in the face of marked deficits in other areas. Syntax and morphology seem to be isolable from other language components and from nonlanguage cognitive abilities.

Data from rare cases like Marta's do not tell us that there is no relationship between language and other mental functions, or that language can develop completely autonomously. Obviously, cognitive development and social interaction contribute to normal language and language use. Normal language is the product of a complex, synergistic relationship among many cognitive systems. Such cases do however, demonstrate that nonlinguistic cognitive abilities are insufficient to account for language. Aspects of language, e.g. syntax and morphology, can emerge independent of putatively prerequisite or commonly governed cognitive systems. Such cases suggest that while some principles affecting language acquisition may be general, encompassing both linguistic and nonlinguistic functions, other principles, some possibly unique to language, may also be involved in language acquisition.

NOTES

[1] As Vicki Fromkin, Dan Kempler, and Marta's father have aptly suggested, it is likely that Marta is using the word *kids* for *siblings* here.

ACKNOWLEDGEMENTS:

Many thanks to Vicki Fromkin, Dan Kempler, and Marta's father for insightful comments and criticisms on earlier drafts of this paper.

REFERENCES

Bates, E., Benigni, L., Bretherton, I., Camaioni, L., and Volterra, V. (1976) From gesture to the first word: on cognitive and social prerequisites. In *Origins of behavior: communication and language*. Lewis, M. and Rosenblum, L. (Eds.) N.Y.: John Wiley and Sons.

Bates, E. (1979) *The emergence of symbols*. N.Y.: Academic Press.

Beard, R.M. (1963) The order of concept development studies in two fields. *Educational Review*, 15, (3): 228-37.

Beilin, H. (1980) Piaget's theory: refinement, revision, or rejection? In *Developmental Models of Thinking*. Kluwe, R. and Spada, H. (Eds.) New York: Academic Press.

Chomsky, N. (1980a) The linguistic approach. *Language and Learning: the debate between Jean Piaget and Noam Chomsky*. Cambridge, Ma.: Harvard University Press.

Chomsky, N. (1980b) *Rules and representations*. New York: Columbia University Press.

Curtiss, S., Fromkin, V., and Yamada, J. (1979) The independence of language as a cognitive system. Unpublished manuscript.

Curtiss, S. and Yamada, J. (forthcoming) *Curtiss-Yamada Comprehensive Language Evaluation*.

Curtiss, S. and Yamada, J. (1981) Selectively intact grammatical development in a retarded child. In *UCLA Working Papers in Cognitive Linguistics*, 3:61-91.

DiLeo, J. (1973) *Children's drawings as diagnostic aids*. N.Y.: Brunner/Mazel Inc.

Elkind, D. (1961) Children's discovery of the conservation of mass, weight, and volume: Piaget replication study II, *Journal of Genetic Psychology*, 98, pt. 2: 219-27.

Flavell, J. (1977) *Cognitive development*. Englewood Cliffs, New Jersey, Prentice-Hall, Inc.

Furth, H.G. (1966) Thinking without language: psychological implications of deafness. N.Y.: Free Press.

Garron, D. (1970) Sex-linked, recessive inheritance of spatial and numerical abilities, and Turner's syndrome. Psychological Review, 77, (2): 147-52.

Gelman, R. (1972) Logical capacity of very young children: number invariance rules. Child Development, 43:75-90.

Gelman, R. and Gallistel, C.R. (1978) The child's understanding of number. Cambridge, Mass.: Harvard U. Press.

Graham, N. (1968) Short-term memory and syntactic structure in educationally subnormal children. Language and Speech, 11: 204-219.

Greenfield, P., Nelson, K., and Saltzman, E. (1972) The development of rule-bound strategies for manipulating seriated cups: a parallel between action and grammar. Cognitive Psychology, 3: 291-310.

Greenfield, P. and Schneider, L. (1977) Building a tree structure: the development of hierarchical complexity and interrupted strategies in children's construction activity. Developmental Psychology, 13, (14): 299-313.

Ingram, D. (1975) If and when transformations are acquired by children. In Developmental psycholinguistics: theory and application. 26th Annual Georgetown University Round Table, Dato, D. (Ed.) Washington D.C.: Georgetown University Press.

Inhelder, B. and Piaget, J. (1964) The early growth of logic in the child. London: Routledge and Kegan Paul, Ltd.

Kellogg, R. (1970) Analyzing children's art. Palo Alto: Mayfield Publishing Co.

Kempler, D. (1977) The function of automatic speech. Honors thesis. U.C. Berkeley.

Kirk, S.A., McCarthy, J.J., and Kirk, W.D. (1968) Illinois Test of Psycholinguistic Abilities. Urbana, Illinois: University of Illinois Press.

Lee, L., and Canter, S.M. (1971) Developmental sentence scoring: a clinical procedure for estimating syntactic development in children's spontaneous speech. J. of Speech and Hearing Disorders, 36: 315-40.

Lee, L. (1974) Developmental sentence analysis. Evanston, Illinois: Northwestern University Press.

Limber, J. (1973) The genesis of complex sentences. In Cognitive development and the acquisition of language. Moore, T. (Ed.) N.Y.: Academic Press.

Lovell, K., Healey, D., and Rowland, A.D. (1962) Growth of some geometrical concepts. Child Development 33, (4): 751-67.

Maratsos, M. and Chalkey, M. (1980) The internal language of children's syntax: the ontogenesis and representation of syntactic categories. In Children's language, Vol. 2. Nelson, Keith (Ed.) New York: Gardner Press, Inc.

Masland, M. and Case, L. (1960) Limitation of auditory memory as a factor in delayed language development. British Journal of Disorders in Communication, 3: 139-142.

Menyuk, P. (1964) Comparison of grammar of children with functionally deviant and normal speech. Journal of Speech and Hearing Research, 7: 109-121.

Money, J. (1964) Two cytogenetic syndromes: psychologic comparisons, I. Intelligence and specific-factor quotients. J. of Psychiatric Research, 2: 223-31.

Money, J., and Alexander, D. (1966) Turner's syndrome; further demonstration of the presence of specific cognitional deficits. J. of Medical Genetics, 3: 223-231.

Muma, J. and Muma, D. (1979) Muma Assessment Program. Natural Child Publishing Co.

Neimark, E. (1970) Model for a thinking machine: an information-processing framework for the study of cognitive development. Merrill-Palmer Quarterly, 16: 345-68.

Pawley, A. (1980) One clause at a time hypothesis. University of Auckland. Unpublished manuscript.

Piaget, J. (1980) Schemes of action and language learning. In Language and learning: the debate between Jean Piaget and Noam Chomsky. Piatelli-Palmarini, M. (Ed.) Cambridge, Massachusetts: Harvard Univ. Press: 163-183.

Piaget, J. (1977) Some recent research and its link with a new theory of groupings and conservations based on commutability. In, The roots of American psychology: historical influences and implications for the future. Annals of the New York Academy of Sciences, 291: 350-357.

Piaget, J. and Inhelder, B. (1967) The child's conception of space. N.Y.: W.W. Norton and Company, Inc.

Piaget, J. and Inhelder, B. (1969) The psychology of the child. New York: Basic Books.

Schwartz, E. (1974) Characteristics of speech and language development in the child with myelomeningocele and hydrocephalus. J. of Speech and Hearing Disorders, 39: 465-68.

Selfe, L. (1977) Nadia. London: Academic Press.

Silbert, A., Wolff, P., and Lilienthal, J. (1977) Spatial and temporal processing in patients with Turner's syndrome. Behavior Genetics, 7, (1): 11-21.

Sinclair, H. (1971) Sensorimotor action patterns as a condition for the acquisition of syntax. In Language acquisition: models and methods. Huxley, R., and Ingram, E. (Eds.) N.Y.: Academic Press.

Sinclair, H. (1973) Language acquisition and cognitive development. In Cognitive development and the acquisition of language. Moore, T. (Ed.) N.Y.: Academic Press.

Sinclair, H. (1975) The role of cognitive structures in language acquisition. In Foundations of language development, Vol. 1. Lenneberg, E.H. and Lenneberg, E. (Eds.) N.Y.: Academic Press.

Sugarman, S. (1979) The development of classification and correspondence from 12 to 36 months: from action to representation. Paper presented at the biennial meeting, Society for Research in Child Development, S.F. March.

Swisher, L. and Pinsker, E. (1971) The language characteristics of hyperverbal hydrocephalic children. Developmental Medical Child Neurology, 13: 746-755.

Uzgiris, I.C. (1964) Situational generality of conservation. Child Development, 35, (3): 831-41.

Vereecken, P. (1961) Spatial development. Groningen: J.B. Wolters.

Wallach, L., Wall, A.J., and Anderson, L. (1967) Number conservation: the roles of reversibility, addition, subtraction, and misleading perceptual cues. Child Development, 38, (2): 425-42.

Wepman, J. and Morency, A. (1973) Auditory memory span test. Chicago: Language Research Assoc., Inc.

Whitaker, H. (1976) A case of isolation of the language function. In Studies in Neurolinguistics, 2. Whitaker, H., and Whitaker, H. (Eds.) N.Y.: Academic Press, 1-58.

Yamada, J. (1981) Evidence for the independence of language and cognition: case study of a hyperlinguistic retarded adolescent. In UCLA Working Papers in Cognitive Linguistics, 3: 121-160.

Yamada, J. and Curtiss, S. (1981) The relationship between language and cognition in a case of Turner's syndrome. In UCLA Working Papers in Cognitive Linguistics, 3: 93-115.

WHAT DO YOUNG CHILDREN SAY TO START PEER INTERACTION?
SOME DISCOURSE PROCESSES AT PRESCHOOL AGE IN THE CHILD-CHILD DYADIC RELATION

Barbara Bokus and Grace Wales Shugar

Department of Psychology, Warsaw University,
ul. Stawki 5/7, 00-183 Warsaw, Poland.

Abstract: An examination was made of a proxemic factor operating in utterance construction, based on the hypothesis that preschool children's utterances, which function to initiate interaction with a same-age peer in a dyadic situation, are constructed according to different characteristic patterns depending upon inter-child distance. The source of the hypothesis was an observational study of child-child pairs in free play conditions without adult presence. Two assumptions (based on patterns noted in the observational study) were treated as independent variables: (a) that in the situation under study preschool children typically initiate interaction with a same-age peer by drawing the partner into the initiator's own action field, and (b) that a reliable device serving this purpose is an appropriately constructed utterance. Inter-child space was experimentally manipulated in two distance variants, the dependent variable being the type of utterance constructed by the initiating child which had the contingent effect of starting interaction. Treated as the intervening variable was the initiating child's perception of action fields proper to self and to the other child as separate or shared. Evidence is presented in support of the hypothesis. Depending on whether children see their respective action fields as separate or undivided, interaction-opening utterances are constructed in characteristically different ways.

Starting interaction with an adult and starting interaction with a peer

The study of social interactions in which the child participates might well start from recognizing the child as a different (from the adult) but competent interpreter (in his own way) of the social world (cf. Mackay, 1974; Speier, 1970). How might such differences be made manifest?

Among the striking differences we have found in

studies contrasting child-adult and child-child dyadic situations (where situations are unstructured and partners unacquainted) (Shugar, 1980; in press) is the way in which the same participants in the two situations establish active interaction. There are some interesting theoretical aspects involved which relate to how the child might see the relationship with an adult partner in contrast to that with a child partner; in the first case a relationship between unlike partners and therefore asymmetrical and in the second case a relationship between similar partners and therefore one of symmetry. The child's view of a dyadic partner in categories similar to, or different from, those which might apply to himself can presumably affect his style of discourse with that partner. In the case of a child-child dyad this style may be supposed to be one very like that which the child would use in self-address.

In the child-adult situation, an invariant pattern (initiated by the adult according to a pre-fixed interactional pattern) was as follows:

(1) Adult (seated at table) Hello, my name is Jola, what's yours?
Child (standing beside table) Piotrek.
Adult: Piotrek.

In the child-child situation, only two instances of self-naming or name-eliciting were encountered in 48 observations.
They are as follows:

(2) $Child_1$ (approaching $Child_2$ who is busy with blocks) What's your name?
$Child_2$: Tania, and yours?
$Child_1$: I'm Magda

(occurring in the first seconds of the 15-minute play session of two girls aged 4;6 - 5;0).

(3) $Child_1$ (jumping up and down on mattress) Whatcher name?
$Child_2$? (end of tape)

(occurring in the final seconds of the 15-minute play

session of two boys aged 3;0 - 3;6, following nearly continuous interactive play).

Whereas in (1) the adult started with a greeting, presentation of own name and request for child's name, in (2) the initiating child does not greet but requests the other's name first, giving own name next on request. In (2) the name interchange is basically similar to the adult pattern and probably not accidentally occurred after this particular child had experienced social interaction with the adult. In the case of (3), occurring at the end instead of the beginning of the session, the name query does not seem to serve any interaction-initiatory function.

From the above, it may be concluded that self-presentation is not the child's typical way of starting interaction. This paper will provide evidence for the suggestion that the child's typical way of starting interaction is action field presentation.

Source of the experimental hypothesis

The hypothesis formulated above emerged from an exploratory observational study (in preparation) which performed a descriptive analysis of the process whereby preschool children (aged three to five) spontaneously initiated interaction sequences in conditions of unfamiliarity with each other and with the play setting, i.e. unaffected by habitual experience linked to partner and place. Opposite sex partners were studied. The study focussed on the points of transition from states of non-interaction to states of interaction, identifying the relations between socially directed behaviors in the stream of activity of each child, using an adaptation of Mueller & Vandell's procedures (1977; cf. Bokus, 1980). Analyses of the interactional sequences revealed a prevailing function for all four pairs studied, viz. to draw the attention of the second child to the initiating child's current activity in a manner such as to cause the second child to abandon temporarily his own current activity and attend to that of the initiating child. Further, among the types of socially directed behaviors identified in the behavior stream of each child as the starting points of interaction sequences (visual-perceptual, verbal, and physical action upon an object), the verbal behavior turned out to be the single necessary component for interaction initiation. However, the visual-perceptual behavior frequently combined with the verbal, occurring usually just prior to the verbal behavior. The specific function of this behavior was thought to be orientational, a visual scan serving to locate the other child and his action space in relation to that of the initiating child. The brevity of the visual search (less than 3 seconds) seemed to support this interpretation. As for the verbal behaviors serving to initiate interaction, they appeared to be widely diverse in form and function when examined together, but when the factor of inter-child distance was taken into account (either $\leq$ ca. 65 cm. or $\geq$ ca. 95 cm.), the utterances fell into two fairly distinct patterns. When inter-child distance was greater, the utterances in question were briefer and consisted mainly of calls and summonses, without elaborated information, whereas when the distance was shorter, the utterances were longer, more detailed and specific in content. (Of the 56 interaction-initiating utterances located in the observational data of 4 same-age dyads, aged 3 to 5, MLU of those uttered at close-range was 5.14, and of those at farther-range, 2.18).

The latter finding was unexpected. It was not obvious to us why children within arms' reach should tend naturally to verbalize their activity in more detail as a way of starting interaction, and on the other hand should tend not to do so when mutually located beyond arms' reach. The increase in verbalization on the approach of one other child in nursery school play has already been remarked upon (Shields, 1979, p. 265) without however noting its contingent effects.

Therefore we undertook to test the validity of our finding by means of a controlled experiment on a larger population, using a design that in its essentials permitted a replication of the observational design. To re-state the hypothesis: In a dyadic, free-play situation, children start interaction with a same-age partner by constructing utterances according to two different patterns depending on the proxemic relations of their action fields: short utterances lacking in referential detail occur when the mutual distance is greater, and longer utterances with richer referential content when the mutual distance is lesser. Further, empirical evidence would be sought for the role of an intervening variable of perceptual assessment, i.e. that the children actually gauge the relation holding between their action fields in terms of separateness or commonality. These perceptual assessments would be strongly linked to proxemic relations between the action fields.

Experimental design and procedure

The experiment was a naturalistic one, woven into ongoing nursery school events. Exploiting the occasion of a visit by children of one nursery school to a neighbouring one, one of us conducted the experiment as a kind of game. Matched pairs of unacquainted children were introduced into a special playroom where each pair spent about 20 minutes in toto playing the experimental game. An adult (the experimenter) played with the children for part of the time, and for the remainder of the time the children played alone. The adult played in such a way as to manipulate the proxemic variable according to the experimental design (changing the children's play locale), interviewed each child apart on the topic of action field relations (separate or shared), and finally, elicited initiation of new child-child interactions by the particular child who had just been interviewed. Each of the two children were tested in this way in both proxemic conditions (close-range and far-range).

48 children aged 3 to 5 years were paired in half-year age brackets (as in the observational study). The order of proxemic arrangements (play locales at close-range first, far-range second) was reversed for 24 of the pairs, equally in each age bracket.

The procedure was as follows: Once the children had started interactive play by themselves, E (who observed from behind a screen) entered the playroom and conducted the first phase of the experiment. She announced that a third child wanted to come in and play too. E posed the question as to what play space could be allocated to that child in the joint opinion of the present children. Then E proceeded to conduct a 'private consultation' with each child apart, following which the opinions of the two were confronted and agreement reached as to where the third child could play. Following this, the third child was brought into the playroom. Experimental data was obtained from the 'private consultations' which were conducted by a pre-set questioning scheme. The scheme was built on the assumption that play space for the unknown child would be allocated outside of the areas appropriated by the present children (which was borne out by the children's actual allocations of play space for the third child). The point of the interview was to obtain from the child an explicit expression of how he/she attributed play spaces to each of the present children - either separately to self and to the other child, or together as joint space. In addition, concrete evidence was obtained by eliciting from the child a delineation of the respective play spaces by means of chalk markings or the equivalent. Access by the second child to the perceptual and manual operations accompanying the interview was precluded by blindfolding (as part of the 'game'). The children enjoyed the procedure and their responses followed in highly similar ways.

In the next phase of the experiment (after the interview with one child), a play interlude occurred. The experimental purpose of this phase was to elicit initiation of interactive play along prescribed lines. Thus, once the children had begun to play freely with objects, E suggested 'privately' to the child who had just been interviewed that he/she get the other child to play together on the current activity (i.e., initiation of a given type of interaction), and then suggested that he/she say something so that the other would start playing with the initiator (i.e., elicitation of an utterance serving to initiate interaction). E then left the room and observed events from behind a screen. Thus interactive play interludes occurred without adult presence. The eliciting procedure turned out to be successful, and in all cases the subject initiated interactive play, using verbal means to this end.

The two phases of the experiment - interviewing phase and elicited interactive play - were repeated in both proxemic conditions with each child.

Experimental results

Three variables were taken into account. Inter-child distance (x) in the free play situation (the independent variable) had two values: $x \leq$ ca. 65 cm. (close-range condition), $x \geq$ ca. 95 cm. (far-range condition). Perceptual assessment of action field relations as separate or shared (the intervening variable) was indicated in the responses of the interviewed child to E's questions. Utterances (the dependent variable) were generated in response to E's elicitation for initiation of child-child interaction.

1. Perceptual assessments under different proxemic conditions

The children attributed play spaces (action fields) as belonging either to self, other child, or both: in the first two cases, as separate, in the second case, as shared. In the far-range condition, 37 subjects assessed play spaces as separate and 11 subjects assessed them as shared; in the close-range condition, 13 subjects assessed play spaces as separate, and 35 subjects assessed them as shared. Assessment frequencies differed significantly ($p < .001$, Chi square = 20.571, McNamara's test for dependent pairs).

These facts indicate that children in the dyadic play setting show reliably a tendency to see play space as shared and undivided when they are located at close range within mutual arms' reach, and as separate and divided when they are located beyond this range. This establishes the reality of the intervening factor of perceptual assessment as affecting children's attitudes toward mutual play space allocation. However the results also show that, though this factor is mainly determined by the proxemic relations between play spaces, it is not totally dependent upon the distance factor. In presenting the further results, we shall therefore distinguish between the data on the effects of these two types of factors. For, having established the existence of the perceptual factor, we expect to find its effect upon the construction of utterances serving to initiate interaction. This prediction is supported by evidence from other experimental studies which take into account the effect upon verbal behavior of shared vs. isolated perceptual access to referential objects (Bokus & Shugar, 1979; Maratsos, 1973).

2. Utterances initiating interactions under different proxemic-perceptual conditions

Forty-eight utterances were constructed by children

with the express intention of starting interactive play with a partner (elicited by the adult) in each proxemic condition, totalling 96. We shall refer to them as I.I. utterances. Systematic differences were found in the characteristics of these utterances according to perceptual assessments under different proxemic conditions.

Utterance length

As concerns the formal feature of length, I.I. utterances were shorter when action fields were perceived as separate (MLU value 3.13), and longer when perceived as shared (MLU value 5.26), this regardless of proxemic conditions. However the proxemic factor operated differently in the two cases. When the shared field assessment was made at close-range, the MLU value of the I.I. utterance was higher (5.59 ± 1.76) and when the same assessment was made at far--range, the MLU value of the I.I. utterance was lower (4.94 ± 1.73). The direction of the difference is in line with our hypothesis about the effect of the proxemic factor. But the reverse direction was noted when action fields were assessed as separate. When the separate field assessment was made at close-range, the MLU value of the I.I. utterance was lower (2.95 ± 1.23) and when the same assessment was made at far-range, the MLU value of the I.I. utterance was higher (3.31 ± 1.10). Apparently in the latter case the proxemic factor worked differently. An explanation was found in the higher frequencies of functional equivalents contained in the I.I. utterances pronounced at far-range (e.g., see, look, watch, o!). With increased inter-child distance, there was more functional redundancy in I.I. utterances, adding length to the utterance. In short, the proxemic factor affected differentially the construction of I.I. utterances in line with the effects of the perceptual factor.

Utterance types

I.I. utterances were grouped according to two patterns which we shall characterize as the Indicative type and the Descriptive type. Indicative utterances merely indicated place or object to attend to, while Descriptive utterances furnished information about states and events. Indicative utterances lacked descriptions while descriptive utterances might also contain indicators (e.g., look, o!). Table 1 shows the distribution of frequencies according to experimental conditions.

I.I. utterance types were distributed in the expected way. Perceptual assessment determined which type of utterance was used in both proxemic conditions. As stated earlier, the most frequent assessment at close range was the shared field assessment, and in this case the typical I.I. utterances was descriptive; if however the speaker perceived the action fields as separate albeit at close range, the typical utterance was indicative. Further, also as stated earlier, the most frequent assessment at far range was the separate field assessment, and in this case the typical I.I. utterance was indicative; if however the speaker perceived the action fields as shared, albeit at far range, the typical utterance was descriptive.

These facts lead to the conclusion that the I.I. utterance is constructed in a way that is determined not directly by the physical aspect of mutual distance between action fields, but by the intervening variable which makes the evaluation of the relation between action fields.

Construction of I.I. utterances

A closer analysis was made of the make-up of the I.I. utterances in terms of content and function. A selected list of recurrent features was drawn up and frequencies of occurrence were tallied. Table 2 provides the frequency data with percentages permitting comparisons across proxemic-perceptual conditions, together with ratio values. There is a different distribution of the identified features in I.I. utterances produced after perceptual assessment of mutual relations between children's action fields (separate or shared). In the first case, the dominant features were calls to look and to come, the expressive indicator "O", use of the localizer "here" and, occasionally, reference to a given object. In the second case, the dominant features were full propositions, reference to an object, often with use of an elaborated noun phrase, the call to look often being an added feature. (Its secondary role in the case of shared fields is suggested by its placement in final or mid position in the utterances whereas in the case of separate fields it occurs most often in first position). The effect of the proxemic factor is seen in the higher percent values for the referentially richer (descriptive) utterances, in accordance with the data of Table 1. Of interest is the use of the feature "Y'know", occurring almost entirely in the case of shared fields at close-range; this suggests that the speaker thinks the listener already knows something about the speaker's action field, and is now being told more.

The different configurations of features (ratio values) characterizing I.I. utterances produced after perceptual assessment of action field relations clarify what the speaker expects the utterances to accomplish. If the mutual relation is seen as separate, the speaker mainly used deictic indicators and general directives which effectively drew the listener into the speaker's field. If the mutual relation is seen as shared and individed, the speaker produced detailed verbalization informing the listener about the contents of his field, which in turn drew the listener to participate in that field.

This point led us to give closer attention to the nature of the action field itself and the structure of its contents.

Organization of play space as action field

Play space has been referred to above by the term 'action field'. This assumes that the child relates himself to his play space as agent to his action field. Applying this view which we hypothetically ascribe to the child, we may also assume that the action field is structured in terms of such parts as Agent - Action - Object as well as some Goal to which the action is moving. An analysis in line with this structural framework was performed on the referential content of the full propositions contained in I.I. utterances. Referential content of all complete propositions under analysis could be categorized under the headings: Agent's work, Action field contents, State of Action field (with its problematic aspect), Directive, and Absent Situation Reference. The analysis concerns 46 utterances (ca. 48 percent of the total number of I.I. utterances). Of these, 1 only contained content extraneous to the speaker's own action field. Of the remaining 45, the great majority (38) were constructed in the condition of shared action field perception, and of these 31 when the fields were located at close-range. Under these circumstances, the speaker detailed most frequently what he or she as Agent was doing, would do, had done or was causing to happen (Agent's work); he also made statements about what objects were contained in the Action field, or about the current state of the Action field. Of interest are the statements of problems arising in the action field, 7 of which occurring when the speaker perceived action fields as shared and none when fields were perceived as separate. To illustrate, here are some examples (translated from the Polish).

Ex. 1. "It doesn't want to come off the square, why not! See?
Ex. 2. "You're not s'posed to make braids on this doll, I guess not, eh?"
Ex. 3. "Dolly doesn't wanna go to sleep y'know?"
Ex. 4. "Oh, my wheel fell off y'know."

The analytical data support the contention that the child's play space is structured as an action field with the speaking child as the Agent of that field. When the child perceives this field as isolated from the other child's field, he constructs utterances that merely draw attention to its existence in order to attract the partner to it. But when the child perceives his own field as included within a shared field, where both overlap physically, he constructs a full proposition which represent those objects, states and events which mark out his own field and his own action within it.

Discussion

The mutual spatial arrangements naturally assumed by children in a free play setting have already been shown to be factors affecting their communication processes (Shugar, 1979). Why, however, should the child who wishes to initiate interactive play with a partner invariably use different kinds of utterances depending on whether his play space is adjacent and overlapping with that of the partner, or whether it is farther removed? More particularly, why should his perception of play space as belonging separately to each child, or shared between them, turn out to be such a critical factor in deciding what he will say? Apparently the interaction-initiating child has reliable expectancies as to how the other child will respond to given types of utterances, regardless of direct knowledge of that child's behavior (we recall that the subjects are unfamiliar pairs). Our contention is that these expectancies have their source in children's perceptions of each other in the same categories that could be applied to themselves. Thus they generate those utterances to which, in like conditions, they would themselves in like manner respond. The categories that have basic reality for young children in peer conditions have to do with agentive action upon objects, action goals and problems. This would explain why the child generates the types of utterance that have often been regarded as egocentric in nature, but are in fact - in conditions such as these - basically social.

One might reflect more deeply upon the very nature of the uniformities revealed in this study of young children's natural responses to spatial aspects of situations where peer interaction is involved. If we consider this question against the background of the situation where adult-child interaction is involved (as illustrated at the beginning of this paper), it is clear that these spontaneous responses in the peer situation contrast sharply with the late acquisition of interactional procedures in the adult world, products of socialization by the adult. We can state the difference this way: In adult-child interaction, children are inducted into the social-cultural life through learning from adults the practised procedures and norms, whereas in child-child interaction, children build their own mutual relations, socializing each other and themselves.

Acknowledgment. This investigation was supported, in part, by the Polish Ministry of Education (Grant W 11.4).

References

Bokus, B. (1980) Initiating social interactions at the preschool age. A method of analysis and some results. Paper to the 22nd International Congress of Psychology, Leipzig, July, 1980. To appear in: POLISH PSYCHOLOGICAL BULLETIN.

Bokus, B. & Shugar G. W. (1979) What will a three-year-old say? An experimental study of situational variation. In O. K. Garnica & M. L. King (eds.), LANGUAGE,

CHILDREN AND SOCIETY, Oxford: Pergamon Press. 65-79.

Mackay, R. W. (1974) Conceptions of children and models of socialization. In R. Turner (ed.), ETHNOMETHODOLOGY. SELECTED READINGS. Harmondsworth: Penguin. 180-193.

Maratsos, M. P. (1973) Nonegocentric communication abilities in preschool children. CHILD DEVELOPMENT 44 (3), 697-700.

Mueller, E. & Vandell D. (1977) A methodology for the study of social interaction. Playgroup Project. Paper to Conference on the Social Network, Educational Testing Service.

Shields, M. (1979) Dialogue, monologue and egocentric speech by children in nursery schools. In O. K. Garnica & M. L. King (eds.), LANGUAGE, CHILDREN AND SOCIETY. Oxford: Pergamon Press. 249-269.

Shugar, G. W. (1979) Peer face-to-face interactions at age three to five. INTERNATIONAL JOURNAL OF PSYCHOLINGUISTICS 5 (4), 12. 17-37.

Shugar, G. W. (1980) Early child discourse in the dyadic interaction unit. Paper to 22nd International Congress of Psychologists, Leipzig, July, 1980. To appear in INTERNATIONAL JOURNAL OF PSYCHOLINGUISTICS.

Shugar, G. W. (in press) Action discourse and topical discourse in learning to use language. Paper to Fifth International Congress of Applied Linguistics. To appear in GRAZER LINGUISTISCHE STUDIEN 16.

Speier, M. (1970) The everyday world of the child. In J. Douglas (ed.), UNDERSTANDING EVERYDAY LIFE, Chicago: Aldine. 188-217.

Table 1. Frequencies of interaction-initiating utterance types according to perceptual assessment of action fields as Separate or Shared, at close and far range.

UTTERANCE TYPE	PERCEPTUAL ASSESSMENT					
	SEPARATE	SHARED	ALL	SEPARATE	SHARED	ALL
	(at close range)			(at far range)		
Indicative	11	3	14	33	3	36
Descriptive	2	32	34	4	8	12
All	13	35	48	37	11	48
Frequency difference value (Pearson's Chi-square test)			26.532[a]			17.337[a]
Inter-variable correlation strength			$r_p = 0.844$			$r_p = 0.729$

[a] $p < .001$

Table 2. Content-functional features of I.I. utterances according to perceptual assessment (Separate vs Shared Action Fields) at Far- and Close-Range, in frequencies (N) and (%), and ratios of utterances for Separate/Shared Fields.

CONTENT-FUNCTIONAL FEATURES in total of utterances:	PERCEPTUAL ASSESSMENTS				RATIOS of UTTERANCES for SEPARATE/SHARED FIELDS
	SEPARATE FIELDS Proxemic		SHARED FIELDS Conditions		
	Far N (%) 37 (100)	Close N (%) 13 (100)	Far N (%) 11 (100)	Close N (%) 35 (100)	
Expressive "O!"	20 (54)	7 (54)	2 (18)	8 (23)	2.70
Call to look	29 (78)	8 (61)	6 (54)	13 (37)	1.95
Call to come	6 (16)	3 (23)	0 (0)	2 (6)	4.5
Localizing "Here"	9 (24)	3 (23)	0 (0)	2 (6)	6.0
"Y'know"	1 (3)	0 (0)	1 (9)	7 (20)	0.13
Referenced Object	8 (22)	3 (23)	8 (73)	30 (86)	0.29
—with elaborated NP	2 (5)	1 (8)	5 (45)	18 (51)	0.13
Full propositional content	5 (13)	3 (23)	7 (64)	31 (88)	0.21

EFFECTS OF DAY-CARE EXPERIENCE ON THE FORMAL AND PRAGMATIC DEVELOPMENT OF YOUNG CHILDREN*

Toni Cross, Gillian Parmenter,
Institute of Early Childhood Royal Children's Hospital,
Development,

Maryla Juchnowski, and Gillian Johnson,
Prahran College (TAFE), University of Melbourne,
                                        Australia

It was thought in the 40's and 50's that studies of the developmental patterns of institutionalized children would elucidate the effects of deprivation of human interaction on aspects of learning and social behaviour (e.g. Ribble 1944; Spitz 1949; Goldfarb 1944; Brodbeck & Irwin 1946). However, we are now familiar with the many shortcomings of this methodology. On the other hand, the careful study of children in full-time group day-care centres can overcome many of these problems and may therefore provide us with a reasonable test as to whether certain kinds or amounts of linguistic experience are crucial to normal language development. In fact, comparison of children in full-time day-care centres with those cared for at home can provide several research advantages:

1. Full-time day-care, in comparison with otherwise matched middle-class home-care, provides us with two normal child-rearing situations in our culture which vary considerably in the amount of, and opportunity for, mother-child (or mother-infant) conversational interaction. Although there is evidence that working mothers preserve some non-working time to interact with their children, such opportunities are not readily available for at least eight to ten waking hours per day, five days per week. Thus we have a naturalistic test of the importance of the amount of linguistic input and adult-child interaction in language acquisition.

---

* Aspects of this research were supported by a grant from the Australian Research Grants Scheme to the senior author.

2. Middle-class children in good quality child-care centres are not *prima facie*, emotionally deprived or 'self-selected' in obvious ways in comparison with middle-class children at home.

3. With regular day-centre attendance, we are not dealing with a situation, such as institutionalization, which is known to have disruptive effects on family relations or child development, either in terms of the reasons for institutionalization (e.g. family breakdown, child abuse or neglect, or bereavement of parents), or in the experiences and events of institutionalization (as in admission to hospital).

Few studies to date have investigated the influence of day-care attendance on young children's language development and most of these have relied on standard tests of language ability (such as the Peabody Picture Vocabulary, the Reynell Developmental Language Scale or the Illinois Test of Psycholinguistic abilities) which generally do not provide sensitive measures of language use (e.g. Tizard, Cooperman, Joseph & Tizard, 1972, Cochran, 1977; Kagan, Kearsley & Zelazo, 1977; Rubenstein & Howes, 1979). In general, these studies have been unable to demonstrate clear differences between children cared for at home and those in regular group daycare centres. However, no previous study known to the authors can escape the criticism that the insensitivity of the measures used may have masked real differences between the children.

This paper reports several small scale studies of child language development in which children from middle-class families, who have been attending day-care centres for substantial amounts of time, are compared with children of similar backgrounds, ages and stages of development cared for entirely at home by their mothers. Each study used different groups of home and day-care families and approached the comparison in different ways and each employed a detailed functional analysis of children's spontaneous speech. In all, five studies will be presented, on the grounds that single studies do not provide convincing evidence of either difference or no difference in an area where there is great scope for systematic variation in child-care arrangements, both at home and in day-care centres.

The investigations commenced in 1973 and spanned nearly a decade in which attitudes to, and conditions of child-care and maternal employment have altered considerably.

They involved a total of 120 children of both sexes, two to three years of age; forty-six in full-time home-care and seventy-four children in either part-time or full-time day-care from over twenty different centres. Most of these children had entered regular day-care centre attendance in the first year of life.

The Amount of "Input"

The first step is to establish that conditions for equivalent children cared for at home or in day-care do in fact create differences in their respective opportunities for participating in one-to-one conversations with adults and, hence, for receiving appropriately adjusted linguistic input. This step was carried out by Gillian Parmenter for a doctoral dissertation at the University of Melbourne (1976). She selected forty-two middle-class first-born children aged between thirty and thirty-three months. Twenty-eight (fifteen boys and thirteen girls) were selected from eleven different day-care centres in Melbourne; twelve children were full-time in divided day-care centres (centres which stratify the children into age groups) and sixteen were full-time in non-divided centres (those in which two to five-year-olds were grouped together). All children had commenced daily day-care attendance at least three months previously; most of them had been there for more than six months. The home group contained fourteen children who had been cared for by their mothers at home on a full-time basis since birth (seven boys and seven girls). The day-care children's average age was 31.8 months and the home-care, 31.1 months (with no difference in age between the divided and non-divided groupings). The families of each group were comparable in terms of socio-economic status, family size and educational level of the parents.

Each child was fitted with a radio-microphone and recorded in spontaneous conversation for at least an hour twice during the week-day, that is, between 10 and 11 a.m. and between 6.30 and 7.30 p.m. In the morning session the day-care children were recorded in the usual routine of play in the centre while the home-care children were recorded at home. In the evening recording, all children were recorded at home with their families. The data was analyzed for both recording sessions, but of particular interest for the moment are the morning sessions which were taken across the home-care and day-care situations. Parmenter made her comparisons using 3 x 2 x 2 analyses of variance designs for care-arrangements, sex of child and time of recording, and examined the following:

(a) The amount of speech output by the child, measured as the total number of utterances over the hour-long recording.

(b) The speech addressed to the child in the same amount of time measured as the total number of utterances observed to be directed to the focal child.

(c) The source of the "input" to the child; that is, whether the speech addressed to the child came from another child in the group, a child-care worker, a parent, other adult relative (or neighbour), or from a sibling or play-mate.

The results showed the following pattern for speech addressed to the child:

TABLE 1

AMOUNT OF SPEECH ADDRESSED TO THE CHILDREN IN THE MORNING

		Adult	Older Child	Peer	Total
Care Arrangements					
Home-Care	Mean	348.50	N/A	N/A	348.50
	SD	113.00			113.00
Divided Day-Care	Mean	145.50	N/A	21.50	167.00
	SD	107.50		17.50	108.00
Non-divided Day-Care	Mean	86.00	33.50	22.00	141.50
	SD	48.50	24.50	19.00	48.00

	df	Mean Square	F	p
Sex	2	2879.39	.39	NS
Care Arrangement	2	177786.75	18.68	<.001
Sex x Care Arrangement	2	3674.65	.38	NS

This table shows the mean amount of speech addressed to the 2½ year-old subjects in each care arrangement, in the morning. There is a significant difference in the amount of speech directed at the children in the three care-arrangements (p < .001) such that home children experienced more than twice as much total verbal 'input' as the children in day-care. However, in terms of adult speech only, the home-care group received 349 utterances per hour on average, the divided day-care group 146 utterances, and the non-divided day-care group 86 utterances. Since both situations of recording probably optimized the adults' tendency to address the subject child, we can probably regard these results as representing the maximum opportunities for adult-child interaction in all three situations.

Amount of "Output"

The pattern for the children's output showed a similar pattern and is presented in Table 2.

TABLE 2
AMOUNT OF SPEECH EMITTED BY THE CHILDREN IN THE MORNING

Category of Addressee

Care Arrangements		Adult	Older Child	Peer	Total
Home Care	Mean	377.50	N/A	N/A	377.50
	SD	123.50			123.50
Divided Day-Care ..	Mean	69.50	N/A	51.00	120.50
	SD	45.50		28.00	90.00
Non-Divided Day-Care	Mean	38.50	31.50	28.00	98.00
	SD	35.50	26.50	31.50	77.50

	df	Mean Square	F	p
Sex	2	379.5	.05	NS
Care Arrangement ..	1	322342.7	43.78	< .001
Sex x Care Arrangement	2	3438.55	.47	NS

As Table 2 shows, the home children produced more than three times as many utterances at home than did the children in the day-care situation. Thus, if opportunity to engage in adult-child or child-child interaction is important in acquiring linguistic and communicative competence, these three regular settings produce considerable variation on both sides of the interaction.

On the other hand, comparison with the results of the evening recording sessions for all children at home shows clearly the depressant effect of the day-care situation.

TABLE 3

TOTAL AMOUNT OF SPEECH TO THE CHILDREN IN THE EVENING CLASSIFIED BY SEX

			Care Arrangements		
			Home-Care	Divided Day-Care	Non-Divided Day-Care
Sex	Female	Mean	461	355	464
		SD	142	91	253
	Male	Mean	483	458	433
		SD	120	229	181

	df	Mean Square	F	P
Sex	1	15563.16	.49	NS
Care Arrangement	2	14123.34	.45	NS
Sex x Care Arrangement	2	15258.94	.48	NS

Table 3 shows that the amount of speech directed to the children at home in the evening increased for all groups, indicating that the slight day-care input was a function of the context and not the children. It is important to recognize that in the evening there were no significant effects of care-arrangement on amount of adult speech to the children (regardless of the child's sex) which suggests that day-care parents were not compensating for their children's day-care experience by increasing their interactions with them at home.

The Effects of Day-Care

Table 4 shows the total amount of speech (number of utterances) produced by the children in the home context in the evening classified by child's sex and day-time care-arrangement.

TABLE 4

TOTAL AMOUNT OF SPEECH BY THE CHILDREN IN THE EVENING
CLASSIFIED BY SEX

			Home-Care	Divided Day-Care	Non-Divided Day-Care
Sex	Female	Mean	375	422	409
		SD	114	75	197
	Male	Mean	466	393	481
		SD	162	159	80

	df	Mean Square	F	p
Sex	1	15496.98	.83	NS
Care Arrangement	2	6081.82	.32	NS
Sex x Care Arrangement	2	15386.10	.82	NS

This result indicates that, in terms of amount of output, the day-care experiences of the child have no effect on his/her language use in the home.

Parmenter also included analysis of the complexity of child and adult speech according to care-arrangement. Using mean utterance length, she compared across care-groups for both morning and evening sessions. On this measure for the morning comparison (where care arrangements differed) the results in Table 5 showed that there were again no significant differences due to care type, despite the large differences in the interpersonal contexts.

TABLE 5

MEAN M.L.U. SCORES OF THE CHILDREN IN THE MORNING

Care Arrangements		Adult	Older Child	Peer	Total
Home-Care..	Mean	3.05	N/A	N/A	3.05
	SD	.64			.64
Divided Day-Care ..	Mean	2.40	N/A	2.75	2.55
	SD	.63		.79	.60
Non-divided Day-Care	Mean	2.70	2.50	2.10	2.85
	Sd	1.40	1.45	1.55	.95

	df	Mean Square	F	P
Sex	1	.53	1.00	NS
Care Arrangement ..	2	.80	1.49	NS
Six x Care Arrangement	2	1.10	2.07	NS

Moreover, as Table 6 indicates (again using MLU as a measure of children's linguistic complexity) there were also no child differences for the evening recordings.

TABLE 6

M.L.U. SCORES OF THE CHILDREN IN THE EVENING CLASSIFIED BY SEX

			Home-Care	Divided Day-Care	Non-Divided Day-Care
Sex	Female	Mean	3.3	2.9	2.8
		SD	.43	.65	.89
	Male	Mean	2.8	2.3	3.1
		SD	.87	.54	.81

	df	Mean Square	F	P
Sex	1	1.05	2.18	NS
Care Arrangement	2	.88	1.82	NS
Sex x Care Arrangement	2	.86	1.77	NS

Thus, on the most commonly used measure of child language growth (whether taken in the centre or at home), we have no evidence of an effect of full-time day-care on the children's language use at 2½ years.

However, it was interesting to find that when M.L.U. was applied to the parent's speech in the evening, significant complexity differences due to care arrangement did emerge. The mothers of the home group produced slightly more complex speech than did the mothers of either day-care group, with the mothers of the divided day-care group producing the least complex speech (Table 7).

TABLE 7

M.L.U. SCORES OF THE MOTHERS IN THE EVENING CLASSIFIED BY SEX

			Care Arrangements		
			Home-Care	Divided Day-Care	Non-Divided Day-Care
Sex	Female	Mean	5.0	4.1	4.4
		SD	.54	.47	.82
	Male	Mean	4.7	3.9	4.7
		SD	.61	.68	.46

	df	Mean Square	F	P
Sex	1	.12	.34	NS
Care Arrangement	2	3.02	8.26	< .001
Sex x Care Arrangement	2	.30	.83	NS

In fact, the pattern observed for the children was similar to their parents' pattern but, in the former case, the differences were not significant in either recording session. However, because the correlations between all parent and child M.L.U.'s were positive and significant, Parmenter suggested that the parents may be responding to real differences in the children's linguistic ability in favour of the 'home' children that were not picked up by the M.L.U. measure.

Parmenter then analyzed the mothers' and children's language for the evening session at a more micro level, using an adapted version of Wells' (1973) conversational code. Since it will not be possible to present her results at this level of detail, suffice it to summarize her findings.

At the functional (utterance-based) level, she found only one difference in the children due to care-arrangement: children in the home-care group expressed more "want" utterances in the interpersonal control subsequence. No differences at any level were found for Parmenter's multi-level conversation code which, at the finest level, reliably differentiated twenty-four speech functions. Moreover no main effects on maternal conversations were attributable to care arrangements. Parmenter therefore concluded that:

> "Although the day-care environment promotes differences in language use and input for 2½ year-olds, it seems that these differences are not carried over into the home situation." (Parmenter, 1976, p.33).

However, since there are serious problems in producing evidence to firmly support the null-hypothesis (the hypothesis that two samples represent the same population), we have continued to research the issue using different samples for comparison, different selections of day-care centres, and different methodological approaches.

Juchnowski (1978, 1982) has conducted two separate and intensive comparisons of the language of children in day-care and at home, this time matching the children specifically for formal language ability (rather than age) and using a functional code based on Halliday (1975).

In her first study, Juchnowski (1978) matched two groups of eight children from full-time day-care and home-care on the basis of the high socio-economic status of the father, the post-tertiary education of both mother and father, and a precise matching for child M.L.U. Her full-time day-care group had been in full-time day-care for at least twelve months and were aged between twenty and thirty-eight months.

However, after considerable screening, the precise match for M.L.U. (home-care children were 2.46 and day-care 2.58) was only achieved at the cost of a small but reliable difference in the ages of the children in the groups (home-care 28.63, day-care 33.25, $p < .05$). This outcome initially suggested a small effect of day-care on rate of development in favour of the home-care children and seemed to confirm Parmenter's suspicion that there were hidden differences between her groups of this same direction. This was further supported by Juchnowski's finding of a significant difference ($p < .05$) in maternal M.L.U. in the direction of greater complexity in maternal speech to home-care children (4.45 versus 5.12).

Juchnowski then compared mother and child conversations at home in a play situation collected during the week-ends or public (school) holidays. She used a code which included some formal measures, conversational devices, and a detailed functional (or speech act) code based within Halliday's (1975) framework and including categories from several other researchers, e.g. McNeill and McNeill (1975), Wells (1973) and Dore (1976). This code categorized twenty-three measures of the children's language use and thirty-eight measures of their mothers' language to them.

TABLE 8

MEANS AND TESTS OF SIGNIFICANCE OF CHILDREN'S SPEECH CATEGORIES

Feature	Day-Care Mean	Home-Care Mean	Mann-Whitney sign. level
Age	32.25	28.63	**
M.L.U.	2.58	2.46	
Turn-grabbing devices	25.50	33.75	
Conversation repair devices	14.00	14.00	
Functional Code:			
Instrumental	7.13	8.50	
Directives	.38	1.25	
Requests	1.13	1.63	
Intentions	5.63	5.63	
Regulatory	27.13	26.63	
Directives	19.38	17.00	
Refusal to comply	2.25	2.13	
Compliance	2.75	2.88	
Suggestions for action	1.75	3.88	
Heuristic	29.00	26.00	
Questions	21.75	23.50	
Clarification questions	2.38	1.38	
Directives	0	.13	
Lack of knowledge	4.88	1.00	***
Informative	123.50	127.00	
Descriptives	87.75	92.25	
Confirmations	31.63	29.88	
Questions	.38	.38	
Total number of Interrogatives	26.63	27.75	
Total number of Imperatives	19.75	18.38	

** $p < .05$ (2tt)
*** $p < .01$ (2tt)

The results of her comparison of children and mothers in the full-time day-care and home-care groups (shown in Table 8) produced only one significant difference in measures of child language, a smaller proportion of expressions of lack of knowledge (I dunno, etc.). The profiles of all other pragmatic categories were remarkably similar.

On the mothers' side, in addition to more complex utterances, three significant differences were found (out of thirty-eight measures).

As Table 9 shows, the mothers of the day-care children used far fewer paraphrases of their own utterances (semantic repetitions), fewer self-repetitions overall and more informative utterances. These few differences led Juchnowski, too, to the conclusion that any reliable effects of prolonged day-care attendance on very young children have yet to be established.

In her more recent study Juchnowski (1982) again made some comparisons based on type of care-arrangement, using new samples of mothers and children. In this comparison, she selected fifteen children in full-time care at home, fifteen children in full-time day-care and eleven children in part-time day-care (1½-3 days per week). The children in day-care centres were selected from twelve formal centres in Melbourne and had been in attendance on a similar time-basis (full- or part-time respectively) for at least twelve months prior to testing and recording. The mothers of all groups had completed or were completing a tertiary qualification. All children spanned eighteen to thirty-eight months and the groups were equated precisely for M.L.U. and Peabody Picture Vocabulary Test scores. Maternal and child speech samples, recorded in spontaneous play situations with all mothers and children at home were compared for all three care-arrangement groupings and coded for eighteen formal and pragmatic maternal speech features and eleven child speech features. The results of the analysis of variance are presented in Table 10.

TABLE 9 MEANS AND TESTS OF SIGNIFICANCE OF MOTHERS' SPEECH CATEGORIES

Feature	Day-Care Mean	Home Care Mean	Mann-Whitney Sig. Lev.	Feature Functional Code:	Day-Care Mean	Home-Care Mean	Mann-Whitney Sig.Lev.
M.L.U.	4.45	5.12	**	Instrumental	10.25	13.88	
Rate of speech	57.60	68.38		Directives	.25	.50	
Proportion of mother-child utterances	1.46	1.34		Requests	6.63	8.25	
				Intentions	3.38	5.13	
Total interruptions	12.63	21.38		Regulatory	34.13	28.75	
Proportion of mother-child interruptions	.43	.73		Directives	30.00	23.75	
				Requests	1.75	1.13	
Proportion of turn-grabbing devices	1.30	.87		Refusals	.25	.13	
				Compliances	1.50	3.00	
Turn-grabbing devices	34.00	28.63		Suggestions	.63	.88	
Prop. of mother-child conversation repair devices	1.96	2.07		Heuristic	30.75	34.63	
Conversation repair devices	20.25	24.00		Questions	17.88	22.13	
Imitations	5.63	5.63		Clarification Questions	9.50	11.25	
Expansions	16.63	20.25		Lack of knowledge	.88	1.25	
Contractions	6.00	4.13		Informative	113.13	101.25	**
Extensions	36.75	40.25		Descriptive	56.38	57.75	
Exact maternal repetitions	9.13	5.75		Confirmation	25.38	20.50	
Partial maternal repetitions	4.87	5.25		Questions	131.38	26.00	
Semantic maternal repetitions	13.90	27.50	***	Total number of interrogatives	57.89	68.75	
Total maternal repetitions	27.90	38.80	***	Total number of imperatives	30.00	24.75	

** p < .05 (2tt)   *** p < .01 (2tt)

TABLE 10

MEAN PERCENTAGE OF AGE, LANGUAGE MEASURES AND LANGUAGE
FUNCTIONS OF CHILD ACCORDING TO CARE ARRANGEMENTS

	Care Arrangement			Significance
	Full-Time Day-Care	Part-Time Day-Care	Home-Care	
Age (months)	29.9	28.9	29.3	
Peabody Vocabulary (Mental Age months)	29.2	20.9	27.9	
M.L.U.	2.57	2.49	2.53	
M.M.L.U.	6.43	6.28	7.05	
Conversational turns	144.2	150.4	139.7	
Child interruptions	8.3	7.8	10.1	
Conversation Grabbing Devices	17.0	18.3	15.4	
Conversation Repair Devices	16.4	22.3	12.6	
Directives	13.6	13.2	12.0	
Suggestions	1.8	1.3	3.5	
Requests	2.3	2.3	1.8	
Intentions	3.3	2.7	4.1	
Total Regulatory Utterances	16.9	16.7	17.2	
Total Questions	19.0	26.6	17.1	
Descriptive Responses	45.5	42.2	49.5	
Descriptive Comments	40.3	51.0	36.4	
Total Informative Utterances	84.4	94.3	86.4	

** $p < .05$
*** $p < .005$

As Table 10 shows, no significant differences were apparent
across the care-groups for the children. Only one difference
approached significance and this was the lower Peabody scores
for the part-time day group. On the mothers' side of the
interaction, the only maternal speech variable differentiating the groups was the strong tendency for the mothers of
the part-time day-care children to use greater frequencies of
self-repetitions--exact and partial repetitions in particular
(Table 11).

TABLE 11

MEAN PERCENTAGE OF LANGUAGE FUNCTIONS OF MOTHER
ACCORDING TO CARE ARRANGEMENT

	Care Arrangement			Significance
	Full-Time Day-Care	Part-Time Day-Care	Home-Care	
M.L.U.	5.16	4.82	4.99	
M.M.L.U.	13.49	12.92	13.19	
Maternal Expansions	10.3	14.5	18.0	
Maternal Extensions	20.5	18.0	22.9	
Maternal Exact and Partial Repetitions	7.9	16.8	7.3	***
Semantic Repetitions	19.0	22.8	16.3	
Total Maternal Repetitions	26.9	39.6	23.6	***
Conversational Turns	192.6	205.7	199.7	
Maternal Interruptions	10.5	11.1	11.6	
Conversation Grabbing Devices	17.2	15.2	15.7	
Conversation Repair Devices	41.7	49.4	42.5	
Directives	23.9	26.4	23.7	
Suggestions	6.8	8.1	7.7	
Requests	3.5	3.0	1.7	
Intentions	4.5	4.7	2.8	
Total Regulatory Utterances	35.5	29.3	33.5	
Total Questions	70.7	67.4	71.0	
Descriptive Responses	31.8	37.3	34.0	
Descriptive Comments	43.3	42.7	36.2	
Total Informative Utterances	75.1	80.0	70.2	

** $p < .05$
*** $p < .005$

When the children in the two day-care situations were grouped into 'long-stayers' (length of attendance over nineteen months) and 'short-stayers' (length of attendance under sixteen months), the only child speech feature to differ was the higher use of conversation-grabbing devices by the short-stayers. The failure to find other differences was important because the long-stayers had begun regular day-care attendance in the prelingual stage of development at between four and eleven months of age.

TABLE 12

COMPARISON OF THE USE OF CONVERSATIONAL ACTS BY HOME-CARE AND DAY-CARE CHILDREN AT TIME 1

Conversational Acts	Mean Home-Care	Std. Dev.	Mean Day-Care	Std. Dev.	2 Tailed Level of Sig.
REQUESTIVES:					
Choice questions	2.8	3.0	3.6	2.8	
Product questions	3.6	3.0	6.6	6.9	
Process questions	-	-	.3	.7	
Action requests	2.4	4.0	1.7	2.2	
Permission requests	.1	.3	.4	.5	
Suggestions	.6	.9	2.5	1.2	**
Requestives (total)	9.6	7.0	15.1	10.7	
ASSERTIVES:					
Identifications/labels	17.6	17.4	14.1	6.5	
Descriptions	24.6	16.4	24.0	7.3	
Internal/Self reports	2.6	2.5	3.5	4.5	
Personal evaluations	.9	.8	.9	1.1	
Personal " of partner	.9	2.5	.8	1.4	
Rules	-	-	-	-	
Explanations	.4	.7	.9	1.4	
Assertives (total)	47.0	24.6	44.1	11.4	
PERFORMATIVES:					
Performatives (total)	.9	1.2	1.7	2.3	
RESPONSIVES:					
Choice answers	17.5	15.1	18.6	10.1	
Product answers	27.2	18.1	18.6	9.2	
Process answers	.4	.5	.3	.5	
Compliances	19.5	30.6	5.8	3.6	
Clarification Responses	3.0	3.2	2.7	3.2	
Qualifications	5.4	5.0	5.1	3.8	
Agreements	7.1	4.2	8.2	5.3	
Acknowledgments	3.8	2.1	5.9	6.1	
Responsives (total)	84.0	40.7	65.5	27.9	
REGULATIVES:					
Regulatives (total)	2.1	4.0	4.0	2.9	
EXPRESSIVES:					
Exclamations/ Accompaniments)	7.1	2.3	9.7	6.7	
Repetition	19.5	11.7	14.7	12.7	

* $p < .05$
** $p < .01$

TABLE 13

COMPARISON OF THE USE OF CONVERSATIONAL ACTS BY
HOME-CARE AND DAY-CARE CHILDREN AT TIME 2

Conversational Acts	Mean Home-Care	Std. Dev.	Mean Day-Care	Std. Dev.	2 Tailed Level of Sig.
REQUESTIVES:					
Choice questions	3.9	4.5	2.4	1.7	
Product questions	7.0	3.6	5.7	4.2	
Process questions	-	-	.4	.7	
Action requests	.9	1.6	2.1	2.7	
Permission requests	-	-	.1	.4	
Suggestions	1.1	2.1	.6	.7	
Requestives (total)	12.9	7.8	11.4	6.4	
ASSERTIVES:					
Identifications/labels	15.4	8.3	19.5	9.6	
Descriptions	39.6	22.3	37.1	11.4	
Internal/Self reports	1.5	1.9	2.6	1.6	
Personal evaluations	.6	1.1	.5	.5	
Personal " of partner	1.7	2.8	.7	.7	
Rules	.5	.7	-	-	
Explanations	3.2	4.9	2.1	1.1	
Assertives (total)	62.6	24.1	62.5	10.9	
PERFORMATIVES:					
Performatives (total)	.4	.7	1.3	1.9	
RESPONSIVES:					
Choice answers	22.9	13.0	18.5	8.5	
Product answers	25.5	23.1	18.9	10.8	
Process answers	.1	.3	.9	2.5	
Compliances	7.7	7.4	4.7	3.3	
Clarification Responses	.6	1.2	2.9	3.3	
Qualifications	1.9	2.9	2.1	1.6	
Agreements	6.3	4.1	12.5	3.8	**
Acknowledgments	6.2	7.0	3.4	1.8	
Responsives (total)	71.2	39.0	63.9	17.8	
REGULATIVES:					
Regulatives (total)	2.2	2.5	4.0	4.6	
EXPRESSIVES:					
Exclamations/) Accompaniments)	6.9	4.8	11.2	5.5	
Repetition	10.6	6.7	12.3	10.4	

*   p $<$ .05
**   p $<$ .01

A final study in Melbourne was conducted by Johnson (1980). She selected eight day-care children who had attended formal day-care in three centres full-time for at least twelve months and eight who had remained in home-care. The groups were closely matched for S.E.S. and age (day-care mean 27.00 months, range 23-33 months; home-care mean 27.25, range 24-33 months). The children were also equated, pair by pair, for M.L.U. (day-care mean 2.42, SD .58; home-care mean 2.23, SD .54), and for scores on the Pre-school Language Scale (Zimmerman, Steiner and Pond, 1979).

Johnson's study tested the hypothesis that children exposed to a formal day-care environment on a full-time basis diverge over time in their functional and expressive language abilities in comparison with their counterparts of the same age at home. Consequently, she recorded the mothers and children in spontaneous interaction at an initial session (Time 1) and then again six months later (Time 2) - i.e. when they were, on average, thirty-one to thirty-nine months old. Her language analysis was based on Dore's (1979) conversational code (with minor adaptations) and compared the children on twenty-eight speech acts (inter-coder reliability = .85-.96) and M.L.U. Her results are presented in Table 12.

Johnson, too, was unable to find reliable differences in either the formal or the functional measures of child language at Time 1, with the single exception of the "suggestions" sub-category which was used infrequently by both groups but more frequently by the day-care group. The analysis of divergence showed that this decreased over the six months.

Moreover, as Table 13 shows, the pattern of results was similar for Time 2 and no divergence occurred. The only reliable difference found six months later was in the higher use by the day-care group of responses indicating agreement.

Conclusions

The results of these five comparative studies of matched children receiving what could be termed 'good quality' care both at home and in day-care centres are highly consistent, and indicate that, in the early stages of language development, continuous and regular experience of day-care, full-time or part-time, seems to have no reliable effects on language development of middle class children. These findings are compatible with more general comparisons in the research literature, which, though they rarely include detailed language measures, have also failed to show that children in full-time day-care are disadvantaged in language development or use (e.g. Tizard, Cooperman, Joseph and Tizard, 1972; Kagan, 1976).

It now seems appropriate to draw some general conclusions about the implications of such findings for the issue of the role of parent-child interaction in promoting language development. At the very least, the evidence suggests that we should reconsider the role (or significance) of parent-child conversational interaction in development. Given that we have established that the opportunities for one-to-one conversation between care-givers and children are severely reduced in the day-care situation, it seems necessary to conclude that the absolute amount of input from adults is not a factor which determines rate (or course) of language development. It also seems necessary to postulate that parent-child interaction, although it may be crucial to satisfactory language development in ways suggested by a number of authors (e.g. Bruner 1975, Snow 1977, Brown 1977, Cross 1978) may have what has been termed a "threshold effect" (Newport 1975, Cross 1978). That is, it may be the case that there are limits on the extent to which interaction with adults (or older children) are necessary for adequate development. Our evidence indicates that it may be productive to think in terms of a certain minimum amount of interaction being both necessary and sufficient; further amounts then being redundant - at least specifically for the language development process. This may not, of course, be the case for other aspects of development (e.g. social or intellectual development).

The data from our several studies also indicates that language development (at both the functional and formal levels) is a relatively uniform and robust process, which, of course, once again raises the question of the importance of maturational constraints on the whole process.

REFERENCES

BRODBECK, A. J. & IRWIN, O. C. (1946) The speech behaviour of infants without families. Child Development, 17, 145-165.

BROWN, R. (1977) Introduction. In C. Snow & C. Ferguson (eds.). Talking to Children. Cambridge: University Press.

BRUNER, J. (1975) The ontogenesis of speech acts. Journal of Child Language, 2, 1-19.

COCHRAN, M. (1977) A comparison of group day-care and family child-rearing patterns in Sweden. Child Development, 48, 702-707.

CROSS, T. (1978) Mother's speech and its association with rate of linguistic development in young children. In N. Waterson & C. Snow (eds.) The Development of Communication. New York: Wiley.

DORE, J. (1976) Requestive systems in nursery school conversations: Analysis of talk in its social context. Paper presented at the Psychology of Language Conference. Stirling, Scotland.

DORE, J. (1979) Conversation and preschool language development. In P. Fletcher & M. Garman (eds.) Language Acquisition. Cambridge: Cambridge University Press.

GOLDFARB, W. (1944) Infant rearing as a factor in foster home placement. American Journal of Orthopsychiatry, 14, 162-167.

HALLIDAY, M. (1975) Learning How to Mean. London: Edward Arnold.

JOHNSON, G. (1980) Language development of two-year-old children in conversational interactions: the communication of meaning intentions. Unpub. Honours Thesis. University of Melbourne.

JUCHNOWSKI, M. (1978) Investigations into the role of the conversational contexts in language development. Unpub. M.A. (Prelim.) Thesis. Psychology Department, University of Melbourne.

JUCHNOWSKI, M. (1982) Some relationships between characteristics of mother, child-care arrangements and language development in young children. Unpublished Masters Thesis, University of Melbourne, Australia.

KAGAN, J. (1976) The effects of infant day-care. Department of Health, Education and Welfare, Washington.

KAGAN, J., KEARSLEY, R. & ZELAZO, P. (1977) The effects of infant day care on psychological development. Evaluation Quarterly, 1, 109-142.

McNEILL, D. & McNEILL, N. (1975) Linguistic Interaction Among Children and Adults. Committee on Cognition and Communication. University of Chicago, Illinois.

NEWPORT, E. (1975) A study of mother's speech and child language acquisition. Paper presented at Stanford Child Language Forum, Stanford.

PARMENTER, G. R. (1976) An investigation into some environmental factors influencing the use of language by the young child. Unpub. Ph.D. Thesis. Psychology Department, University of Melbourne.

RIBBLE, M. (1944) Infantile experience in relation to personality development. In J. McV. Hunt (ed.) Personality and Behaviour Disorders. New York: Ronald.

RUBENSTEIN, J. & HOWES, C. (1979) Caregiving and infant behaviour in day care and in homes. Developmental Psychology, 15, (1), 1-24.

SNOW, C. (1977) The development of conversation between mothers and babies. Journal of Child Language, 4, 1-22.

SPITZ, R. A. (1949) The role of ecological factors in emotional development in infancy. Child Development, 20, 145-156.

TIZARD, B., COOPERMAN, O., JOSEPH, A. & TIZARD, J. (1972) Environmental effects on language development: A study of young children in long-stay residential nurseries. Child Development, 43, 337-58.

WELLS, G. (1973) Coding Manual for the Description of Child Speech. University of Bristol.

ZIMMERMAN, I. L., STEINER, V. G. & POND, R. E. (1979) Preschool Language Scale. Revised Edition. Columbus: Charles E. Merrill.

FUNCTIONAL DIVERSITY AS A DEVELOPMENTAL PHENOMENON
IN CHILD AND PARENT CONVERSATION*

Maggie Kirkman,   Toni Cross,
University of   Institute of Early Childhood
Melbourne,   Development, Victoria,
Australia.   Australia.

The issue of functional diversification as an aspect
of the child's developing communicative ability has
been the subject of speculation but has not been
directly examined. Wells (1975) claimed that increasing diversity of function is an index of
language acquisition, but research has usually
focussed on the likelihood of a universal sequence
of emergence of communicative functions (Halliday,
1975; Greenfield and Smith, 1976, for example).
This begs the question of whether such an increase
occurs independently of consistent order.

For the purpose of this paper, functions are defined
as the specific, differentiable purposes for which
language is used in a particular context and at a
particular time.

Dale (1980) has concluded that there is no evidence
to support the notion that children acquire types of
communicative function in a universal sequence. He
did find, however, that diversity of function (like
mean length of utterance) was highly correlated with
age. The fact that syntactic and functional
measures were not directly correlated was attributed
by Dale to the apparent rapidity of functional
development during the one-word and early two-word
phases. He argued that the number of pragmatic
functions is a valid measure only at the one-word
stage because of a ceiling effect. If this is so,
there should be no major differences in diversity of
function (that is, the number of functional types

---

* Aspects of this research were supported by a grant
from the Australian Research Grants Committee to the
second author.

used) between children with mean utterance lengths of 1.0 and 3.0.

On the other hand, Curtiss, Prutting and Lowell (1979) considered diversity to be so important that it was selected as their sole measure of communicative competence for deaf children with a range of syntactic abilities. We believe that two assumptions are implicit in this (and related) work. One is that structural and communicative aspects follow separate developmental paths; there is some evidence to support this view. For example, Blank, Gessner and Esposito (1979) report the case of a child who at three years, three months,used age-appropriate syntactic and semantic structure but was ineffective in terms of interpersonal communication. Similarly, Snyder (1978) reports discrepancies in the pragmatic development of language-delayed children compared with normal children of equivalent mean utterance lengths, and Cross and Ball (1981) have reported marked deviance in functional ability of autistic children matched for formal language ability with younger, normal children. In contrast, however, Cross and Ball found few differences between matched dysphasic and normal children on the same functional measures. Rees (1978) has argued that mentally retarded children have also been assessed as communicating effectively despite impoverished verbal ideation. (However, Yamada (1981) has provided a contrary case report.)

The second assumption is that of the continuity (or, more strongly, stability) of functional diversity from the prelingual period through to the emergence of patterned speech. Griffiths (1979), for instance, explicitly claims that the transition from early asyntactic utterances to the first syntactic constructions is bridged by functional continuity. The possibility that the emergence of language may serve to increase functional differentiation and diversity is often obscured by assertions that a great deal of communicative development occurs prior to language use or in the very early stages (for example, Bates, Camaioni and Volterra, 1976; Dale, 1980). The role of language in functional development is further complicated by arguments that the context in which communication takes place forms part of the child's linguistic system (as in Greenfield and Smith, 1976).

In contrast (following Dore, 1975), we have chosen to stress the logical necessity of associating linguistic functions only with the beginnings of speech, and of considering prelingual communicative behaviour (incorporating gesture and context) as a prerequisite of later language use rather than as its equivalent. The context remains undeniably crucial in constructing the meaning attributed to communicative intentions. In measuring diversity of functional usage, then, we focus on speech whilst taking account of context and non-verbal communication.

A further essential source of meaning to a participant in conversation, having a significant effect on subsequent conversational contributions, is the effect of communication on the other participant(s). In fact, results achieved by Gallagher and Craig (1978) suggest that functional diversity may be most sensitively measured within a conversational context; they found an increasing ability to implement the demands of conversational conventions in children at Brown's stages I, II and III. The concept of "conversational act" (Dore, Gearhart and Newman, 1978) encompasses these aspects of communicative functions and has therefore been selected as the basis for this study.

The present study examined diversity in children conversing with their mothers. Matching of either age or language ability in the child groups permitted us to examine the relative importance to conversational skills of these two features. Our adoption of such an interactive approach also allowed us to investigate maternal language to discover whether functional aspects, like many formal measures, are adjusted to the linguistic ability of the child. As a strong test of this, mothers talking to pre-lingual children were included to determine whether maternal functional diversity was altered by the absence of language in the child. Furthermore, prelingually deaf as well as hearing children were included, on the grounds that such children present a test of the importance of formal language skills to the development of communicative intentions in the child and also to adjustment in maternal functional diversity. If, as Curtiss et al. (1979) claim, deaf children (with delayed oral language ability) exhibit the same range of conversational acts as their age-matched hearing peers, we would have support for the notion of separate development of the formal and functional aspects.

Method

Our subjects were forty Australian middle class children and their mothers, selected into five groups of eight mother-child pairs on the basis of the child's age, formal language ability and hearing capacity. Group data are set out in Table 1.

A group of eight five-year-old deaf children was equated for age with a group of eight five-year-old hearing children and for receptive and expressive language with a group of eight hearing two-year-olds. The mean length of utterance of the deaf five-year-olds was 1.61 and that of the hearing two-year-olds was 1.94.

TABLE 1
MEAN AGES, TEST SCORES; M.L.U.[1] AND M.M.L.U.[2] OF THE FIVE GROUPS OF CHILDREN

Groups	Hearing			Deaf	
	1 Year	2 Years	5 Years	2 Years	5 Years
Age (months)	11.55	26.25	62.10	29.30	65.59
Peabody Vocabulary	0	21.75	54.30	0	26.60
Sentence Comprehension[3]	0	32.88	98.90	0	36.10
M.L.U.[1]	0	1.94	3.85	0	1.61
M.M.L.U.[2]	0	3.80	9.43	0	3.17

1. Mean length of utterances
2. Mean length of 10 longest utterances (mean maximum length of utterance)
3. Devised by Cross (1977)

Similarly, a group of eight prelingual deaf two-year-olds was matched with the hearing two-year-olds for age and with a group of eight hearing one-year-olds for language. All deaf children had been tested audiologically within a period of three months before data were collected. Hearing losses in the better ear ranged from severe to profound, with a loss in excess of 70 dB SPL HL at frequencies of 500, 1000, 2000 and 4000 Hz being a necessary criterion for inclusion in the study. Aided thresholds exceeded 40 dB SPL HL over the same frequency range. Deafness was congenital in all cases, although the aetiology was unknown for some children. Known aetiologies included maternal rubella, ototoxic drugs and genetic factors. Children with additional handicaps were not included in the study. All of the deaf children and their mothers were attending at least one parent guidance programme in Melbourne. Each hearing child had undergone free-field audiological testing at seven to nine months of age and none had demonstrated a significant hearing loss.

Each mother and child pair was video-taped in spontaneous conversation at home whilst playing with a dolls' house and furniture (or with favourite toys, in the case of the youngest group). Recording was commenced only after the pair had been playing for a few minutes and seemed relaxed.

The functional coding scheme devised by Dore et al. (1978) was chosen; a network representation of the scheme is set out in Figure 1.

This scheme was chosen for the following reasons:

1. It has a sound theoretical basis in speech act theory (Austin, 1962, 1963; Searle, 1969, 1971) and in the analysis of conversational constraints (Grice, 1968; Sacks, Schegloff and Jefferson, 1974).

FIGURE 1

CONVERSATIONAL CODE ADAPTED FROM DORE (1979)

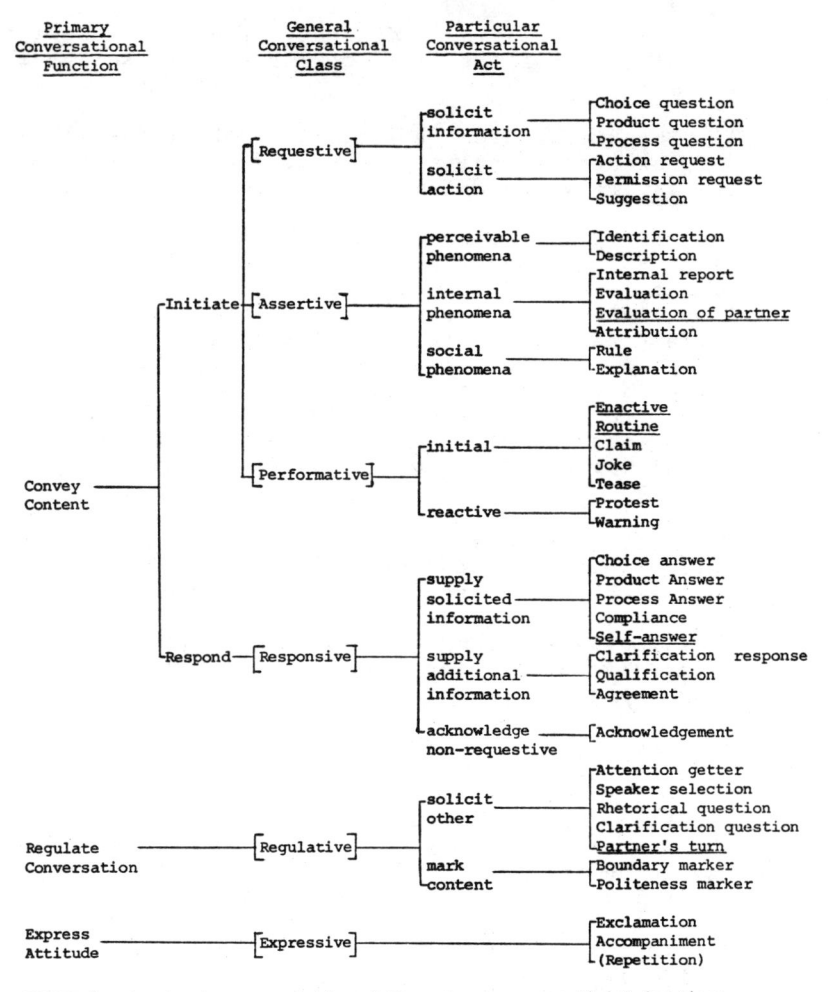

Primary Conversational Function	General Conversational Class	Particular Conversational Act	
Convey Content	Initiate — Requestive	solicit information	Choice question Product question Process question
		solicit action	Action request Permission request Suggestion
	Initiate — Assertive	perceivable phenomena	Identification Description
		internal phenomena	Internal report Evaluation Evaluation of partner Attribution
		social phenomena	Rule Explanation
	Performative	initial	Enactive Routine Claim Joke Tease
		reactive	Protest Warning
	Respond — Responsive	supply solicited information	Choice answer Product Answer Process Answer Compliance Self-answer
		supply additional information	Clarification response Qualification Agreement
		acknowledge non-requestive	Acknowledgement
Regulate Conversation	Regulative	solicit other	Attention getter Speaker selection Rhetorical question Clarification question Partner's turn
		mark content	Boundary marker Politeness marker
Express Attitude	Expressive		Exclamation Accompaniment (Repetition)

FIGURE 1: A network representation of the primary conversational functions, general conversational classes and particular conversational acts in the coding scheme. Adapted from Dore (1979). The underlined act categories are additions; parentheses indicate the omitted act category.

2. Its focus on conversational acts permits the effects of utterances to be assessed by the responses they produce.

3. The conversational framework provides immediate situational functions for each conversational act.

4. The hierarchical structure of the code allows concurrent analysis of specific or more general levels where appropriate.

The original code was modified by the addition of five types of particular conversational acts at the finest level of analysis and the omission of one (see Figure 1). These changes accommodated the differences attributable to the dyadic exchanges of mother and child. The diversity score was calculated at the finest level of analysis and achieved an intercoder agreement of 92% (84-98%). The initial use by a subject of each particular conversational act added a score of 1 to the diversity measure.

The first 100 consecutive conversational acts (as defined by Dore, Gearhart and Newman, 1978) of each verbal child were used for calculating the functional diversity score. Other mother and child measures were based on the first consecutive 200 maternal conversational acts and all contributions from the child within this period.

Supplementary measures of the participation of the children were also recorded. The child's failure to respond (verbally or non-verbally) to maternal questions was recorded to provide an index of non-participation. The number of non-verbal responses was noted in order to determine whether the prelingual or linguistically immature children could register recognition of the illocutionary force of maternal questions, even though they did not respond verbally. In addition, we recorded each occasion on which a maternal conversational act was contingent on an action by her child, as a means of assessing maternal responsiveness.

In summary, the conversational coding scheme and supplementary measures were used to establish:
(i) whether the diversity of child conversational acts increased with either age or language ability (a prediction of an increase with age in the hearing children was made);
(ii) whether the diversity of mother's conversational acts increased with either the child's age or language ability;
(iii) the diversity of conversational acts used by deaf children whose ages were equivalent to one group of hearing children but whose language level matched a younger group.

Results and Discussion

Results pertinent to the children will be discussed first; details are set out in Table 2.

One-way analyses of variance were performed when the assumptions of the test were fulfilled; otherwise the Kruskal-Wallis one-way analysis of variance by ranks was used. Planned comparisons were made in all cases (t - tests, Kruskal-Wallis or Mann-Whitney U test where appropriate).

TABLE 2

MEAN SCORES AND TEST RESULTS OF MEASURES MADE OF THE CONVERSATION OF CHILDREN

Groups	Diversity	Non-Response of Questions (% of maternal questions)	Non-Verbal Response to Questions (% of maternal questions)	Number of Conversational Acts (to mother's 200)
Hearing:				
1 Year (H1)	-	53.7	27.6	-
2 Years (H2)	17.0	25.0	18.2	139.9
5 Years (H5)	22.3	17.1	9.9	155.6
Deaf:				
2 Years (D2)	-	52.2	20.4	-
5 Years (D5)	12.9	25.9	19.8	81.8
Comparisons				
Overall	*	*	*	*
D5(H2+H5)	*			
H2/H5	**			

* $p < .01$ (2tt)
** $p < .05$ (1tt)

As predicted, the two-year-old hearing children displayed significantly less diversity than the hearing five-year-olds (U (8,8) = 10; p < .01, one-tail). This indicates that contrary to Dale's finding, a measure of diversity within a structured code can usefully differentiate children beyond the one-word stage. The fact that this has emerged in the present study is probably attributable to the use of Dore's scheme of conversational acts. Because this is interactional it may capture a higher-order differentiation of meaning than is usual, in that it classifies conversational acts on the basis of their relation to the preceding acts of the partner, thus revealing the child's response when required to take account of the conversation of another person.

It is interesting to note that the range of diversity scores for the five-year-old hearing group (19-24) is identical with that of the mothers of the hearing one-year-olds, although the children have a slightly higher mean. It thus appears that children of this age are capable of using a range of conversational acts similar to that used by adults talking to young children. However, the competence of the five-year-olds in this scheme is not really surprising given that Dore developed it on the basis of conversations between nursery school children and adults.

The deaf five-year-old children gave evidence of a significantly more limited diversity of conversational acts than both their age and language peers ($\underline{H}$ (1) = 9.00; p < .01). When we examined the distribution of their conversational acts, we found that the deaf children scored a particularly low rate of Requestives and Assertives: Requestives formed 1.53% of their total utterances (compared with hearing two-year-olds, 3.84%; and five-year-olds, 8.99%) and Assertives accounted for 13.3% (compared with 25.92% and 23.46%). This suggested to us that the verbal hearing children led the conversation more than the deaf five-year-olds who tended to respond to their mothers rather than to initiate interaction (either verbally or nonverbally).

It can also be seen from Table 2 that noticeably fewer conversational acts in total were recorded for the deaf children (a mean of 81.8 to the mother's 200) than for either of the two lingual hearing groups (139.9 and 155.6), although the comparisons were not statistically significant. However, the deaf five-year-olds' rate of non-response to questions (25.9%) and non-verbal response to questions (19.8%) was on a par with the language-matched two-year-olds (25.0% and 18.2%). The deaf five-year-olds seemed to the observers to be no less attentive than their hearing language peers, thus suggesting that the reduced diversity range stemmed chiefly from limited conversational initiative on the part of the deaf children.

The finding of considerably reduced diversity in deaf five-year-olds, in comparison not only with hearing children of the same age but also with hearing children of the same formal language ability, is contrary to the conclusion drawn by Curtiss et al. (1979). These researchers claimed that deaf children use a range of (verbal and non-verbal) "conversational acts" (based loosely on Dore's early categories) equivalent to that of hearing children. However, the present study actually found greater verbal diversity than Curtiss et al., for whose subjects the major contribution was non-verbal. The children studied by Curtiss et al. were observed in the unstructured setting of the playground and their gestures were interpreted without the requirement of a conversational context. The current finding suggests both the easier flow of spoken communication when a deaf child is with a familiar and co-operative conversational partner, and also the greater ease (and credibility) of interpreting the illocutionary force of the child's conversational acts when observed within the structure of conversation.

The analysis of maternal conversational acts did not reflect the pattern of the children. As can be seen from Table 3, the diversity scores of the five groups of mothers offer little evidence that this measure of maternal speech is adjusted to either the

TABLE 3

MEAN SCORES AND TEST RESULTS OF MEASURES MADE OF
THE CONVERSATION OF MOTHERS

Groups	Diversity	Response to non-verbal acts
Hearing:		
1 year	21.1	57.3
2 years	23.6	7.4
5 years	23.5	2.9
Deaf:		
2 years	21.1	39.5
5 years	22.8	21.5

Comparisons

| Overall | NS | * |

* $p < .01$ (2tt)

formal or functional abilities of the children. The maximum possible measure of diversity was thirty-nine. No mother scored higher than twenty-eight and only one act type (Claims) was not scored at all, which suggests that the failure to find a significant difference between the maternal groups cannot be directly attributed to a ceiling effect imposed by the scheme. The failure to find evidence of adjustment in this facet of maternal speech may be interpreted in several ways:

1. As reflecting responses to similar communicative patterns in the children. The statistically significant differences found in measures of the children's communication, seen particularly in the extremes of the deaf two-year-olds and hearing five-year-olds, demand that this interpretation be rejected.

2. Alternatively, that mothers behave <u>as if</u> their children make broadly similar contributions to the conversation; and

3. As implying that there is a certain minimum variety of conversational acts likely to be present in adult conversation; that is, having achieved competence in self-expression and behaviour appropriate to social interaction, adults do not easily relinquish those skills when confronted with a considerably less competent interlocutor. This reliance on practised linguistic skills may produce a floor effect not imposed by any coding scheme, which militates against fine tuning for this measure.

Both of these latter arguments have a certain face validity. The similarity of the diversity counts of the mothers encourages the interpretation that to some extent they do behave as if their children were participating equally, whereas the slight (non-significant) differentiation between the diversity of the mothers of verbal and non-verbal groups suggests that the participation of the child has a slight influence. However, more detailed analysis (to be reported elsewhere) showed that child participation was reflected more clearly in the relative <u>proportions</u> of maternal conversational acts (which were significantly related to the language level of the child). (A summary of these data is presented in Table 4.)

There is, in fact, no intuitive reason why there should be greater diversity in the mothers of hearing five-year-olds; it could be argued that the greater participation of the child may equally be expected to <u>reduce</u> the diversity of the mother by influencing her to use more Responsives in adjusting to the increased initiatives of the older child.

The fact that the diversity of the hearing five-year-olds was equivalent to the adult level suggests another contributing factor to the absence of differences in maternal diversity:

4. A further interpretation is that this level of the child's ability may represent the language stage at which the variety (if not the relative proportions) of adult conversational acts in the conversation reaches a ceiling imposed not by the scheme itself but by the context of adult-child interaction. This suggests, with regard to child language, that functional diversity may only be a useful measure of child communicative skill prior to the stage of language development represented by these hearing five-year-olds.

TABLE 4

Mean scores of particular types of conversational acts in mothers' speech (total of 200 utterances per subject).

Conversational act code	Hearing			Deaf	
	H1	H2	H5	D2	D5
REQUESTIVE					
Solicit information	41.3	59.0	58.0	41.5	59.3
Solicit action	29.4	17.6	11.9	23.6	13.3
ASSERTIVE					
Perceivable phenomena	26.3	21.8	32.4	47.4	22.6
Internal phenomena	14.4	6.4	9.6	5.9	8.9
Social phenomena	4.1	5.3	10.0	2.3	4.8
PERFORMATIVE					
Initial	18.6	0.8	0	8.6	7.0
Reactive	1.8	1.3	0.4	3.3	2.0
RESPONSIVE					
Supply solicited information	3.1	6.4	11.0	5.3	6.0
Supply additional information	13.1	39.1	36.1	6.0	32.0
REGULATIVE					
Solicit other	25.4	32.0	9.0	38.9	33.3
Mark content	3.3	1.1	3.1	3.4	3.4
Expressive	17.9	7.6	8.6	11.5	4.4
Uncodable	1.3	1.4	3.5	1.9	2.6
Unintelligible	0.5	0.4	4.6	0.6	0.6

Floor and ceiling effects extraneous to the coding scheme may be invoked as explanations, but the scheme itself may also impose limitations on adult conversation. The scheme may be adequate for young children but is possibly insufficiently subtle - lacking depth, or fine distinctions within categories, rather than breadth across categories - for the sophisticated gradations of meaning found in adult conversation. This issue demands further exploration.

Analysis of the mothers' responses to non-verbal child acts (Table 3) showed more similar frequencies for groups matched for language than for age. The higher rate for children with little or no verbal fluency indicated that apparently uncommunicative acts (as well as communicative gestures) were treated as conversational contributions. This permits the inference that the expressions of intention by the children were gradually guided by the mothers to suit conversational conventions, and suggests that it is not the contribution of the child which develops before language (and therefore remains constant) but, as Snow (1977) argues, the contribution of the conversational partner acting within a conventional communication system which imposes a stable structure.

The way in which mothers treat children as at least potential communicators (Shotter, 1974) and construct "scaffolding" within which they experience successful communication (Bruner, 1975; Bruner & Sherwood, 1976) has implications for the speech act approach and particularly for any attempt to score diversity. The interactive system of communication thus studied cannot escape the inextricable factor of maternal attribution. Although this is, in one sense, a research limitation, we may also postulate that this is what aids in the development of a range of conversational acts by associating language with meaning and with its perlocutionary effect.

A serious problem in studies which demand the attribution of intent to children and the interpretation of the meanings they wish to convey is that no assessment of accuracy is possible. However, this is inevitable even in adult conversation; the problem of other minds has provided grist to the philosophical mill for centuries. Child language researchers may well have to accept this problem, learn to treat infants as intentional beings (as Shotter, 1974, 1978 argues) and pursue the question of how those intentions come to be expressed conventionally. The way in which the child's presumed intentions are interpreted and fed back to him is bound to be a central component in learning the conventional means for expressing them. Even if the child's meaning is misconstrued, this may be one way in which the child comes to relate his intentions to their conventional expression. By being helped to respond appropriately to the mother's communicative acts (through Bruner's notion of the 'scaffolding' she constructs and the situational cues available to both) the child may learn to interpret the illocutionary force of utterances whose grammatical form may be opaque in terms of the desired perlocutionary effect. Dealing with pragmatics, or speech acts, does not require the attribution of detailed grammatical knowledge to the child; for the child to interpret the illocutionary force requires (as Garvey 1975 argues) only a recognition of the salient contextual features and that his interlocutors may be requiring something of him in relation to them. The child may in fact use and interpret speech acts as unanalysed routines.

Moreover, the problem of interpretation may be overcome, at least partly, by the adoption of the interactive mode used in the present study because it permits the inclusion of the effects of communicative acts as part of the essential data available both to child and researcher. It has been argued, even in syntactic studies, that an understanding of the interactive language environment is crucial to understanding the way in which the child acquires language (Cross, 1980).

Halliday (1975) has suggested that the major developmental issue is not increasing diversity of function but increasing subtlety and complexity within particular functional categories, plus the emergence of multi-functional utterances. Dore's hierarchical scheme was chosen partly to deal with the issue of subtlety and also to reveal appropriately finer or broader distinctions. Even so, it was subjectively apparent that increasing sophistication of quality within categories accompanied greater diversity in the children, and qualitative differences were apparent in the conversations of mothers with children of varied linguistic ability, but this was not accessible to analysis in the scheme we selected.

However, in overview, the <u>pattern</u> of maternal adjustments (summarised in Table 4) suggested a move from the clearest conventional expression of communicative intent (such as Requests for Action, Exclamations, Attention-Getters) and joint activity (Routines) to more subtle acts which demand interpretation possibly a little in advance of the child's expressive ability (Suggestions, Explanations) and which increasingly respond to the child's spontaneous expressions. This indicates the child-attuned adjustments made by mothers by which conventional communication may be acquired.

In conclusion, it may be stated that functional diversity is measurable in the context of conversation and can be seen to increase in children in relation to formal language development. The fact that maternal diversity does not appear to change in a corresponding manner may illustrate the readiness of mothers to accept the child (even the profoundly deaf child) as a conversational partner, from an early age.

REFERENCES

AUSTIN, J., How to Do Things with Words. Oxford, Clarendon Press, 1962.

AUSTIN, J., Performative - constative. In C. Caton (ed.), Philosophy and Ordinary Language. Urbana, University of Illinois Press, 1963.

BALL, J. CROSS, T. & HORSBOROUGH, K. A comparative study of the linguistic abilities of autistic, dysphasic and normal children. Paper presented at the Second International Congress for the Study of Child Language. Vancouver, Canada, 1981. Published in this volume, pp. 502-515.

BATES, E. CAMAIONI, L. & VOLTERRA, V., Sensorimotor performatives. In E. Bates, Language and Context: the Acquisition of Pragmatics. New York: Academic Press, 1976.

BLANK, M. GESSNER, M. & ESPOSITO, A., Language without communication: a case study. J. Child Language, 6, 1979, pp. 329-52.

BRUNER, J., The ontogenesis of speech acts. J. Child Language, 2, 1975, pp. 1-19.

BRUNER, J. & SHERWOOD, V., Early rule structure: the case of 'Peekaboo'. In R. Harre (ed.), Life Sentences. Wiley, 1976.

CROSS,T.G., Mothers' speech adjustments: The contribution of selected child listener variables. In C.E. Snow and C.A. Ferguson (eds.) Talking to Children. Cambridge, Cambridge Univ. Press, 1977.

CROSS, T.G., The linguistic experience of slow language learners. Paper presented at The National Conference on Child Development, Perth, W.A., August, 1980.

CURTISS, S. PRUTTING, C. & LOWELL, E., Pragmatic and semantic development in young children with impaired hearing. J. Speech and Hearing Res., 22, (3), 1979.

DALE, P., Is early pragmatic development measurable? J. Child Language, 7, (1), 1980, pp.1-12.

DORE, J., Holophrases, speech acts and language universals. J. Child Lanaguage, 2, 1975, pp.21-40.

DORE, J., Conversation and pre-school language development. In P. Fletcher & M. Garman (eds.). Language Acquisition. Cambridge, Cambridge Univ. Press, 1979.

DORE, J. GEARHART, M. & NEWMAN, D., The structure of nursery school conversation. In K. Nelson (ed.). Children's Language, Vol.I, 1978.

GALLAGHER, T. & CRAIG, H., Structural characteristics of monologues in the speech of normal children: semantic and conversational aspects. J. Speech and Hearing Res., 21, (1), 1978.

GARVEY, C., Requests and responses in children's speech. J. Child Language, 2, 1975, pp.41-63.

GRICE, H., Utterer's meaning, sentence-meaning and word-meaning. Foundations of Language, 4, 1968, pp.1-18.

GREENFIELD, P. & SMITH. J., The Structure of Communication in Early Language Development. New York, Academic Press, 1976.

GRIFFITHS, P., Speech acts and early sentences. In P. Fletcher & M. Garman (eds.). Language Acquisition. Cambridge, CUP, 1979.

HALLIDAY, M., Learning How to Mean. London, Edward Arnold, 1975.

REES, N., Pragmatics of language. In R. Schiefelbusch (ed.). *Normal and Deficient Language*. University Park Press, 1978.

SACKS, H. SCHEGLOFF, E. & JEFFERSON, G., Simplest systematics for the organisation of turntaking for conversation. *Language, 50*, (4), 1974.

SEARLE, J., *Speech Acts*. Cambridge University Press, 1969.

SEARLE, J., What is a speech act? In J. Searle (ed.). *The Philosophy of Language*. Oxford Univ. Press, 1971.

SHOTTER, J., The development of personal powers. In M. Richards (ed.). *The Integration of a Child into a Social World*. Cambridge Univ. Press, 1974.

SHOTTER, J., The cultural context of communication studies: theoretical and methodological issues. In A. Lock (ed.). *Action, Gesture and Symbol*. London, Academic Press, 1978.

SNOW, C., The development of conversation between mothers and babies. *J. Child Language, 4*, 1977, pp.1-22.

SNYDER, L.S., Communicative and cognitive abilities and disabilities in the sensori-motor period. *Merrill-Palmer Quarterly, 24*, 1978, pp.161-180.

WELLS, G., *Coding Manual for the Description of Child Speech*. Univ. of Bristol, Revised Edition, 1975.

YAMADA, J., On the independence of language and cognition: evidence from a "hyper linguistic" retarded adolescent. Paper presented at The Second International Congress for the Study of Child Language. Vancouver, Canada, 1981. Published in this volume, pp. 297-321.

Discourse Universals and the Development of Linguistic Structures from the First to the Fifth Year. Part 1. First Words.

Maureen Shields

The study of child language, like the study of human communication in general, should be an interdisciplinary study and, possibly one day it will be, though the departmentalisation of academic life casts a heavy shadow over this prospect.

Linguistics in all its variety of phonology, syntax, semantics, pragmatics and discourse is now joined by philosophy, logic, sociology, ethnography, ethnomethodology, genetics, biology, developmental psychology, cognitive psychology, social psychology, communication theory, information theory and theories of artificial intelligence all of them staking a claim to make their contributions at some stage of the language learning process.

This rich variety of contributory knowledge has much in its favour, because it has made the study of child language one of the liveliest areas of academic life, but it also has disadvantages. For one thing it is almost impossible for the speaker of any of these disciplinary metalanguages to refrain from imputing to the language learner as though it were a learning mechanism or a skill, some element of the theoretical apparatus which helps them as third party onlookers to understand what they have under observation and communicate about it to other like-minded observers.

Developmental psychologists also have the temptation to read forward from early non-verbal performances to linguistic ones and find continuity where there may only be analogy. In this great market of theoretical ideas, what the child's personal equipment might be, and how it might orient him or her towards facing a young communicator is often passed over with the briefest acknowledgement as the expert hastens on to a discussion of function, context or input. This conceals the fact that the child chooses the context and input by attending selectively to some features and not others. This paper sets out to look at this selectivity, and to ask why the child should pick on the structural features of discourse rather than on particular contents of meaning when he acquires his first words.

Human communication requires the mastery of a kind of orchestral score in which elements of messages are transmitted in parallel by posture, gesture, gaze, intonation, stress, pitch, phonetic contrast, lexis and syntax, all playing over a shared base of prior knowledge of the world, the characteristics of human beings and the social relations, rules and conventions which govern their behaviour. The score is dynamised by affectivity and intention and paced by rhythmicities of utterance and exchange. The mastery of such a system would seem to be a formidable task, more formidable, indeed, than that envisaged by Chomsky when he postulated a language acquisition device capable of extracting from an input of variable and sometimes defective quality, the basic structural features of syntax. The child has to do more than that, for she has to extract from this immense and many stranded orchestration those features which will enable her to tune her own set of instruments and to become a player in turn.

This task requires the assembly of a varied set of inbuilt or native potentials some of which may be specialised for language, but most of which are of a more general nature and functional in other spheres. I think the implausibility of a Language Acquisition Device based exclusively on syntax, especially T.G. syntax should not lead us to underestimate the more general claim that intrinsic properties of mind and self directed activity may play a major role in the acquisition of language.

The child is faced with the task of assembling these diverse abilities into a language learning strategy and thus it may be more appropriate to speak of a Language Acquisition Assembly (LASS) than a Language Acquisition Device (LAD).

This Assembly can get some purchase on the communication system not only through the pressure of a highly communicative environment but also because human discourse itself has certain rather simple and obvious structural features which are part of the intrinsic logic of communication, and necessary whatever the medium that carries the message. This paper maintains that it is these quite general features of human discourse which assist the development of language for the reason that they are salient in any human exchange, though like syntax they are not usually objects of direct metalinguistic attention by speakers.

Before discussing these discourse universals, it might be as well to enumerate at least some of the native abilities that the child brings to the learning task, because these, though cursorily acknowledged, are rarely spelled out in discussions of the language learning process. There is no space to do them justice here, but even a brief enumeration of some of them should remind us not to underestimate the child's potential. Those who have to work with children who have part of this endowment missing or defective are only too well aware of the problems thus created, but students of normal development too often take it for granted. Indeed there are some who would maintain that the proposition that human beings do what they do because they are what they are is basically uninteresting. But students of common human abilities such as visual perception or motor development sometimes make more mileage than those who surrender to the temptation to consider what is different rather than what is common. It would need a neuropsychologist and a geneticist to do justice to what is here mentioned in quite general terms. So this must be a bare reminder which picks selectively some of the areas worthy of further attention.

In the first place the child is endowed with a CNS adapted by evolution to deal with time and space. The CNS is specialised to deal with the one way flow of time by conserving the sequence of observed behaviour. Which segments the child will chunk out for attention may vary, and the child will not retain or produce them all, but those that are retained will tend to be reproduced in the same sequence in which they were noted. This ability to conserve temporal sequence will come in handy for the acquisition of important features of morphology and syntax. Moreover the cross modal co-ordination of sight and hearing and the sensorimotor feedback and feed-forward between output and input in action are already partially present in the CNS at birth, and rapidly develop during the first two years of life.

Secondly, there is the ability of the CNS to retain experience in memory, especially the primary and largely unconscious ability which enables persons and animals to recognise situations they have met before, though recall is a skill of slower development. A third ability which appears to have innate foundations is the ability to use an observed input as a model for producing a roughly isomorphic output. The close observation of infants has shown that mouthing in response to adult vocalisation and motor imitation such as tongue protrusion are part of the inbuilt equipment of the human baby. This particular skill seems to disappear and reemerge in a more elaborate form as development proceeds. Confusion between imitation and mimicry has led to an underestimation of the role of imitation in language learning. Imitation is more properly considered as observational learning and is profoundly bound up with the child's social propensities and the ambition to do the done thing and say the said thing in the familiar contexts of interaction. Without the ability to form a model of what is said and then to attempt to reproduce it, the child could not begin to drive towards the mastery of the phonology of his language, or to associate words with their appropriate contexts of utterance, or participate in the many scripted episodes of everyday life. Ruth Clark has pointed out the importance of imitation in the formation of language patterns which can later become productive (Clark 1974, 1977, 1978). Nelson (1981) however points out that those who are able to use their language patterns productively do better than those who spend more time imitatively, but nevertheless at the initial stage imitation may be an important aid to forming such patterns in the first instance. Direct repetition or imitation of previous utterances are only a small part of a large iceberg formed by the accumulated cognitive schemes concerning human behaviour which watching and listening to people form in the child's memory store. Such schemes can then be combined, intercalated and nested one within another to form functionally new behaviour. Guy Ewing (1982) gives examples of the combination of limited formulae in early utterance formation.

Fourthly, there is the relevant sensory equipment which channels input into the system, with its cross modal structure both endogenous and learned. Those who deal with handicaps are well aware of the difficulties caused for the development of communication by deficiencies in the main distance receptors such as sight and hearing. In the fifth place there is the motor system which drives the movements of some speech-specialised and some speech-adaptable structures and co-ordinates them in the production of communicative vocalisations. The larynx is specialised for the production of sounds but the lungs and mouth are not. Nor are gaze or limb movement, though some aspects of facial expression seem to be endogenously programmed. All of these need co-ordination and orchestration and each has an inbuilt feedback system or servo-mechanism to control and space out its movements and this also has to be co-ordinated with re-afferent visual and auditory feedback systems which the child must learn to use to adjust her organised activity to its goals. There is of course one built in ready-organised behaviour, the cry, which co-ordinates both breathing and the vocal articulators and also specific accompanying limb movement. Even crying comes under a degree of voluntary control in the course of time. The modification of this inbuilt vocalisation into a nasalised summons for help may be the origin of one of the earliest words...*mum*, *ma*, *mama* (Lock 1980).

Sixthly, but probably first in importance, there is an inbuilt social orientation which subtends a preferential interest in and attachment to human beings. This, though reinforced by the satisfaction of needs is, as Bowlby convincingly suggests part of the phylogenetically programmed behaviour of a social species (Bowlby 1971).

This is a formidable array, and the problem for the child is one of assembling, co-ordinating and developing these inbuilt behavioural potentials driven by the social need to become a communicator in a world of communicators as well as a doer in a world of action.

What problems does the child have to solve to make headway in this task? That the child has such problems has tended to be masked both by a theoretical orientation which focuses on the effect of context and over emphasises the role of the child's care givers and by artifacts arising out of the observational situations in which much of the data on child language is collected. Typically, the mother and child pair are either brought into a laboratory playroom, or the investigator armed with the recording or video equipment visits the child's home. The mother is then instructed to interact normally with the child, and no doubt her interaction is normal, it is simply the prolonged occasion for interaction which is abnormal.

If the normal experience of the child is made up of rather brief and intermittent interactions centered on routine care-giving episodes embedded in longer periods when the mother is giving only partial or absent minded attention, or even ignoring the child altogether, the child has a different quality of experience than that deduced from the more prolonged and intensive interactions artificially induced by experimental observation.

In the natural environment of the home where the mother has many other tasks and preoccupations, a much greater onus for setting up communication falls on the child. Firstborn singletons have in this respect a more favourable interactional environment, for as soon as there are two or more children under school age the weight of domestic tasks and the greater demands of both older and younger siblings makes the mother less available as a communicative partner. Furthermore, it is part of the childbearing ethos of our culture that toddlers should learn to occupy themselves in a specially designated play sphere while their care-givers occupy themselves in the work sphere appropriate to their roles. The objects and implements of the mother's work sphere and the toys and artifacts of the child's play sphere are segregated sets. Some mothers are more permissive about the child crossing the boundary of the work sphere provided the pressure to 'get on' is not too great, but intensive interaction between mother and child seems to occur at particular occasions such as washing, dressing, potting and nappy changing and mealtimes where there is a strong instrumental context. The more unbuttoned and relaxed encounters of which the primary purpose is the exchange of affective tokens such as kissing, cuddling and tickling seem to occupy the fringes of the instrumental episodes. The mother's speech during these episodes often consists of monologue 'jollying along'. The child's contribution is largely non-verbal. After all the required response to '<u>Come along darling...where's that little foot</u>' is to proffer a foot rather than a comment.

These observations are based on a re-reading of all the transcripts from the 15 month old children of the language sample collected at Bristol by Gordon Wells, which are available in mimeograph. As you well know, this unrivalled study is based upon recordings made by microtransmitter carried by the child and timed to record for ninety seconds every fifteen or twenty minutes during one day every three months over two and a quarter years. There are 24 recorded episodes in each three monthly session. The first session of the younger of the two overlapping samples was recorded when the children were 15 months of age, and each of the two overlapping samples consists of sixty-four children, half boys and half girls. The day's recordings were played over to the mother when the transmitter and recorder were fetched in the evening so there is some background provided by the mother's recall (Wells 1980). No investigator was present during the recording. The recordings of the sixty-four children of the early samples who were recorded between 15 months and three and a half years are the most substantial naturalistic sample of the communicative life of toddlers entering the stage of communication where spontaneous or socially structured vocalisation together with a few lexical words starts to advance towards more recognisable attempts at conventional speech. This data shows that the child indeed has a problem in setting up communication and it is by working on this problem that the child becomes aware of basic structural features of human communication which are so much part of normal talk that their role is literally 'beneath notice' for practised speakers.

For communication to take place, mutual attention or primary intersubjectivity has to be established between two separate centres of awareness and activity. The studies of young babies in arms have picked out early devices for attracting attention (Trevarthen 1974, Trevarthen & Hubley 1978). These studies however have made the whole transaction look too easy. The toddler has to attract attention from a distance and across role boundaries and is therefore forced to consider discourse devices which can bridge the gap such as address, summons and terms for attracting attention. Re-establishing the physical contact of babyhood by touching and clinging tends to be discouraged, and children who use affective exchange to get their care-givers' attention are often referred to in Wells' sample as 'soft soapers' or 'monkeys' who can 'get round' their mothers.

Once mutual attention has been established there is a second problem, namely how to keep the attention of the other and prolong the exchange. The rather slender vocal and verbal resources of the child have to be recycled energetically, a process which is manifest in the repetitious and imitative character of many early exchanges. Taking and eliciting 'turns' also raises problems of 'fit' between turns, or functional cohesion and rules have to be learned about asking and responding to questions and requests, making and responding to demands and commands and the social rules which govern the relations between the interacting persons on each occasion. Please may be tutored but can and can't as markers of social possibility are winkled out of the data by the child herself.

Each scenario of interaction in which the child participates will have a script in the sense that there will be recurrent patterns of words which adjust the behaviour of one participant to that of the other. These however are frequently embedded in redundant chat, though those elements which serve as cues for some expected behaviour of the child may be made more salient either by formula or intonation. The primary intersubjectivity which structures interpersonal transactions for babies-in-arms is focussed on the states and behaviour of each of the interactants, and this probably builds the child's disposition to give close attention to the pragmatic consequences of her actions and vocalisations on the behaviour of others, and so to select out of the input features of language which serve to maintain interpersonal cohesion and adjust interpersonal behaviour.

The problem of gaining and keeping the attention of the significant but hard-to-get adult in due course makes salient the need to interest them in something. Pure interpersonal focus is gradually being discouraged in the toddler as 'attention seeking'. Demands for attention mediated only by terms of summons pass largely ignored. The child as person watcher has to figure out what things are likely to hook the vagrant attention of these autonomous and busy beings. A simple call is rarely effective, reliable attention getters such as wee wee or potty are liable to produce diminishing returns. The child can raise some topic which has previously been a focus of adult interest such as showing a duck and saying quack or mentioning bow-wows or birds. She can observe the adult's activity and attempt participation by uttering some associated items from the script such as washit when the mother is engaged in doing the laundry. She can keep up a stream of concurrent activity and vocalisation to keep herself at least on the periphery of attention, keeping the communicative field 'live' so that the adult may occasionally hook into the child's activity. The tactic of searching for some focus of joint interest and labelling it appears to be the strategy which pays off best. Fortunately much of the adult tutorial effort is directed at giving the child labels for things, these labels then become part of the child's discourse sustaining strategies.

A follow up of twelve of the fifteen month Bristol sample by the examination of the recordings to session four (34 months) suggest that the children who succeed best in catching and sustaining the interest of adults are those who learn to associate their approaches with some theme for joint attention Those who rely on summons and address and attention seeking devices do less well because mutual attention seeking is less approved than joint attention seeking. It may be however, that children who repeatedly call for maternal attention by address and who obtain little response may have some deeper problem concerning the level of responsitivity which does not allow them to exploit joint attention (Wooton 1981).

The toddler then, by virtue of her new independence of movement and her new role which our local child rearing practices build up through independence training has new and complex problems to solve which the baby-in-arms does not face. It is true that the baby-in-arms also has to work for adult attention but her extreme dependency means that she will in any case get more of it. Things are harder for the toddler who has to secure attention from both physical and socially defined distance. This will focus her attention on those discourse devices which serve to bring communicating persons together which adjust their mutual behaviour and which adjust their joint attention within the interpersonal field.

Some preparation for this task may be built up in the earlier period of primary intersubjectivity when communication is very closely centered on mutual states and activities.

A diagram of this pre-verbal communication network showing its possible discourse potential is shown on the next page. The infant designated me is entering into relations with the adult designated you. Some continuity between this and the first word stage is indicated. However care must be taken not to assume too much developmental continuity between this and the protoverbal stage, because, for instance, behavioural turntaking in care routines and verbal turntaking may be analogously arranged rather than developmentally continuous simply because given the one way flow of time there is no other way of effectively organising interaction (Bretherton & Bates 1979). Diagram 2 however is built up round the most frequently used first words of children first collected from many different studies, by Roger Brown (1973) and added to from subsequent studies. This is designed to demonstrate that these early words are related to primary discourse functions, and that their early acquisition provides evidence for the child's focus on the structure of discourse as an interpersonal system rather than on particular performative or referential meanings which may at the very early stages play a subsidiary role in relation to the child's main motivation. This may be aimed at how to be a communicator, rather than at the communication of specific meanings.

It is tempting to read back into the child's early adventures in interpersonal speech the kind of meaning that an adult or even an older child might have, given the context of utterance. Studies on the functional value of early utterances have tended to this kind of 'rich' interpretation, and valuable as these have been, they are likely to attribute more specific meaning and intention to the child than the child in point of fact has. The child may often have participant motivation rather than commitment to a particular message and may come to attribute illocutionary force and semantic meaning to her own utterances by noting their perlocutionary effect and the interpretations put upon them by others.

ESTABLISHMENT OF PREVERBAL COMMUNICATION

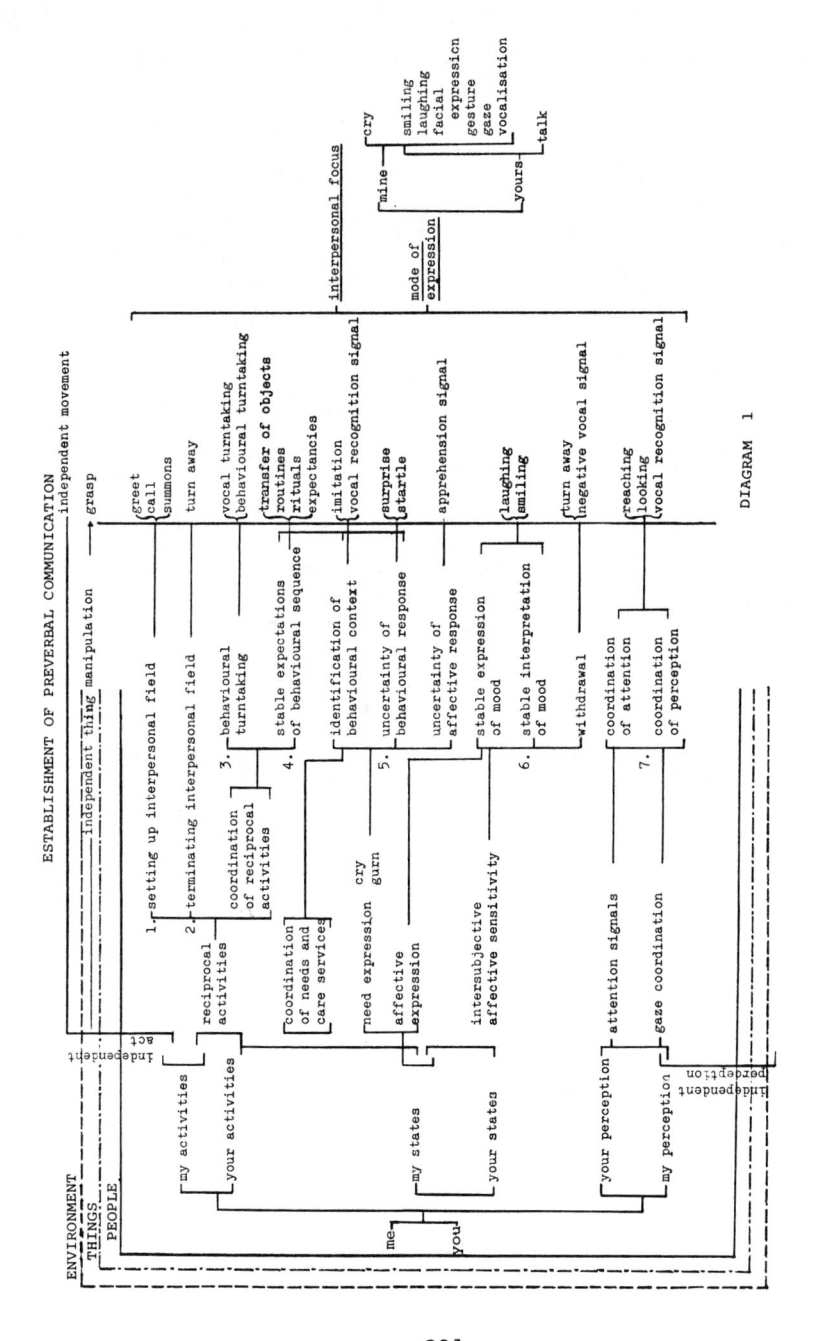

DIAGRAM 1

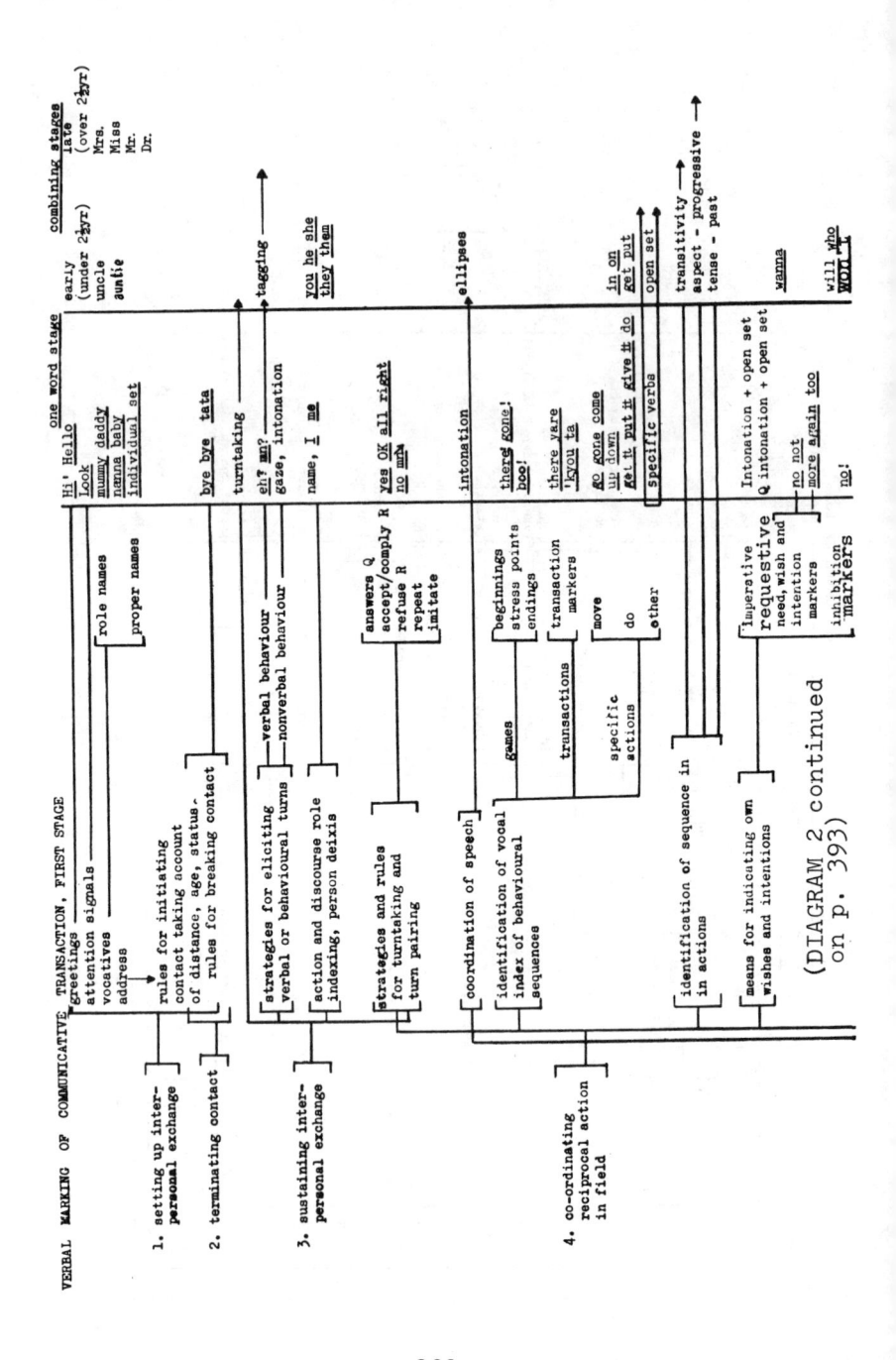

VERBAL MARKING OF COMMUNICATIVE TRANSACTION, FIRST STAGE

		one word stage	early (under 2½yr)	combining stages late (over 2½yr)
1. setting up inter-personal exchange	greetings attention signals vocatives address ──┬── role names └── proper names	Hi' Hello Look mummy daddy nanna baby individual set	uncle auntie	Mrs. Miss Mr. Dr.
	rules for initiating contact taking account of distance, age, status- rules for breaking contact			
2. terminating contact		bye bye tata		
3. sustaining inter-personal exchange	strategies for eliciting ──┬── verbal behaviour verbal or behavioural turns └── nonverbal behaviour	turntaking eh? mm? gaze, intonation	tagging ↑	
	action and discourse role indexing, person deixis	name, I me	you he she they them	

	strategies and rules ──┬── answers Q
	for turntaking and ├── accept/comply R
	turn pairing ├── refuse R
	                        ├── repeat
	                        └── imitate
		yes OK all right
		no mm		

	coordination of speech	intonation	ellipses	
	identification of vocal ──┬── games ──┬── beginnings index of behavioural │ ├── stress points sequences │ └── endings	there's gone! boo!		
	├── trunsactions ── transaction markers	there yare 'Iyou ta		

	└── specific ──┬── move
	                              actions ├── do
	                                          └── other
		no gone come
		up down
		get it put it give it do
		specific verbs
			in on
			get put
			open set
				transitivity →
				aspect - progressive →
				tense - past

4. co-ordinating reciprocal action in field	identification of sequence in in actions ──┬── Imperative
	                                            ├── requestive
	means for indicating own wishes and intentions ── need,wish and
	                                                   intention
	                                                   markers
	                                          └── inhibition markers
		Intonation + open set
		Q intonation + open set
		no not
		more again too
		no!
			wanna
			will who
			won't	

(DIAGRAM 2 continued on p. 393)

392

DIAGRAM 2

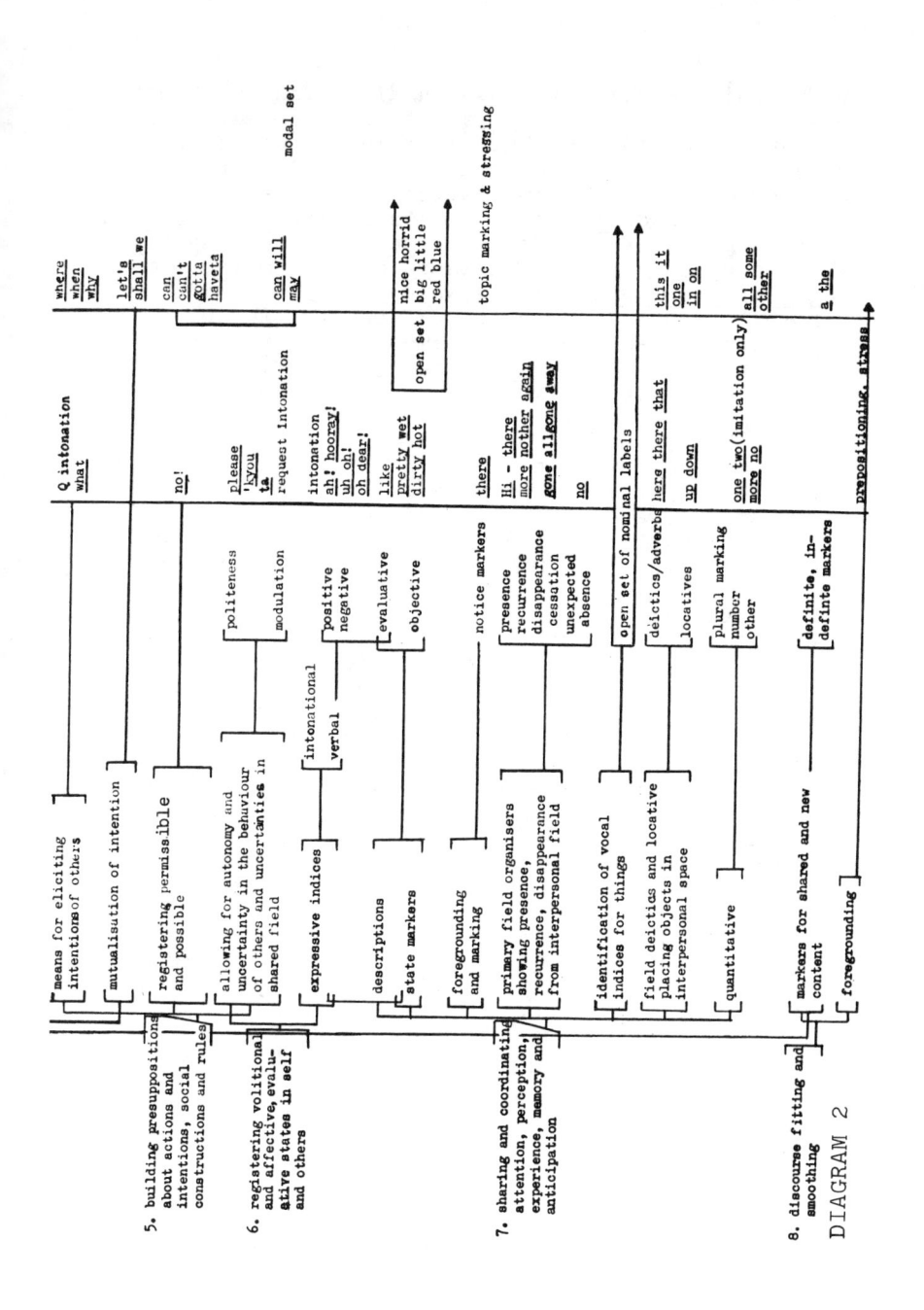

A complex branching diagram (rotated 90°) with the following categories listed down the left side:

5. building presuppositions about actions and intentions, social constructions and rules
6. registering volitional and affective, evaluative states in self and others
7. sharing and coordinating attention, perception, experience, memory and anticipation
8. discourse fitting and smoothing

Branches and labels (reading across):

- means for eliciting intentions of others — Q intonation — *what* — *where when why*
- mutualisation of intention — *let's shall we*
- registering permissible and possible — *can can't gotta haveta* — *can will may* — modal set
- allowing for autonomy and uncertainty in the behaviour of others and uncertainties in shared field — *no!*
- expressive indices — politeness — *please 'lyou 'ta* — request intonation
- — modulation
- descriptions — intonational — positive/negative — intonation *ah! hooray! uh oh! oh dear!*
- state markers — verbal — evaluative/objective — *like pretty wet dirty hot* — *nice horrid big little red blue* — open set
- foregrounding and marking — notice markers — *there*
- primary field organisers showing presence, recurrence, disappearance from interpersonal field — presence, recurrence, disappearance, cessation, unexpected absence — *Hi – there more nother again gone allgone away no* — topic marking & stressing
- identification of vocal indices for things — open set of nominal labels
- field deictics and locative placing objects in interpersonal space — deictics/adverbs — *here there that* — *this it*
- — locatives — *up down* — *one in on*
- quantitative — plural marking, number, other — *one two* (imitation only) *more no* — *all some other*
- markers for shared and new content — definite, indefinite markers — *a the*
- foregrounding — PREPOSITIONING STRESS

The child's primary focus on discourse leads her to
select out for special attention those words which
function in the regulation of mutual and joint
attention, hence the prominence in the first set of
words of address terms, attention getters like
look, yes and no responses, turn elicitors, social
exchange markers such as there y'are and thank you,
field deictics and organisers such as more, 'nother,
gone and all gone all of which early enter into
combinations with more specific words to form
strings. These terms have meaning only as part of
discourse structure and, indeed play more than one
role within that structure. This variability might
make them difficult to pick up, but the child does
pick them up among the first words of his native
tongue, and they continue to play a major role in
child (and adult) utterance. It is their role in
the structure of interpersonal discourse syntax
combined with the child's drive to participate in
discourse which bring them early into repertory.

When the first words are beginning to appear, the
Bristol records show that the major part of the
child's vocalisation still consists of non-verbal
items. First there are spontaneous and involuntary
noises such as sneezing, yawning and coughing. The
last two however have response evoking potential
and can then be produced voluntarily for effect.
Then there are semi-voluntary affective vocalisations such as crying, shouting, screaming, sighing,
whining, laughing and grunting. In addition there
are learned vocalisations such as lip smacking,
sucking, bubble blowing and making raspberries. All
these can be repeated if they attract attention.
In addition there are semi-socialised vocalisations
capable of deployment as a turn in an exchange such
as uh, ah, oh, ow, mm and mhm. These may actually
carry a specific meaning which depends on the context. There is also socialised onomatopoeia such
as meow, wow-wow, moo, of animals, and noises such
as beep-beep and drur drur of vehicles. For some
reason this appears to be a heavily tutored area

and can serve not only to animate the artifacts of the child sphere but also to act as labels for joint reference. Then there are the fully socialised vocalisations such as greetings, attention getters, farewells, address terms and the other items listed in Diagram II which serve to co-ordinate action and attention. All the lexical items in the Bristol data fall within the first words apart from a few individual labels.

Here is an example of the discourse use of mm to produce and maintain interpersonal affect; it is taken from the data of Gordon Wells.

Chr. D. of B: 2.4.72   D. of R. 9.7.73

Context   Chr. is sitting on his potty. M. with him.

M. Do you know what I'm going to call you?... The hunchback of Notre Dame...That's exactly what you look like....a hunchback... that's what you look like....yes....you're bad.

Chr. (unstructured noise)

M. yes...mm (kisses him)

Chr. Mm

M. Mm

Chr. Mm

M. Mm,mm.mm

Chr. Mm..mm...mm...mm...mm

M. Mmmmmmmmmmmmmmmmmmm

Chr. Ooooooooooooo

M. Mmmmmmmmmm

Chr. Ooooh.....mmmmmmmm

In that example turntaking sustained by mm serves an affective exchange, the child entering imitatively to a sequence initiated by the mother, who uses the term for an affective repair. In the next one a version of a question form is used by the child to elicit turns from his mother in a prolonged chain.

Pat: D. of B. 6.6.72   D. of R. 7.9.73

Context   Pat is fingering mother's blouse

M.   Hello, what've you got...got some flowers on mummy's blouse?.....They are pretty, aren't they?

Pat   Zat?

M.   That's a big flower....that's a little flower

Pat   Zat?

M.   That's a little flower.....that's a big... (pause)

Pat   Flower

M.   That's a little flower....flower....yes, that's right

Pat   Zat?

M.   There's a big flower

Pat   Zat?

M.   There's a big flower....there's a big flower....look...big one

The child is not seeking information; he is keeping his mother talking using Zat? as a turn elicitor. He may also have underlying motivation in poking his mother's emblousoned bosom, and the mother's tutorial response may be diversionary. The topics of any of these exchanges are recycled rather than developed, with the recycling serving the objective of maintaining the exchange. Even the extract below which is slightly less repetitious has the same features.

Tim: D. of B. 10.1.72   D. of R. 10.4.73

Tim and father looking at a dog on T.V.

    F.   Look at the bow wow......

           Where?

    Tim   Bow wow.....bow wow

    F.   Bow wow....doggy........doggy

    Tim   Doggy

    F.   Doggies

    Tim. A goo' way (possibly all gone away)

    F.   What?

    Tim   Bah ba (possibly bye bye)

    F.   Bow wow?

    Tim   Ba wa

    F.   Look, Tim, Tim ba wa

The last extract shows repetition and imitation, but one of the most interesting features is the adaptation of Tim's utterance of <u>Ba ba</u> possibly meaning bye bye to his father's interpretation of bow wow. This shows the child considering his own performance in the light of the response of another.

These three extracts are from a bare two dozen in the 15 month old corpus which show an interaction of more than two turns and are quite clearly structured by the child's determination to participate in verbal exchanges. Message sending is not really part of the act at this stage.

However the great majority of the child's vocalisations, even those directed at adults within earshot meet with no response. It is possible that the highly intermittent responses of the adults serve as a schedule of intermittent rewards which we are told by learning theorists increases the strength of the behaviour. Perhaps also the threshold effect which is mentioned by Toni Cross and her colleagues (this volume) may also be operating. Given the initial equipment of the child and her high motivation, the small amount of adult response is sufficient.

The suggestion embodied in this paper is that the endogenous equipment of the child encounters certain necessary features of discourse and by selecting these out the child learns how to become an active communicator. The paradox is that parental interest in the child's vocalisation and parental response appear largely elicited by the child as the child acquires more skill in attempting conversation....a case where the building precedes the 'scaffolding'. The child's own efforts are worthy of the greatest respect.

References

Bretherton, I & Bates, E 1979 — The Emergence of Intentional Communication. <u>New Directions for Child Development</u> 4 81-100

Brown, Roger 1973 — A First Language. London Allen & Unwin

Bowlby, John 1971 — Attachment and Loss. London Penguin

Clark, Ruth 1974 — Performing without Competence. <u>J of Child Language</u> 1 1-10

Clark, Ruth 1977 — What's the Use of Imitation? <u>J of Child Language</u> 4 341-358

Clark, Ruth 1978 — Some Even Simpler Ways to Learn to Talk. In Natalie Waterson & Catherine Snow (Eds) The Development of Communication. London Wiley

Cross, Toni
Parmenter, Gillian
Juchnowski, Maryla
& Johnson, Gillian 1982 — Effects of Day-care Experience on the Formal and Pragmatic Development of Young Children. Paper presented at the Second International Congress for the Study of Child Language, Vancouver, Canada, 1981. Published in this volume, pp. 337-359

Ewing, Guy 1982 — Word-order Invariance and Variability in Five Children's Three-Word Utterances: A Limited Scope Formula Analysis. In Carolyn Johnson & Carol Thew (Eds) Proceedings of the Second International Congress for the Study of Child Language, Volume I. Washington, D.C., University Press of America, 151-165

Lock, A   1980   The Guided Re-invention of
                          Language. London Academic
                          Press

Nelson, Keith   1981   Language-Learning Styles that
                          Combine Semantic, Syntactic
                          and Discourse Components. Paper
                          presented at the Second Inter-
                          national Congress for the Study
                          of Child Language, Vancouver,
                          Canada, 1981

Wells, Gordon   1980   Apprenticeship in Meaning. In
                          Keith Nelson (Ed) Children's
                          Language, Volume 2 New York
                          Gardner

Wooton, A.J.   1981   Children's Use of Address Terms.
                          In Peter French & Margaret Mac-
                          lure (Eds) Adult-Child Conver-
                          sation. London Croom Helm

Talkativeness as a Source of Individual
Variation in Children's Language Use

Anne Van Kleeck
The University of Texas at Austin

and

Richard Street
Texas Tech University

While the concept of reticence has been studied for decades by researchers in a variety of disciplines under a variety of labels (e.g., audience anxiety, shyness, stage fright, communication apprehension), it has been virtually ignored by scholars in the area of language acquisition. Regardless of particular disciplines or labels, the work to date has in common that it has dealt primarily with adults and has focused on variables "surrounding" reticence such as what occurs before (causes), alongside (correlates), and after (consequences). There has been little attempt, however, to study either the ontogenesis or the actual communicative behaviors of reticence. While it is clear that talkative and reticent children differ in the quantity of language they contribute to a conversation, the important question is to determine if qualitative differences exist as well. By using methodology developed by language acquisition researchers, the actual linguistic behaviors that distinguish talkative from reticent children can be determined.

In our recent efforts to understand variation in the language acquisition process, the existence and nature of the communicative behaviors which differentiate talkative from quiet children have not been considered. Indeed, most spontaneous language sample data upon which our knowledge of normal development is based have systematically eliminated the quiet child or selectively chosen the more talkative child (e.g., Brown, 1973). This practice, while expedient for the researcher, has perhaps narrowed our understanding of the true range of individual differences in language acquisition.

The purpose of the present study was to conduct an investigation of the language behaviors of reticent children and to ascertain how these compare with the language behaviors of more talkative children. Rather than attempting to cover all aspects of language in depth in this initial attempt, the purpose was to sample each area, thereby pointing to those areas that might be most productively explored in future research.

METHOD

Subjects

Children. This study looked at the language produced by four normal three and one half year-old girls (two talkative and two reticent) and their adult conversational partners. Two of the children had participated in a previous study (Van Kleeck & Carpenter, 1980) where it was informally noted that they differed in the amount of talk they each contributed to spontaneous conversations with adults. Two other children were randomly selected from lists generated by their teachers, since research has shown that teachers' rankings of students' verbal interaction frequencies are most highly correlated with the children's actual interaction rate in preschool settings (Greenwood, Walker, Todd & Hops, 1979). All four children attended preschool.

The results of several standardized tests indicated that all four children were developing language structure normally for their chronological age. Tested were receptive vocabulary (Peabody Picture Vocabulary Test, Dunn, 1959), receptive syntax (Test for Auditory Comprehension of Language, Carrow, (1973), and spontaneous expressive language (developmental sentence scoring procedure from Developmental Sentence Analysis, Lee, 1974). Standardized scores in the form of percentiles are presented for each child in Table 1. For all three measures, scores fell within approximately one standard deviation of the mean, with no observable differences within this range between the performance of the talkative and reticent children.

Following data collection, a post-hoc definition of talkativeness was generated on the basis of the average number of child utterances per 100 adult utterances. On this basis of this computation, the average number of utterances per 100 adult utterances was 38 for the reticent children and 78 for the talkative children. For each child, the means, standard deviations, and sample sizes these values were based on are presented in Table 1. Based on this data, it can be noted that the means for the two reticent children were well within one standard deviation of each other, and separated from the means of the talkative children by at least one and a half standard deviations. The most talkative child varied more than the other talkative child in the mean number of utterances she produced per interaction. Using this larger standard deviation, the two talkative children were also within one standard deviation of each other (although this was not true using the smaller standard deviation). This post-hoc analysis, then, supported the pre-experimental labelling of the children as either talkative or reticent.

Adults. The adults were 28 college-educated females from the Austin and Seattle areas who spoke American English as their native language.

Procedures

Each child interacted individually with six to eight previously unfamiliar adults so that differences would occur only if the children were longitudinally consistently different in their use of language in a similar social context. This assured that child differences were not solely a function of interacting with a particular adult conversational partner. That is, the design ruled out the possibility that the adult member of the conversational dyad was the primary cause of the child's response pattern.

Each child played with the adults for one half hour in a small room at a university speech and hearing clinic. The investigator was not present during the play session. Each session was videorecorded using a camera mounted in the room that was operated from behind one-way observational mirrors or from a control room. Prior to each session, the adult was simply told to interact naturally with the child for the duration of the one-half hour session.

Data

The data consisted of child talk occurring during the free play session. To obtain samples for analysis, each videorecorded session was transcribed until 100 adult utterances were obtained for each of the 28 adults who participated. In total, there were 2,800 adult utterances and the accompanying child utterances. For all the samples, both adult and child language and the nonlinguistic situational context were transcribed according to conventions set forth by Bloom, Hood and Lightbown (Bloom & Lahey, 1978, Appendix A.1).

Analytic Scheme

Both the structural complexity and language use aspects of the children's language were analyzed. The structural measures were intended to provide estimates of various aspects of language complexity and included (1) mean length of utterance (MLU) computed by determining the average number of morphemes per 100 child utterances (in cases where 100 child utterances were not obtained in the one half hour sample, the maximum number of child utterances available were used); (2) lexical diversity, computed by determining a lexical type-token ratio based on the first 100 words; (3) a noun, verb, adjective, adverb ratio, computed by adding the number of nouns plus verbs and dividing by the number of adjectives plus adverbs in the first 100 words (a smaller ratio indicates greater grammatical complexity); (4) a word length index, computed by determining syllables per word based on the first 100 words (see Lynch, 1970, for a discussion of measures 3 and 4); and (5) the proportion of complex sentences was also determined.

The pragmatic functions included two broad categories, assertives and requestives, and subcategories of each. Assertives were subdivided into (1) evaluative comments, (2) complies, (3) noncomplies, and

(4) other comments. Requestives included (1) verbal obliges (requiring a verbal response) and (2) requests for physical action. Requests for physical action were further coded into categories indicating direct versus indirect linguistic form.

The children's participation in ongoing discourse was considered by looking at their responses to comments and obliges posed in adult-initiated utterances. The nature of their own self-initiated utterances was also categorized into comments and obliges. This analysis was approached using a matrix categorization scheme which allowed the simultaneous coding of the behaviors of both partners in the conversational interaction. The categories, presented in Table 2, were adapted from Blank, Gessner, and Esposito (1979). At the most general level, this scheme determined who initiated the topic. At the next level, the utterance of the initiator was classified broadly into either an oblige or comments. Obliges require responses, either verbal or nonverbal. They are frequently in question form. The comment category included all other utterances. The third and final level of analysis considered the responses of the non-initiator, if any. The four categories included here were (1) adequate response, (2) inadequate response, (3) no response, and (4) other. In the present study, the adequate response category was further divided into those which merely met the conversational obligation, and those which met but also elaborated or expanded in giving information.

Reliability

Four randomly chosen samples were both transcribed and scored by three independent judges to obtain reliability. For transcription, percent agreement for segmentation of the corpus into utterances, morpheme agreement, description of the nonlinguistic context, and for categorization of utterances as a question ranged from 89 to 99 percent. For scoring procedures, interjudge agreement ranged from 85 to 99 percent for the structural complexity measures and from 72 to 92 for the pragmatic and discourse function measures.

Statistical Analysis

For all measures of the four children's language t-tests were conducted using each dyadic interaction as the source of variation. Thus for the two talkative children combined, there were a total of fourteen adult-talkative child interactions, since one child interacted with six different adults and the other with eight. Likewise, there were fourteen adult-reticent child dyadic interactions. With this total of 28 interactions in both groups combined, confidence levels were determined at 26 degrees of freedom.

Since they are computed by equalizing the quantity of utterances or words that go into the various calculations, the structural complexity measures all address qualitative differences. Thus, a higher MLU for the talkative children, for example, would indicate a comparatively greater proportional frequency of longer utterances (given that the standard deviations indicated similar distributions). This would mean that quiet children not only talk less (a quantitative issue), but also that the utterances they do use when they talk tend to be less structurally complex (a qualitative difference).

For the pragmatic functions and discourse functions of the children's language, in order to adjust for quantitative differences, proportional data (arcsin transformations) were used. For example, for the two major pragmatic function categories of assertives and requestives, the proportion of each child's total number of utterances that fell into each category was used. For the subcategories of assertives, for example, the data consisted of the proportion of the total number of assertives that fell into each category.

Since the analytic scheme employed contained several categories and subcategories within each language domain investigated, it was necessary to take precautions against the corresponding increased probability of committing a Type I error. This was done by dividing the traditionally accepted probability level of .05 by the number of tests being conducted in each particular category. The allowable probability level thus varied depending upon the number of tests being conducted within a particular domain --be it structural complexity, pragmatic function, or discourse function.

RESULTS

As shown in Table 3, on the structural complexity measures, the talkative children had a significantly higher MLU, significantly more lexical diversity, and a greater proportion of complex sentences than the reticent children. Differences were not observed on the noun-verb-adjective-adverb ratio or on the word length index.

Regarding pragmatic function measures, Table 4 gives the proportion of the total talk produced by the two types of children that were categorized as assertives, requestives, and subcategories of each. On all measures, excluding requests for verbal response, the proportional frequencies were signigicantly different for the two groups. Compared to the reticent children, the talkative children had a lower proportion of assertives in their talk, with a lower proportion of comments but a higher proportion of complies within that category. Correspondingly, the talkative children had a greater proportional frequency of requestives, with the subcategory of requests for physical action accounting for this difference. Both groups of children encoded their requestives in a direct form the vast majority of the time. However, the proportional frequency of indirect requestives was significantly higher for the talkative children.

The analysis of discourse functions, displayed in Table 5, revealed no significant differences between the two groups of children. A second analysis of the children's language at the discourse level considered the nature of the child-initiated utterances. In Table 6 it can be seen that the talkative children had a lower proportion of comments and a correspondingly higher proportion of obliges in their self-initiated speech.

DISCUSSION

The analysis performed in the present study revealed numerous differences between the language of the two talkative and two reticent children observed. These differences were noted in structural complexity, in pragmatic functions, and in the discourse functions of the children's self-initiated speech.

Structural complexity. Concerning structural complexity, pre-testing established that the reticent children had age appropriate knowledge of language structure. This was established both receptively and expressively. That is, the reticent children's disinclination to engage in conversation was not due to pathological or delayed development of the formal aspects of their language. The significant differences on three of the five measures tapping structural complexity indicates a qualitative difference between the groups. It was not the case that the reticent children talked less. They also were less inclined to use the full range of complexity they demonstrate on standardized tests when engaged in spontaneous conversation. Regarding the implications of this finding, one might question the potential impact of the consistent use of less complex language on the language development of the reticent child. Snyder-McLean and McLean (1977) discuss how talkativeness may be one strategy children use for furthering their knowledge of language. If this is the case, reticence may actually be deleterious to the language acquisition process. Reticent children might simply get less practice and as such may eventually fall behind in their knowledge of language form.

Research on both normal and delayed language development frequently uses mean length of utterance (MLU) as an indicator of language development. Often groups of subjects are matched on this criterion alone. The findings in the current study that MLU did not equally reflect the syntactic knowledge of talkative and reticent children raises some perplexing issues. Have we been systematically biasing research findings by the assumption that MLU is a good indicator of syntactic development? Is it possible that quiet children have been systematically eliminated from much research in which children were matched on MLU, simply because their MLU's have made it appear that their syntactic development was inadequate for their chronological age? If so, those included in much research may represent a special subset of children developing language normally--that is, those who are more loquacious. Biasing of the samples included in studies would have the effect of narrowing our understanding of the true range of individual differences in the normal development of language.

In other research where children have not been orignally matched for MLU, it is possible that not distinguishing between talkative and reticent children may have served to obscure the results obtained. That is, there may be an interaction effect between a child's talkativeness and the type of response she or he has to different situational variables. In data collapsed over these two types of children, such differences would be obscured. This concern was raised in a study of stimulus conditions used in language sampling that was conducted by Longhurst and File (1977). Further research using larger numbers of talkative and reticent children is needed to corroborate the present results regarding language complexity in general and MLU specifically. Determining a consistent influence of the talkative/quiet dimension on MLU's obtained from spontaneous language samples would clearly be important to interpreting previous research and designing future studies.

Pragmatic functions. The data support the position that there are qualitative differences in the pragmatic functions used by talkative versus reticent children, since the reticent children did not exhibit the same proportional use of the various functions measured.

While both groups of children had more assertives than requestives in their speech, the reticent children had a significantly higher proportion of comments. Correspondingly, they had a significantly lower proportion of requestives, accounted for by less requests for physical action. This pattern of findings suggests that the reticent children were less inclined than their more talkative peers to use language to manipulate others. This tendency is further corroborated in that noncomplies, a subcategory of assertives, occurred only in the speech of the talkative children (an average of .5 occurred in the talkative children's talk, while none were observed in the reticent children's talk) even though post hoc analyses indicated that the adults addressed a similar number of requests for physical action and significantly more requests for verbal responses to the reticent children. This overall pattern may indicate a power-sharing or symmetry in the conversations of the adult-talkative child dyads that was not present in the adult-reticent child dyads.

The reticent children appeared in general to be more restricted in their use of language. No instances of positive or negative evaluation or noncomplies, two subcategories of assertives, were found in their language samples. Complies were present, but there were proportionally significantly fewer of them. In the course of language development, children learn to verbally encode a greater range of language functions (e.g., Halliday, 1973, 1975). As such, the more restricted range of functions observed in the reticent children could be regarded as evidence for a skill delay. The fact that the talkative children encoded a significantly greater proportion of their requests in indirect forms further bolsters the argument for a delay in skill acquisition, since the indirect forms are later emerging.

Discourse functions. Regarding the discourse parameter of the children's language, the proportion of each type of child's total number of adequate responses that were to comments as opposed to obliges was not significantly different. This finding indicates that the two groups of children showed similar response patterns to adult-initiated utterances.

The pattern which emerged for both types of children regarding expanding upon required information in response to both comments and obliges warrants further discussion. The children's responses to adult obliges and comments were analyzed into those which met the conversational obligation and those which met and also offered additional unsolicited information. For example, if a child responded "yes" to a yes/no question posed by an adult, she or he was merely meeting the response obligation. On the other hand, when asked "How old are you?," the child might respond, "Three and my sister is nine." All of the children very rarely offered additional information in response to obliges. This finding supports other empirical evidence that questions can inhibit spontaneous conversation in children (see Hubbell, 1977, for discussion).

On child-initiated utterances, a qualitative distinction did emerge. The reticent children had a greater proportion of comments and a correspondingly smaller proportion of obliges. This finding regarding child-initiated utterances reflects the findings regarding the general pragmatic functions of the children's talk, where more comments than obliges were observed. Again, since the talkative children were requiring more adult responses in their self-initiated utterances, they appeared to be more active and controlling participants in the conversations. This resulted in a more symmetrical discourse pattern, since the onus of maintaining the conversation was lightened for the adult member of the dyad. In this sense, the adult-talkative child dyads resembled more the symmetrical interactions characteristic of conversations between equal status (for adult) or equal age (for children) participants (e.g., Giles, 1973, 1977; Lougee, Grueneich & Hartup, 1977, Van Kleeck & Cooper, 1980). It appears, then, that symmetry of conversational exchange may be one further parameter which distinguishes talkative from less talkative children.

CONCLUSIONS

While conclusions regarding talkative and reticent children in general must remain guarded due to the small sample size in the present study, this preliminary investigation contains numerous findings which

offer insights into the nature of reticence. Two
noteworthy causal explanations emerged from patterns noted in the current data that deserve further examination.

Several findings suggest a skill delay in the social
use of language on the part of the reticent children. As is characteristic of normal younger children, these children had a narrower range of pragmatic functions coded linguistically and a smaller
proportion of questions in their speech. In some
ways, the adult talk addressed to the reticent children resembled talk to younger children. For example, other research has found that the rate of direct requestives (imperatives) decreases as the age
of the child being addressed increases (Bellinger,
1979; Glanzer & Dodd, 1975; Newport, 1976; Rondal,
1978). Also, the number of questions addressed to
the child also decreases as a function of age
(Cross, 1977; Longhurst & Stepanich, 1975). In general, the number of declaratives also increases
with an increase in the age of the child being addressed (Glanzer & Dodd, 1975; Newport, 1976). In
the present study, post hoc analyses (not reported
here due to space limitations) indicated that these
same adjustments characteristic of talk to younger
children were also found in the talk addressed to
the reticent children. In many ways then, the reticent children were both acting and being treated
conversationally as if they were younger than their
more talkative peers. While any broad generalization regarding these findings is premature, it does
appear that there may at least be a subgroup of
reticent children who exhibit a delay in the social
use of language. Since it has been established
that knowledge of language structure was not delayed for these children, these findings suggest a
communication deficiency. While such a distinction has been suggested in the literature (e.g.,
Bloom & Lahey, 1978; Nelson, 1978), there have been
no empirical reports of actual children fitting
such a description. The reticent children in the
present study provide an initial characterization
of the actual language behaviors of such a child.

An alternative, or perhaps complementary, explanation of the current findings resides in regarding the behaviors of the reticent children as an individual difference. Implicit in the skill delay model is the notion that the reticent children might eventually "catch up" with their more loquacious peers. One might view the reticent children's behavior instead as reflecting an individual difference in social style, i.e., a personality characteristic that is not outgrown. The reticent children displayed a general pattern of conversational "nonassertiveness" that would fit well with explanation. Indeed, some of the same findings that support a skill delay model (e.g., low rate of question asking) could also be construed as evidence of nonassertiveness. Moreover, responses of the adults (indicated by post hoc analyses) may simply be characteristic of adjustments to less sociable interactants, including, but not exclusively consisting of, younger children. Research focusing on the language behaviors of reticent adults might provide a fruitful approach for further exploring this personality characteristic explanation of reticence.

Regardless of which of these possible explanations holds, the negative consequences for the reticent child and thus the need for intervention in more extreme cases remains. A recent study by Furman, Rahe, and Hartup (1979) offers one possible avenue for intervention. These researchers found significant increases in the sociability of socially withdrawn preschoolers during and after 10 play sessions with chronologically younger children. Since prosocial behavior in general increases with age (see Hartup, 1970), these mixed-age dyads provided a better match in number of social overtures. With the better match, a more symmetrical communication exchange is established, giving the socially withdrawn child a communicative experience denied in interactions with more talkative age-peers.

Normal language acquisition. This preliminary investigation suggests that caution is due in using MLU as an indicator of syntactic development in studies of language development. Undoubtedly, further research is needed to unequivocally establish

the contribution of the talkativeness dimension to
this recently documented variation in MLU.

BIBLIOGRAPHY

Bellinger, D. Changes in the explicitness of mother's directives as children age. Journal of Child Language, 1979, 6, 443-458.

Blank, M., Gessner, M. and Esposito, A. Language without communication: A case study. Journal of Child Language, 1979, 6, 329-352.

Bloom, L. and Lahey, M. Language development and language disorders. New York: John Wiley, 1978.

Brown, R. A first language: The early stages. Cambridge, Mass.: Harvard University Press, 1973.

Carrow, E. Test for Auditory Comprehension of Language. Austin, TX: Urban Research Group, 1973.

Cross, T. Mothers' speech adjustments: The contribution of selected child listener variables. In C. Snow and C. Ferguson (eds.), Talking to children: Language input and acquisition. Cambridge, Eng.: Cambridge University Press, 1977.

Dunn, L. Peabody Picture Vocabulary Test. Circle Pines, Minn.: American Guidance Service, 1959.

Furman, W., Rahe, D. and Hartup, W. Rehabilitation of socially withdrawn preschool children through mixed-age and same-age socialization. Child Development, 1979, 50, 915-922.

Giles, H. Accent mobility: A model and some data. Anthropological Linguistics, 1973, 15, 87-105.

Giles, H. Social psychology and applied linguistics: Towards an integrative approach. ITL: Review of Applied Linguistics, 1977, 27-40.

Glanzer, P. and Dodd, D. Developmental changes in the language spoken to children. Paper presented at the biennial meeting of the Society for Research in Child Development, Denver, April, 1975.

Greenwood, C., Walker, H., Todd, N. and Hops, H. Selecting a cost-effective screening measure for the assessment of preschool social withdrawal. Journal of Applied Behavior Analysis, 1979, 12, 639-652.

Halliday, M. Learning how to mean. London: Edward Arnold, 1975.

Halliday, M. Explorations in the functions of language. London: Edward Arnold, 1973.

Hartup, W. Peer interaction and social organization. In P. Mussen (ed.), Carmichael's Manual of Child Psychology, (3rd ed.), Volume 2, New York: Wiley, 1970.

Hubbell, R. On facilitating spontaneous talking in young children. Journal of Speech and Hearing Disorders, 1977, 42, 216-231.

Lee, L. Developmental sentence analysis. Evanston, IL: Northwestern University Press, 1974.

Longhurst, T. and File, J. Comparison of DSS from Headstart Children collected in four conditions. Language, Speech and Hearing Services in Schools, 1977, 8, 54-64.

Longhurst, T. and Stepanich, L. Mothers' speech addressed to one-, two-, and three-year old normal children. Child Study Journal, 1975, 5, 3-11.

Lougee, M., Grueneich, R. and Hartup, W. Social interaction in same- and mixed-age dyads of preschool children. Child Development, 1977, 48, 1353-1361.

Lynch, M. Stylistic analysis. In P. Emmert and W. Brooks (eds.), *Methods of research in communication.* New York: Houghton Mifflin, 1970.

Nelson, K. Early speech in its communicative context. In F. Minifie and L. Lloyd (eds.), *Communication and Cognitive Abilities - Early Behavioral Assessment.* Baltimore: University Park Press, 1978.

Newport, E. Motherese: The speech of mothers to young children. In N. Castellan, D. Pisoni and G. Potts (eds.), *Cognitive theory, Volume 2,* Hillsdale, NJ: Lawrence Earlbaum Associates, 1976.

Rondal, J. Maternal speech to normal and Down's syndrome children matched for mean utterance length. In C.E. Meyers (ed.), *Quality of Life in Severely and Profoundly Mentally Retarded People: Research Foundation for Improvement.* Washington, DC.: American Association on Mental Deficiency, 1978.

Snyder-McLean, L. and McLean, J. Verbal information gathering strategies: The child's use of language to acquire language. *Journal of Speech and Hearing Disorders,* 43, 306-325.

Van Kleeck, A. and Carpenter, R. The effects of children's language comprehension level on adult's child-directed talk. *Journal of Speech and Hearing Research,* 1980, 23, 546-569.

Van Kleeck, A. and Cooper, C. Children's communication strategies in a cooperative learning task with developmentally delayed and normal partners. Paper presented at the annual convention of the American Educational Research Association, Boston, April, 1980.

Table 1. Percentile scores for each child on Lee's Developmental Sentence Scoring (DSS), the Test of Auditory Comprehension of Language (TACL), and the Peabody Picture Vocabulary Test (PPVT). Also included is the breakdown of the amount of talk each child produced in spontaneous interactions with the adults. Provided are the sample sizes (number of interactions), means ($\bar{x}$), and standard deviations (SD).

	Subject	DSS	TACL	PPVT	Child Utterances per 100 Adult Utterances		
					(sample size)	($\bar{x}$)	(SD)
Quiet	1	85*	75	69	6	40	15
	2	26	84	64	8	35	19
Talkative	3	47	54	87*	8	63	17
	4	39	83	88*	6	92	29

*NOTE: The percentile ranking at one standard deviation below the mean is 15.9 and at one standard deviation above the mean is 84.1. The scores with asterisks are slightly above plus one standard deviation.

Table 2. Matrix used for the discourse analysis of the adult-child interactions (adapted from Blank, Gessner, and Esposito, 1979).

Child as speaker-responder	Adult as speaker- initiator	
Response types	Comments	Obliges
Adequate a) meets b) expands Inadequate No response Other		

Adult as speaker-responder	Child as speaker-initiator	
Response types	Comments	Obliges
Adequate a) meets b) expands Inadequate No response Other		

Table 3. Means ($\bar{X}$), standard deviations (SD), and t-test values for the structural complexity measures of the talkative and reticent children. P values are for a two-tailed test at 26 degrees of freedom.

Complexity Measures	Talkative $\bar{X}$ (SD)	Reticent $\bar{X}$ (SD)	t-value
MLU*	3.8 (.30)	2.8 (.45)	4.04***
LTTR*	1.77 (.09)	1.53 (.14)	3.15***
NVAAR*	2.63 (.66)	3.08 (1.83)	.36
WLI*	1.14 (.04)	1.12 (.04)	.50
PCS*	.513**(.23)	.089**(.07)	7.26***

*MLU= Mean length of utterance.
*LTTR= Lexical type/token ratio.
*NVAAR = Noun-verb-adjective-adverb ratio.
*WLI= Word length index.
*PCS= Proportion of complex sentences.

**Mean reflects arcsin transformation.

***Significant at p<.01.

Table 4. Proportions of talkative and reticent children's total talk that were assertives and requestives (actual mean proportions are provided for conceptual clarity; the t tests were conducted using arcsin transformations of these values). Where sufficient data allowed, the proportion of total assertives and requestives that fell into the subcategories of each was also analyzed. P values are for a two-tailed test at 26 degrees of freedom.

Pragmatic Function	Talkative $\bar{x}$ ∅(SD)	Reticent $\bar{x}$ ∅(SD)	t-value
Assertives	77 2.22(.34)	91 2.62(.37)	2.62*
Comments	75 2.12(.31)	90 2.58(.35)	3.68**
Complies	2.14 .24(.17)	.64 .07(.15)	2.83**
Requestives	21 .92(.35)	9 .51(.40)	2.88**
Function verbal response	84.6 .64(.34)	51.6 .48(.40)	1.13
physical action	48.5 .55(.32)	15.4 .40(.13)	4.07**
Form indirect	.60(.40)	1 .06(.18)	3.86**
direct	2.5(.39)	99 3.03(.16)	4.08**

*Significant at p<.025

**Significant at p<.01

Table 5. Qualitative analysis of discourse functions. Numbers entered in table represent proportion of total number of child adequate responses or no responses that were to comments or obliges (actual means are provided for conceptual clarity; t tests were conducted using arcsin transformations of these values). All t values were nonsignificant at 26 degrees of freedom.

	Talkative		Reticent	
	$\bar{x}$	∅(SD)	$\bar{x}$	∅(SD)
Adequate response rates to COMMENTS				
A. meets and expands categories combined	26	1.04(.19)	19	.87(.30)
B. expands only	75	2.20(.53)	71	1.67(99)
Adequate response rates to OBLIGES				
A. meets and expands categories	74	2.10(.19)	80	2.13(.61)
B. expands only	25	2.20(.53)	29	1.67(.99)
No response rate to COMMENTS	73	2.05(.25)	70	1.98(.18)
No response rate to OBLIGES	26	2.05(.25)	30	1.98(.18)

421

Table 6. Proportion of total child-initiated speech that were comments or obliges (actual means are provided for conceptual clarity; $\underline{t}$ tests were conducted using arcsin transformations of these values). $\underline{P}$ values are for a two-tailed test at $\overline{26}$ degrees of freedom.

	Talkative		Reticent		
	$\bar{x}$	∅(SD)	$\bar{x}$	∅(SD)	$\underline{t}$ value
Proportion COMMENTS	65	1.96(.72)	90	2.70(.53)	3.07*
Proportion OBLIGES	35	2.70(.53)	10	1.96(.72)	3.07*

*p<.025

A MODEL OF BILINGUAL SEMANTICS: INTERSECTING AND NON-INTERSECTING MORPHEMES AND THEIR ACQUISITION

by Marlene Dolitsky, Université de Paris VII

Haugen (1956) suggests that the sum of the linguistic knowledge at the disposition of a bilingual is greater than that of a monolingual but not large enough to equal that of two separate systems. His knowledge can then be schematized as two intersecting sets.

Thus the bits of linguistic knowledge of a bilingual can be classed as an element of L_1 ($\not\subset L_2$), L_2 ($\not\subset L_1$) or $L_1 \cap L_2$. This knowledge is at all levels of language:

Phonetic: Some traits are pertinent for only one language and others for both;

Syntactic: There are similarities and differences in tense formation, usage, morphology ... etc.

and Semantic: The signifieds of analogues overlap to a certain extent and have characteristics that belong uniquely to only one language.

Thus where two languages reside in a single individual, a single language system whose characteristics are the same as a monolingual's, i.e. totality, transformability and self-regulation (Piaget, 1968) will develop, the difference being, however, that it will extend over two languages.

Weinreich (1970) distinguishes three types of bilingualism: compound, subordinate and coordinate.

The signifieds of the analogues are combined and equivalent in the compound sign:

```
    'boat-bateau'        (signified)
      /      \
   (bot)   (bato)        (significand)
```

In such a case the signified of L_1 equals the signified of L_2, or $L_1 \cap L_2 = L_1 = L_2$. For both languages there is a direct word-thing relationship*. The compound sign is similar to the monolingual's sign, differing only in that it has a double significand for a given signified, while the monolingual has only a single significand. Interference, which Weinreich defines as the deviation from the norm of a language as a result of the knowledge of more than one language is potentially high for this type of sign (Lambert, 1972).

A subordinate sign is characterized by the perfect overlapping of the signifieds of the two analogues, where the signified of the weaker one is totally dependent on the signified of the stronger one:

```
   'boat'          (signified)
     |
   (bot)           (significand L₁)
   ─────
   (bato)          (significand L₂)
```

Only the dominant sign has a direct word-thing relationship. Interference for this type of sign tends to be from the dominant into the subordinate. Thus the signified of L_1 is equal to the signified of L_2 where $L_1 \cap L_2 = \frac{L_1}{L_2}$.

The signifieds of the analogues differ in the coordinate sign:

424

```
    'boat'     'bateau'      (signified)
      |           |
     (bot)      (bato)       (significand)
```

In this case there is no intersection of L_1 and L_2. A coordinate sign is highly resistant to interference (Lambert, 1972).

Lambert has been carrying out a number of experiments on adult bilinguals on the hypothesis that there is a functional neurological difference between coordinate and compound bilinguals. But even so, he does admit that his work is based on extremes and that intermediate positions of bilingualism do exist where a given bilingual will develop a compound relationship for some of his experiences and a coordinate one for others. Weinreich too, states "that a person's bilingualism need not be entirely of one type." As the adult's bilingualism is in only a minority of cases purely compound or coordinate and in a majority of cases a mosaic of these two types, it would seem that to understand his bilingualism an analysis of its development in the child would be of great import.

Haugen (1972) likens the child's acquisition of bilingualism to that of acquiring a skill such as acrobatics. However, it would seem that these "gymnastics" are not present from the beginning of the learning process. Leopold (1949), Imedadze (1967) and Volterra and Taeschmen (1978) have found that at first the child has an undifferentiated system. While he is being presented with two languages at once, he confronts his linguistic environment in the same way as the child who hears only one language. It is only subsequently that he becomes aware of the bilingual situation.

In this paper we study how within a single individual the various undifferentiated signs found at the start of bilingual acquisition develop into compound, coordinate or subordinate bilingual signs as schematised by a model of intersecting sets.

SUBJECTS

The acquisition of English and French by David, a child living in France, whose mother is American and father is French, was followed from age 2.0 to 3.0 at the stage of two-word utterances (in MLU: French 1.0 - 2.0; English 1.0 - 2.5). He spent most of his time with his English-speaking mother. He did not yet attend school. His father addressed him in both English and French as did his older bilingual sister, while his baby-sitter addressed him in English. Infrequent but long visits to the father's family were the main source of French interaction. Verbatim phonetic transcripts of the recordings of his speech in conversation with adults were typed and used to carry out this study.

A preliminary study of the same type was carried out on Liza, a child whose mother is French and father, American. However, Liza saw little of her father who was her sole source of native English input, and the study ended soon after the parents decided the mother's English was not good enough and that she should address the child in her native French. At this time Liza stopped responding to English and stopped using it, so that for our intents and purposes she was considered monolingual.

Both children come from upper-middle-class socio-economic backgrounds, and the parents all have university degrees.

Thus the following theory has its roots in a case study. And while David's language learning strategy is only one of a number (which is probably limited) of bilingual language acquisition strategies, this should not invalidate the ulterior model of bilingualism being presented. It would seem, rather, that his particular process of acquisition has cleared the camouflage off the case of the bilingual acquisition question.

BILINGUAL DEVELOPMENT

At the holophrasic stage the separate systems do not present a great source of confusion. The child may use the English "doggie" as well as the French "coq". The fact that these morphemes belong to two different systems does not hinder the communication process.

Children at this stage have just acquired a rudimentary phonemic system consisting of only a few distinctive traits which both systems employ. <u>Consistent</u> distinctions made by David at 2,1 were a closed front vowel (i:) from back vowels, and labial, dental and back consonants. He showed no differentiation of the two languages on the phonetic level. In order for the child to demonstrate his awareness of the bilingual environment in spite of his restricted lexicon, he would have to demonstrate some sort of discrimination toward his interlocutor. This, in fact, has not been observed. "Doggie" and "coq" were employed by Liza (age 1,9) regardless whether she was addressing her French-speaking mother, or her English-speaking father. A distinctive use of a limited vocabulary does not occur at the holophrasic stage. This then supports the argument that the child originally perceives all linguistic input as belonging to a single system. For him there is no differentiation of L_1 from L_2. The input is received as if it were part of a single set of stimuli, L.

It is at the two-word stage that the child becomes aware of the two distinct codes. He finds in trying to reproduce "the system" he is presented with, that there are certain sequences which appear together. The child's awareness of others and his ability to differentiate between himself and among them also helps him to distinguish the different linguistic systems they use.

At this stage we can now consider that L_1 and L_2 are beginning to emerge from L. However, L_1 and L_2 form only a small part of the intersecting sets, while the greatest part is their intersection itself.

David's awareness of the bilingual situation was already apparent at age 2,5 when the experimenter spoke to him in French rather than her usual native English. His personality changed. He became shy and less verbal, turning into himself. However, when a native French speaker was brought into the taping sessions, David laughed and played with him in the same way he had with the English-speaking experimenter. And although his grasp of English was better than that of French, he refused to use it with this French person. He categorically "refused" to use a recognized "English" word when speaking French, i.e. when addressing a French person.

In spite of David's clear awareness of the bilingual situation, a number of his sentences were formed "across languages". However, a detailed examination of these mixed sentences spanning ages 2,5 to 2,6 turned out a limited number of morphemes being used consistently in this type of sentence. These were: "un autre", "encore", "là", "no", "me" as in: "no eyes" (no ai:s), "no bateau" (no papo), "là cow" (la kau), "là bateau là" (la pato la), "ça là" (ža la), "un autre là" (not la), "voilà me" (wala mi:), "me un autre" (mi: ʌno), "me encore" (mi: aka), "encore kitty" (ʌka dɨki:), "mommy encore" (mami: aka).

To the question, "Does the child mix English and French?" the answer when taken from an adult point of view would be "yes". But just as it has been shown that a child's grammar must not be conceptualized in the same way as the adult's, so his bilingualism must also be taken from his point of view. The restricted number of "mixing" morphemes in David's data has lead to the hypothesis of an $L_1 \cap L_2$ category. It would seem that when taken from the child's point of view, mixing does not in fact occur due to the existence of this category. Thus any unmixed two-word sentence can be formed following any one of the following rules: French + English, French + (French ∩ English), English + English, English + (French ∩ English), (French ∩ English) + (French ∩ English), where order is impertinent. English words combine with English or (French ∩ English) words; French words combine with French or (French ∩ English) words and (French ∩ English) words can also combine with each other. However, a uniquely French word cannot combine with a uniquely English one.

As the languages become more and more differentiated, the set (French ∩ English) will become smaller and smaller, but it will NOT disappear. Few morphemes will belong exclusively to L_1 or L_2. These groups are made up uniquely of morphèmes that have no translation in the other language. The strength of the liason between analogues of the two languages is dependent on:

- the development of the analogues per se
- the similarity of their phonemic shapes
- the amount of overlap of their signifieds

The intersection of the two systems cannot be over-emphasized in the discussion of bilingual development, as can be seen in the evolution of the first-person pronoun and the demonstrative:

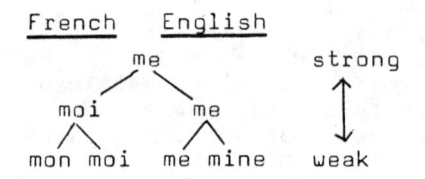

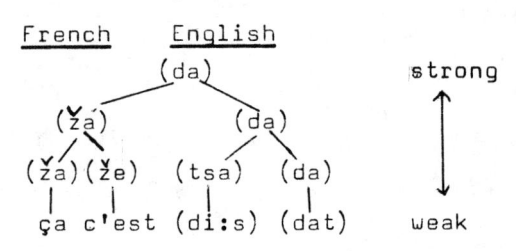

```
French      English
        me              strong
      /    \              ↑
   moi      me            ↓
   / \     /  \
mon moi  me  mine        weak
```

```
French           English
            (da)                strong
         /       \                ↑
      (ža)       (da)              ↓
      /  \      /    \
   (ža)(že)  (tsa)  (da)
    |    |    |      |
    ça  c'est (di:s) (dat)       weak
```

Historically, "me" first belonged to (English French) as did (da); both were used in both French and English constructions. In each case there seems to be an inability on the part of the child to differentiate the phonemic shapes of the English and French analogues: the strength of the shared (m) dominated a distinction between (wa) and (i:), while for the demonstrative there is no distinction between the fricatives (š) and (s). On the other hand the signifieds of the analogues and the syntactic use of their morphemes are similar. It is not until the child 1) can more finely distinguish phonemes, and 2) notes their differences of co-occurrence, i.e. that the utterances in which they occur belong to different systems, that he will be able to separate out and produce morphemes belonging exclusively to each language, which is in fact what occurs at the next level.

The bonds between analogues in the adult can be hierarchically classified according to their temporal proximity to the original (English French) morpheme, and the intersections of their signifieds, their phonetic shapes, and their syntactic uses. However, not all adult analogues develop out of an element of (English∩ French). Some develop out of unrelated morphemes or are learned by translation. This potential difference then accounts for later differences among individual adults.

ACQUISITION OF BILINGUAL SIGNS

For a child learning two languages simultaneously, functional signs will be compound if the particular function exists in both languages. Functions develop from a single morpheme and then follow parallel courses in each language as we have seen for the first person pronoun and the demonstrative. A function existing in both languages does not appear in only one at a time. The only case where this occurs is if it only exists in one language, for example, the differentiation of the feminine and masculine in French which has no counterpart in English. Lexical signs may be compound, coordinate or subordinate depending on their development in the individual. Bilingual functional signs develop similarly across the population while the development of lexical signs depends on individual learning situations.

The classification of compound, subordinate or coordinate seems to reflect, in fact, the quality of the intersection of the given sign. A compound sign is one whose analogues developed from a single $L_1 \cap L_2$ morpheme and whose final $L_1 \cap L_2$ forms a great part of the total $L_1 \cup L_2$ sign. For David, the first person could be considered compound as the etymon of the analogues derives from the single (English - French) morpheme, "me". The sign of the demonstrative would also be compound for the same reasons. David's 'dog-chien' sign will be compound as it developped from the single blend (dai:n).

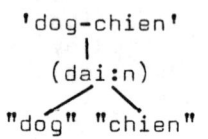

```
    'dog-chien'
         |
      (dai:n)
       /    \
    "dog"  "chien"
```

From strong words of one language, from which the analogue in the second will be learned by translation will develop a subordinate sign, as David's 'kitty'.

```
    'kitty'
       |
    (gɨdi:)
    ───────
      (ša)
```

A subordinate analogue grows out of a dominant one and is more restricted. Its signified remains dependent on the dominant analogue's. The only differentiation between the two analogues remains phonetic. As learning of the second analogue continues, more of its signified becomes differentiated from that of the dominant one's. However, wherever L_2 intersects L_1 it remains subordinate to it:

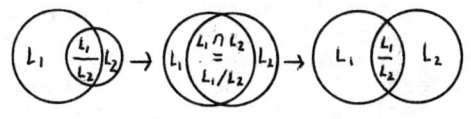

$$\left(L_1 \; \overline{\left(\frac{L_1}{L_2}\right)} L_2\right) \rightarrow \left(L_1 \left(\begin{array}{c} L_1 \cap L_2 \\ = \\ L_1/L_2 \end{array}\right) L_2\right) \rightarrow \left(L_1 \left(\frac{L_1}{L_2}\right) L_2\right)$$

A coordinate sign presents some tricky problems to solve, the main one being that if the analogues do not have similar signifieds, as the diagram seems to indicate, they cannot, by definition, be translations of one another. What then can be the real difference between a compound and a coordinate sign? It would seem then, that the key lies not, in fact, in the signified so much as in the interlocutor. It is seen that when looking at the same picture, the child will use either "cow" or "vache" depending on who he is talking to. The coordinate sign thus differs from the compound one not so much by a differentiation of its signifieds as by an additional element in its composition, the interlocutor with whom only one significand is correct.

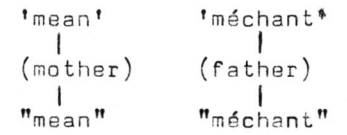

```
    'mean'           'méchant'
      |                 |
   (mother)          (father)
      |                 |
    "mean"           "méchant"
```

The analogues thus develop parallelly through different contexts and interlocutors, but are ultimately similar. The intersection of L_1 and L_2 in a coordinate sign, like for a compound sign, is made up mainly of the similarity of the signifieds and significands, but it will in no way include the development of the analogues, and while the "interlocutor-as-point-of-reference" is somewhat important in the compound sign, it is all-important in the coordinate sign. It is the interlocutor-as-reference which renders a coordinate sign resistant to negative interference, thus the importance of Ronjat's (1913) rule "one person, one language"; if every adult in the child's surroundings uses only one language with him, the development of this component is favored and ergo of the coordinate signs which tend to preclude surface level interference. Lambert (1972) and Ervin-Tripp's (1954 in Lambert, p. 300) work further substantiates this hypothesis.

There also exists a mediated coordinate sign whose analogues developed separately, but which were linked by an original intermediary $L_1 \cap L_2$ sign, such as the onomatopoeic "moo" which linked 'cow' and 'vache' for David and is itself, compound.

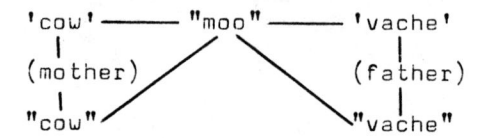

```
'cow' ——— "moo" ——— 'vache'
  |                    |
(mother)           (father)
  |                    |
"cow"               "vache"
```

Sometimes the child begins using equivalent morphemes of the two languages at the same time. In such a case it is difficult to determine whether they have risen from a common source or separately. It would seem insofar as they are consistently used correctly in context, i.e., with a French or English interlocutor, they might be considered of a coordinate type with an unknown mediator, e.g.:

```
"mordre"   -----  ?  -----  "bite"
"un, deux" ---    ?  -----  "one, two"
"mal"      --------  ?  -----  "hurt"
```

INTERSECTION - CONCLUDING REMARKS

Obviously, the intersection of the two languages a bilingual possesses depends on their similarity taken as a whole; the intersection in a French/English bilingual is much greater than that in a Chinese/English one, while it is certainly less so in a Slovak/Czech one.

Intersection is a tool with which to study various problems in bilingualism. For example, interference is in fact the misassignment of an exclusively L_1 element into $L_1 \cap L_2$. A bilingual tends to encompass more elements into $L_1 \cap L_2$ than he should, and the greater the intersection of L_1 and L_2, the more the bilingual will tend to generalize it; thus the more similar two languages are, the greater the potential of interference is for the individual bilingual, which is in agreement with Ruke-Dravina's (1965) conclusion. It would seem then that studies on interference should begin by delineating and describing the actual intersection of the two languages. Individuals' systems could then be compared to this.

On the other hand, while interference is the negative aspect of assigning elements to $L_1 \cap L_2$, there is a positive aspect to this in that it simplifies the learning process both for the first and for the second language learner. In the latter case the intersection of L_2 and the native language should not be ignored. The real problem of second language education is not so much one of teaching a completely new and unique linguistic system, but one of helping the student find what of the new language agrees with the linguistic knowledge he already possesses and what does not. At first all L_2 signs are subordinate to their L_1 analogues. $L_1 \cap L_2$ is great, only a gross difference in the phonemic shape of the analogues belongs uniquely to L_1 or L_2. As for the child, the learning process should bring him to reduce this intersection, assigning various semantic, syntactic and finer phonetic traits to their respective set while at the same time retaining in the intersection those traits that are common.

It would seem then that the intersection and non-intersection of two languages is the key to any study on bilingualism and that this concept should particularly be considered in work on child bilingualism, as a finished edifice is more easily understood when we possess the components and progression of its construction.

REFERENCES

Haugen, E. <u>Bilingualism in the Americas.</u>
    Alabama: University of Alabama Press, 1956.
Haugen, E. <u>The Ecology of Language.</u> Stanford,
    Calif.: Stanford University Press, 1972.
Imedadze, N. "On the psychological nature of child formation under conditions of exposure to two languages". <u>International Journal of Psychology,</u> 1967, 2, pp. 129-132.
Lambert, W. <u>Language, Psychology and Culture.</u>
    Stanford, Calif.: Stanford University Press, 1972.
Leopold, W. <u>Speech Development of a Bilingual Child,</u> Vol. I-IV. Evanston, Ill.: Northwestern University Press, 1939 - 1948.
Meillet, A. <u>Linguistique Historique et Linguitique Générale.</u> Paris: Champion, 1965.
Piaget, J. <u>Le Structuralisme.</u> Paris: Coll. "Que sais-je", PUF, 1968.
Ronjat, J. <u>Enfant Bilingue.</u> Paris: Librairie H. Champion, 1965.
Ruke-Dravina, V. "The process of acquisition of apical /r/ and uvular /R/ in the speech of children". <u>Linguistics,</u> 1965, 17, pp. 56 - 68.
Volterra, V. and Taeschner, T. "The acquisition

and development of language by bilingual children". <u>Journal of Child Language</u>, 1978, 5, pp. 311 - 326.

Weinreich, U. <u>Languages in Contact</u>. La Hague: Mouton, 1970.

<u>FOOTNOTE</u>

* I would like to thank Frédéric François for directing my attention to the differences between a direct word-thing relation and other indirect relations the significand can have to a signified.

Language elicitation techniques
in bilingual discourse: A comparison

Mel Greenlee
TESOL/Linguistics
University of Northern Iowa*

Introduction

During the past several years, sociolinguistic research on adult-child discourse has been extended to the study of specialized situations, such as language in the classroom (Cazden et al, 1980; Mehan, 1979a, 1979b). It has also been expanded to encompass a wide range of individuals with varied linguistic and cognitive characteristics; conversations of bilingual dyads have been examined (E. García, 1980; M. García, 1980; Zentella, 1981) as well as the communication of mentally handicapped persons (Bedrosian & Prutting, 1978; Price-Williams & Sabsay, 1979; Rosenberg, 1981).

In this paper, I will draw together two pieces of the extended research on child discourse, showing how bilingualism and situation may interact in the speech of a single developmentally disabled individual. The subject of this study, Ricky, is a 16-year-old boy with an estimated mental age of 4.3 who has been continuously exposed to two languages, English and Spanish. Table 1 summarizes results of formal cognitive and linguistic testing conducted by his school and brief accounts of his developmental history as given by his mother.

*Present address: Department of Linguistics
Stanford University
Stanford, CA 94305

Table 1

Estimates of Ricky's cognition and language

a. IEP for 1980 notes: Ricky has "good verbalization skills," but is "distractible" and "has trouble following verbal directions." His hearing is normal.

b. Leiter (age 12.7): Ricky's cognitive function estimated within the severe range of mental retardation.

c. English Peabody Picture Vocabulary Test (age 9.9): Ricky's mental age estimated at 2.4.

d. Developmental History: Ricky's mother reported that R. learned Spanish and English simultaneously, saying his first word at age 3. His schooling has been in English.

In remarks to follow, Ricky's language will be examined on only one very specialized situation. Ricky's conversation with adults in an 'instructional' or 'language elicitation' task will be compared to results earlier reported for bilingual preschoolers and their mothers in a roughly similar situation (E. Garcia & Carrasco, 1981).[1] Of specific interest in the comparison will be not only the language which the children used, but also the interplay between the children's speech and the techniques which the adults used in attempting to elicit the child's less-often-used language, Spanish.

It will be seen that, despite individual variation and some procedural differences, Ricky's interaction with adults shares a number of pragmatic and discourse features with the earlier-reported preschool data. I hypothesize that these similarities result from parallel aspects of the communication setting, i.e., (1) the purpose of the sessions--language elicitation, (2) the perceived and/or actual abilities of the children to respond in a linguistically appropriate way, and (3) the constrained nature of the task itself, in which the adults generally maintained control of topics, asking for display of knowledge they (the adults) presumably already had. The elicitation sessions seem to build on a process of mutual linguistic adjustment, such that adults more familiar to the child are most successful in adapting their elicitation strategies to what the child can or will do.

Procedures

1. García & Carrasco (1981) tape-recorded four mothers and their 3-1/2 year-old children during a picture description task in a preschool where the mothers also sometimes served as teachers. On alternate days, the mother-child pairs performed the task either in English or in Spanish; however, the mothers' Spanish questions were often answered in English by the children. In discussion of results from García & Carrasco's study, the focus of this paper will be on those conversations in which the mothers used Spanish, since the goal of those sessions was closest to the perceived goal of adult talk with Ricky.

2. Ricky's speech was tape-recorded at his home in a single day. Participants in the conversation were his mother (MC), his sister (S), and an Anglo researcher (M) who also spoke Spanish. Although there were no pre-set conditions on language use, it soon became clear that the adults perceived the goal of the session to be Spanish production by Ricky, and they questioned him about picture books and events, attempting to elicit this language. Table 2 provides frequency data on the use of Spanish and English by all participants in Ricky's session.

Table 2 on next page.

From Table 2, it can be seen that although the adults were trying to elicit Spanish from Ricky, they did not often use Spanish themselves. Neither were the adults overwhelmingly successful in their aim; less than one-quarter of Ricky's utterances were in Spanish.

Table 2

Language choice by participants in Ricky's session*

	English	Spanish	Mixed	Neutral**	Unintell.	Total	% Spanish
R	612	249	99	58	20	1038	23.9
MC	299	185	36	52	1	573	32.2
S	35	56	8	16	--	115	48.7
M	171	315	127	102	--	715	44

* Numbers represent turns.

** The column marked Neutral represents words like "no" or names, which could not be assigned to either language.

Instructional Model

In analyzing Ricky's session, I followed García & Carrasco in using an instructional discourse model (Mehan, 1979a, 1979b). García & Carrasco had found that mother-child talk in their recordings held to a three-part sequential pattern common in genuine classroom lessons (Mehan, 1979a, 1979b; Sinclair & Coulthard, 1975). This sequential pattern is shown in Table 3.

Table 3 on next page.

Table 3 provides examples from the classroom (3a is from Mehan, 1979a), from García & Carrasco (3b), and from Ricky's conversation (3c). In the three-part instructional sequence, the adult initiates a topic by questioning ("What's it about?"), the child responds ("The map."), and finally, the adult replies, evaluating or otherwise prompting the child's response ("That's right."). The examples in Table 3 illustrate one of the simplest types of questions with which an adult can begin a sequence, a product elicitation, to which the child is expected to provide a factual response (Mehan, 1979a; García & Carrasco, 1981). Product elicitations made up over half of teacher's questions in Mehan's observations of elementary school lessons (Mehan, 1979a). Nevertheless, although product elicitations are extremely common, more complex types of adult questions occur, as well as child answers, and variations on adult replies. A list of major coding categories for each step of the sequence (I-III) is shown in Table 4, with brief definitions and/or English examples. To those categories used by García & Carrasco, I have added two: (I) IIIe, REPAIR REQUEST, representing a request by the adult for a restatement, or indication of noncomprehension on the adult's part (2) ACKNOWLEDGE-

Table 3

The three-part instructional sequence and examples

I: Adult elicitation
II: Child response
III: Adult reply

    a) Mehan (1979 a)

    T: Edward, what's it about?
    E: The map.
    T: The map. That's right. This says "the map."

    b) García & Carrasco (1981)

    M: ¿Qué es eso? (What is that?)
    C: Casa. (House.)
    M: Una casa, muy bien. (A house, very good.)

    c) Ricky

    I: (MC) What's bed in Spanish?
    II: (R) Cama. (bed)
    III: (MC) Cama, yeah.

MENT, a type not listed in Table 4, but which represents a simple 'back-channel' utterance (such as "Mmmmm..." or "Ah...") in which the hearer notes that something was heard, but does not overtly add to it.

In coding the data from Ricky's session, each move (Coulthard, 1977) by each of the four participants was classified as a 'micro' sub-category of one of the three 'macro' interactional steps (I-III).[2]

Table 4 on next page.

Results

In order to show how the three-part sequence functioned in Ricky's session, I will first survey the overall frequency of the various utterance sub-types within each step of the sequence (I-III). In this initial overview, I will leave aside for the moment variations in language code and in strategies used by the three different adults conversing with Ricky. Two questions will be addressed:

(1) What subtypes of adult initiations occurred most often?

(2) How closely did Ricky's responses match the adults' questions, in order of frequency?

After considering these questions, the focus will narrow to Spanish utterances, comparing the types of Spanish utterances participants used in Ricky's session to those observed in Garcia and Carrasco's picture description task. Finally, some clear differences in style between the three adults interacting with Ricky will be described.

Table 4

Major coding categories for each part of the instructional sequence and examples

I. Adult Elicitations

   a. PRODUCT: "What's that?" (requires factual response)
   b. PROCESS: "What's she doing?" (requires opinion or interpretation)
   c. CHOICE: "Is that a horse?" (yes/no or alternative response required)
   d. INFORMATIVE: "That's a small microphone."
   e. DIRECTIVE: "Pay attention." "Let's look at this one."

II. Child Responses

   a. NR: No response within 2 seconds, or irrelevant (e.g., singing).
   b. PRODUCT: (Cf. questions above) "A cat."
   c. PROCESS: "She's making pancakes."
   d. REPEATS: "Microphone." "That's a small microphone." (Child repeats adult utterance.)
   e. BIDS: "I wanna go to the show." (C attempts to change subject, get the floor).
   f. DON'T UNDERSTAND: "Huh?" "What?"

III. Adult Replies

   a. REPEATS: "The show." (A repeats all or part of C's utterance.)
   b. POSITIVE EVALUATION: "No." "That's right." "Good."
   c. NEGATIVE EVALUATION: "No." "That's not a cat."
   d. PROMPT: (A corrects wrong or incomplete C response) "You know what that is..." "That's a dog."
   e. REPAIR REQUEST: "Huh?" "What?"

Table 5

Overall frequency of interaction types in Ricky's session (percentages)

I: Adult elicitation	%	II: Child response	%	III: Adult reply	%
PRODUCT	39.8	PRODUCT	35.7	REPEATS	23.6
CHOICE	22.0	BID	23.9	ACKNOWLEDGE	14.7
PROCESS	19.6	PROCESS	11.2	PROMPT	14.2
DIRECTIVE	13.3	CHOICE	9.5	POS. EVAL.	13.8
INFORMATIVE	4.4	REPEATS	7.9	NEG. EVAL.	11.7

1. *Overview* Table 5 presents frequency data in percentages for the various sorts of adult elicitation, child response, and adult reply in Ricky's session. A quick glance at the left column shows that product questions were frequent, as they had been in the classroom. Turning to the child's responses (column II), it can be seen that, with the exception of child bids, answers Ricky gave are roughly parallel (in order of frequency) to the types of questions adults asked. Although Ricky did not always give typologically appropriate answers, he most readily responded to product questions, followed by process (or "what-doing?" type) questions, and finally to choice (alternative) questions.

Child bids at step II formed a relatively large percentage of Ricky's utterances. This could be accounted for by several situation factors: (1) the length of the session -- two hours with breaks, (2) Ricky's "distractibility" as noted in school records, or (3) quite understandable boredom with a language game in which the adults consistently controlled the interaction. The great majority of Ricky's bids were at least partially in English (220 out of 260), and very few of these attempts to change the topic were successful.

While the adults usually ignored Ricky's bids, Table 5, column III shows that they responded variously to his other utterances. The most frequent adults replies were repetition (23.6%) while acknowledgements, prompts, and evaluative responses were similar in frequency (between 11% and 15%).

To summarize this preliminary survey of Ricky's session, adults initiated most topics with simple question types, sustaining the conversation through repetition or prompting. Responses given by Ricky, except for bids which the adults largely ignored, matched the adults' questions rather closely.

2. Spanish utterances In comparing those portions of Ricky's session in which Spanish was used with earlier work by García & Carrasco (1981), both parallels and divergence were found in interaction strategies. However, as will be seen below, interaction patterns differed among the three adults who conversed with Ricky; this, in turn, contributed to divergent patterns between the two adult-child sessions.

A comparison of adult elicitation strategies in the two studies is shown in Figure I. Data from adults in García & Carrasco's study is shown in the blank bars, while the three adults conversing with Ricky are represented by separate, filled bars in the figure.

Figure I on next page.

For the moment considering all three of the adults in Ricky's session together, it is clear that both the bilingual mothers in García & Carrasco (1981) and adults conversing with Ricky used mainly simple product elicitations in their attempts to elicit Spanish, while process and directive utterances were less frequent. However-process questions were comparatively more frequent in Ricky's session than among the pre-school mother-child pairs, while informative utterances were less frequently spoken to Ricky. These differences could be due to greater Spanish abilities on the part of the child (since Ricky is able to answer Spanish process questions), or they might reflect other, procedural differences. For example, one could speculate that since mothers in García & Carrasco (1981) were actual teachers at least part of the time, they extended information-giving to the descriptive task as a carry-over from their classroom role. A more mundane explana-

FIGURE I: ADULT ELICITATIONS IN SPANISH

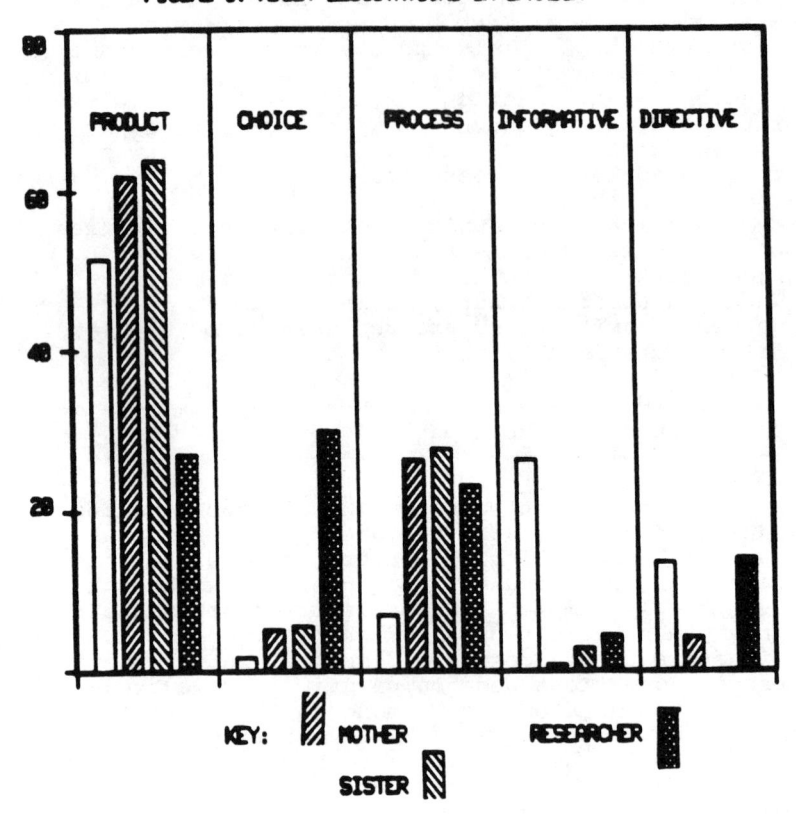

tion might have to do with the differences in defining Spanish interactions between the two studies.[3]

Figure II on next page.

Figure II compares the children's responses in Spanish context in the two studies. The most striking similarity is in the frequency of <u>product</u> answers, which could have been predicted from data in Figure I. Also common to both sets of conversations are the lower frequencies for <u>process</u> answers, as compared to <u>products</u>, and indications of non-comprehension.

The most apparent differences are in <u>choice</u> responses and in <u>repetition</u>. García & Carrasco's dyads rarely used alternative questions or answers in Spanish context. In Ricky's session, most of these questions were asked by the Anglo researcher, with Ricky answering in kind.

The striking frequency of repetition in García & Carrasco's data had to do with "phonetic pronunciation activities" bilingual mother-teachers carried out with their children. García & Carrasco (1981:258) reported that the mother "stated or stressed a word, the child repeated, and then the mother repeated the same word." Such drills did not occur in Ricky's session, although adults did present models which they expected him to repeat.

I would speculate that the lack of overt pronunciation drills in Ricky's session is at least partially a function of the chronological age of the person filling the child's role. It may also be attributable to the true status of García & Carrasco's mothers as teachers. However, there are many other possible explanations. For example, I have not checked to see how often the adults

FIGURE II: CHILD RESPONSES IN SPANISH

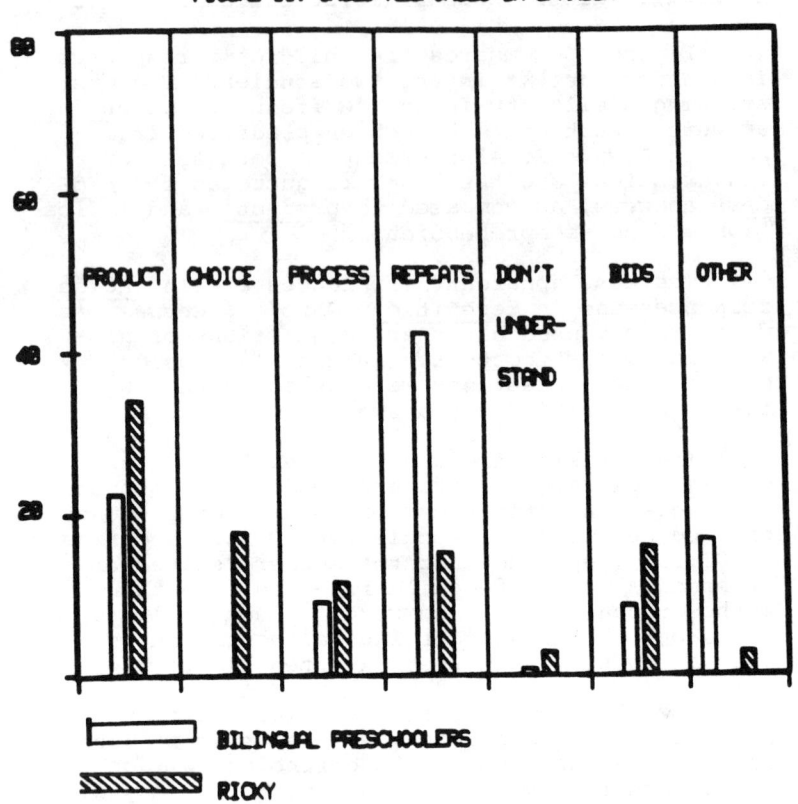

might have presented a model which Ricky failed to repeat. If such models were not often imitated, the adults may have accommodated the child by not presenting them.

Figure III on next page.

Figure III shows that in both data sets, repetition and prompting were strategies adults used to keep the interaction going. Evaluations, whether positive or negative, occurred more rarely. Included in Figure III is the category of adult requests for repair, which was not used in coding by García & Carrasco (1981). In Ricky's session these requests were sometimes used by adults as a tactic for getting him to switch from English to Spanish. They were also often used in cases of genuine adult puzzlement, which more often occurred in the case of the adult least familiar with the child.

To summarize the information from the three figures, while the strategies identified are certainly not identical, in both data sets, the interactional pattern seems to be created through mutual cooperation and tailoring of questions to the perceived capabilities of the child to respond, since the relative frequency of various response categories fairly closely match the relative frequency of question types. Although adults in García & Carrasco's study placed much more emphasis on pronunciation and repetition than those in Ricky's session, both sets of adults relied on repetition and prompting in conjunction with the simplest question type -- product -- to keep the interaction going.

FIGURE III: ADULT REPLIES IN SPANISH

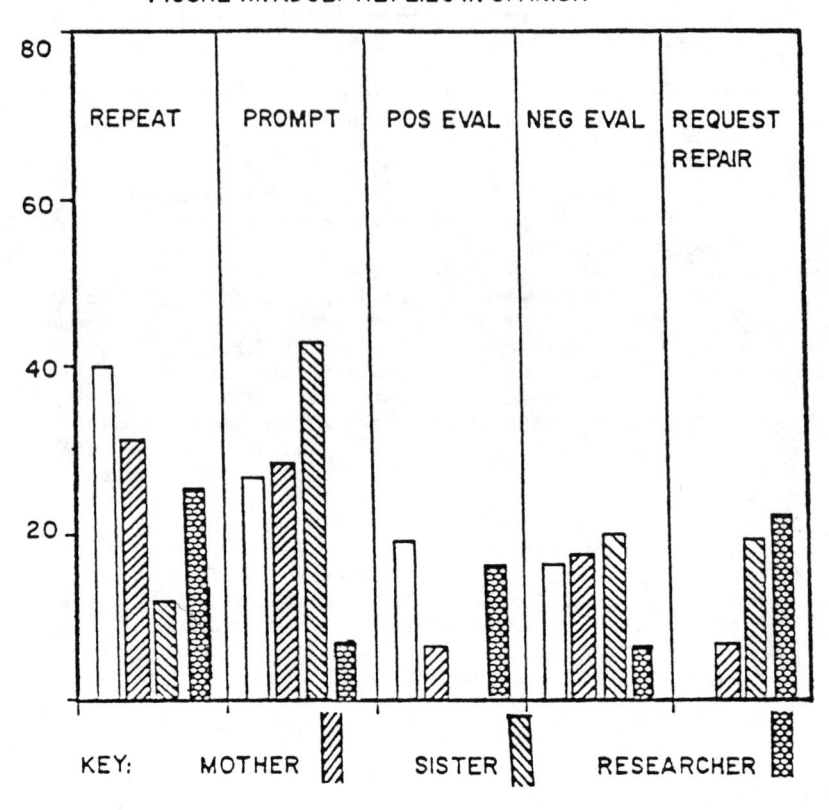

KEY: MOTHER SISTER RESEARCHER

3. _Individual variation in interactional style_ However, the three figures also illustrate differences in interactional style among the three adults who conversed with Ricky. In eliciting (see Figure I), the Anglo researcher used many more _choice_ questions and _directives_, while Ricky's mother and sister used _product_ and _process_ questions which, on the face of it, would require more complex answers from the child.

In her responses (see Figure III), the Anglo researcher tended to evaluate the child's responses positively and to prompt less than his mother and sister, thus unwittingly using two strategies which would tend to cut the conversation short. Moreover, over 20% of the less familiar adult's replies were _requests for repair_, indicating that she often had difficulty in understanding Ricky. The Anglo researcher's different style seems to be accounted for by her difficulties in glossing Ricky's remarks and also, in part, by her lack of knowledge of Ricky's capabilities; therefore, she asks less than he can do. While the two adults who know Ricky best are acting in complementary fashion with him, prolonging the interaction until they get the 'right' answer, the researcher accepts Ricky's response if she can understand it, thus necessitating another question to get the conversation flowing again.

To illustrate the extended nature of the familiar adults' attempts to get Ricky to speak Spanish, observe the examples in Table 6.

Table 6

Examples of extended Spanish elicitation sequences

a. A process elicitation (R126a)

S: ¿Qué está haciendo? (What's he doing?)
R: El libro. (The book.)
S: ¿Qué está haciendo con el libro? (What's he doing with the book?)
R: Reading it.
S: ¿En mejicano? (In Spanish?)
R: Leyendo el libro pa la escuela. (Reading the book for school.)

b. An extended interaction between Ricky and MC illustrating Spanish elicitation strategies (R378b)

1. MC: Look at that. (Picture of boys throwing water).
   R: Throwing some water in...
2. MC: Throwing some water, yeah, yeah.
   M: Yeah, yeah, there.
3. MC: What is he doing in Spanish?
   R: Peanuts, eating peanuts.
4. MC: ¿Qué está haciendo en mejicano el muchachito? (What's the little boy doing in Spanish?)
   R: Comiendo peanuts. (Eating peanuts.)
5. MC: No, aquél, este otro, ¿qué estaba haciendo? Este, ¿qué estaba tirando? (No that one, this other one, what was he doing? This one, what was he throwing?)
   R: Wa - (starts to say 'water.')
6. MC: ¿Tirando qué? (Throwing what?)
   R: Wa-water.
7. MC: ¿Tirando qué? (Throwing what?)
   R: Agua. (Water.)
   M: Yeah, muy bien. (Real good.)

8. MC: Now say it, the whole thing.
   R: Water.
9. MC: Estaba tirando agua. (He was throwing water.)
   R: Tirando agua. (Throwing water.)
   M: M-hm, OK, yeah.
10. MC: All right.

Example 6a shows that Ricky can answer Spanish process questions with prompting. Example 6b illustrates several prompting tactics Ricky's mother used in attempting to elicit Spanish. In turn 1, she elicits the 'answer' in English. In turn 3, she asks for a translation, and in 4, switches to Spanish herself. When Ricky misconstrues her question, she clarifies it (in 5), staying in Spanish, but now asking not a <u>process</u> but a simpler <u>product</u>-type question. In turns 6 and 7, when <u>Ricky</u> fails to give a Spanish answer, she prompts him, and finally switches to English (turn 8) to elicit a long Spanish phrase, which Ricky dutifully repeats. While Ricky's answers do not match her questions language-wise, there is discourse agreement between question and answer which shows he has understood her question.

Summary and Conclusion

This paper has reviewed language elicitation techniques in two rather unusual mother-child or child-adult interactions in which the object was to get the child to speak Spanish. In both, the child's responsiveness and the adults' close knowledge of the child's language allowed cooperative discourse to take place, although the adults never relinquished control. While not identical, discourse in both language-elicitation sessions fell largely within the confines of an instructional model, with the most frequent questions being among the simplest to answer. However, those adults who were most familiar with the developmentally disabled child's capabilities expected and got more complex responses than an unfamiliar adult whose interaction pattern might be described, in comparison, as struggling to keep the conversation going. It has been suggested (Oksaar, 1981) that bilingual conversation of a directed sort provides an apt window for viewing pragmatic and metalinguistic development. I would suggest, in conclusion, that equally important are the ways in which the "window" itself is constructed in the joint adult-child interactions which make up a significant part of language learning.

Notes

Research was supported by an NEH Summer Seminar for College Teachers (1980) and by the Graduate College of the University of Northern Iowa. I would like to thank the director of the seminar, Dr. Bernard Spolsky, and fellow participants for their helpful comments. I am particularly grateful to Mariscela Amador Hernandez for help in transcribing Ricky's conversation.

[1] Factors which make the two studies only roughly comparable include the following: (1) the number and relationship of participants (2) single-language (Garcia & Carrasco) versus either or both as the medium of communication (3) setting -- Ricky was recorded at home, while Garcia & Carrasco's dyads were recorded at school (4) length of data collection -- Ricky was recorded in a single long session, while mother-child dyads were recorded in short sessions over several months.

[2] Garcia & Carrasco (1981:253-4) used the utterance (roughly equivalent to the turn) as the unit of discourse analysis. "An utterance was defined as any word...or set of words separated from one another by a 2-second time interval of silence, or by the occurrence of an utterance by a second speaker."

Since I found that participants in Ricky's session sometimes used two micro-interactional categories within the same utterance or turn (for example, a positive evaluation combined with an initiating question), I used the move as the unit of discourse analysis. Using moves, each of the micro-interactional categories could be coded separately. Analysis of adults' questions revealed occasional use of chained questions within the same initiating utterance; decomposition of such questions into component types helped in identifying differences in adults' questioning strategies.

[3] In García & Carrasco's study, utterances "in Spanish context" were those which were said by either participant during the sessions in which mothers had been instructed to use Spanish. Thus, if the mother asked a question in Spanish and the child replied in English, utterances in this interaction would have been coded as "in Spanish context."

In Ricky's session, "in Spanish context" refers to those utterances which were actually spoken in Spanish, as opposed to those which were said in English or with an intra-sentential code-switch.

A further coding difference between the two studies concerns the "confirmation question." In this type of question, one participant repeats the previous utterance of another with a rising intonation. Such questions in Ricky's session were coded simultaneously as instances of I: Choice question, and III: Repetition. This coding procedure doubtless inflated the number of choice questions in comparison to those asked in sessions recorded by García & Carrasco.

References

Bedrosian, J. & C. Prutting. 1978. Communicative performance of mentally retarded adults in four conversational settings. Journal of Speech and Hearing Research 21:79-95.

Cazden, C., R. Carrasco, A. Maldonado-Guzmán, & F. Erickson. 1980. The contribution of ethnographic research to bilingual bicultural education. In J. Alatis (Ed.) Georgetown University Round Table on Language and Linguistics, 64-80. Washington, D.C.: Georgetown U. Press

Coulthard, M. 1977. An introduction to discourse analysis. London: Longman

García, E.E. 1980. Mother and child use of Spanish and English in bilingual preschool environments. Education and Treatment of Children 3:183-194.

García E.E. & R. Carrasco. 1981. An analysis of bilingual mother-child discourse. In R.P. Duran (Ed.) Latino language and communicative behavior, 251-269. Norwood, N.J.: Ablex

García M. 1980. Linguistic proficiency: How bilingual discourse can show that a child has it. In R.V. Padilla (Ed.) Ethnoperspectives in bilingual education research, Vol. III: Theory in bilingual education, 62-74. Ypsilanti, Mi: Eastern Michigan University.

Genishi, C. 1981. Code-switching in Chicano six-year-olds. In R.P. Durán (Ed.) Latino Language and communicative behavior, 133-152. Norwood, N.J.: Ablex

Greenlee, M. 1981a. Communicative competence in Spanish/English developmentally disabled persons. Paper presented to the Council for Exceptional Children Conference on the Exceptional Bilingual Child, New Orleans, Louisiana, Feb. 18, 1981.

Greenlee, M. 1981b. Specifying the needs of a 'bilingual' developmentally disabled population: Issues and case studies. Los Angeles: NABE Journal 6: 55-76.

Mehan, H. 1979a. Learning lessons. Cambridge, Mass.: Harvard U. Press

Mehan, H. 1979b. "What time is it, Denise?" Asking known information questions in classroom discourse. Theory into Practice 18:285-294.

Oksaar, E. 1981. Linguistic and pragmatic awareness of monolingual and multilingual children. In P.S. Dale & D. Ingram (Eds.) Child language: An international perspective, 273-286. Baltimore:University Park Press

Price-Williams, D. & S. Sabsay. 1979. Communicative competence among severely retarded persons. Semiotica 26:35-63.

Rosenberg, S. 1981. Editor's overview. Applied psycholinguistics 2:1-4.

Sinclair, J.M. & M. Coulthard. 1975. Toward an analysis of discourse. N.Y.: Oxford U. Press

Zentella, A.C. 1981. 'Tá bien, you could answer me en cualquier idioma: Puerto Rican code-switching in bilingual classrooms. In R.P. Durán (Ed.) Latino language and communicative behavior, 109-131. Norwood, N.J.: Ablex

THE ACQUISITION OF INTERACTIONAL COMPETENCE IN BI- AND TRILINGUAL ENVIRONMENTS

Els Oksaar

1. INTRODUCTION

My study is concerned with the acquisition of the interactional competence in an environment, where children were exposed to and used two or three languages every day. The present paper examines two aspects of it: the acquisition of culturemes such as <u>thanking</u> and <u>greeting</u> and the <u>comprehension of indirect requests</u>. The data are mainly from my longitudinal Multilingual Language Acquisition Project that is part of the Paedolinguistic Projects of Language Acquisition at the Pre-School Age[1] at the Institute of General Linguistics at Hamburg University. It is undertaken to establish a theory of the acquisition of linguistic and interactive competence in the early years. The subjects are children in a mono-, bi-, tri- and quadrilingual environment. The focus of data collection is on spontaneous speech in natural play and family-life settings at the children's homes and surroundings, but various tests and role-plays were also carried out; we may speak of modified laboratory conditions in these cases.

The <u>bilingual data</u> of the project are derived from 8 Swedish-Estonian children (age 1;8 - 6;7) in Stockholm, 6 German-Swedish children (age 1;7 - 7;0) in Hamburg, 6 German-English children (age 1;10 - 6;8) in Hamburg. See also 3.3.1 and 3.3.2.

The <u>trilingual data</u> of the project are derived from 3 Estonian-Swedish-German children (age 2;1 - 7) in Stockholm and 4 Swedish-English-German children (age 2;8 - 6;7) in Hamburg.

The parents' and caregivers' behaviour was

taped and protocolled, too. The socio-economic status of the parents varied from lower to upper middle class.

1.1. First I shall give some preliminaries and the theoretical frame of the study, define some concepts which I am working with, and then discuss empirical evidence.

What I mean by <u>interactional competence</u>, however, must be explained now to avoid misunderstandings: I define <u>interactional competence</u> as the ability of a person - in interactional situations - to perform and interpret verbal and nonverbal communicative actions according to the socio-cultural and socio-psychological rules of a group.[2] Failure to acquire this competence could have unfavourable consequences for interpersonal relations.

1.1.1. The following preliminaries are important for our paedolinguistic research:
A child first receives language, that is the <u>verbal</u> means of communication, in the role of a <u>listener</u>, long before it is active in the role of a speaker.
A child first receives interactional items - <u>culturemes/behavioremes</u> (see 2.1) - through looking at the behaviour of others, together with listening, long before it is actively interacting himself by these means.
Investigations of the development of interactional competence have to work with at least two concepts of <u>context</u>: the <u>linguistic</u> and <u>situational context</u>.
Learning a language as a means of communication not only requires that a child masters the linguistic material according to the grammatical rules, but also that he acquires the ability to judge the conditions for using this material and that he masters the rules of these conditions, including change of register and strategies of code switching, as is the case for multi-lingual children.

When acquiring interactional competence, the child must develop the ability to recognize the sociocultural and the linguistic demands for each different situation and to react appropriately to them. If a German or Estonian child understands the semantic structure of the word <u>man</u> and can use the sentence <u>here comes a man</u> correctly, still he must learn which sociocultural rules do not allow the sentence <u>hello, man</u> and demand instead <u>hello, Mister Miller</u>. A child has to learn how to greet, how to ask for something, how to express emotions, how to avoid conflicts, what cannot be talked about, strategies of contact, etc.

A child has also to learn that when people interact, most linguistic utterances seldom fulfill only one function - according to Karl Bühler's (1934) <u>organon model</u> a word can be used in its <u>referential</u>, <u>expressive</u> and <u>appelative</u> functions. Roman Jakobson (1960) has added three more functions, the <u>phatic</u> function being of great importance. The child has to learn, however, that there is <u>functional dominance</u>, which depends <u>partly</u> on the situation and <u>partly</u> on the sociocultural frame in which something is said. This is the case of indirect requests when a declarative sentence like: <u>the door is open</u> is said in the appelative function: <u>please close the door</u>.
   A child learns the socio-cultural and sociopsychological rules of a group gradually, whereby it must also learn to synchronize verbal actions with nonverbal ones: <u>to say</u> Hello, Mister Miller, <u>to look at him</u>, <u>extend hands</u> etc.

1.1.2. <u>Hello</u> belongs to the verbal behavioremes of greeting. Greeting, thanking, excuses and other sociocultural behaviour patterns constitute culturemes. The question of how and when a child learns the appropriate realization of culturemes has for a long time been fully ignored in research. First in the seventies there was awaking interest in these matters (Gleason and Weintraub, 1976; Ochs and Schieffelin,1979).

So far, attention has been paid to the verbal part of the greeting only. But the nonverbal part of it and its synchronization with the verbal one are equally important in interaction: the action of the eyes, head, hands. To smile or not when greeting somebody and so on.

We know from previous research that parents prompt verbal behavioremes (Greif and Gleason, 1980). How and when do children learn to behave nonverbally in interactional situations? - This question has not been asked. We are asking and trying to find answers to it in our ongoing projects. So much can be said from this ongoing research: children are prompted concerning the action with hands and bowing. Smiling, however, has been acquired through imitation of the partner, usually parents.

Different nations such as Estonians, Swedes, Englishmen and Germans may have different sociocultural patterns. Thus also the interactional competences of the people may differ.
Bi- and trilingual children acquire their different interactional competences through direct tutelage - prompting and through indirect tutelage - imitation and through the so called partner-pressure.

2. THEORETICAL FRAME

2.1. The theoretical frame of my paper starts with two concepts: cultureme and behavioreme. The mere fact that people greet each other is a cultureme, a culturally determined behavioral pattern; how they express it, is a behavioreme. The so called routine does not cover this necessary difference. A behavioreme is the realization of a cultureme. It can be nonverbal, verbal or both simultaneously. Thus in German culture: nodding the head only, or saying Guten Tag, literally "good day" or doing both and also shaking hands. An approach to the communicative and interactive behaviour of the child is necessarily an <u>integrative</u> approach, combining verbal and nonverbal factors in the <u>communicative act</u> (Oksaar, 1975a, 1981).

What happens, when a child is growing up in a bi- or trilingual environment having to learn different kinds of realizations of culturemes as his interactional competence? Theoretically there is the possibility of situational interferences.

<u>Situational interferences</u> are deviations from the norms of communicative behaviour (verbal and nonverbal) of one community through the influence of another. For example when German-English children use only one form of addressing - Du - instead of two - <u>Du</u> and <u>Sie</u>. It is necessary to differentiate between <u>linguistic</u> and <u>situational interferences</u>, because you may be linguistically correct, but situationally wrong when answering with <u>please</u> in English when somebody has said <u>thank you</u> to you. In German <u>bitte</u> "please" is correct in this situation. In language contact studies the concept of <u>interference</u> has usually been understood as <u>linguistic</u> interference. But this concept cannot account for interferences we find in <u>interactional settings</u>, therefore I have suggested (Oksaar 1976) to differentiate between <u>linguistic</u> and <u>situational interferences</u>.

3. POLITENESS CULTUREMES

3.1. Bilingual Environment
The bilingual children heard Swedish and Estonian or German and Swedish or German and English every day. There were 80 culturemegenerating communicative acts in every language together with fathers, mothers, and/or caregivers and acquaintances during a period of 6 months for thanking and 70 cultureme -generating communicative acts for greeting.

466

3.1.1. Thanking

Spontaneous thanking occured in 22% (105) of cases only (n = 477), being highest in case of the older children (age 4;6 - 7), who also prompted the younger ones. However, most spontaneous production of the behavioremes was observed in Estonian speaking environment, 62% of the spontaneous thankings (65 of 105), least in the English one 11%, followed by Swedish 13% and German 14%.

A bilingual child (4;2) with an Estonian mother and Swedish father thanked 33% more in equal situations (having received a toy or a cake; having been passed a thing etc.), when speaking Estonian than when speaking Swedish.

This fact is interesting, because adult Swedes thank in considerably more situations than Estonians, among other things both before receiving something and after. It shows that prompts from parents play an important role in the acquisition of the cultureme. Estonians prompted their children 46% more than Swedes, mothers and fathers equally. Swedish mothers prompted more (28%) than Swedish fathers.

There was no mixing of languages in this special cultureme, however, a few mixings of situations could be observed. One case concerning a German-English child (4;0): He gets a sausage at the butchers in the morning and starts eating. His mother says: (in German) What do you say? - Child: (silence). Mother: Don't you know what to say? Child: Good morning! - That is what to say first when you meet an acquaintance in the morning! The child behaved according to the rules of person and time, however, not observing the rules of action and acted upon.

As all of the children had learned their languages through the principle: one person - one language, there were hardly ever code switchings with linguistic interferences during the same communicative act. Only a few cases of situational interferences occured. 2 German-English children, age 4;6 and 5;2, sometimes used <u>please</u> in English according to the German model, where the English model has silence (or the American one <u>you are welcome</u>). Type: When handing over a newspaper to his father and he said <u>thank you</u> the child answered <u>please</u>.

3.1.2. Greeting

Spontaneous greeting occured in 31% (137) of cases (n = 422), there were, however, no such environmental differences, as was the case with thanking. Spontaneous greeting was highest in case of the older children (4 - 7), the younger ones (2 - 4) had 12% more spontaneous greetings than thanking.

What concerns <u>nonverbal</u> behavioremes of the politeness cultureme, the younger children (age 2 - 4) generally did not want to shake hands when greeting, though they were prompted to do so (only 2 children did so in 42% of the greeting situations). The cultureme <u>greeting</u> requires, when speaking Estonian or German, in many situations also hand-shaking. Children were prompted to shake hands, but the younger ones, up to 4 often refused. However, the cultureme <u>greeting</u> also requires that people usually have eye contact and smile or at least do not look angry. Pre-school children seem to learn these features mostly by imitating their parents or caregivers. They were actively prompted what to do with their eyes, when greeting somebody, only by Estonian parents: in Estonian <u>vaata otsa</u>, literally "look at the top".

3.2. Trilingual Environment

The <u>trilingual</u> children heard <u>Estonian</u>, <u>Swedish</u> and <u>German</u> or <u>Swedish-English</u> and <u>German</u> every day. I have in earlier publications (Oksaar 1975b; 1978) analyzed the <u>functionality</u> of their <u>code switching</u> and the <u>creative aspects</u> of their <u>interferences</u>. Concerning the behavioremes of politeness culturemes there were no significant differences between bilingual and trilingual children. Children older than 3;6 - 4 years, were accomplishing more items of thanking and greeting than the younger ones.

3.3. Awareness of the Politeness culturemes

3.3.1. Little research has been done on the children's knowledge of sociocultural and pragmatic rules for language use. When Kirsten 1;9 says in German (fi: daŋk), that is <u>vielen Dank</u> "thank you very much" when someone offers her something, this need not yet be the result of her awareness of this interaction rule in the realm of politeness. From the analysis of our corpus it can be seen that, while playing with their dolls and teddy bears, Estonian, Swedish and German speaking children around the age of 2;6 to 3 were all aware of the cultureme <u>greeting</u> and realized it through the most common verbal behavioremes in their respective languages: Estonian <u>tere</u>, Swedish <u>goddag</u>, German <u>guten Tag</u>. When Christina, age 2;6, prompts her Swedish doll: <u>säg goddag</u> "say hello", this shows that a certain knowledge of the interaction rules may be present. More information was gained through the following study of pragmatic understanding with 10 German-English bilingual children (2;5 - 7;0) in Hamburg. They were shown four teddy bears, which all looked the same. The teddies asked (on tape) in German, in different ways for an apple and thanked, except one of them, again in different ways, after having received the apple.

The children had to decide which had asked the nicest, and which had said <u>thank you</u> in the nicest way after he had received the apple. Eight children between the age of 2;7 and 4;2 found the indicative sentences with German <u>bitte</u> and <u>danke</u> the nicest. Conjunctive sentences with <u>könnte</u> "could" and dürfte "may" such as <u>dürfte ich einen Apfel bekommen</u>, indicative in <u>English</u> "may I have an apple" or <u>Ich bedanke mich</u> "I thank you", were reacted to only by children older than 5. Non-use of thank you was considered bad by 90% of the children. The youngest 2;5 did not react to non-use of the politeness routine.

Three weeks later the same procedure was carried through in English. There were interesting differences: requests such as may I have an apple were found nicest also by children age 3;7 upwards.

3.3.2. Concerning nonverbal behaviour, 10 German-English bilingual children, 5 boys, 5 girls, age between 7 and 8 years, were asked, in single conversations, whether they have to shake hands, when greeting somebody in German. The answer was yes, only one boy did not know. Three weeks later they were asked the same question in English, the answer from all was no.

4. INDIRECT REQUESTS

4.1. The use and understanding of indirect requests is an important part of interactional competence. There is little empirical research done in this area. Clark and Lucy (1975) were among the first to study adult comprehension of different types of indirect requests. Children's abilities in this area have been looked upon primarily from the point of view of productive competence. One of the recent studies of children's comprehension of various specific types of indirect requests by Carrell (1981), which is carried out in an experimental mode, showed that children, age between 4 and 7 years, are able to comprehend a wide variety of indirect requests, that there is a general developmental pattern of acquisition, and that the relationship between request type and ease of comprehension is strikingly similar for both children and adults. This experimental approach, however, has to be extended to testing children's comprehension of indirect requests also in "contextualized settings, in order to begin to synthesize the 'decontextualized' experimental findings with the contextualized, observational data" (Carrell 1981:344). The current study focuses on comprehension of indirect requests in natural contextualized settings.

4.2. So far most research has been carried out on the basis of the English language only. Furthermore, no investigations have been made with bi- and trilingual children. The question arises: Do the general developmental pattern vary in various languages? How well does a bi- or trilingual child aged 4 to 7 understand the same type of indirect requests in his various languages?

My data in <u>contextualized settings</u> (87 indirect request-generating communicative acts in every language) show that there is a difference between Indoeuropean and Nonindoeuropean (in our study Estonian, a Finno-Ugric language) languages. Certain kind of declarative forms seemed to be more difficult to understand than interrogative forms. The Estonian question <u>kas sa pead ukse lahti tegema</u>? "must you open the door?" as an indirect request "please don't open the door" was understood by all Swedish-Estonian children and responded by action. The declarative form: <u>uks on lahti</u> "the door is open", was correctly understood only by the older children (aged 5 to 7 years), and acted upon: the door was closed.

However, when addressed in Swedish (on another occasion): <u>maten är färdig</u> "the meal is ready", also the 4 year old followed the indirect request. Methodologically it is important to state that not the <u>type</u> of the indirect request alone, but also the <u>token</u> is important. The frequency of the <u>tokens</u> in the environment of the child seems to be a basic factor for their acquirement. The child learns behavioral tokens matching to situations first and afterwards the types.

Results, based on English language only and

on tests in laboratory situations, stating that "interrogative forms of indirect requests are more difficult than declarative forms", and "conveyed negative requests are more difficult than corresponding conveyed positive requests" (Carrell 1981:329) must thus be relativized in the light of data from other languages and natural settings.

5. SUMMARY

This study has shown that the verbal and the nonverbal part of a behavioreme are both important in case of the politeness culturemes. They are "taught and drilled", often using indirect requests. There were no significant differences between bi- and trilingual children; children older than 3;6 - 4 performed more items of the total behavioreme of the politeness cultureme than the younger ones. Spontaneous thanking occured in 22% of cases, spontaneous greeting in 31%. There were only a few situational interferences, and hardly ever code switchings with linguistic interferences during the same communicative act. Already the 2;5 year old were aware of the politeness culturemes in the sociocultural frame of their various languages. The microlevel of analysis showed interesting differences in verbal and nonverbal behaviour.

There were separate models of prompting: generally mothers prompted more than fathers. Estonian mothers and fathers prompted their children most, Swedish fathers the least. Children were prompted not only concerning the verbal behavioremes of a cultureme, but also the nonverbal ones: action with hands and bowing, but not smiling. Only Estonian parents told their children to have eye contact when greeting somebody.

The analysis of comprehension of indirect requests in natural settings showed that not the type of the indirect request alone, but also the token is important. In the light of data from other languages than English and from non-laboratory settings, we get new results in this field. A comprehensive analysis will be reported (Oksaar in preparation).

NOTES

1) For information about these projects and methodological questions see Oksaar (1980) and (1981).
2) For the discussion of communicative and interactional competence see Oksaar (1977:138-141).

REFERENCES

Bühler, K. (1934). Sprachtheorie. Jena. Gustav Fischer.
Carrell, P.L. (1981). Children's understanding of indirect requests: comparing child and adult comprehension. J. Child Lang. 8, 329-345.
Clark, H.H. and Lucy, P. (1975). Understanding what is meant from what is said: a study of conversationally conveyed requests. JVLVB 14, 56-72.
Gleason, J. Berko and Weintraub, S. (1976). The acquisition of routines in child language. Lang. Soc. 5, 129-136.
Greif, E. Blank and Gleason, J. Berko (1980). Hi, thanks, and goodbye: More routine information. Lang. Soc. 9, 159-166.
Jakobson, R. (1960). Linguistics and poetics, in Th.A. Sebeok, (ed.) Style in Language. New York, 350-377.
Ochs, E. and Schieffelin, B.B. (eds.) (1979). Developmental pragmatics. New York. San Francisco. London. Academic Press.
Oksaar, E. (1975a). Spracherwerb und Kindersprache. Pädolinguistische Perspektiven (Language acquisition and child language. Paedolinguistic perspectives). Zeitschrift

für Pädagogik 21, 719-743.
Oksaar, E. (1975b). Code switching as an interactional strategy for developing bilingual competence. Word 27, Child Language, 377-385.
Oksaar, E. (1976). Interference and bilingual interaction, in G. Nickel (ed.) Proceedings of the 4th International Conference of Applied Linguistics, Vol. 2, Stuttgart.
Oksaar, E. (1977). Spracherwerb im Vorschulalter. Einführung in die Pädolinguistik. Stuttgart. Kohlhammer. Engl. translation (1982). Language acquisition in the early years. An introduction to paedolinguistics. London. Batsford Academic.
Oksaar, E. (1978). On becoming trilingual, in F.C.C. Peng and W. von Raffler-Engel (eds.) Language acquisition and developmental kinesics. Hiroshima. Bunka Hyoron.
Oksaar, E. (1980). The multilingual language acquisition project. Intern. Rev. of Appl. Psychology 29. 268-269.
Oksaar, E. (1981). Linguistic and pragmatic awareness of monolingual and multilingual children, in Ph.S. Dale and D. Ingram (eds.) Child language - an international perspective. Baltimore. University Park Press.

A Comparison of Order of Grammar
Acquisition between French Immersion
Students and Francophones*

Robert R. Roy
Faculty of Education
University of British Columbia

The order of acquisition of the grammatical elements of first or second languages has been the object of numerous studies in the last decade. Many of these studies have served to infer learner strategies, to reflect cognitive development, to reveal the logic of a language, or to determine how the situation affects learning. The relative order of learning, order of importance, or order of difficulty has been assessed through frequency studies,[1] through cognitive development studies,[2] or error analyses.[3] The result of the growing amount of evidence is the conclusion that there is in natural language learning situations a nearly universal order of acquisition of phonology, morphology, and even syntax, a conclusion which is not without its detractors.[4] According to Ervin-Tripp, there is even evidence to show that second-language order of acquisition in a natural situation conforms to first-language order of acquisition. "... We can reject, at least, the hypothesis that children's interpretations of second-language sentences are directly processed through a translator."[5] It is self-evident, however, that in a formal language teaching situation the order of acquisition can be controlled by selective experience.

If by definition language acquisition in a natural situation is functional, school instruction can provide a variety of blends of functional and formal instruction.[6] The first emphasizes the ability to communicate, to function linguistically in a natural situation; the second, the ability to demonstrate primarily control of the elements of a language. In the formal instructional setting the ability to communicate may be of secondary importance.

Immersion, or language-switch instruction, a second-language instruction strategy which has gained a wide acceptance in Canada in the last two decades, has been shown to be effective in developing functional competence in French.[7] It is claimed that instruction in an immersion setting is distinguished from traditional second-language instruction in that it creates a functional setting to achieve its purpose.[8] This study undertook to determine whether the order of acquisition of certain grammatical elements of French is the same for children learning French as a second-language in an immersion setting as it is for native-speakers in a natural situation.

A sample of language for analysis was obtained from a group of thirty-seven speakers of English who had almost completed their grade three in immersion and were therefore 8-9 years old. They represent a non-selected population which opted for immersion in grade one after taking kindergarten in English. All instruction in grades one and two was in French and also in grade three except for an hour a day given to English language arts. The community in which the children live is anglophone. About half of the school population was instructed in English and the other half was in French immersion.

The instrument used to elicit the samples of speech was L'évaluation de syntaxe bilingue (ESB)[9] adapted from The Bilingual Syntax Measure.[10]

The test was administered individually in private to ten students whose names had been drawn at random five from each class. The conversations were recorded, transcribed, and analyzed according to a method adapted from Dulay and Burt.[11] In responding to the questions, the child creates "obligatory occasions" --

contexts that require the use of certain morphemes e.g. a present tense marker, a feminine singular third person possessive adjective. Each of the obligatory occasions is assessed and scored 2, if correct; 1, if partly correct; and 0, if incorrect. For example an article which represents a correct definite/indefinite distinction and is correct according to number but not for gender is scored 1, a verb which is correct semantically but is not properly inflected is scored 1 also. The total thus produced for each grammatical element by the whole student sample is divided by the number of obligatory occurrences multiplied by two. The quotient is multiplied by one hundred to produce a group score for each element. A group score of 100 would represent correct production of the element in question by every member of the group. A score of 90 or more is defined as mastery. Contrary to Dulay and Burt who counted only examples produced by subjects who used the functor five or more times, in this case the investigator retained all the occurrences. A group mean was used because Dulay and Burt found that results obtained by this method were not significantly different from using an average of individual scores. A cogent criticism and defence of Dulay and Burt's study has been reported by Tarone.[12] The Dulay-Burt technique effectively avoids the possibility that the kinds of structures produced is an artifact of the test since it makes conclusions only about the mastery of the forms used and makes no statement about the mastery of forms not encountered in obligatory occasions.

By the method described above it was possible to generate a score for a number of grammatical elements produced by the immersion students and to determine whether or not they were mastered and to identify those which were still farthest away from mastery. Bautier-Castaing[13] as a result of the administration of the test to 60 francophone 4-5 and 7-8 year olds identified the structures that had been mastered by four year old francophones, by eight year old francophones, and not yet by eight year old francophones thus producing an order of acquisition of the mother tongue in a natural situation. Bautier-Castaing did not report how she quantified her results.

Verbs

Four verb forms were used with sufficient frequency for analysis: the present indicative, the past indefinite, the infinitive after a verb, and the infinitive after a preposition. Of the 35 verbs used, 17 were irregular and 30 are in Gougenheim's list of the 1500 most frequently used words.[14] Regular and irregular verbs were not distinguished in the analysis. One would have to analyze production before age 9 to distinguish between the acquisition of regular and irregular verbs in the present indicative.

Table 1

Order of Verbs Used in Gougenheim's Frequency List

34	aller	19	faire	55	pouvoir
x	appartenir	59	falloir	77	prendre
422	apporter	x	habiller	216	regarder
2	avoir	438	habiter	x	ressembler
517	chanter	205	laisser	529	rire
x	crier	689	laver	717	sauter
883	danser	166	manger	304	tomber
28	dire	585	manquer	347	vivre
105	donner	85	mettre	43	voir
417	dormir	x	mouiller	64	vouloir
508	enlever	1023	nager		
1	être	1052	nettoyer		

x - not in frequency of first 1500.

As reported in Table 2 a score of 94 indicates the subjects have mastered the present indicative of the verbs they used. Surprisingly the evidence points to a mastery of the present tense equal to that of 8 year old native speakers but does not exclude the possibility, however, that the range of verbs used by native speakers is greater.

Table 2

Verb Mastery Scores

	Obligatory Occurrences	Incomplete	Wrong Inflection	Correct Inflection	Raw Score	Score
Present indicative	234	5	16	213	442	94
Past indefinite	35	-	11	24	59	84
Infinitive after verb	41	2	8	31	70	85
Infinitive after preposition	14	1	1	12	25	89

The subjects are approaching mastery of the past indefinite tense (84). Verbs conjugated with être are the main problem that remains.

The use of the infinitive after a verb (85) and after a preposition (89) approaches mastery but lags considerably behind native speakers who master this element by age 4.

Subordinate Clauses

In the use of complex sentences, the grade 3 immersion students are more like 8 year olds than 4 year olds. In the sample, 11 adjectival clauses beginning with qui or que were used and 99 adverbial clauses beginning with parce que. All of the subordinate clauses were appropriate in a discourse sense; the distinction between qui and que was always correctly made;

finally, parce que was used correctly except for elision in 8% of the cases. Some of the failures to elide are due to hesitation. The questions by calling for the use of subordinate clauses forced the respondents to show their mastery of those structures. A younger child would have a way to answer without using a subordinate clause.

Pronouns

The third person subject pronouns (il, elle) were almost always used correctly in the singular (99) except for a rare mistake in gender. The plural forms (ils, elles) still showed some mistakes in gender or number (83). French children who reportedly master person and number first have mastered gender by age 8.

Ce was used correctly in a simple sentence (94) as do French 4 year olds. The following are examples of the structures used:

>   c'est une fleur
>   c'est sale
>   c'est tout sale
>   c'est dans l'eau
>   c'est le gros
>   c'est le chapeau du monsieur
>   c'est la maison de _____.

However, ça/cela was used incorrectly in the few cases observed.

Possessives

Third person possessive adjectives are mastered (95) but the few gender mistakes indicate that unlike native speakers, second language learners are slower to acquire gender than number.

Descriptive Adjectives

With native speakers the gender of

descriptive adjectives, is mastered by 4, number by 8, and position after age 9. The performance score of 70 obtained by the grade 3 students indicates non-mastery generally but the mistakes are mainly of gender. The L2 learner is different from the L1 learner in that it is the gender that he masters last. Could it be because the plural is rarely marked in the adjectives used? As for position there were no occurrences of adjectives whose meaning varies with position.

Articles

The article (definite, indefinite, partitive) is also almost mastered (89) insofar as obligatory/defi/indefinite use is concerned. No mistakes in number or elision were found. Gender accounted for most errors. In this respect native speakers differ from second language learners - they master number after gender. In the Bautier-Castaing study children mastered the contraction of the article with de after age 4 and with à after age 8. In this sample neither contraction has been mastered but control of the de contraction gave a score of 50 compared to 31 for the à contraction; order of acquisition is therefore the same for both groups.

In conclusion can it be said that the order of acquisition of selected grammatical elements by L2 learners in a functional immersion setting corresponds to the order of acquisition of the mother tongue in infancy? The answer seems to be at least partly, no. Some of the difference which may be related to the different starting age and the associated cognitive difference, may account for the rapid mastery of the complex sentence or of the irregular verbs, others related for example to gender may be mainly due to an experience differential.

To summarize, Bautier-Castaing indicates that the present tense of irregular verbs is acquired after the present tense of regular verbs,

Table 3

Comparison of Order of Acquisition of Grammar

L1 learners	L2 learners
present indicative regular infinitive after a verb infinitive after a preposition past indefinite --- before --- present indicative irregular	present indicative regular present indicative irregular --- before --- past indefinite infinitive after verb infinitive after a preposition
present indicative regular infinitive after verb infinitive after preposition --- before --- subordinate clauses	subordinate clauses --- before --- past indefinite infinitive after a verb infinitive after a preposition
gender of articles, possessive and descriptive adjectives --- before --- number	number of articles, possessive and descriptive adjectives --- before --- gender
contraction of article with de --- before --- with à	contraction of article with de --- before --- with à
subject pronoun number --- before --- subject pronoun gender	subject pronoun singular --- before --- subject pronoun plural

the past indefinite, and the infinitive after a verb or a preposition all of which are mastered before age 4 by the native speaker. The L2 learner in this sample mastered the past indefinite, and the infinitive after the present regular and irregular.

The control of subordinate clauses by the L2 speaker is the same as for an 8 year old L1 speaker. Compared to the verbs, the use of subordinate clauses is acquired sooner by the immersion students. The francophones mastered the present indicative, the infinitive, and the past indefinite before mastering the subordinate clause.

For articles and descriptive adjectives the L2 speaker acquires the gender last while the L1 speaker acquires number last. Contractions of the articles with de are acquired before contractions with à by both groups but they are mastered considerably later by L2 learners.

For subject pronouns, L1 speakers master gender last while L2 speakers master the plural after the singular.

It can be hypothesized that age, cognitive maturity explains in part the different order of acquisition of immersion students. The 9 year old may be better at distinguishing the non-conformity of the irregular verb; the subordinate clause is no longer beyond his maturity.

Another possible explanation is that immersion instruction is not completely like functional natural learning. The range of language used may be smaller than in a natural situation. The teacher likely takes corrective or avoidance measures to deal with problems which he feels should have been overcome earlier.

Another persistent problem has to do

with the mastery of gender. Generalizations formed at an earlier age by anglophones do seem to make them unattentive to some gender signs.

But the order of acquisition for native speakers and for primary school children in French immersion is generally not the same. One cannot tell whether the instruction plan should be changed to bring the two to conformity or whether the differences are plainly to be accepted.

Footnotes

[1] Jacques Vachon. A Proposal for Structural Analysis of the Language Development of the Child as a Base for Learning a Mother Tongue. Rapport non-publié présenté au Ministère de l'Education de l'Ontario au sujet de recherches effectuées dans le cadre de Contractual Research. Ottawa. 1973. 670 pp.

[2] L. Desjarlais et A. Lazar. Etude du potentiel d'apprentissage des concepts grammaticaux chez l'enfant de 9 à 13 ans. Editions de l'Université d'Ottawa. 1976.

[3] M. F. Buteau. Student Errors in the Learning of French as a Second Language. I R A L. 1970, 7, 2. 133-46.

[4] J. de Villiers and P. de Villiers. A Cross-Sectional Study of the Acquisition of Grammatical Morphemes in Child Speech. Journal of Psycholinguistic Research 2. 1973.

[5] Susan M. Ervin-Tripp. Is Second Language Learning Like the First? Second Language Acquisition: A Book of Readings. E. M. Hatch, editor. Rowley: Newbury House Publishers, 1978. 190-205.

[6] H. H. Stern. The formal-functional distinction in language pedagogy: a conceptual clarification. Fifth International Congress of Applied Linguistics: Montreal, 1978. mimeo.

[7] Fred Genesee. Scholastic Effects of French Immersion: An Overview after Ten Years. Interchange. 1978-9, 9, 4. 20-29.

[8] Robert R. Roy. Immersion defined by strategy. The Canadian Modern Language Review. 1980, 36, March. 403-407.

[9] Elisabeth Bautier-Castaing. Acquisition comparée de la syntaxe du français par des enfants francophones et non francophones: étude expérimentale de quelques stratégies d'apprentissage. Etudes de linguistique appliquée. 1977, 27, juillet-septembre. 19-41.

[10] Marina K. Burt, Heidi C. Dulay, and Eduardo Hernández. Harcourt, Brace, Jovanovich, inc. 1973.

[11] Heidi C. Dulay and Marina K. Burt. Natural Sequences in Child Second Language Acquisition. Working Papers on Bilingualism. 1974, 3, June. 44-67.

[12] E. Tarone. A Discussion of the Dulay and Burt Studies. Working Papers on Bilingualism. 1974, 4. 57-70.

[13] Les théories syntaxiques et l'enseignement. Le français dans le monde. 1977, 129, mai-juin. 54-59.

[14] G. Gougenheim et al. L'élaboration du français fondamental (1er degré). Paris: Didier, 1964.

ON THE PREDICTIVE VALUE OF THE LINGUISTIC LEVEL AND
PRIMARY SYMPTOMS CONFIRMED IN PRE-SCHOOL AS REGARDS
SUBSEQUENT SCHOOL AND LINGUISTIC PERFORMANCES

Eila Alahuhta
University of Jyväskylä
Finland

INTRODUCTION

The present investigation is the follow-up study for the research reported in Tokyo in 1978. The subjects of the earlier investigation were a sample of 100 preschoolers (aged 5;9 to 6;9). They were tested linguistically and divided accordingly into four speech level groups (I, II, III, IV). In addition, their primary abilities were tested by the BMA test battery in the areas of auditory discrimination, spatial orientation and structural ability, and motor orientation ability. The results revealed significant relations between low speech level and the difficulties occurring on the primary ability tests and the fact of belonging to the low Apgar group. The test subjects were divided into different groups according to the Apgar score given right after the test subject's birth: 10 Apgar, 9 Apgar and 8 Apgar (Alahuhta 1979, 1980). The material for the follow-up study was collected in November-December, 1980. At that time the test subjects were in Grade IV.

PROBLEM AREA

The problem was to investigate whether there is any relation between the variables of the primary ability level confirmed at preschool and the variables collected four years later relating to school achievement and school adaptability. In addition, there was a desire to clarify whether there occurs any disparity between the different speech level groups, on the other hand, in regard to the present state of mastering the written language or any other school ability which is regarded to have connection with the above mentioned primary ability variables. The reason for that was to make it possible to draw conclusions about the prognostic value of the different speech level groups and Apgar groups regarding the future mastering of written language, and other school ability.

The first task was to find out where the test subjects now attended school. This mapping was relatively successful, in other words, information was obtained in about 90 percent of the cases. However, failure to answer was remarkably bigger as far as concerned the filling out of the questionnaire sent to the teachers, or the return percentage of the questionnaire presented to the parents. Nevertheless, information about the marks in different school subjects, and the dictation test result was obtained from about 70 pupils. The questionnaires sent to the teachers revealed information on about 60 pupils.

HYPOTHESES

The following hypotheses were derived from the research problems:
1. The preschool speech level is related to school achievement and linguistic performance, and school adaptability in Grades III-IV.
2. The preschool Apgar group is related to school achievement and linguistic performance, and school adaptability in Grades III-IV.
3. The preschool primary symptoms (measured by the BMA test) are related to school achievement and linguistic performance, and school adaptability.

RESEARCH PERFORMANCE

Serving as a starting point for data collection were the basic data collected from test subjects of preschool age. By sending the questionnaire to the teachers, information was obtained about the spring semester school marks in Grade III and the teachers' evaluation in the fall semester in Grade IV regarding the pupils' linguistic (23 variables), motor (28 variables), spatial and musical ability (9 variables) and the pupils' adaptability and ability to perform the school work (30 variables).

In addition, a questionnaire was sent to the parents in order to obtain information about the child's interests, school attitudes and certain behaviour patterns, among other things.

The fact that there was less information available than expected limited the data handling. The conclusion was to use a one-way analysis of variance in order to establish the differences between the observation groups formed at preschool (speech level I, II, III and IV as well as the Apgar groups of 10 Apgar, 9 Apgar and 8 Apgar). In order to detect possible connections between the primary symptoms tested by the BMA test and the information obtained from home as well as between school achievement and linguistic, motor ability etc. evaluated by the teachers, Pearson's correlation coefficients were calculated. Factor analysis was performed on the available material regarding the present school situation.

RESULTS

Speech level groups

One-way analysis of variance revealed the following most significant differences between the various preschool speech level groups (Table 1-2) regarding some variables which describe school achievement. The average in reading marks in the best speech level group (I) was 8.18 and in the weakest one (IV) 6.50. The difference was thus quite noticeable. As far as the whole analysis is concerned, the F ratio was 4.36 which meant a statistical significance on a one per cent risk level. An equally significant difference was detected in the groups in regards to the use of scissors in delicate assignments ($p < .01$). A distinct difference of a similar nature was revealed among the various speech level groups in movements ($p < .02$), in the ability to choose independently, in arts, in the neatness of handwriting, in realistic drawings of human shapes as well as in writing. It seemed that the weak speech level is thus especially connected with the future performance in reading and motor ability.

The Apgar groups

As concerns the Apgar groups, the variance analysis gave the most significant differences between the groups in writing marks (Table 3). The average of the writing marks was in the 8 Apgar group 6.57 and in the 10 Apgar group 8.06. There was a distinct difference between the groups, and the F ratio for the whole analysis was 4.58. Consequently, the significance is in the order of $p < .01$. There were other significant differences in physical endurance ($p < .02$), in mathematics and in arts ($p < .05$). In molding ability and in dictation writing as well as in pupils' taste for writing and in the realism of spatial relations in drawings, there turned out to be similar differences on the average level. However, regarding significance, the differences did not represent even the level of

TABLE 1. Comparison of school achievement in the various speech level groups based on the school marks

Variable	I speech level group N=34		II speech level group N=		III speech level group N=		IV speech level group N=		One-way variance analysis	
	x̄	s	x̄	s	x̄	s	x̄	s	F (F prob)	p<
Reading	8.18	.30	8.19	.83	7.80	1.23	6.50	.58	4.36 (.0073)	.01++
Arts	8.00	.74	7.52	.51	7.70	.95	7.25	.50	2.98 (.0378)	.05+
Writing	7.97	1.17	7.61	1.03	7.30	1.16	6.75	.96	2.11 (.1067)	-

TABLE 2. Comparison of school achievement in the various speech level groups based on information obtained from the questionnaire

Variable	I speech level group			II speech level group			III speech level group			IV speech level group			One-way variance analysis	
	x̄	s	N	x̄	s	N	x̄	s	N	x̄	s	N	F (F prob)	p<
Use of scissors in delicate assignments	2.42	.86	26	3.00	.85	12	2.33	.87	9	4.00	.00	3	4.35 (.0089)	.01++
Movements	2.64	1.16	28	2.79	1.05	14	1.78	.85	9	3.75	.96	4	3.42 (.0240)	.02+
Ability to choose independently	1.72	.96	29	2.33	.82	15	1.75	.89	8	3.00	1.41	4	3.12 (.0343)	.05+
Neatness of handwriting	2.47	1.25	30	3.12	1.17	17	2.11	.50	9	3.25	.60	6	2.69 (.0548)	.05+
Realistic drawings of human shapes	2.46	.88	28	3.14	.95	14	2.67	1.22	9	3.67	.58	3	2.58 (.0630)	-

TABLE 3. Comparison of school achievement in the various Apgar groups as based on information about the school marks and the questionnaire

Variable	10 Apgar			9 Apgar			8 Apgar			One-way variance analysis	
	x̄	s	N	x̄	s	N	x̄	s	N	F (F prob)	p<
Writing	8.06	.85	16	7.57	1.15	41	6.57	1.27	7	4.58 (.014)	.01++
Enduring good shape	2.50	1.31	12	2.45	.96	31	3.83	.75		4.59 (.015)	.02+
Mathematics	8.13	.89	16	7.76	1.34	41	6.71	1.38	7	3.14 (.050)	.05+
Arts	8.06	.77	16	7.76	.70	41	7.29	.49	7	3.07 (.054)	.05+
Dictation test	8.31	1.25	13	7.33	1.55	24	6.60	1.52	5	3.07 (.058)	
Molding abilities	2.55	.73	9	2.50	.76	20	3.40	.55	5	3.16 (.057)	
Pupil's taste for writing	2.13	.92	15	2.18	.98	33	3.17	1.47		2.56 (.088)	
Sense of spatial relations in drawings	2.25	.82	12	2.71	1.08	28	3.33	.82	6	2.50 (.094)	

$p < .05$, but the p-value was still $< .10$. To belong in the weaker Apgar group, even if the group still represented the relatively high level of the 8 Apgar, seemed thus to mean a risk to perform poorer at school than the pupils with higher Apgar scores, not only in writing but as well in some other tasks presupposing motor and spatial ability.

The girls and boys

The research performed at preschool revealed a linguistic inferiority on the part of the boys as compared with the girls. In addition, it appeared that the weaker the speech level, the larger the number of boys concerned. Thus it was naturally interesting to make comparisons between the girls and boys, based on information obtained from school marks and the questionnaire (Table 4). It became evident that in the neatness of handwriting, conscientiousness, music, arts, in the shape and quality of the letters, and in behaviour the difference between the sexes was in terms of statistics significantly in favor of the girls ($p < .001$).

A similar type of difference was found also in the rhythmic movements ($p < .01$), in the coherence of writing ($p < .02$), in the pupil's taste for writing, in the ability to draw by pattern, in singing ability, in the handling of tools, in the ability to use small and capital letters as well as in the concentration and self-restraint ability ($p < .05$). It can thus be verified that the boys were poorer than the girls in some tasks which require motor, auditory, and spatial ability. The results were quite logical, for the previous research results have shown that motor, auditory, and spatial abilities are related to linguistic ability level.

On the relation of the primary symptom complex as verified at preschool to future school achievement and linguistic ability

While calculating Pearson's correlation coefficients (by the BMA test) between the primary ability variables verified at preschool and the spring semester school marks in Grade III as well as the results obtained in Grade IV from the questionnaire sent to the teachers, the following correlations, among others, were established (Table 5). Examined closely were those test variables which in the previous studies (Alahuhta 1976, 1979,

TABLE 4. Comparison of the girls' and boys' school achievement as based on the school marks and the questionnaire

Variable	Girls			Boys			One-way variance analysis		
	$\bar{x}$	s	N	$\bar{x}$	s.	N	F	(F prob)	p <
Neatness of handwriting	2.12	.82	33	3.30	1.0	27	24.20	(.000)	.001+++
Conscientiousness	9.18	.66	33	8.38	.95	34	16.20	(.000)	.001+++
Music	8.37	.88	35	7.63	.83	36	13.02	(.001)	.001+++
Arts	8.03	.66	35	7.50	.70	36	10.70	(.002)	.002+++
Behaviour	9.69	.47	32	9.09	.98	35	9.93	(.003)	.003+++
Shape and quality of the letters	2.33	.85	33	3.07	1.0	27	9.23	(.003)	.003+++
Rhythmic movements	2.43	1.03	28	3.04	.62	24	6.42	(.014)	.01++
Drawing by pattern	2.16	.94	25	2.83	1.04	20	5.43	(.024)	.02+
Coherence in writing	2.33	.99	33	3.00	1.14	27	5.86	(.018)	.02+
Pupil's taste for writing	2.03	.88	33	2.63	1.14	27	5.22	(.026)	.05+
Singing ability	2.00	1.00	29	2.57	.79	23	4.92	(.031)	.05+
Molding abilities	2.45	.67	22	3.00	.87	17	4.92	(.033)	.05+
Concentration ability	1.70	1.05	30	2.27	1.00	26	4.25	(.044)	.05+
Adherence to the rules	1.43	.68	30	1.85	.83	26	4.17	(.046)	.05+
Handling of tools	2.40	.89	30	2.94	.77	16	4.13	(.048)	.05+
Ability to use small and capital letters	1.91	.91	33	2.44	1.15	27	4.02	(.049)	.05+
Ability to self-restrain	1.67	.84	30	2.15	1.00	16	3.88	(.054)	.05+
Writing speed	2.30	.92	33	2.93	1.23	27	5.00	(.029)	.05+

1981) have proved to be mapping the primary abilities in which the children with linguistic problems differed most significantly from those with no linguistic problems. The next step was to examine whether the poor primary ability verified at preschool has any correlation with future school success and linguistic ability level.

The test variables subject to examination represent three subareas: auditory discrimination, spatial orientation and disposition ability, and tactual discrimination and motor orientation ability (mastering of body image).

Both items of auditory discrimination measure the discrimination ability of temporal rhythm. In the first task, the rhythm patterns to be heard have to be repeated in motor movements. In the second task, these rhythm patterns coincided with those rhythm patterns which symbolize them and are to be read.

TABLE 5. Intercorrelations of primary ability as tested by the BMA test **in preschool and of some school ability variables** as collected in grades III-IV

(Preschool age) Variables of the BMA test	Reading	Writing	Music	Arts and crafts	Drawing	Physical activity	Mathematics	Willingness to write	Faultless writing	Ability to write short essays	Willingness to read	Ability to act by the written instructions	Sense of rhythm as evaluated by the teacher	Having therapy in reading-writing difficulties	Willingness to play at school	Expressive speaking	Understanding the verbal instructions	Unaffected speaking	Clearness of drawings	Spatial relations	Drawing by the pattern or instructions	Handling of tools
					School marks (grade III)				Results from the teachers' questionnaire (grade IV)													
Auditory discrimination																						
Repetition of rhythm			.27/.01				.16/.10						.24/.05		.19/.10			.24/.05			.23/.10	
Rhythm (to read as heard)	.29/.01	.31/.001	.25/.02		.21/.05		.39/.001	.26/.02	.31/.01	.28/.02	.32/.01	.26/.01	.37/.001		.35/.003	.33/.01	.44/.001	.43/.001	.27/.02	.38/.003	.34/.01	
Spatial orientation and composition																						
Sector	.16/.10	.17/.10		.22/.05	.24/.02	.37/.001	.30/.01		.18/.10		.23/.05	.28/.02	.20/.10	.27/.02	.29/.01	.27/.02	.32/.01	.26/.02	.26/.03	.25/.05	.20/.10	
Pierons squares	.18/.10	.20/.05	.16/.10	.30/.01	.20/.05		.30/.01	.25/.05	.29/.01		.23/.05	.28/.02	.20/.10	.29/.02		.17/.10				.23/.05	.37/.003	.29/.05
Semicircles and straight lines	.26/.01	.28/.01			.25/.02	.21/.05	.29/.01	.25/.05	.25/.05	.29/.01	.25/.05	.28/.02		.21/.06	.32/.01			.25/.03			.20/.10	
Mosaics to be completed	.35/.001	.38/.001	.27/.01	.20/.05	.21/.05	.32/.001	.45/.001	.18/.10	.26/.02	.27/.02	.25/.05	.27/.02	.28/.02	.21/.05	.30/.01			.19/.10	.29/.02		.25/.05	
Curves to be completed	.26/.01	.32/.001			.24/.02	.38/.001	.36/.001	.20/.10	.26/.02	.35/.003	.34/.01	.44/.001	.22/.05	.23/.05	.21/.05			.30/.01	.17/.10	.31/.01	.32/.01	.35/.01
Right-angled triangle: arrangement equilateral		.24/.02		.29/.01	.34/.001	.18/.10	.30/.01	.35/.003	.33/.01	.46/.001	.31/.01	.35/.003	.20/.10	.28/.02	.23/.05			.26/.05	.21/.05	.43/.001	.40/.001	.26/.05
Equilateral triangle: arrangement		.11		.41/.001	.29/.01		.24/.02			.20/.10	.20/.10	.21/.10		.21/.06				.18/.10		.39/.002	.38/.003	.33/.01
Spatial position — bottle glass	.16/.10	.16/.10		.17/.10			.20/.05		.21/.05	.17/.10		.32/.01	.26/.02		.41/.001			.19/.10	.24/.05	.34/.01	.30/.02	.23/.10
Spatial position — glass		.10		.10														.10	.05	.01	.02	.10
Spatial position — cheeses		.26/.02			.22/.05	.24/.02	.17/.10		.32/.01	.27/.02	.26/.02	.29/.01		.26/.02		.28		.28/.02	.31/.01	.40/.001	.29/.05	
Completion of profile				.15	.34/.001			.18/.10	.20/.10	.18/.10	.26/.02	.22/.05		.32/.01		.32/.01	.28/.02	.33/.01	.31/.01	.29/.02	.31/.02	.37/.01
Motor orientation body image																						
Tactile discrimination			.16/.10				.21/.05	.29/.02	.37/.002	.35/.003	.24/.05	.23/.05		.39/.001					.26/.03	.37/.003	.39/.004	
Motor orientation -hands				.38/.001						.17/.10									.31/.01	.35/.02	.30/.02	.35/.01
Motor orientation -arms		.16/.10	.28/.01							.21/.05									.23/.05	.18/.10	.22/.10	.26/.10
Motor orientation by picture					.21/.05			.28/.02	.27/.02	.31/.01	.20/.10	.23/.05						.24/.05		.21/.10		
N	71	71	71	71	71	71	71	60	59	60	61	60	52	57	60	60	59	59	53	53	45	46

The results (Table 5) indicated that the ability to read the heard rhythm patterns, as tested at preschool, correlated very significantly (p< .001) with the marks in writing and mathematics and significantly (p< .01) with the marks in reading and music in the Grade III spring certificate. The corresponding correlation with the following variables describing the linguistic ability as obtained from the teachers' questionnaire in Grade IV was very significant: unaffected speaking, ability to understand verbal instructions, sense of rhythm (p< .001) as evaluated by the teachers and willingness to play at school (p< .003). The correlation was very significant (p< .003) regarding the spatial relations' realism. The corresponding correlation concerning willingness to read, faultless writing, expressive speaking, ability to act by written instructions was p< .01, and p< .02 as far as willingness and ability to write short essays was concerned. The correlation was significant (p< .01) also in the ability to draw by pattern or instruction, and in the clearness of drawings.

On the basis of the facts presented above, the conclusion can thus be drawn that the so-called weak rhythm manipulation ability which I have indicated in various studies (Alahuhta 1976, 1979, 1980, 1981) to be the quite significant primary symptom in linguistic difficulties, has to be seen--as confirmed at preschool age--as a symptom of linguistic and some other school difficulties in the future. In addition, the ability to succeed at preschool in many different BMA test items measuring spatial orientation and composition ability appeared to correlate positively with many dependent variables in this study at the level of p< .001 and p< .01. The prognostic value of 'mosaics to be completed', for instance, proved to be very significant with regard to future school performance: it correlated on the level of p< .001 with the marks in reading (.35), writing (.38), mathematics (.45) and physical activities (.32). The correlation was also significant (p< .01) with music (.27) and willingness to play (.30) and (p< .02) with faultless writing (.26), ability to write short essays (.27), ability to act by written instructions (.27), sense of rhythm as evaluated by the teacher (.28) and unaffected speaking (.29). The item 'curves to be completed' correlated very significantly with the marks in writing (.32), physical activities (.38) and mathematics (.36), ability to act by written instructions (.44) and ability to write short essays (.35). The correlation was, furthermore, significant (p< .01) with the marks in reading (.26), willingness to read (.34), ability to understand verbal instructions (.30), ability to draw by pattern or instruction (.35), spatial relations' realism (.32), clearness of drawings (.30) and arts (.24, p<.02). Successful performance in the above-mentioned items correlated positively (p< .05) with the therapy for reading-writing difficulties.

In my view, the above-mentioned outcome examples indicate quite clearly that weakness in spatial orientation and composition ability, which has been proved to be, in various studies, the primary symptom of linguistic difficulties, can be considered, with good reason, as verified at preschool, to be the symptom of later linguistic as well as other difficulties at school.

The test results regarding the level of motor orientation ability and mastering of body image correlated most clearly with the ability to write short essays (.31, p< .01), willingness to write (.28, p< .02), faultless writing (.27, p< .02) and ability to act by written instructions and ability to understand verbal instructions (.23, p<.05).

The level of tactile discrimination--as one of the items closely related to mastering of body image and body knowledge--correlated very significantly (p< .001) with the ability to write dictation (.40), therapy for reading-writing difficulties (.39), faultless writing (.37, p< .002) and ability to write short essays (.35, p< .003) and coherence in writing, and significantly p< .01 with fluent reading (.30) and willingness to write (.29, p<.02). The correlation was significant, p< .05, with willingness to read (.24), and ability to act by written instructions (.23).

The results indicate that the sensitive tactile discrimination ability, which has been proved to be related closely to ability to correct articulation (Alahuhta 1976) has its effect on the level of mastering the written language. The result is quite logical because writing presupposes activating of articulatory engrams (pharyngobuccal proprioceptive) (Alahuhta 1976, 1979).

School adaptability and primary symptom complex as confirmed at preschool

The following school adaptability variables from the questionnaire had been examined here: 'ability to do independent work', 'ability to organize own work', 'paying attention to teaching', 'ability to decide independently and make choices', 'ability to do homework', 'ability to finish work without delay', 'restlessness during a school hour', 'concentration disturbed by outside noise'. (Results scores were 1 to 5, dimensions from 'nearly always' to 'never'.)

The results indicated (Table 6) that many primary symptom variables, collected at preschool by the BMA test, correlated significantly with the above school adaptability variables. The correlation in question was found in variables representing spatiotemporal as well as motor orientation ability. In other words, those who performed poorer at preschool age in test items presupposing spatial orientation and composition ability, and whose body image and temporal orientation ability--inability to read the rhythm patterns they heard--were poorer, were four years later less able to work and choose independently. They also were less able to organize their work, and their concentration ability was more easily disturbed. Those who performed poorer in the items of spatial orientation and composition ability, were more restless during a school hour and were not able to do their homework well. The situation of those who performed well, was quite the contrary.

In my view, from the above-described there can be drawn the conclusion that the primary symptoms of the linguistic disorders and difficulties, and thus the linguistic difficulties, are related to the difficulties to adapt to some school working norms.

About the questionnaire sent home

The following variables from the questionnaire sent home are examined here: 'concentration ability to listen to fairy tales', 'willingness to begin school', 'feeling comfortable at school', 'concentration on tasks requiring patience', 'willingness to prepare lessons', 'number of friends', and 'reading of cartoon magazines'.

Examination of the results (Table 7) revealed that 'concentration ability to listen to fairy tales', as reported by the parents, correlated very significantly with the marks in writing and coherence in writing,

TABLE 6. Intercorrelations of primary ability as tested by the BMA test at preschool and school adaptability variables collected in grade IV from the teachers

Variables School adaptability → Test variables of the BMA test ↓	Ability to work independently	Ability to organize own work	Attending to teaching	Ability to decide independently and make choices	Ability to do homework	Ability to finish work without delay	Restlessness during school hours	Concentration disturbed by outside noise
Ability to read rhythm patterns previously heard	.30 .01	.34 .01	.15 –	.33 .01	.19 .10	.20 .10	.12 –	.31 .01
Sectors	.34 .01	.32 .01	.24 .05	.41 .001	.34 .01	.29 .02	.15 –	.26 .05
Semicircles and straight lines	.20 .10	.12 –	.16 –	.24 .05	– –	.16 –	.34 .01	.31 .01
Spatial position bottle + glass	.24 .05	.35 .004	.35 .004	.23 .05	.21 .10	.29 .02	.34 .01	.26 .02
Spatial position cheeses	.25 .05	.34 .01	.35 .004	.22 .05	.23 .05	.27 .01	.17 –	.21 .10
Completion of profile	.24 .05	.31 .01	.29 .01	.34 .01	.18 .10	.19 .10	– –	.17 –
Curves to be completed	.38 .002	.23 .05	.29 .01	.34 .01	.30 .01	.26 .05	– –	.18 .10
Motor orientation by the picture	.33 .01	.23 .05	– –	.20 .10	.13 –	– –	.27 .05	.30 .01
N	55	56	56	56	56	55	53	56

497

TABLE 7. Intercorrelations of variables from home questionnaire and of variables describing school performance and school adaptability

Variables (Home questionnaire)	Reading	Writing	Music	Foreign Language	Physical Activities	Mathematics	Liking for Physical Activities	Graceful-Clumsy movements	Coherence in writing	Writing Speed	Ability to draw following instructions	Handling of Scissors	Speed of movements	Preciseness of movements	Carefulness
Concentration ability in listening to fairy tales	.15 / — / —	.39 / (51) / .003	.30 / (51) / .02	.34 / (47) / .01	.24 / (51) / .05	.34 / (51) / .01	— / — / —	— / — / —	.36 / (53) / .004	.42 / (53) / .001	.46 / (42) / .001	.35 / (46) / .01	.25 / (41) / .10	.40 / (40) / .01	.33 / (47) / .01
Willingness to begin school	.19 / (52) / .10	.26 / (52) / .05	.28 / (52) / .02	.21 / (48) / .10	— / — / —	.19 / (52) / .10	.30 / (50) / .02	.33 / (50) / .01	.33 / (54) / .01	.30 / (54) / .01	.38 / (42) / .01	.29 / (47) / .02	.43 / (41) / .003	.32 / (40) / .02	.24 / (48) / .05
Feeling comfortable at school	.34 / (52) / .01	.52 / (52) / .001	.15 / (52) / —	.35 / (48) / .01	.14 / (52) / —	.40 / (52) / .002	— / — / —	— / — / —	.28 / (54) / .02	.24 / (54) / .05	.41 / (42) / .004	.34 / (47) / .01	.30 / (41) / .03	.30 / (40) / .03	.16 / (48) / .10
Concentration on tasks requiring patience	.40 / (52) / .002	.44 / (52) / .001	— / — / —	.37 / (48) / .004	.47 / (52) / .001	.61 / (52) / .001	.15 / (50) / —	.29 / (50) / .02	.25 / (54) / .03	.36 / (54) / .01	.29 / (42) / .03	.28 / (46) / .03	.41 / (41) / .004	.38 / (40) / .01	.29 / (48) / .02
Willingness to prepare lessons	.27 / (50) / .05	.42 / (50) / .001	— / — / —	.41 / (46) / .002	.31 / (50) / .02	.43 / (50) / .001	.21 / (49) / .10	.27 / (49) / .05	.45 / (53) / .001	.38 / (53) / .003	.47 / (41) / .001	.33 / (46) / .01	.47 / (40) / .001	.55 / (39) / .001	.19 / (46) / .10
Number of friends	—	—	—	—	—	—	.48 / (50) / .001	.26 / (50) / .05	—	.20 / (54) / .10	—	.13 / (47) / —	—	—	—
Willingness to read cartoon magazines	—	—	—	—	—	—	—	—	.45 / (50) / .001	.22 / (50) / .10	.36 / (42) / .01	.11 / (47) / —	—	.17 / (40) / —	—

(N in parentheses)

498

writing speed and ability to draw by instructions. The correlation was also significant with the marks in foreign language, mathematics, music and conscientiousness as well as with preciseness of movements and handling ability of scissors. 'Feeling comfortable at school' correlated most strongly with the marks in writing and mathematics, but the correlation was significant with the marks in reading and foreign language as well as with the ability to handle scissors, writing speech, preciseness of movements and coherence in writing. 'Number of friends' had not any other correlation than that the fewer friends the child had, the less he liked physical activities and the clumsier he was in his movements. 'Number of friends' did not correlate with any other variables. 'Willingness to read cartoon magazines' had not any significant correlation with any other variables except with 'coherence in writing' and 'ability to draw from instructions'. The correlation meant that the more the child read cartoon magazines the more incoherent his writing was and the weaker 'the ability to draw by instructions'.

As stated above, it can be confirmed that the child's motor ability and his performance ability in both linguistic and other areas at school have a significant correlation with 'ability to listen', 'willingness to begin school', 'feeling comfortable at school', 'willingness to prepare lessons' and 'ability to concentrate on tasks requiring patience'.

DISCUSSION

As a starting point for discussion, I briefly present the established evaluation of the hypotheses:
1. The speech level, as confirmed at preschool is related to school success and linguistic performance level in Grades III-IV. The preschool speech level groups differed from each other in terms of statistics significantly in favour of the better speech level groups, especially in reading and motor performance and in the tasks requiring spatial orientation ability: the relation, thus, exists.
2. Placing in the so-called Apgar group, as confirmed at preschool, is related to school success and linguistic performance level in Grades III-IV.

The Apgar groups, as founded at preschool, differed from each other very significantly in the marks in writing--those having poorer Apgar scores performed poorer--

and significantly in the marks in mathematics and arts. Some type of difference was also to be found in some tasks requiring motor and spatial ability: the relation, thus, exists in this case too.

3. The primary symptom complex, as confirmed at preschool by the BMA test--is related to school success and linguistic performance level as well as school adaptability in Grades III-IV.

Those having weaker sense of rhythm and spatial orientation and composition ability at preschool, performed in Grades III-IV significantly, even very significantly, poorer in reading, writing, mathematics and arts. The linguistic performance ability and school adaptability of those children were significantly poorer than that of the children having better primary qualifications. Therapy for reading-writing difficulties proved to correlate positively very significantly, significantly or nearly significantly with some variables representing primary ability: presupposed relation was thus verified in these items, too. If we regard the language disorders and other related school difficulties as an indication of lack of adaptability for the surrounding world--as I have verified in many contexts, quoting Mucchielli--and if we hold on to this conception that the weak spatiotemporal orientation ability and weak body image are the background factors of this lack of adaptability, the research result is very logical. The basic factors for lack of adaptability exist in the child already at preschool age and even noticeably earlier reflecting speech difficulties (speech level groups). At school, these difficulties are revealed much more concretely as difficulties in written language and school adaptability.

References:

Alahuhta, E. (1976) On the Defects of Perception, Reasoning and Spatial Orientation Ability in Linguistically Handicapped Children. Ann.Acad. Sci. Fenn. Ser. B. Diss. TOM 6, Helsinki.
Alahuhta, E. (1976) Puhumisen, lukemisen ja kirjoittamisen häiriöiden yhteiset primaarit oireet tri R. Hussonin kuvaaman aivotoiminnallisen mekanismin valossa. Publications of the Institute of Phonetics University of Helsinki, 30.June 1976.
Alahuhta, E. (1979) On the Primary Factors Predicting Linguistic Abilities of Pre-School Children Research Reports 20/1979.

Department of Special Education University of Jyväskylä, Finland.
Alahuhta, E. (1980) On the Primary Factors Predicting Linguistic Abilities in Pre -School Children, Proceedings of the First International Congress for the Study of Child Language, Ingram, Peng, Dale, University Press of America.
Alahuhta, E., Laakso, K. (1981) Findings concerning school achievement primary symptoms predicting it, and to concentrate on school work, among pupils with speech defects, Research reports n:o 23/1981, Department of Special Education University of Jyväskylä, Finland.

A COMPARATIVE STUDY OF THE LINGUISTIC ABILITIES OF AUTISTIC, DYSPHASIC AND NORMAL CHILDREN

Jillian Ball, University of Melbourne

Toni Cross, Institute of Early Child Development

Kim Horsborough, Institute of Early Childhood Development, Australia

In normal language development, advances at the pragmatic level have been defined in different ways by different authors. Wells (1973) sees pragmatic development as being accompanied by an increasing diversity of speech acts and de Villiers and de Villiers suggest there will be an increased probability of reference to subjective opinions, hypothetical constructs and non-present referents. Slobin (1977), Bates (1976) and Keenan (1977) predict an increasing tendency to use language to manipulate the interlocutor and to cater for the communicative needs of the listener by framing utterances that are appropriate and sequiturial. However, little research is available to determine whether advances in such abilities do in fact accompany development in other aspects of language in normal children. Even less is available on the pragmatic development of communicatively impaired children.

The general profile of dysphasic (developmental receptive aphasic) children portrayed in the literature, suggests that in many respects they shadow normal patterns of development, but with marked developmental delay in the formal aspects of language use (e.g. Morehead and Ingram, 1972; Morehead, 1975). However, Menyuk (1975) argues that this pattern of straightforward delay is often complicated by some signs of deviance in application of grammatical rules. At the level of pragmatic abilities, a comparison by Snyder (1976) of specifically language-delayed and normal children matched for mean length of utterance, has suggested that such children are even more delayed pragmatically than syntactically.

On the other hand, amongst those autistic children who eventually develop some spontaneous speech, both formal and pragmatic deviances from normal have been described. For instance, Savage (1968) and Boucher (1976) note that the language use of autistics is limited and stereotyped. Bartak, Rutter and Cox (1975) observe that they use language less in social contexts than do other language-disabled children, and that most of their remarks bear no relationship to the ongoing conversation. Several researchers comment that questions and informative statements are infrequent or absent (e.g. Cunningham and Dixon, 1966; Wing, 1969; Goldfarb, Levy & Meyers, 1972).

Thus, in broad terms, the indications are that the speech of the autistic child provides evidence of both formal and pragmatic deviance from normal as well as major delay in general developmental milestones; whereas dysphasic speech suggests delayed rather than deviant development, in both aspects. However, there are some who dispute this conclusion. Churchill (1972), for instance, has argued that the language disability in autism is essentially the same as that which occurs in dysphasia, but often more pronounced. Though not postulating a common aetiology, Churchill has contended that a central linguistic disorder is both the necessary and the sufficient cause of autistic and dysphasic behaviour.

It is clear, then, that a detailed pragmatic analysis of the spontaneous language of both groups in comparison with normal children would shed light on these issues, and help to clarify the relative contributions of social, communicative and specific linguistic impairments to both syndromes. The present study therefore asked whether there were differences in the expressive, performative and discourse abilities of language-using autistic, dysphasic and normal children at equivalent levels of verbal intelligence.

METHOD

The sample comprised eight autistic, eight dysphasic and sixteen normal children, the relatively small group sizes being a direct reflection of the rare occurrence of diagnostically clear cases of the clinical syndromes. The groups of autistic and dysphasic children were matched in pairs over each group on the basis of verbal mental age, as measured by the Peabody Vocabulary Test (Dunn, 1965). Two normal children were than matched on the same basis with each of these pairs.

The autistic group comprised five males and three females between the ages of six years five months (6-5) and 14-10 (mean 9-11). They had been diagnosed by a clinical psychologist as Class 1 autistics, using a taxonomic system of childhood psychosis devised by Prior, Boulton, Gajzago and Perry (1975).

The dysphasic group comprised five males and three females aged between 4-10 and 6-4 (mean 5-8) and diagnosed by both a psychologist and speech therapist as suffering from specific developmental receptive aphasia.

The normal group contained ten males and six females with ages ranging from 2-10 to 4-7 (mean 3-8). They were assessed by a psychologist as being normal in language and cognitive development on the basis of verbal scales.

Psychometric Language Tests: All children were also tested with the Reynell Expressive and Receptive Scales to provide measures of their formal language levels.

Spontaneous Language: Each child's spontaneous speech was recorded in two separate twenty minute conversations, first with a parent and then with another familiar adult. Different interlocutors were used to overcome the possibility that the child's conversational style or functional patterns would merely reflect the particular style of the adult. The conversations were recorded in settings familiar to the child using portable audio and video equipment. Recordings were not commenced until both adult and child seemed relaxed and involved in a reciprocal conversational exchange.

The Functional Codes: Each transcript was segmented into "primary functional utterances" to provide the basic unit of analysis using the operational definition proposed by McNeill and McNeill (1975). This was independent of the utterance unit used for Mean Length of Utterance (M.L.U.) and Maximum Mean Length of Utterance (M.M.L.U.) which was defined by Brown (1973).

The code, adapted from McNeill and McNeill (1975), distinguished two hierarchical levels of function - macro and micro functions - which permitted selection of a dominant conversational function for each utterance and subdivision of each category into more specific speech acts where necessary. Differentiations were guided by information from nonlinguistic context, gesture, intonation, use of explicit performative verbs, preceding and subsequent utterances, and the reaction of the adult. Inter-coder reliability averaged at 86% agreement for two independent coders.

The pragmatic code also differentiated speech used by the child into performative initiatives and discourse aspects. Performatives are defined by Bates (1976) as 'the purpose an utterance is intended to realize in the context in which it occurs, e.g. request, command or question.' (p. 6). The discourse aspect, on the other hand, includes the regularities governing interaction between participants. This involves consideration of the sequiturial structure of conversation (e.g. that questions require relevant answers, statements should be acknowledged or commented upon, etc.), the production of utterances to convey purpose or intent, and the selection of content that can be understood and responded to by the interlocutor.

RESULTS AND DISCUSSION

Formal Linguistic Measures

The means, standard deviations and significance levels between groups on measures gleaned from formal language tests and spontaneous language indices, are shown in Table 1.

TABLE 1

MEAN PERCENTAGES, STANDARD DEVIATIONS AND SIGNIFICANT LEVELS FOR LINGUISTIC MEASURES AND AGE USING THE T-TEST (TWO-TAILED)

Functions	Normal (n=16) Mean %	S.D.	Autistic (n=8) Mean %	S.D.	Dysphasic (n=8) Mean %	S.D.	Significance Levels Norm./Aut.	Norm./Dys.
Chronological Age (yrs.mos.)	3-8	.60	9-11	3.00	5-8	.60	***	***
Verbal Mental Age (Peabody)	4-0	.77	4-3	1.03	4-2	.55		
M.L.U.	3.93	.98	3.36	.99	3.16	1.27		
M.M.L.U.	9.95	2.71	8.32	3.05	8.07	3.35		
Reynell Comprehension	4-4	.73	4-1	.73	3-10	.59		
Reynell Expression	3-9	.61	3-7	.51	4-0	.79		

* $p < .05$ (2 tt)
** $p < .01$ (2 tt)
*** $p < .001$ (2 tt)

As can be seen from Table 1, no significant differences occurred between the groups on measures of their receptive and expressive language abilities, nor in the complexity of their spontaneous speech. The three groups must be viewed, therefore, as similar in formal linguistic abilities despite their considerable differences in chronological age. Any differences that emerge in pragmatic aspects must, therefore, be interpreted beyond a specific impairment in stage of formal linguistic development.

THE FUNCTIONAL ANALYSIS

A. Performative Aspects

Of the five macro-functional (conversation-act) categories, Table 2 shows that significant differences between the autistics and normals were found in three categories - utterances serving informative functions (of which the autistics produced very few indeed), utterances serving regulatory functions (again reduced for the autistics) and utterances serving commenting functions (fewer for the autistics). There were no significant differences at this global level between the dysphasic and normal groups.

At the micro-functional (individual speech-act) level, fourteen of the twenty possible speech acts significantly differentiated the autistics and normals, whereas only six differentiated the dysphasics and normals. Both sets of results support the contention that the dysphasic group's use of language is more comparable with the normal pattern than is the autistic children's speech. Closer examination of the specific speech acts, which differentiate the normals and dysphasics, indicates that the pattern for three of the six differences is such that, while large differences exist between the autistics and normals, the dysphasics produced an intermediate frequency. This is the case for statements of affect, commentaries on self-actions and comment-

TABLE 2 MEAN PERCENTAGES[+] OF PERFORMATIVE ASPECTS AND THE SIGNIFICANCE LEVELS USING THE T-TEST (TWO-TAILED)

		Normal		Autistic		Dysphasic		Significance Levels	
	PERFORMATIVE ASPECTS	Mean %	S.D.	Mean %	S.D.	Mean %	S.D.	Norm./ Aut.	Norm./ Dysphasic
A.									
I.	Informative Functions	11.24	5.25	2.07	1.57	10.33	3.36	***	
	Statement of Knowledge	3.55	1.87	1.23	1.35	4.06	2.67	**	
	Statement of Affect	3.90	2.79	.24	.34	1.76	1.30	***	*
	Statement of Intent	1.19	.69	.04	.11	1.51	1.25	***	
	Report	2.06	2.46	.50	.46	3.31	3.12	*	
	Hypothetical Statement	.49	.53	0	0	.13	.27	*	
II.	Regulatory Functions	6.69	2.32	1.46	1.17	10.96	5.29	***	
	Request	1.71	1.94	.48	.54	5.09	2.16	*	***
	Command	1.62	1.16	.43	.51	1.12	.92	**	
	Rejection	1.22	1.04	.19	.42	1.89	1.73	**	
	Attention Directing	2.13	1.33	.37	.43	2.78	2.31	***	
III.	Interrogative Functions	11.02	2.89	10.19	12.30	6.91	5.82		
	Information Question	5.94	2.54	4.16	4.92	4.84	4.74		
	Query Name	2.58	1.67	4.51	8.23	1.80	1.48		
	Clarification Question	1.62	1.56	1.88	3.35	.27	.35		**
	Quiz Question	.87	.94	.08	.23	0	0	**	*
IV.	Commentative Functions	30.53	9.97	20.37	13.50	23.96	6.78	*	
	Self Actions	4.86	2.73	1.36	1.16	2.55	1.48	***	*
	Labelling	4.72	2.83	8.94	6.52	4.06	2.77		
	Description of Object	8.67	5.11	4.32	2.87	6.17	3.18	*	
	Description of Event	3.29	2.27	3.89	4.69	4.28	2.80		
	Location	3.71	3.12	1.35	1.05	2.86	2.20	*	
	Enactment	3.33	2.07	.15	.41	1.54	1.79	***	*
	Sensorimotor Play	1.93	2.68	.69	.86	.68	.68		
V.	Other	3.21		6.04		5.01			

* $p \leq .05$ (2tt) ** $p \leq .01$ (2tt) *** $p \leq .001$ (2tt)

[+]Note that the Mean Percentages of utterances in Tables 2 & 3 combined total 100%.

aries on enactment.

The dysphasic children were found to use considerably more requests to regulate the adult than the normals, suggesting a greater degree of interpersonal purpose in their conversations. The younger normals and autistics used very few such speech acts. The other two differences included the extremely low figures found for the use of clarification and quiz questions, and may be said to indicate deviance on the part of the dysphasics. The paucity of the former speech act could reflect a reluctance on the part of the dysphasic child to engage in attempts to repair communication breakdowns. Alternatively, the low percentage of both clarification and quiz questions could also be argued to be a direct consequence of maturity in comprehending conversational intention.

The autistic pattern, on the other hand, indicates a much poorer level of conversational initiative. They show slight use of any category of speech act designed to convey knowledge, feelings, opinions and intentions to a conversational partner (informative functions), to convey interpersonal meanings (regulatory functions), or to comment on themselves, on environmental events, or on the behaviour of others (commentative functions). The fact that they achieved a score similar to normals on interrogative functions was primarily a function of their stronger tendency to merely request the labels for things in repetitive "What's that?" type of questions.

B. Discourse Aspects

The pattern of deviation from normal language use by the autistic children is further strengthened in examination of the responses made by the children to adult initiatives. Table 3 indicates at the macro-functional level, that the autistics produced much higher percentages of non-sequiturs (utterances which did not conversationally supply the appropriate speech act adjacency pair to the

TABLE 3 MEAN PERCENTAGES AND STANDARD DEVIATIONS OF DISCOURSE ASPECTS AND THE SIGNIFICANCE LEVELS USING THE T-TEST (TWO-TAILED)

		Normal		Autistic		Dysphasic		Sign. Levels	
Functions		Mean %	S.D.	Mean %	S.D.	Mean %	S.D.	Norm./Aut.	Norm./Dys.
B. DISCOURSE ASPECTS									
I. Responses		32.61	10.10	39.05	11.46	40.04	6.36		
Content Response		14.67	7.68	26.58	9.48	21.92	5.95	**	*
Yes No Answer		7.77	4.32	7.23	3.50	9.14	1.08		
Acknowledgement		7.39	3.71	5.06	5.03	7.81	2.13	***	
Contradiction		2.68	1.54	.19	.38	1.23	1.46		*
II. Non-Sequiturs		3.91	3.76	13.84	8.83	4.59	2.43	*	
New Topic		3.18	3.14	3.93	3.33	3.72	1.86		
Nonsensical		.05	.13	3.71	3.14	.23	.33	***	
Other		.68	1.20	6.19	9.54	.65	.40	*	
III. Repetitions		3.69	3.02	12.99	12.81	3.70	2.22	**	
Repetition of Others		1.09	.83	7.91	11.33	1.92	1.46	*	
Repetition of Self		2.59	3.01	5.13	2.85	1.78	1.13		
IV. Inappropriate Utterances		.20	.43	7.56	5.50	.82	.64	**	**
V. Uncoded (Ambiguous Utterances)		.73		.75		.71			

* p ≤ .05 (2tt)   ** p ≤ .01 (2tt)   *** p ≤ .001 (2tt)

adult's initiative), repetitions of their own or the adult's utterance, and totally inappropriate utterances (those which bore no meaningful relation to the conversational context). The dysphasic group showed only a slight increase over the normals in the use of inappropriate utterances. The autistic children, therefore, differed in their greater tendency to disregard the social and conversational context in which communication occurs.

At the micro-level, the autistics differed from the normals in five of the ten sub-categories of responses. The dysphasics differed from the normals in only two sub-categories, both of which involved appropriate responses which contained some semantic content and the tendency to contradict the adult. Again the proportional use of such speech acts puts the dysphasics between the normals and autistics. The autistics, in contrast, displayed a marked conversational inadequacy in terms of resorting to entirely nonsensical replies to adults' questions, which, though often appropriate in terms of the adjacency pair, were semantically unrelated. The autistics were further found to repeat more frequently the adults' utterances (and their own utterances, though this was not significant), than was the case for either the dysphasic or the normal children.

CONCLUSIONS

In general, the data provide a consistent picture of differences between dysphasic and autistic children in terms of the purpose for which they use language, and in their ability to participate in conversations in a coherent, sequiturial manner. When autistic children acquire language, it would seem that they function at a level of pragmatic ability that appears to be less mature than their dysphasic counterparts. When normal children of the same comprehension and production levels are used as a standard of comparison, the impression of immaturity is given by their restricted range of language functions, their use of less cognitively complex speech acts and in terms of their lack of awareness of sociolinguistic rules for effective social interaction.

However, the results also suggest that autistic children do not merely shadow the process of normal children in the acquisition of pragmatic abilities. The prevalence of contextually inappropriate utterances indicates a lack of specific communicative intent in their language use and violation of Grice's (1968) principle of co-operation, i.e. that only relevant information be offered.

The pragmatic abilities and pattern of development of the dysphasic children suggest a delayed pattern which is similar to that of normal children. On the relatively few occasions where they differed from their linguistically-matched normal counterparts, these differences made sense in terms of their specific problem with formal aspects of language, particularly in comprehension. Many of the dysphasic children's differences in incidence of speech function and measures of discourse competence seemed to reflect their tendency to rely more heavily on simpler, less mature, conversational devices and their inability to avoid, or to repair, comprehension breakdowns. The results for this group seem more consistent with a picture of straightforward delay in both performative and discourse aspects of pragmatic ability. This delay seemed to be roughly in synchrony with their delay in formal language acquisition and, indeed, may be caused by it.

In the case of the autistic group, two alternative conclusions may be drawn. One is that their sociocommunicative development is very different from normal children at comparable stages of language development. Not only were they in chronological terms further behind the normal group in formal language abilities than the dysphasics, but their pragmatic abilities could be classified as both delayed and deviant - deviant particularly in the sense that they rarely used speech for interpersonal purposes. Because of this finding, it seems reasonable to posit that their incapacity with this aspect of communication may have caused their formal language delay, given that many of the defining criteria of autism can be viewed generally as exhibiting an overall inability to be sociable, or develop beyond an egocentric social perspective. However, it could be alternatively concluded that the results provided evidence that autistic children are more severely retarded in pragmatic aspects of development in comparison with their comprehension of language, than could be measured in the present design. That is, it is possible that the autistics may not have emerged as deviant had they been compared with even younger normals and dysphasics. Unfortunately, there is insufficient research currently available on normal pragmatic development to make a judgement about this.

Finally, irrespective of whether the pattern of language use for the autistics is eventually regarded as deviant or severely delayed (which itself may create deviances in development), the fact that discussions of normal development now provide a prerequisite role for the prelinguistic acquisition of most of our major speech functions, has some relevance. It becomes possible to speculate (and test empirically) the notion that autistic children are, first and foremost, impaired in the predisposition to be intentionally interactional with other human beings, and to postulate that the language learning deficiency they exhibit is a consequence of this interactional deficit, not, as many researchers have attempted to claim, that autism is a result of a primary difficulty in acquiring language. For autistic children, the social preconditions for this later acquisition may, in fact, never have been met (or at least met only inadequately) because of a prior sociocommunicative disability.

REFERENCES

Bartak, L., Rutter, M. & Cox, A. (1975). A comparative study of infantile autism and specific developmental receptive language disorder. B. J. Psychiat., 126, 127-145.

Bates, E. (1976). Language and Context - the Acquisition of Pragmatics. Academic Press, New York.

Boucher, J. (1976). Is autism primarily a language disorder? Brit. J. Diseases of Communic., 11, 135-146.

Brown, R. (1973). A First Language - the Early Stages. Harvard University Press, Cambridge.

Churchill, D.W. (1972). The relation of infantile autism and early childhood schizophrenia to developmental language disorders of childhood. J. Aut. Child. Schizophrenia, 2(2), 182-197.

Cunningham, M. and Dixon (1966). A five year study of the language of an autistic child. J. Child. Psychol. Psychiat. 7, 143-154.

Dunn, L.M. (1965). Peabody Picture Vocabulary Test. American Guidance Service.

Goldfarb, W., Levy, D., and Meyers, D. (1972). The mother speaks to her schizophrenic child; language in childhood schizophrenia. Psychiatry, 35, 217-226.

Grice, H.P. (1968). Utterer's meaning, sentence-meaning and word meaning. Foundations of Language, 4, 225-242.

Keenan, E.O. (1977). Making it last: repetition in children's discourse. In S. Ervin-Tripp and C. Mitchell-Kernan (eds.) Child Discourse. Academic Press, New York.

McNeill, N. and McNeill, D. (1975). Linguistic Interactions among Children & Adults. Committee on Cognition & Communication, University of Chicago, Chicago, Illinois.

Menyuk, P. (1975). The language-impaired child-linguistic or cognitive impairment. In Aaronson, D. & Rieber (eds.). Developmental Psycholinguistics & Communication Disorders. New York Academy of Sciences, New York.

Morehead, D. (1975). Language deficient children. Paper presented at the Third International Child Language Symposium, London.

Morehead, D.M. & Ingram, D. (1973). The development of base syntax in normal & linguistically deviant children. J. Speech Hear. Res., 16, 330-352.

Prior, M., Boulton, D., Gajzago, C. and Perry, D. (1975). The classification of childhood psychoses by numerical taxonomy. J.Child. Psychol. Psychiat., 16, 321-330.

Savage, V.A. (1968). A review of the literature with particular reference to the speech & language structure of the autistic child. Brit. J. Dis. Communic., 3, 75-87.

Slobin, D.I. (1977). Language change in childhood & in history. In Macnamara, J. (ed.) Language, Learning & Thought. Academic Press, New York.

Snyder, L.S. (1976). The early presuppositions & performatives of normal & language disabled children. Papers & Reports on Child Language Development 12, Stanford University, California.

Wells, G. (1973). Coding Manual for the Description of Child Speech, University of Bristol School of Education, Bristol.

Wing, L. (1969). The handicaps of autistic children - a comparison study. J. Child. Psychol. Psychiat., 10, 1-40.

TABLE OF CONTENTS
VOLUME I
PRESPEECH

Bénédicte de Boysson-Bardies 1
THE SPECIFICITY OF INFANT BABBLING IN THE LIGHT OF
CHARACTERISTICS OF THE MOTHER TONGUE

Diane Fujitani, Patricia M. Greenfield & James Argiro 8
A YOUNG BABY'S PROSODIC DIFFERENTIATION BETWEEN A
PERSON AND A TOY

Nina Petrovich-Bartell, Nelson Cowan, & Philip A.
 Morse 23
PERCEPTUAL AND ACOUSTIC ATTRIBUTES OF INFANT
DISTRESS VOCALIZATIONS

Adele Proctor 29
EFFECTS OF SOCIAL CONTEXTS ON VOCALIZATION AND HAND
GESTURE IN EARLY INFANCY

David Woods & Ida Stockman 43
A FEATURE HIERARCHY OF NONLINGUISTIC CONSONANT
ARTICULATIONS

PHONOLOGY

Harold Clumeck 58
THE EFFECT OF WORD FAMILIARITY ON PHONEMIC RECOGNITION
IN PRESCHOOL CHILDREN AGED 3 to 5 YEARS

Brian King 78
TONE ACQUISITION: SOME GENERAL OBSERVATIONS

Chieko Kobayashi 88
THE ACQUISITION OF JAPANESE PITCH-ACCENT

Anne Watson & Amy Swenson 103
THE RELATIONSHIP BETWEEN PHONOLOGY AND SYNTAX IN
30 CHILDREN AGED 2;0 to 2;6

Branka Zei 118
CHILDREN'S AWARENESS OF THEIR OWN PHONO-ARTICULATORY
ACTIVITY

TABLE OF CONTENTS
VOLUME I
MORPHOLOGY AND SYNTAX

William J. Baker & Bruce L. Derwing 134
TOWARD AN EMPIRICAL DEFINITION OF "STAGE" IN
LANGUAGE DEVELOPMENT

Guy Ewing 151
WORD-ORDER INVARIANCE AND VARIABILITY IN FIVE
CHILDREN'S THREE-WORD UTTERANCES: A LIMITED-SCOPE
FORMULA ANALYSIS

Christine Howe 166
THE FUNCTION OF NOUN PHRASES IN PRODUCTION AND
COMPREHENSION: SOME FURTHER EVIDENCE ON THE
CONTRIBUTION OF SEMANTICS TO EARLY GRAMMAR

Henriette Lempert 180
LEARNING NEW WORD ORDER: THE ROLE OF ANIMATE
REFERENTS

Yonatha Levy 193
THE NON-INTERACTION OF LINGUISTIC AND COGNITIVE
NOTIONS OF GENDER IN THE LANGUAGE OF YOUNG ISRAELIS

Clifton Pye 201
MAYAN TELEGRAPHESE: STAGE I SPEECH IN QUICHE MAYAN

David N. Shorr & Philip S. Dale 220
GRAMMATICAL COMPREHENSION: A QUESTION OF STYLE?

Jan Vorster 231
THE LAST SHALL BE FIRST: ON THE ACQUISITION OF THE
AFRIKAANS DOUBLE NEGATIVE

SEMANTICS

Camille Hanlon 245
FREQUENCY OF USAGE, SEMANTIC COMPLEXITY, AND THE
ACQUISITION OF SET-RELATIONAL QUANTIFIERS IN EARLY
CHILDHOOD

Willem Kaper 261
THE USE OF SOME COMPLEMENTARY OR ANTONYMOUS VERBS BY
CHILDREN AND ADULTS

Stan A. Kuczaj II & Denise R. Clark 272
THE ACQUISITION OF THE MEANING OF MOOD TERMS

TABLE OF CONTENTS
VOLUME I

Judith A. McLaughlin & Roy D. Pea 284
CHILDREN'S COMPREHENSION OF RELATIONAL TERMS: TWO DEVELOPMENTAL LEVELS

Roy D. Pea & Bernard Kaplan 294
LEXICAL DEVELOPMENT FROM THE PERSPECTIVE OF GENETIC-DRAMATISM

Ida J. Stockman & Fay Boyd Vaughn-Cooke 312
SEMANTIC CATEGORIES IN THE LANGUAGE OF WORKING-CLASS BLACK CHILDREN

PRAGMATICS AND DISCOURSE

Michael F. McTear 328
REPAIRS: LEARNING TO DO IT YOURSELF

Jacqueline Sachs 344
"DON'T INTERRUPT!": PRESCHOOLERS' ENTRY INTO ONGOING CONVERSATIONS

Christine Tanz 357
AN EXPERIMENTAL INVESTIGATION OF CHILDREN'S COMPREHENSION OF THE LOCUTIONARY VERB ASK

Hans Vejleskov 372
A FUNCTIONAL ANALYSIS OF NATURAL LANGUAGE IN PRE-SCHOOL CHILDREN

MOTHER-CHILD INTERACTION

Maria Silvia Barbieri & Antonella Devescovi 386
DIFFERENT WAYS OF EXPLANATION IN TWO SOCIAL CLASSES: STORY TELLING TO CHILDREN FROM 18 TO 36 MONTHS

Kevin Durkin, D.R. Ruther, Susan Room & Patricia
  Grounds 405
PROPER NAME USAGE IN MATERNAL SPEECH: A LONGITUDINAL STUDY

Karen L. Rembold 413
AN EXAMINATION OF THE EFFECTS OF VERBAL AND NONVERBAL FEEDBACK ON MATERNAL SPEECH TO 2½ YEAR-OLD CHILDREN

Ragnhild Söderbergh 429
LINGUISTIC EFFECTS BY THREE YEARS OF AGE OF EXTRA CONTACT DURING THE FIRST HOUR POST PARTUM

TABLE OF CONTENTS

VOLUME I

Lynn H. Waterhouse 442
MATERNAL SPEECH PATTERNS AND DIFFERENTIAL DEVELOPMENT

LITERACY

Aviva Freedman 455
DEVELOPMENT IN REALIZATION OF STORY STRUCTURE IN
WRITTEN PRODUCTIONS OF SCHOOL CHILDREN

Rosa Needleman 473
A LINGUISTIC EVALUATION OF HYPERLEXIA

Mary Rees Nishio 482
JAPANESE/CHINESE KANJI - WHAT THEY CAN TELL US
ABOUT NONVERBAL CHILDREN AND EARLY SYMBOLIC LANGUAGE

P.G. Patel 492
CHILD LANGUAGE AND FAILURE IN READING ACQUISITION:
A TWO-WAY RELATIONSHIP

Sybil Schwartz 504
A DEVELOPMENTAL LINGUISTIC ANALYSIS OF SPELLING
ABILITY IN LEARNING-DISABLED CHILDREN

Christopher M. Sterling & Philip T. Smith 517
SPELLING ERRORS IN THE COMPOSITIONS OF NORMAL
CHILDREN

LANGUAGE DEVELOPMENT IN EXCEPTIONAL CHILDREN

Ken Bleile 531
CONSTRAINTS IN THE PHONOLOGY OF A CHILD WITH DOWN'S
SYNDROME

Sandra Bochner 546
A STUDY OF INTENTIONAL VOCALIZING IN HANDICAPPED,
INSTITUTIONALIZED INFANTS

Pamela Grunwell 561
FRICATIVES AND AFFRICATES IN THE SPEECH OF CHILDREN
WITH PHONOLOGICAL DISABILITY

Leija V. McReynolds & Mary Elbert 576
PHONOLOGICAL PROCESSES: WITHIN OR ACROSS PHONEME
CLASS GENERALIZATION IN ARTICULATION TRAINING

TABLE OF CONTENTS
VOLUME I

Frances O. Pappas 587
THE USE OF MELODIC INTONATION THERAPY AND SIGNING
IN LANGUAGE TRAINING OF AUTISTIC CHILDREN

Sally M. Rogow 594
RIDDLES AND RHYMES: THE IMPORTANCE OF SPEECH PLAY
FOR BLIND AND VISUALLY HANDICAPPED CHILDREN